Transformative Justice

Law, Meaning, and Violence

The scope of Law, Meaning, and Violence is defined by the wide-ranging scholarly debates signaled by each of the words in the title. Those debates have taken place among and between lawyers, anthropologists, political theorists, sociologists, and historians, as well as literary and cultural critics. This series is intended to recognize the importance of such ongoing conversations about law, meaning, and violence as well as to encourage and further them.

Series Editors: Martha Minow, Harvard Law School
                    Elaine Scarry, Harvard University
                    Austin Sarat, Amherst College

Transformative Justice

Israeli Identity on Trial

Leora Bilsky

With a Foreword by Richard J. Bernstein

The University of Michigan Press

Ann Arbor

To my mother, and in memory of my father.

Copyright © by the University of Michigan 2004
All rights reserved
Published in the United States of America by
The University of Michigan Press
Manufactured in the United States of America
⊗ Printed on acid-free paper

2007   2006   2005   2004   4   3   2   1

A CIP catalog record for this book is available from the British Library.

Library of Congress Cataloging-in-Publication Data

Bilsky, Leora, [date]
   Transformative justice : Israeli identity on trial / Leora Bilsky ; with a foreword by Richard J. Bernstein.
      p.   cm. — (Law, meaning, and violence)
   Includes bibliographical references and index.
   ISBN 0-472-03037-x (pbk. : alk. paper)
   ISBN 0472-11422-0 (cloth : alk. paper) —
   1. Trials (Political crimes and offenses)—Israel.   2. Justice and politics—Israel.   3. Democracy—Israel—Religious aspects.   I. Title.   II. Series.

KMK40.P64B55   2004
345.5694'0231—dc22   2004012107

Foreword

Leora Bilsky, a law professor at Tel Aviv University with a strong philosophical background and sensitivity to literary issues of narrative, has written a remarkable book that can be read on a number of levels and from a variety of perspectives. She begins by asking an apparently straightforward question, "Can Israel be both Jewish and democratic?" When the State of Israel was founded in 1948, its Declaration of Independence embodied a bold confidence that Israel would be a Jewish state based on strong democratic principles—one that recognizes the rights of *all* its citizens regardless of religion. But during the more than fifty years of its history, there have been extraordinary tensions in reconciling its commitment to being a Jewish state and its democratic aspirations. With nuanced lucidity Bilsky brings forth the complexities of this uneasy tension by examining four extremely controversial trials: the Rudolf Kastner trial (1954–58); the Adolf Eichmann trial (1960–62); the Kufr Qassem trial (1956–57); and the Yigal Amir trial (1996).

The Eichmann trial is the most famous, but the other three, which occurred at crucial stages in the history of Israel, also raised fundamental questions about Israeli collective identity. Rudolf (Israel) Kastner was a Hungarian Zionist who negotiated with Nazis (including Eichmann) in order to save Hungarian Jews from extermination. He did succeed in saving more than a thousand Jews, then immigrated to Israel and became an important member of the Mapai (Labor) party. When a polemical pamphlet was published in Israel condemning him for his collaboration with the Nazis, Kastner sued the author for libel. Although Kastner was the plaintiff, the trial turned into a prosecution of Kastner (and the Mapai party). In the original trial (there was appeal in which the judgment was reversed), the presiding judge, Benjamin Halevi, condemned Kastner for having sold his soul to the devil. The Kufr Qassem trial dealt with the conduct of a unit of Israeli soldiers who murdered forty-nine Arab civilians for violating a curfew of which they had not prior knowledge. Yigal Amir was notorious because he claimed at his trial that his assassination of Yitzhak Rabin, the popular Israeli general who became prime minister, was "justified" on the basis of Halakhah (Jewish law). Because these trials were not primarily concerned with the status of Jewish law, they are not typically considered relevant to Israel's status as a Jewish democratic nation-state. Bilsky brilliantly demonstrates not just their relevance but their centrality to the question of Israel's future as an open democratic society. But there is much more to what Bilsky has achieved.

All four of these trials were political trials, trials in which government authorities sought to advance a political agenda through a criminal prosecution. Normally we think of "political trials" in a negative manner, as "show trials" in which legal procedures are a mere facade concealing the cynical use of brute power. But one of the most provocative features of Bilsky's study is its defense of the legitimacy and importance of political trials. Political trials need not be "show trials." Indeed, Bilsky develops a positive theory of political trials based on a creative appropriation of themes from the work of Hannah Arendt. In this respect, *Transformative Justice* has legal and political significance far beyond the book's Israeli context. A political trial, as Bilsky characterizes it, is a transformative one. Its purpose is to foster a transformation in the collective consciousness of a people. Bilsky at once articulates the criteria for such trials and defends their importance in furthering democratic practices. Thus, her work connects with the larger issue of transitional justice. But Bilsky argues that transitional justice is not just a problem that occurs at moments of crisis when legal procedures are used to judge those accused of committing criminal political acts. Because Israel has been in a constant and continuous process of *transition,* transformative trials play a critical role in the ongoing process of defining a democratic identity.

Bilsky does not restrict herself solely to what occurs within each of these trials, but also examines some of the striking commentaries that they provoked. In each of these trials there was a battle between a dominant narrative and a counternarrative. The Israeli poet Nathan Alterman, for example, incisively challenged the simplistic binary opposition between Jewish collaborators and heroes of the Holocaust that dominated the Kastner trial. Hannah Arendt was insensitive to the important role of testimony by Holocaust survivors in the Eichmann trial, but she nevertheless raised important philosophical and political issues about the conduct of the trial and Israeli society. *Transformative Justice* thus addresses the subject of the role of narrative in shaping legal processes. Although Bilsky is a master of details, she is always raising more general questions about the limits of the law, the criteria for legitimate political trials, the ways in which they can deeply influence collective identity. She concludes by relating her discussion to the practice and principles of the truth and reconciliation commissions that have sprung up in different parts of the world.

Bilsky's book is engaging and stimulating because she deftly moves among these different levels and perspectives. She has constructed a compelling narrative that is at once gripping and thought-provoking, raising profound questions about the relationship of politics, history, social identity, and the law.

Richard J. Bernstein
New School for Social Research

Contents

Acknowledgments

This book originated while I was a faculty associate of the Ethics and the Professions Program in Harvard University in 1998–99. The program provided me with financial support as well as a most encouraging and congenial environment. I am grateful to director Dennis Thompson for suggesting that I expand my interest in Holocaust trials to investigate the broader notion of political trials, and to my fellow associates for discussing the initial ideas for the book.

Since then, many individuals and institutions helped in completing this book. I wish to thank the Minerva Center for Human Rights, the Cegla Center, and Tel Aviv University for their generous financial support; the libraries and archives of Tel Aviv University, in particular the Law Library, the Wiener Collection, Sourasky Library, the Nathan Alterman Archive, and the Israel Defense Forces archive. All provided a helpful hand in digesting the often dusty and dispersed materials.

I wish to thank my friends and colleagues in the Faculty of Law at Tel Aviv University, in particular Daphne Barak-Erez, José Brunner, Chaim Gans, Hanoch Dagan, Eyal Gross, Ron Harris, Assaf Likhovski, Asher Maoz, and Menachem Mautner for discussing the various chapters with me and offering helpful comments. Special thanks go to my dean Ariel Porat and vice dean Omri Yadlin, who provided me with a free semester to finish working on the book.

Bruce Ackerman, Morton Horowitz, Duncan Kennedy, Anthony Kronman, Mark Osiel, and Dennis Thompson all read drafts of chapters and discussed them with me, as did my students in the seminars on "Holocaust and the Law" and "Political Trials," and the participants in the workshop on "Law and History" at Tel Aviv Faculty of Law. Special thanks go to Martha Minow and Jennifer Nedelsky, whose example was always with me when struggling with the manuscript, and who offered their critical reading, good advice, and their warm friendship throughout these years. Both believed in this book even before the first chapter was written. I also wish to thank Jeremy Shine, my first editor at the University of Michigan Press, and Jim Reische, the editor with whom I finished the manuscript. In addition, the detailed and most pertinent comments of Don Herzog, the reviewer for the University of Michigan Press, have helped to make this a better book than it would otherwise have been.

I am grateful to my various research assistants who helped me at different stages of writing: Ori Aharonson, Yael Broide, Ori Herstein, Ofer Sitbon, and Gal Weingold. Doreen Lustig provided me not only with research assistance but also with vast technical help in the final stages of the project.

Philippa Shimrat provided expert editorial advice and perceptive reading of the manuscript in its various stages. Philippa accompanied me on this journey from the very beginning and her advice and balanced criticism helped make this project come true. My deep thanks go to Analu Verbin whose contribution to this book is evidenced on each page. Initially, a research assistant, Analu edited, commented, inspired, and with her friendship has shown me what miracles can happen if we only believe.

I am also grateful to the following persons and institutions for inviting me to present earlier versions of material in this book: Ariella Gross, University of Southern California; Richard Bernstein, The New School for Social Research; Jennifer Nedelsky and David Dyzenhaus, University of Toronto Law School; Michael Marrus and Janice Stein, Munk Center for International Studies, University of Toronto; Catherine Franke, Center for the Study of Law and Culture, Columbia University; Phil Thomas, Cardiff University; Christopher Tomlins, American Bar Foundation.

This book is the fruit of friendship no less than it is the fruit of research and thinking. My dear friend Pnina Lahav, who engendered the idea of this book when she first learned of my interest in the Eichmann trial, has generously given me her good advice, reading each of the chapters and always finding new horizons to explore. My friends Hagi Kenaan and Ariel Meirav have offered me their time, wisdom, comments, and love in so many ways, that I cannot imagine this book being written without them. And finally, my dearest friend, Vered Lev-Kenaan, was always there for me, never tiring of hearing yet another thought about Hannah Arendt. Her will, conviction, and love were the materials from which this book has been created.

Finally I would like to thank my family for their patience and love, for having to hear about this book at so many Friday dinners, and for accepting my always being in a hurry to try and finish another paragraph. My deepest thanks go to my beloved mother, Tamar Bilsky, who has made this book into a reality in countless ways, always wanting to give much more than I knew how to take. Her love, faith, and the freshness of her thinking always accompanied me in my writing, in places close and far away.

My daughter Ruth-Clio was born just as I submitted the complete manuscript to the University of Michigan Press for review. She has made the abstract terms, natality, narrativity, and plurality into a living reality. Giving birth to my child and to this book simultaneously symbolizes, maybe more than anything else, my belief in the future of this country and its people.

Tel Aviv, May 2004

Portions of this book have appeared in substantially different form in the following publications.

Chapter 1 appeared as "Justice or Reconciliation? The Politicisation of the Holocaust in the Kastner Trial," in *Lethe's Law*, ed. Emilios Christodoulidis and Scott Veitch (Oxford and Portland, OR: Hart Publishing, 2001).

Chapter 2 appeared as "Judging Evil in the Trial of Kastner," *Law and History Review* 19 (1) (spring 2001): 117–60.

Parts of chapters 3 and 6 appeared as "In a Different Voice: Nathan Alterman and Hannah Arendt on the Kastner and Eichmann Trials," *Theoretical Inquiries in Law* 1 (2) (July 2000): 509–47.

Chapter 5 appeared as "When Actor and Spectator Meet in the Courtroom: Reflections on Hannah Arendt's Concept of Judgment," *History and Memory* 8 (2) (fall-winter 1996): 137–73.

A small portion of chapter 8 appeared as "Law and Politics: The Trial of Yigal Amir" (in Hebrew), *Plilim* 8 (December 1999): 13–75.

Introduction
Transformative Trials and
Dilemmas of Democracy

Can Israel be both Jewish and democratic? This question has haunted Israeli society ever since the establishment of the state and came to a head during the Oslo peace process. On 4 November 1995 Israeli prime minister Yitzhak Rabin was assassinated at the end of a mass peace rally held in Tel Aviv. The shock waves from that traumatic event were felt in subsequent political developments and can still be felt throughout Israeli society. The assassin, Yigal Amir, later justified his act by citing a rule, Din Rodef (the law of the persecutor), from the Halakhah (Jewish religious law), which permits killing someone who is about to commit or bring about the murder of another Jew.[1] For a brief moment the two fundamental values of the State of Israel—the "Jewish" and the "democratic"—seemed to be clashing in a violent life and death struggle. The need to engage in a collective reckoning about the democratic rules of the game and the use of political violence was expressed in all sectors of Israeli society. These questions were channeled into a legal process with very high visibility: the trial of Yigal Amir.

This book will trace the constant tension between the Jewish and democratic values in Israeli society through four dramatic political trials that helped shape the Israeli collective identity and memory over a period of forty years. This tension can already be discerned in what is considered the foundational moment of the State of Israel: the 1948 Declaration of Independence. That declaration describes the new political entity that is about to be born as a Jewish state committed to ensuring "complete equality of social and political rights to all its inhabitants irrespective of religion, race or sex," as well as "freedom of religion, conscience, language, education and culture."[2] However, the word *democracy* does not appear in the declaration,[3] even though an earlier draft suggested by one of its framers, Zvi Berenson (later a justice of the Supreme Court), stated that Israel would be "a Jewish State, free, independent and *democratic* in the Land of Israel in accordance with the borders delineated in the partition decision of the United Nations."[4] It was only during the 1990s, with the legislation of two Basic Laws that formed the beginning of an Israeli "civil rights" bill, that the dual definition of Israel as a Jewish and democratic state was given formal constitutional status.[5] This definition triggered a stream of academic symposiums and law review articles and books on whether the two values were indeed contradictory or whether they could be reconciled, and if so in what ways and at what cost.[6]

Rabin's assassination brought this debate on Israel's identity to the center of the public stage. In order to decode the origins of this crisis the book first takes us back to the second decade of the State of Israel, to three successive criminal trials in which a fierce struggle was conducted over the meaning of the foundational values of the young state. The Kastner trial (1954–58), which dealt with the activity of the Jewish leader Rudolf (Israel) Kastner in Hungary during the Holocaust, focused attention on the legitimacy of Jewish leaders' attempts to negotiate and collaborate with the Nazis in order to save Jewish lives. It also led to the first political assassination in the independent State of Israel. The Kufr Qassem trial (1956–57), which dealt with the conduct of a unit of soldiers from the Border Police who murdered forty-nine Arab civilians for violating a curfew order of which they had no prior knowledge, raised the issues of the obligation to obey an illegal order and the weak status of Arab citizens in the State of Israel. The trial of the Nazi criminal Adolf Eichmann (1960–62), which dealt with the defendant's crimes against humanity in general and the Jewish people in particular, offered the first opportunity for survivors to tell the story of the Holocaust on a public stage. This was also the only trial in which a death sentence was imposed by an Israeli court and subsequently carried out. After locating these three trials on a historical/political continuum, the book leaps forward to the trial of Yigal Amir (1996) in order to examine the transformation that had taken place in the intervening decades in the two competing narratives of Israel's collective identity.

Every trial discussed in this book was first of all a political trial, a trial in which the political authorities sought to advance a political agenda through a criminal prosecution. However, they were not "show trials" in the derogative sense of trials in which the legal procedure is a mere facade concealing the brute use of power by the political authorities against a political opponent. The distinction between a political trial and a show trial hinges on the element of risk to the authorities, present in the former and absent in the latter, as I will elaborate subsequently.[7] Moreover, all of these trials had a transformative potential, which was fulfilled to different degrees in each. In all of these trials the practical, sometimes even the existential, implications of the abstract terms *Jewish* and *democratic* were exposed in the political reality of Israel. They transformed the struggle over the content of these terms into an agonal and dramatic conflict between an accuser and an accused, a conflict whose result could not be reduced to the mere question of the conviction or acquittal of the defendant. Rather, their legal result determined to an important degree the content of the collective memory, and therefore also of the Israeli collective identity, for years to come.

A central issue that the book addresses is the ability of a trial to serve as a consciousness-transforming vehicle: what kind of politics is advanced by it and how can it be used to promote the formation of a democratic society?[8] A courtroom, in particular during criminal trials, is first of all a field of human drama. The political struggle waged in the courtroom transforms dry and distant history or abstract ideological worldviews into a living story with a name, a face, and a body. It turns the theoretical dilemma into actuality and makes it accessible to the larger public. In this way it provides a unique forum in which society as a whole can confront its moral, historical, and political dilemmas in a more concentrated and intensive way.[9] Another advantage of the courtroom in comparison with other political forums is its subordination to dictates of procedural justice, which allows both parties to articulate their stories. In this way members of a minority group (such as criminal defendants or victims who are brought to testify) can advance a "counterstory" that can compete with the more dominant understanding of the basic values of society and otherwise is rarely heard. This alternative forum sometimes becomes the only public stage on which a political minority can express its criticism of the authorities (if only in a curbed way). These advantages, however, should not blind us to the inherent limitations of the courtroom. Whatever social transformation the court can induce, it is never as radical as the one achieved by a political revolution.[10] Moreover, as some of the trials show, some transformative narratives advanced by the court are subsequently stripped of their material effect by the intervention of political power holders, and sometimes such transformative trials even stall change by creating a false impression of a commitment to change. This will be called the legitimization effect of political trials.[11] The main danger in a transformative trial, I will argue, is also its main strength: the transformation of a multilayered political debate into a binary conflict. The adversarial structure (at least in Anglo-American legal systems) and the need to translate the rich complexity of reality into familiar legal categories almost inevitably result in reducing the real world problem to a binary representation. While this certainly serves to rivet public attention, it can often also distort reality and promote a black and white solution. The translation of the conflict into legal discourse often obfuscates the political nature of the competing stories and diverts attention from the need to explore a political resolution. Therefore, the central question raised by transformative trials is how to reimagine the structure of a trial and legal procedures in order to take full advantage of the political trial while reducing its risks to a minimum. The book seeks to present such a theory by confronting the concrete dilemmas raised in these four political trials in Israel.

The book is concerned with Israeli transformative trials, but the questions it poses are being raised today in a variety of societies that are undergoing a transition to a democratic system, from Eastern Europe to South Africa. The Israeli case is of special interest because it presents the dilemmas of a modern state that was established in 1948 on the basis of Western conceptions of nationalism, the right of self-determination, minority rights, and democracy. In traditional societies or states with long histories the formation of collective memory and identity is achieved, if at all, through a long, diffuse process, through religious and communal rituals that have nothing to do with the law. By contrast, Israel, which was designed to be a state consisting of Jewish immigrants, along with native Palestinians (both Arab and Jewish), had to forge a collective identity through conscious, central planning and by deliberately adapting old myths to the needs of a modern state.[12] Thus, collective memory was not left to the private realm, to be nourished in family gatherings and by tribal traditions, but was taken up by the state, through direct legislation and court decisions, where it was given its shape and direction.[13] The centrality of the law in these political processes of shaping a collective identity for a newly established state raises difficult questions about the power and limits of the legal arena with regard to these issues. These problems are not unique to Israel and are likely to receive more attention on the part of the international community as other new states are faced with the difficult task of striking the proper balance between nationalist aspirations and democratic commitments.[14]

Unique to Israel is the attempt to weave together two basic values of being a Jewish and democratic state. These values, as the trials discussed here show, were often in conflict and posed a constant challenge for the courts. Israel is peculiar in its attempt to combine liberal values with a state religion, but I argue that the role that political trials played in the development of an Israeli collective identity is not solely attributable to this fact. Political trials in a liberal democracy reflect the dynamics of group conflict within a pluralist society, as well as the basic commitment of liberalism to open its most fundamental values to revision. This renegotiation of collective identity often occurs in major political trials that have an intricate relationship to one another and therefore should be studied together.

For many years the legal community in Israel has focused its attention on the decisions of the Supreme Court sitting as a High Court of Justice, the main arena in which the content of the identity of the state as "democratic" and "Jewish" was challenged and sometimes transformed.[15] In this context special attention was given to court decisions that dealt with such questions as "Who is a Jew" (the nationality rubric in Israeli identity cards);[16] the limits of the democratic system (what parties could be banned from participating in elections to the Knesset);[17] the relations between religion and state (the drafting of Ultra-Orthodox Jews into the army, the recognition of civil marriages, the opening of stores on the Sabbath and the importation of pork);[18] and the distribution of land between national groups in Israel.[19] This literature examined important legal precedents that made vital contributions to the shaping of the Israeli Supreme Court and Israeli democracy. However, not much scholarly attention was given to the way this unique legal forum (the High Court of Justice) influenced the terms of collective memory and identity.[20] Several factors may have contributed to this neglect. Notwithstanding the high visibility of trials in this court, the legal argument is divorced from its human drama and agonal competition, since it is carried out mainly in affidavits and written pleas, and no witnesses testify or undergo cross-examination. Moreover, the High Court of Justice serves as the sole arbitrator of the conflict, being a court of first and last instance, hence not allowing for much social mobilization around the trial.[21] The debate in the High Court of Justice is considered to be theoretical and philosophical, and the decisions resemble in their structure and tone a political-legal essay. The structure of the trial and the theoretical character of the decisions therefore serve to focus public attention on the final verdict and not on the tedious legal arguments that preceded it. The main object is the legal precedent, not the human drama.

By concentrating on the decisions of the Israeli Supreme Court, in particular in its sessions as a High Court of Justice, researchers have overlooked the criminal trials considered in this book, which were no less important, and in some respects, which I will explore, even more important, to the formation of the Israeli collective identity. These trials included long testimonies and cross-examinations with shocking revelations. They lasted for many months and continued over several instances (a trial court and an appellate court), all the while closely followed by the media. These were trials that ignited the public's imagination and emotions, thus instigating a wide public debate. Their adversarial structure helped transform abstract ideas into a struggle between particular individuals, who became, through the trial, living symbols of conflicting worldviews. They became, in Pierre Nora's words *lieux de mémoire* (sites of memory), that is, sites in which the struggle over the interpretation of the past is perceived by the public as having enormous import for the politics of the present and the shaping of society in future years.[22] It was these trials, rather than the trials conducted in the High Court of Justice, that had the potential to become a source of public mobilization for various groups in Israeli society that were struggling to influence how the foundational values of the state would be interpreted.

The trials examined in this book—Kastner, *Eichmann*, Kufr Qassem, and *Amir*—are considered by the Israeli legal community to be exceptional trials that do not constitute a coherent theoretical category that contributes to the development of jurisprudential or constitutional theories of law. The only legal discussion around these trials involved narrow legalistic points that were mainly apologetic in tone—whether these trials could be justified according to ordinary criteria of fair criminal trials or whether the many deviations from ordinary procedure turned them into show trials. Until recent years, the Kastner trial did not receive much attention from the Israeli legal community. It was only in the 1990s that local legal scholars began to study the trial seriously.[23] Likewise, for a long time the Eichmann trial was discussed only in the context of international law or in books written by the lawyers involved in the trial.[24] The Kufr Qassem trial was also studied in the narrow legalistic context of obedience to manifestly illegal orders.[25]

The jurists focused on the precedential value of these trials (their possible contribution to international or domestic law), ignoring almost completely the fierce legal struggle over the historical narrative that was present in each of them. Historians, on the other hand, concentrated precisely on the latter aspects of the trials, overlooking the way in which legal considerations, to a large extent, shaped the historical narrative produced in each trial.[26] As a result until recent years these trials have been virtually absent from the law school curriculum, in particular from courses on constitutional law, and there has been no sustained effort to develop an Israeli jurisprudence that takes account of the function and importance of these trials in Israeli law and the shaping of Israeli democracy.

This book views these trials over a historical continuum and as an integral part both of Israeli constitutional law and of the struggle over the basic values of Israeli society. My claim in a nutshell is that the Zionist revolution did not end with the Declaration of Independence and the establishment of the State of Israel but has continued for the last fifty years, transformed through "constitutional moments," many of them involving a transformative trial.[27] These trials had an important role in the ongoing shaping of the Zionist revolution, and each ignited a heated public debate over its most basic values. The compartmentalization of the discussion into "legal" and "historical" departments has prevented us from understanding these trials as one category, as transformative trials that fulfill an essential function in a democratic society by exposing the hegemonic narrative of identity to critical considerations. In order to open up a conceptual space for such a discussion we first have to overcome two widespread erroneous assumptions: first, that every political trial is necessarily a show trial; and, second, that the formation of a new political-legal entity is completed with the enactment of a constitution or after conducting several transitional justice trials (such as criminal trials of the crimes of the previous regime or some type of truth commission). These assumptions were long considered to be an integral (not to say natural) part of a liberal conception of law. Over the years they have been criticized by several liberal writers, such as Otto Kirschheimer, Judith Shklar, and Bruce Ackerman, who argue that liberal legal theory needs to be revised in such a way as to make it capable of dealing with a reality in which a complete separation of law and politics is both impossible and undesirable. In particular, these writers sought to clarify how certain political trials contribute to constituting and maintaining society's commitment to the rule of law. In other words, they began to explore the way transformative trials create the conditions for a process of "constitutional revision" characterized by moments of transformation and a renewed commitment to the rule of law.

Two basic assumptions shape the discussion of transformative trials in this book. First, instead of a binary understanding that divides trials into show trials and just trials this book develops a theory that places transformative trials on a spectrum between the political and the legal. Instead of engaging in legal apologetics, the book evaluates the extent to which a transformative trial can remain loyal to the basic liberal value of the rule of law while seeking to perform its unique function as a legal forum in which society's fundamental values can be examined in the light of counterstories competing for hegemony.

My second assumption is that the constitution and transformation of collective identity are a continual process. As I have stated, the constitution of a political entity is not completed by a single constitutional act at the moment of its birth but is an ongoing process of evaluation and revision whose political context is revealed in transformative trials. Public trials can have an immense effect on these moments of transformation since they acquire high visibility through media coverage and often kindle a public debate in which prominent intellectuals intervene at crucial points, presenting counternarratives of their own (often critical, but sometimes supportive, of the power holders). The book gives special attention to this indirect dialogue between the social critic and the court. In particular it focuses on the public intervention of two renowned Israeli poets, Nathan Alterman and Haim Gouri, and a political philosopher, Hannah Arendt. All three took it upon themselves to report one or more of the trials but found themselves developing critical positions that conflicted either with the court or with the political authorities.

The reluctance of liberals to acknowledge these two assumptions, which enable political trials to be included in our theory of law, is not unfounded. It stems from the understanding that such trials involve an irreducible risk to the democratic system. The conflict exposed through the fierce competition of narratives during the trial is not a mere matter of rhetoric. It threatens the very fragile web of solidarity in society, confronting us with the constant need to protect the democratic structure of society by a willingness to change what has hitherto been considered sacred.[28] Moreover, there is no guarantee that following such a trial society will have the resources to renew its commitment to democracy and to rebuild social solidarity on firmer grounds. Violence is never far from such conflicts, and the danger they pose to society may explain why liberal theory has been hesitant to see such trials as an integral part of law. Nonetheless, I shall argue that a deeper understanding of the important role fulfilled by transformative trials will reveal them to be a source of strength to a democratic society. For this purpose, these trials should not be examined in isolation—as an exception that cannot be explained as part and parcel of a liberal theory of law—but in dialogue with one another over a period of time, presenting both a challenge to our theories of law and an opportunity to further develop our jurisprudence so as to accommodate transformative trials.

The book relies on several theories that offer alternative ways of understanding the relations between law and politics as opposed to the hostile attitude of traditional liberal legal theory toward political trials. Each theory helps us decode certain transformative trials, but none provides a framework that can explain all the trials discussed in this book. The book will therefore seek to provide such a framework.

Transitional justice theory addresses trials and other processes that take place during the transition from an authoritarian regime to a democracy.[29] This literature acknowledges the futility of trying to separate law from politics in such processes and instead discusses the constructive role trials can play in building society's commitment to a democratic regime. We can trace the origins of this approach in the writings of the political philosopher Judith Shklar, who in her book *Legalism* called for a revision of liberal theory to make it capable of adequately addressing the phenomenon of the Nuremberg and Tokyo trials.[30] This field has gained prominence following the democratization processes in South America, Eastern Europe, and South Africa in which

transitional justice became the focal point of public debate and imagination. However, while candidly recognizing the political aspects of
trials in transitional periods, this approach confines its acceptance of
political trials to this period alone. The assumption that transformation
occurs once and for all during the period of transition has prevented
the many theoretical insights of this literature from being applied to trials in established democracies.

Critical theory focuses on trials in established democracies and challenges the liberal assumption that they can be effectively insulated
from the influence of political forces. One of the unrecognized fore-
bears of this body of literature is the jurist and political scientist Otto
Kirschheimer, who in his book *Political Justice* rejected the common liberal effort to attribute the phenomenon of political trials to undemocra-
tic regimes.[31] Kirschheimer also advanced the distinction between a
show trial, in which the element of risk (the uncertainty of outcome)
has all but disappeared and the legal proceedings are merely a sham,
and political trials, which retain the element of risk. He also pointed to
the important mechanism of legitimization, which can explain the relationship between the court and the political authorities in these trials. It
was only in the 1980s that these ideas were systematically developed
and expanded by writers of the Critical Legal Studies (CLS) movement.[32] Although they rejected the very category of "political trials" as
legitimizing the rest of law as apolitical, their critical insights can help
us explore many of the aspects of transformative trials discussed in this
book, in particular, the extent to which a political lawyer or an independent judge can use the system against itself in order to expose the
underlying hegemonic narrative that is taken for granted in most day-
to-day trials.[33]

The political element of Holocaust trials could not easily be overlooked, and yet it could not be attributed to a "transition period." In
fact many of the Holocaust trials—such as the Eichmann, Demjanjuk,
and Barbie trials—took place many years after the events and were conducted in national courts of democratic states (France, Germany, and
Israel). Nonetheless, their politics could not be simply equated with the
politics of "ordinary trials" (as CLS writers would have it) since many
of them were directed at changing the terms of collective memory of
the society in which the trial took place. *Holocaust trials theory* therefore
serves to overcome an important lacuna: it recognizes the transforma-

tive role of these trials but, in contrast to transitional justice literature, does not restrict this recognition to the moment of transition to a democracy.[34] Instead it discusses two dimensions of the Holocaust trial: its ability to do justice to the defendant and its ability to do justice to history.[35] This theory sheds important light on two of the trials discussed in this book (Eichmann and Kastner), but since it treats Holocaust trials as a special category, a trauma that transcends ordinary legal doctrines, it cannot offer an interpretive framework for studying the Holocaust trial within the Israeli political context as a whole, and it fails to notice the important relations these trials have with non-Holocaust transformative trials.

To summarize, this book takes from transitional justice theory the understanding of the constructive role the political trial performs in constituting a democratic society but refuses to limit this recognition to the moment of transition. The book takes from the insights of critical theory the understanding of the legitimization effect of the political trial and the possibilities it provides for using the system against itself and exposing what claims to be apolitical as simply one kind of politics among others. However, it refuses to see all trials as political in the same way and seeks to identify the unique politics that characterizes transformative trials. Finally, the book takes from the theory of Holocaust trials the understanding of the dual role of transformative trials (justice and didactic history) but enlarges the frame of discussion to encompass other non-Holocaust trials. I argue that only by bringing these diverse theories together can we begin to develop a normative theory that can explain the phenomenon of transformative trials, which has only recently begun to attract attention. In this book I suggest critical criteria for evaluative transformative trials.

In developing a normative theory of transformative trials I rely on certain insights from Hannah Arendt's writings. In contrast to the prevailing view that Arendt adopted a narrow legalistic stance in *Eichmann in Jerusalem,* I seek to show that we should go beyond the polemics of the book and address the profound insights it provides regarding the possibilities of a transformative trial.[36] Indeed, it was only because Arendt realized these possibilities that she became so critical of what she considered the failure of the Israeli prosecution and the limited success of the judges in the Eichmann trial in exploring these possibilities. Moreover, Arendt was the first to point out that the Eichmann trial should not be read solely in relation to the Nuremberg trials but should be located in the Israeli context of political trials such as Kastner and Kufr Qassem. This shift in perspective, I maintain, helps resist the tendency to read the Eichmann trial as unique. Instead, it directs our attention to the political challenge that the trial posed to the Israeli court: whether the trial could bring Israel closer to its ideals of a democratic society or whether it would push it further in the direction of an ethnocratic society. Although Arendt herself did not have the opportunity to develop this insight and elaborate a rich reading of the three trials as they connect and conflict with each other, her book nonetheless opens up a new direction to reading Israeli transformative trials.

By addressing the insights Arendt expressed in *Eichmann in Jerusalem*, and in her theoretical writings on reflective judgment and political action, I seek here to explicate a new theory of transformative trials. I propose examining the trials in light of three criteria taken from Arendt's theory of reflective judgment: natality, the human capacity for regeneration; plurality, the recognition of the irreducible multiplicity of perspectives of human action; and narrativity, the importance of story-telling as an integral part of political action.[37] I will take these ideas, which were developed in the realm of political theory in general, and apply them to the specific phenomena of political trials.

I argue that a legitimate transformative trial has to fulfill all three criteria, and herein lies its difference from an ordinary trial. To put it differently, in a transformative trial the act of reflective judgment (which is constituted by respecting the three criteria) has to overcome the tendency to resort to determinative judgment (which subsumes a fact under a preordained legal category). Unlike ordinary trials, where most effort is directed to applying old precedents to new facts, transformative trials confront us with novel situations and the need to develop innovative legal categories to accommodate them (the component of natality). Thus, for example, the trials had to develop innovative interpretations of new legal concepts such as "collaboration," "crimes against humanity," "universal jurisdiction," "manifestly illegal order," and so on. In an ordinary trial the story advanced by the parties is auxiliary to the legal argument, while in a transformative trial, in which the disagreement often concerns the very rules of the game, the story (or rather the competition of stories) becomes the most important element in resolving the case. Only through this competition can a new common basis for interpreting the different laws be created. This is what I call the narrative component of the trial. The component of plurality, though closely related, is concerned with the court's ability to use the different legal procedures at its disposal, and create new ones, in order to allow the different stories to be fairly heard. In other words, the trial is evaluated according to its capacity to allow a competition of stories, and in particular to allow a counterstory that challenges the hegemonic narrative of identity. The element of plurality, however, should not be confused with the duty to respect due process considerations. For example, in the Eichmann trial, although the defendant enjoyed due process, the condition of plurality was frustrated by opening the trial to the testimonies of about a hundred Holocaust survivors while effectively blocking the defendant's ability to bring witnesses on his behalf. The competition was between live testimonies and written documents. While this did not damage the defense, since the judges were exposed to both sides, the public at large was exposed mainly to one testimony from the defense—that of Eichmann himself.[38] Likewise, in the Kastner trial the defense (due to its marginal political position) was effectively blocked from calling upon "respected" public figures to testify while the prosecution tried to influence the public with a long list of prominent public figures as witnesses. Nonetheless, as we shall see, the defense managed to turn this disadvantage into an advantage during the trial.[39] Together these three components—natality, narrativity, and plurality—provide insights into the different ways in which Israeli courts chose to confront early challenges to the dominant understanding of the meaning of a "Jewish and democratic state."

The terms *Jewish* and *democratic* received different interpretations in the four trials discussed in this book, but by placing the four trials on a historical continuum we can begin to see the recurrence of certain questions that were avoided or deliberately repressed and continuities in the way the court sought to address these issues. The first part of the book discusses the Kastner trial. This trial addressed the opposition between the New Jew and the Diaspora Jew for the first time in the context of a criminal trial, seeking to infer from its legal resolution concrete directions for political action. The "Jewish" identity of the state was explored in the trial by examining the different courses of action taken by Jews during the Holocaust. The trial raised for the first time the issue of self-blame and the "gray area" of Jewish leaders' cooperation and collaboration with the Nazis in order to save Jewish lives. The verdict of the district court strengthened the binary understanding of Israeli collective identity by placing the way of resistance in opposition to the way of negotiations and collaboration. The trial also made the past relevant to deciding the outcome of fierce political controversies that concerned Israeli society at the time, in particular the question of the cooperation of the leaders of the Jewish community in Mandate Palestine with the British authorities. The way of negotiations, despised by the right-wing opposition parties and supported by the ruling Mapai party, as opposed to military resistance, was identified with Kastnerism and presented as illegitimate and necessarily leading to a national catastrophe. This black and white depiction of the Jews' political possibilities during the Holocaust became the cornerstone of Judge Benjamin Halevi's verdict, in which he described Kastner as having "sold his soul to the devil." This approach was strongly criticized by the poet Nathan Alterman, in his widely read weekly newspaper column, who attempted to convince the public of the wrongness of the decision and the need to avoid making false analogies between Europe under Nazi occupation and Palestine under British rule.

The attempt to develop a more pluralistic view of the political options open to the Jewish leaders came to a halt in the trial of Adolf Eichmann. This time it was the attorney general who used the trial to present a simplistic picture consisting of only two categories—victimizer versus victim. This picture allowed Israeli society to empathize for the first time with the Holocaust victims as human beings with faces, voices, and stories. However, as Arendt warned, it also posed great dangers to Israel's political culture. It encouraged thinking in ethnic terms about the relations between Israel and the rest of the world (relying on the category "crimes against the Jewish people"), and it distorted the perception of relations with the Arab inhabitants of the state. However, as we shall see, Arendt's counterstory did not become an integral part of the public debate about the Eichmann trial in Israel. Rather, every effort was made to insulate the trial from the preceding Kastner trial and there was no attempt to reconcile the two very different images of the Holocaust and Israeli-Jewish identity that emerged from the two trials. Here I seek to create a more plural space in which the narrative of the prosecutor in the Eichmann trial, Gideon Hausner, will be compared to the narrative of the philosopher Hannah Arendt in order to examine the very different ways in which they sought to address the basic problems of Israeli democracy. I argue that this trial played an enormous role in transforming Israeli collective memory and identity. The transformative power of the trial consisted not only in determining the guilt of a Nazi perpetrator by a Jewish court, nor even in representing the story of the Jewish Holocaust for the first time on a public stage through survivors' testimonies. Rather, its transformative importance lay in the public forum it created for translating the memory of the past into a concept of the state's Jewish and democratic identity.

The Kufr Qassem trial (which preceded *Eichmann*) reveals the other side of this equation—how well Israel kept its promise to develop a democratic society. This was the first time that the Arab victims of brutal violence at the hands of Israeli soldiers were heard on a public stage, forcing the Israeli public to confront the collapse of the moral code as revealed in the massacre. The court, once again presided over by Benjamin Halevi, tried to address the problem by erecting new boundaries—placing the rule of law above the rule of the army. Through a long narrative Judge Halevi tried to transform the de jure recognition of the rights of Arab citizens into a sustained effort to include them in the Israeli collective. The trial provided a moment of recognition of the need for Israeli society to set limits on the use of power and to develop a more inclusive civil society. The Eichmann trial that followed undermined this understanding, by encouraging the analogy between Nazis and Palestinians (with reference to the sympathy for Hitler of the Mufti of Jerusalem) and by emphasizing the Jews' victimization by these enemies.

The book ends with a discussion of the trial of Rabin's assassin. In Israel's short history, there is a huge leap in time from 1962 to 1996, but this is precisely what gives us an opportunity to reexamine the questions raised in the early trials in historical perspective. In this sense it comes full circle. The trial of Yigal Amir brings us back to the stories that were presented in both the Kastner and the Kufr Qassem trials. Amir's political defense relied on the exclusion of an imagined Other— in the dual form of the Arab and the collaborator. Amir presented the course of negotiation with the Palestinian leaders endorsed by the Rabin government as fundamentally illegitimate, as treason, and hence as justifying the use of illegitimate countermeans such as murder. In response, the court offered a narrative that sought to create solidarity by invoking the two most traumatic moments in the life of the nation— the destruction of the Second Temple and the subsequent expulsion from the Land of Israel in ancient times, and the Holocaust in modern times. This response followed in the footsteps of the *Eichmann* court, stressing the Jewish aspect of Israeli identity over the civic aspect. The trial of Amir revealed in all its poignancy the danger to Israeli democracy presented by a direct challenge to the sovereign in the name of the Jewish Halakhah. The competition of stories based on ideological rivalry, which had been employed over the years more as a rhetorical weapon, was transformed by *Amir* into a life and death struggle over the meaning of the state as Jewish and democratic.

One of the burning issues in Israel today, and in the world at large, is the meaning of democracy in multinational and multiethnic societies.[40] What is the role of the law, and the court in particular, in shaping a collective identity that provides space for conflicting, and at times irreconcilable, narratives of identity by the different groups within these societies? This is the challenge this book hopes to address.

The Kastner Trial

Chapter 1

Performing the Past
The Role of the Political Lawyer

It was not the trials of Nazi perpetrators such as Adolf Eichmann that first brought the Holocaust to the attention of Israeli courts but rather trials involving their Jewish victims. In the 1950s the Israeli Law of Punishment of the Nazis and Their Collaborators led to a number of trials in which judges were obliged to confront the actions of Jewish leaders and functionaries during the Holocaust.[1] These trials did not receive much public attention and were mainly discussed in the communities of survivors involved in them. One trial, however, stands out as the exception: criminal case 124/53 *Attorney General v. Malchiel Gruenwald*, better known as "the Kastner trial," which took place in the district court in Jerusalem during the years 1954–55.[2] This was the first Holocaust trial that succeeded in making itself relevant to the Israeli public at large. No doubt, the Kastner trial differed in important respects from other "Holocaust trials." Not only was it the first (and only) trial that dealt with the actions of a Jewish leader as opposed to those of low-ranking Jewish functionaries (*kapos* and policemen), but the central issue it raised—the negotiations Rudolf Kastner conducted with Adolf Eichmann in the hope of saving Jewish lives—had the power to capture the imagination of ordinary people. Moreover, the fact that this case was brought to court as a criminal libel trial concerning the free speech of an Israeli citizen endowed it with far more immediate interest for the Israeli public than the trials judged under the retroactive and extraterritorial Law of Punishment of the Nazis and Their Collaborators. Nonetheless, these differences were not sufficient in themselves to explain the fierce political debate about Israeli collective identity and memory that the Kastner trial engendered. In order to understand the dynamics of public interest around the trial, I suggest reading it as a political trial in which the parties engaged in a heated debate about the historical lessons that the Holocaust held for the ethos of the new state and its future code of behavior. Although the politicization of the trial began with the insistence of the attorney general, Haim Cohn, that criminal charges of libel be pressed against a man who had accused a public official of collaboration with the Nazis, it did not end there. Rather, it was a brilliant defense lawyer, Shmuel Tamir, one of the founders of the right-wing Revisionist party (Herut), the main opposition to Mapai, who was largely responsible for its transformation from a trial about past events in a distant land into a full-blown political trial perceived by the Israeli public as touching on the most urgent issues of the day. This chapter is devoted to exploring that transformation and the role of the defense lawyer in effectuating it.

The Kastner trial began as a libel trial against an elderly Hungarian Jew, Malchiel Gruenwald, who was accused of defaming the Zionist leader, Rudolf (Israel) Kastner, by alleging that he had collaborated with the Nazis.[3] Kastner lived in Budapest during World War II and organized, together with other Zionist activists (among them Joel and Hansi Brand), a committee for the rescue of Jewish refugees who were fleeing to Hungary in an attempt to escape the Nazi terror in neighboring countries (known by its Hebrew name of Va'adat Ezrah Vehatzalah).[4] After the 1944 German takeover of Hungary, Kastner served as chief negotiator with Adolf Eichmann, the top Nazi official responsible for the deportation of Jews to German concentration camps, and with other Nazi officials on behalf of Hungary's Jewish community (although he was never a member of the Judenrate—the Jewish councils appointed by the Nazis in the ghettoes). The "blood for goods" deal sought by Kastner and seriously considered by the Nazis was intended to save the lives of nearly a million Jews in exchange for ten thousand trucks to be delivered to the German army. Although Joel Brand was even sent to Turkey to persuade members of the Jewish Agency to tell the Allies of the proposal, this ambitious goal was not achieved and approximately 400,000 Hungarian Jews were eventually sent to their deaths in Auschwitz. Kastner did succeed in saving a group of 1,685[5] Jews, who were shuttled to safety in Switzerland. This transport included a disproportionate number of Kastner's friends and relatives.[6]

After the war Kastner's involvement in this capacity was questioned; at the 1946 Zionist Congress he was accused by a Hungarian activist of being a cynical opportunist who had selfishly sacrificed

Hungarian Jewry in return for his personal safety. Kastner responded with a libel suit against the accuser, submitted to the Congress's Honor Court. He also wrote a long report accounting for all his wartime activities in Hungary.[7] However, the panel decided that it did not have enough evidence to reach a conclusive decision and recommended that the matter be investigated in depth in the future.[8] Thereafter, Kastner emigrated to Israel and became active in the ruling labor party, Mapai; by 1952 he was serving as spokesman for the Ministry of Trade and Industry. Kastner was also on the Mapai candidate list for the first and second elections to the Knesset (Israeli parliament). Although he was not elected, there was a good chance he would be successful in the third elections, to be held in 1955.

It was at this time that Malchiel Gruenwald embarked on a campaign against Kastner. A devoted member of Ha-Mizrahi (the religious wing of the Zionist movement) and a refugee who had lost most of his family in Hungary, Gruenwald had a political as well as a personal agenda. In addition to seeking to expose Kastner's crimes, Gruenwald hoped to denounce Mapai, demand Kastner's removal, and facilitate the appointment of a commission of inquiry to investigate the events that had led to the decimation of Hungary's Jews. The target of his criticism was the negotiations that Kastner had conducted with Adolf Eichmann, which Gruenwald asserted had facilitated the destruction of Hungarian Jewry while benefiting Kastner personally. In a pamphlet he sent to Ha-Mizrahi members in the summer of 1952 Gruenwald phrased his charge that Kastner had collaborated with the Nazis in vivid and offensive terms.

> The smell of a corpse scratches my nostrils! This will be a most excellent funeral! Dr. Rudolf Kastner should be eliminated! For three years I have been awaiting this moment to bring to trial and pour the contempt of the law upon this careerist, who enjoys Hitler's acts of robbery and murder. On the basis of his criminal tricks and because of his collaboration with the Nazis . . . I see him as a vicarious murderer of my dear brothers.[9]

According to Gruenwald's allegations, Kastner had become friendly with the Nazis through their negotiations and as a result had been allowed to save his relatives and a small number of Jewish dignitaries. In return, Kastner had allowed himself to be used by the Nazis by not informing Hungarian Jews of the real destination of the deportation trains. Gruenwald also alleged that Kastner, in collusion with some Nazis, had stolen Jewish money and after the war had helped save the life of Kurt Becher, one of the Nazi officers with whom he had negotiated, with favorable testimony at the Nuremberg war crimes trials.[10] Warned by Attorney General Cohn that he must either sue Gruenwald for libel or resign from his government post, Kastner sued, and since he was a senior government official he was represented at the trial by the attorney general himself.[11] In the course of the trial, however, it was Kastner, not Gruenwald, who found himself on the defensive.

Shmuel Tamir,[12] the defense attorney, answered the accusation against his client with the response: "He spoke the truth." Tamir did not deny that Gruenwald had written the offending pamphlet. Quite the contrary—he set out to prove that everything in it was true. Tamir claimed that had the Jews been informed of the Nazi extermination plan, many of them could perhaps have escaped to Romania, revolted against the Germans, or sent calls for help to the outside world, all of which could have significantly slowed the Nazi killing process.

Due to the two main protagonists, Cohn and Tamir, the Kastner trial was politicized from its very inception.[13] However, while Cohn wanted to use the legal device as a simple way of refuting and silencing political criticism against a government official, it was Tamir who immediately understood the trial's political potential to serve as a public stage for embarrassing the political authorities.[14] In the background lurked the political controversy over Prime Minister Ben-Gurion's decision to enter into negotiations with Germany over reparations. Herut's leader, Menachem Begin, used this debate as a political tool to delegitimize Mapai's willingness to negotiate with Germany and he succeeded in transforming a political disagreement into a matter of morality.[15]

Tamir's main aim was to turn the proceedings into a subversive political trial and a means of delegitimizing the ruling Mapai party. But here he confronted formidable obstacles. In the 1950s the Israeli public regarded the Holocaust as belonging to "another planet" and saw the survivors who had immigrated to Israel as "Others," outside the Israeli collective. This attitude was supported by the prevailing Zionist ethos of "the negation of the diaspora," according to which the State of Israel epitomized a rupture with two thousands years of Jewish life in the diaspora. It envisioned a "New Jew" who would develop in the Land of Israel with characteristics diametrically opposed to those of the Diaspora Jew. The New Jew was to be connected to the land, leading a productive life and relying on self-help in economic and security matters, as symbolized by the figures of the *halutz* (pioneer farmer and builder) and the *shomer* (defender and warrior).[16] This ideological background can explain why the Holocaust trials of the 1950s had until then been perceived by the Israeli public as internal matters involving the communities of survivors alone. Thus, Tamir had to find a way to make a trial that dealt with events that had occurred on that "other planet" of occupied Europe relevant to the political controversies of the day. In this he was greatly helped by the weekly *Ha-Olam Ha-Ze,* a lively Israeli newspaper that gave extensive coverage to the trial in a way that was sympathetic to Tamir.[17] Until the Kastner trial the press coverage of the kapos' trials had been minimal, and at first this was also the fate of the Kastner trial. The only newspaper that reported on Gruenwald's pamphlet was *Herut* (which was affiliated with the Revisionist party). But as the trial proceeded other newspapers began to give it more and more coverage, and within a few months the trial had to be moved to a larger auditorium because of the masses of people who came to listen. When the verdict was announced the public's interest reached its peak and the newspapers devoted huge headlines and full pages to the trial. The fact that the verdict was announced only a few weeks before the general elections contributed to its politicization.[18]

The Kastner affair could have signaled a first questioning of the Zionist ideology that opposed the proud "New Jew" of the Land of Israel to the submissive Jews of the diaspora. After all, Kastner was a *Zionist* leader who had chosen negotiations and cooperation with the Nazis rather than military resistance. This moment of recognition, when the simplified stereotype of myth confronted the complexities of concrete historical reality, had an explosive potential. It could have led to a searching critique of this aspect of Zionist ideology, and in particular of its disparaging treatment of Holocaust survivors who had not belonged to the resistance. Tamir, however, who had no intention of undermining an ideology he himself upheld, chose to take the trial in another direction, one that could be used to sully the Zionist credentials of his political opponents. Thus, instead of examining the ideology in light of the historical reality of occupied Europe, he chose to interpret the historical facts in accordance with his own ideological beliefs, thus strengthening the blinders that this ideology produced. Tamir sought to show that it was not the ideology that was at fault but the leaders

(Kastner and, by association, Mapai) who had failed to live up to it. Tamir skillfully used the legal process to sustain this argument, building his case on three central strategies, which involved (1) adapting historical reality to the binary structure of Zionist ideology, (2) reenacting the past trauma in the courtroom, and (3) manipulating the legal discourse of "truth."

1.   A Sociolegal Binary Structure

The legal process of Israeli law is adversarial. The struggle between the two sides—the prosecution and the defense—generates a drama, which is intensified in criminal proceedings that are held on a daily basis and take place within a relatively short period of time. The decision of the attorney general to prosecute forced the complex affair into the binary structure of the trial, which created the impression that there were only two possibilities—acquittal or conviction. However, this structure was also perfectly suited to the story Tamir wished to promote, according to which people were faced with two mutually exclusive choices—heroic resistance or collaboration and treason. The formal positions of prosecution and defense in a criminal trial thus came to symbolize two ideological positions: cooperation versus defiance. Kastner's actions were associated with the cowardly path of collaboration while Tamir's political stance was associated with the heroic path of resistance. The entire intermediate range of actions between these two poles—such as the different ways in which the underground movements had cooperated with the Judenrate—was disregarded. The binary framework thus excluded serious consideration of the issues actually faced by Kastner and other Jewish leaders who had had to take life and death decisions without the benefit of hindsight: the immense difficulties of saving the victims, the impending end of the war, and so on. Moreover, this binary structure (both ideological and legal), which was imposed on the facts, obscured the tragic nature of the decisions taken by people who were forced to make the cruel choice of sacrificing the few in the hope of saving the many.

Tamir presented his arguments within the framework of the prevailing Zionist narrative. According to Tamir, Kastner's compliance with the authorities was typical diaspora behavior, which had led to full collaboration with the Nazis and to the annihilation of the Jewish people of Hungary. The Zionist alternative to "Kastnerism," however, could

not come from Tamir's client, Malchiel Gruenwald, himself a typical
Diaspora Jew who was ultimately a marginal character in the legal
drama.[19] Rather, it was defense attorney Tamir who offered himself as
a model of the proud Sabra (native born Israeli Jew).[20] The contrast
between the new and old Jew was especially evident in the cross-examination of Kastner. Tamir's eloquent rhetoric and perfect fluency in
Hebrew were in stark contrast to the broken Hebrew of Kastner's testimony, which was filled with "foreign" expressions.[21] Moreover, by
managing to transform his position in the trial from that of a formal
defense lawyer into that of a de facto prosecutor, Tamir reenacted the
national myth of heroism—the weak and few overcoming the strong
and many by turning a defense into a victorious offensive.

The familiar Zionist narrative, which Tamir so skillfully put to use in
the trial, made the Israeli audience receptive to his critique. Although
Tamir's criticism failed to reveal, for the most part, the sordid secrets
and sensational facts that he had promised, he succeeded in transforming his defense of Gruenwald into a political attack by extending the
patterns of behavior he had identified in Nazi-occupied Hungary to the
situation in prestate Palestine, implying that the leadership of the
Yishuv (the organized Jewish population in Mandatory Palestine) during the war had played the role not of "heroic Zionists" but, like Kastner, of collaborators with the foreign ruler.

During World War II, one of the main divisions among the different
Jewish political groups in Palestine had concerned the relationship
with the British authorities. Mapai, the leading party, had chosen to
cooperate with the British in their war efforts against the Nazis, while
the Revisionists had believed that the military struggle for liberation
from the British in Palestine should continue. On several occasions, as a
result of the often bitter conflict between the groups, Revisionists who
were believed to be terrorists had been handed over to the British by
members of the opposing political party. At first glance, the Kastner
trial seemed irrelevant to this controversy since it dealt with the actions
of Jewish leaders in Nazi-occupied Hungary. However, in his effort to
discredit the Mapai party, Tamir used Kastner's political affiliation
with Mapai leaders to imply an underlying resemblance in their political approach. Both, he argued, had preferred negotiations and cooperation to military resistance, thus, by implication, betraying their people.[22] In Europe this choice had proved to be catastrophic since it had
facilitated the Nazi annihilation of European Jewry. The trial, in

Tamir's vision, should serve to demonstrate this "lesson" to the younger generation, a warning against the pragmatic path of negotiations and collaboration. "We should remember," he admonished in his closing argument, "that never in the history of humankind have so many been annihilated in such a short time and in such a criminal and degrading manner. When we discuss this chapter, in addition to discovering the truth we are obliged to scrutinize ourselves. . . . There is a young generation growing up in Israel that has to be told what was done to their parents, brothers and sisters, has to know the whole affair. There is a young generation that has to have a value system that will direct them to what is right and what is wrong."[23] This was the essential meaning of the Zionist message of the negation of the diaspora, since Jews in the diaspora throughout the ages had relied on compliance and cooperation with the authorities for their survival. This ideological line is particularly striking in Tamir's cross-examination of the Judenrat member Pinchas Freudiger.

> *Tamir:* I think Sir that you were not given a revolutionary education. Forgive my asking, I would be right in saying that your and your group's mentality was that of a Diaspora Jew. I am sorry to use this expression but I'm afraid this is so.
> *Freudiger:* Is there such a thing?
> *Tamir:* I think so.
> *Freudiger:* I was a religious man in the Diaspora and I am still a religious man in Israel.
> *Tamir:* That is not what I mean. I mean that the general view, the way of life, was one of accepting the reality in the Diaspora, and in times of trouble, of resorting to bribery and petitioning [of the authorities].
> *Freudiger:* But it is explicitly written [in the Bible] "strive for the peace of the city."
> *Tamir:* That's why I'm asking whether this was your mentality.
> *Freudiger:* Yes.
> *Tamir:* Did Dr. Kastner urge you and your group to join the underground?
> *Freudiger:* No.[24]

This line of questioning implied that the Israelis, as the New Jews, should abandon this path and criticize the Mapai leadership for demonstrating a "diaspora mentality." In short, the trial should serve to legitimate the Revisionist approach as the only authentic Zionism capable of guarding against the recurrence of similar catastrophes to the Jewish people in the future. It was here for the first time that the political path of "negotiations" with the enemy acquired the defeatist connotation that was to be evoked in future political debates concerning the legitimacy of negotiations between Israeli and Arab leaders.[25] Tamir emphasized this in his concluding remarks, saying: "We do not oppose negotiations even with the devil in order to save souls from Israel. However, once you have entered such negotiations, and you see that the devil himself is sitting opposite you and talking to you, then you have to ask yourself the initial question: What does he want? Aren't I serving his interests?"[26]

According to Tamir, the right-wing underground movements, which had urged that all contacts with the British cease, were the only ones fit to bear the title of "heroic Zionists."[27] Tamir's critique entailed merely switching the positions of the protagonists in a narrative with clearly defined roles rather than a challenge to the prevailing ideology. He completed his subversive narrative by representing the Jewish population in occupied Europe not as passive victims but as heroes ready for battle who had been misled by incompetent leaders and had therefore gone "like lambs to the slaughter."[28] His narrative could help ordinary people assuage their guilt feelings for not having done enough during the war to save their Jewish brethren, since the failure could now be attributed to an incompetent and deceitful leadership.

Tamir's portrayal of the events in his closing arguments was deliberately nonlinear and nonchronological, constantly shifting back and forth between places (Israel and Hungary) and time periods (wartime and trial time) in order to draw analogies between Kastner's leadership in Hungary and Mapai's leadership in Palestine.[29] This analogical storytelling helped create a black and white drama in which historical time, with its elements of contingency, uncertainty, and ambiguity, was expelled from the courtroom. Moreover, this method transformed the audience into active participants in the legal drama because each one was invited, on the basis of his or her personal knowledge about present day politics, to draw further analogies between what had happened in Mandatory Palestine and wartime Europe. Since the actions of the leaders in both cases were depicted as determined by innate tendencies (the diaspora mentality) rather than external exigencies, knowledge of historical details was not required. This narrative also elided the significant differences between past and present—between the situations in Hungary and in Palestine during the war and between the actions of leaders under colonial rule and in a sovereign state. In this way, Tamir's strategy helped turn the trial into a political trial since, unlike ordinary trials, which are directed toward determining the truth about past events, the Kastner trial under Tamir's influence became oriented toward the future, encouraging the public to draw lessons from the affair in order to choose between different courses of political action.[30]

2.   Reenacting the Past Trauma in the Courtroom

"The Prominent" versus "The Masses"

In order to render historical events part of a living collective memory, it was not sufficient merely to switch the roles of the participants in the Zionist narrative. It was essential to revive the past and re-create the trauma in the courtroom. For this purpose Tamir relied on testimonial witnessing. Tamir's early recognition of the value of survivors' testimonies as a privileged site of memory preceded the proliferation of current studies on the subject. Indeed, testimony has recently become a prevalent and important genre of nonfiction, and witnessing—typically witnessing based on memory—has emerged as a widely used mode of access to the past and its traumatic occurrences. Recent studies reveal that testimonial witnessing transforms the audience itself into a secondary witness but that the reception of testimony depends on the extent to which the audience is capable of real empathic listening.[31] However, as we shall see, since Tamir's purpose was not to deepen historical understanding of the full complexity of the events but to reinforce his own political message, he was not concerned with the need to create a proper framework for real listening.[32]

Tamir used the structure of the testimonies in the trial in order to re-create the painful moment of "selection" between the "prominent Jews" who were rescued and the "Jewish masses" who were sent to their deaths. This tactic was made possible by the prosecution's unwise decision to call Kastner as its first witness in order to allow him to present his full version of events. After Kastner had testified for three days, Judge Halevi turned to the defense and asked if it would like to change its plea to guilty. Gruenwald refused, and Tamir's subsequent cross-examination of Kastner became a turning point in the trial.[33] Kastner's tendency to exaggerate, to be somewhat vague, and sometimes to take more credit than he deserved may have worked to his advantage in his negotiations with the Nazis when he had had nothing substantial to offer, but it was exploited by Tamir to Kastner's detriment in the trial. Through his aggressive cross-examination Tamir exposed many weak points in his testimony. One of the most dramatic moments in the trial occurred on the second day of Tamir's cross-examination (25 February 1954). When questioned about the affidavit Kastner had given on behalf of the Nazi officer Kurt Becher in the Nuremberg trials, Kastner denied that he had intervened in order to gain Becher's release from prison. Tamir confronted Kastner with a letter he had sent to the Israeli finance minister in July 1948 in which he had written: "Becher was released thanks to my personal intervention."

> *Tamir:* Do you confirm that you wrote it?
> *Kastner:* Yes.
> *Tamir:* A minute ago you claimed that it was a lie that Becher was released thanks to your personal intervention. Do you still claim this?
> *Kastner:* I confirm what I said in the trial.
> *Tamir:* And in your letters to the ministers of Israel do you write the truth?
> *Kastner:* Yes. I write the truth in these letters.
> *Tamir:* And in court, do you testify the truth?

Kastner then explained that in court he had told the truth but in his letter to the minister of finance he had exaggerated. "If I were to be accused of formulating my words carelessly, I would admit it. I take responsibility for the way I expressed myself. [But] there is no lie here . . . what I wrote to Kaplan is exaggerated. I tell you that it is a lie that thanks to my personal intervention Becher was released."[34]

As a result of Kastner's poor performance in cross-examination, the prosecution decided to call a large number of "political" witnesses who had worked with Kastner to substantiate and complete his testimony. The witnesses for the prosecution included Menachem Bader, Ehud Avriel, and Yoel Palgi, prominent political figures and cultural heroes who had played key roles in rescue operations in Europe.[35] Some, like

David Berman, had been Judenrat members and some had held public positions in the young State of Israel.[36] Tamir exploited the desperate attempt of the prosecution to corroborate Kastner and turned a disadvantage into an advantage. Instead of countering the prosecution's well-known political witnesses with other prominent political figures—a move that in any case was not possible for Tamir because of his marginal position in Israeli politics—he decided to call a number of mostly unknown Holocaust survivors whose voices had not yet been heard by the Israeli public. These people, from various walks of life and representing a broad range of political views, formed a vivid contrast with the witnesses for the prosecution, most of whom belonged to the Israeli socioeconomic elite and were affiliated with Mapai.[37] Tamir emphasized the fact that his witnesses were not affiliated with any particular political party, arguing that this proved that "the spontaneous truth" was on his side. He claimed that their testimonies were being repressed by the authorities who had initiated the libel trial in order to keep them from public knowledge. The contrast between the prosecution's list of prominent political figures and the unknown witnesses of Tamir had the powerful effect of re-creating the traumatic moment of "selection" within the courtroom between those who had been chosen to board Kastner's rescue train and those who had been forced to board the death trains leading to Auschwitz. The result was a complex tale of a dual act of selection—the original selection of the few privileged Jews who had boarded Kastner's train reenacted by this second selection of "privileged witnesses" by the prosecution who had been summoned to defend Kastner.

In order to better understand Tamir's procedural tactic we should consider the legal method of proving the truth through firsthand testimony and direct observation.[38] Since the law privileges the human voice as the basis for proving the truth, establishing the trustworthiness of the witness becomes an issue of critical importance in the trial. As Lawrence Douglas observes, "in this jurisprudential model, the witness identifies himself to the court before he tells the court what he has seen. His identity, once defined and secured, is considered anterior to, and enabling of, the act of bearing responsible witness."[39] Tamir was doubly burdened in this respect. Throughout the 1950s the only historical accounts of the Holocaust in Israel were written by people associated with the Jewish resistance. The prevalent Zionist ideology of the day rendered the "ghetto fighters" and "resistance members" as the only trustworthy witnesses of the period. Ordinary survivors, on the other hand, were deemed suspect. Their very survival was taken by Israelis to be a sign of their moral failure, an attitude that has been succinctly captured by Primo Levi, who wrote that "the worst survived, that is the fittest: the best of all died."[40] These survivors were transformed into "victims" in the extreme sense of the word described by Lyotard, as indicating those who cannot even express their victimization because their words are considered unreliable.[41] The prosecution used this "economy" of uneven credibility and packed its list of witnesses with "heroes" and "political leaders." Nonetheless, through the witnesses' symbolic reenactment of the past trauma of selection, Tamir managed to present the very "respectability" of the prosecution's witnesses as a sign of their unreliability, implying that they were the ones most interested in "covering up" the preferential selection of people like themselves for rescue. With this performative hyperbole Tamir transformed the "ordinary survivors" into reliable witnesses who were perceived by the public as doubly wronged—once by their Nazi persecutors and again by Israeli prosecution.

Giving Voice to Holocaust Survivors

The defense repeatedly declared its intention to allow the survivors, who had never before been given the chance to tell their stories in public, to report "the whole truth." However, a scrutiny of the actual testimonies reveals a different view of what went on in the trial. Legal rules of procedure limit the testimonies of witnesses in court, mainly by subjecting them to the form of questions and answers that are controlled by the attorneys and the court. Tamir's questions did not allow for hesitation or confusion in his witnesses' testimonies. Their words were meant to be heard only insofar as they supported the Zionist "lesson" in favor of military resistance. Consequently, he repeatedly asked the survivors, "What would you have done if you had known about the secret of Auschwitz?" The answer was inevitably that they would not have boarded the trains.[42] Tamir's question took advantage of the understandable anger felt by the passengers of the death transports who had not been fortunate enough to be rescued by Kastner's train. His questions were intended to elicit a simple answer—one that would place all the blame squarely on the leaders who had known about the atrocities but had not warned their communities about them. Any other answers, which suggested that the leaders' decision to cooperate with the Nazi authorities had been complex and was influenced by the Nazis' own deceptions and extremely uncertain circumstances, were presented by Tamir as efforts to conceal the truth.[43] Moreover, he ignored the crucial issue of whether "knowing" about Auschwitz at that time could have been the same as comprehending its meaning. Thus, by summoning a long list of Holocaust survivors as witnesses, Tamir created the impression of breaking the silence about the Holocaust without actually giving the public a chance to listen to the accounts of Holocaust survivors in all their complexity and ambiguity.

The difficulty of listening to testimonies of Holocaust survivors within an ideological framework and the constraints of legal questioning is particularly evident in the court's examination of Hillel Danzig, who had been affiliated with the Jewish Council in Kastner's hometown, Cluj. Despite Danzig's efforts to explain the difficulty of judging past events in today's courtroom, his words were dismissed as perjurious and unreliable.

> *Question:* If you had known that the train was going to Auschwitz, how would you have acted in relation to your family and yourself?
>
> *Answer:* I don't know . . . I can think about it today and give you an answer, but it has nothing to do with the situation then, with what I would have done under those circumstances.
>
> *Question:* Why doesn't it have anything to do with it?
>
> *Answer:* Because we are sitting here today in completely different circumstances. What one asks and answers here in the state of Israel, ten years later, is not at all related to the situation then.
>
> *Question:* Can you remember the situation then?
>
> *Answer:* I remember. But I can't tell you what I would have done given the way things are now. Since all the Jews boarded those trains, I guess that my family and I would probably have gotten on the train too, if there had been no other possibility.[44]

In his study of the testimonies of Holocaust survivors, Lawrence Langer discovered a disjunction between past and present experiences, which prevented the survivors from presenting a coherent chronological account of their lives.[45] The rules pertaining to legal evidence are based on the assumption that there is chronological continuity between the past and the present, and any discrepancy is interpreted as a sign of lying or evading the truth. The law is accustomed to dealing with a witness who either does or does not remember, but it lacks tools that are sensitive enough to deal with a witness who remembers all too well but is incapable of reproducing the past in the present. Thus, in Kastner's trial the silencing of the survivors took on a new dimension—even when they came to testify in public, their testimonies were not really heard.

Several years later, in the *Eichmann* trial, Attorney General Gideon Hausner faced a similar problem. In order to facilitate meaningful listening to survivors' testimonies he decided to relax some of the rules of procedure—in particular, the format of questions and answers.[46] This decision may have been influenced by the Kastner trial, in which the traumatic moment was reenacted without resolution. Relying on the ordinary rules of procedure, Tamir's examination of the Holocaust survivors furthered his legal defense but failed to respect the difficulty of testifying about the Holocaust. The survivors were deprived of a sense of control and empowerment in relating their stories. They were brought as defense witnesses, were asked very focused questions, and were expected to limit their answers to pointing an accusatory finger at Kastner (but for his silence we would have never boarded the trains).[47] In *Eichmann,* by contrast, survivors were brought as witnesses for the prosecution, a structural change that allowed them to direct their accusations where they really belonged—toward the Nazi perpetrators. With no legal resolution of the painful past (the acquittal of Gruenwald was not accompanied by the conviction of Kastner), the emotions aroused by the Kastner trial were left without catharsis.

3. A Libel Trial as a Political Trial

Debunking National Myths

Two testimonies were particularly important in creating Tamir's iconoclastic image. One of the main heroic myths in the Israeli memory of World War II was that of young Jewish paratroopers in Palestine who were sent in 1944 by the British to war-torn Europe on a mission of espionage and who also undertook to help the Jews organize resistance to the Nazi occupiers. Three of the thirty-two paratroopers were sent to Hungary (Yoel Palgi, Peretz Goldstein, and Hannah Senesh), of whom only Palgi survived to tell the story of their heroic mission. On 16 March the prosecution summoned Palgi to testify on his relations with Kastner in the hope that he would corroborate the latter's version of events. However, during his cross-examination Palgi revealed rather ambivalent feelings toward Kastner.[48] Tamir challenged the accuracy of the paratrooper's story in the trial, seeking to discredit Palgi, who was a witness for the prosecution, and through him the Mapai party with which he was affiliated.

National myths, woven on the basis of actual events but replete with historical inaccuracies, are not likely to withstand a cross-examination in court. Palgi, was known for an autobiographical book, *And Behold a Great Wind Came,* published immediately after the war, which described the mission and its failure but glorified the courage of the paratroopers, particularly that of Hannah Senesh, who was executed by the Hungarians.[49] In his cross-examination Tamir questioned the story told in the book, suggesting that Palgi had covered up Kastner's role in the failure of the paratroopers' mission. For this purpose Tamir sought to establish that Palgi had told Kastner about the paratroopers' military espionage mission (and about the hiding place of the radio transmitter that they had brought with them) and that Kastner had convinced Palgi (and later Goldstein) to give himself up to the Gestapo in the guise of a representative of the Jewish agency who had come to negotiate with the Nazis. Kastner hoped in this way to prevent the cancellation of the rescue train. Tamir's aim was to make Palgi admit that he had deliberately concealed these facts in his book.

> *Tamir:* I tell you that you did not disclose your military mission to Kastner.
>
> *Palgi:* If you say so, you are lying.
>
> *Tamir:* But on page 116 to your book you write: "to sum up, for the moment we should not disclose our military mission."
>
> *Palgi:* The book lies intentionally about this point. . . . I wrote a novel and not a history book, there are two points in the book that I intentionally blurred and changed.
>
> *Judge Halevi:* Why did you find it necessary to change the truth about Kastner and the transmitter?
>
> *Palgi:* Maybe it is a bad habit of a liar—when he does not want to tell the truth he exaggerates. I did not know what would be the implications of my writings. There were numerous trials in Europe

against people who betrayed Allied soldiers and were later executed. Dr. Kastner, technically, delivered Goldstein to the enemy.
This is why I did not write the true version about Goldstein's
arrest. Not only in order to save Goldstein, if he was still alive, but
also to protect Kastner and the whole affair. And as to the transmitter, I added that Kastner did not know about it as an emotional
reaction to the lie. I wanted to emphasize that Kastner had nothing to do with it.[50]

Tamir restricted his criticism of the paratrooper affair to the fact that
Palgi had been willing to cooperate with Kastner, betray his original
mission, and hand himself over to the Nazis. He refrained from investigating whether the paratroopers' mission could have offered a realis-
tic alternative to Kastner's rescue efforts and was unwilling to admit
the possible "price" of such heroism—the undermining of the rescue
plans of Kastner's committee. Instead, he exploited the structure of the
criminal process to offer a simple solution to the discrepancy between
the myth of heroism as related in the book and the reality of collaboration with the Nazis that was exposed in the trial.[51] Tamir presented
Kastner as an all-knowing figure whose actions had sabotaged the
paratroopers' mission from the outset. This dichotomous view of heroism and treason was reinforced by the testimony of Katherine Senesh,
Hannah Senesh's mother, who was brought by Tamir as a witness for
the defense. Senesh presented a pure version of heroism in the eyes of
a mother who had unsuccessfully tried to meet Kastner in order to
deliver a package to her imprisoned daughter. Cohn, the prosecutor,
decided not to cross-examine Senesh, sensing that her story touched a
sensitive chord in the heart of the young nation. Tamir, thus, could
strip Palgi of his heroic aura and reconstruct the myth of heroism
around Hannah Senesh, "the paratrooper who did not return."[52]

Drawing Analogies: Brand's Mission

Tamir drew a sinister analogy between the failure of the paratroopers'
mission and the failure of Joel Brand's mission. About a month after the
beginning of the "trucks for blood" negotiations, Eichmann had proposed to send Brand to Turkey to persuade representatives of the Jewish Agency to deliver a message to the Allies about the Nazis' proposal
to stop the murder of Hungarian Jews in return for ten thousand trucks,

which the Germans would deploy only on the Eastern Front. Eichmann had promised that the death transports would be postponed for several weeks until Brand's return. Brand had intended to warn the Jewish leaders in Palestine about the Nazis' plans of annihilation and to convince them to cooperate with Eichmann's proposal. For this purpose he asked to meet with the top-level leaders, in particular Moshe Sharett, head of the political department of the Jewish Agency (who at the time of the trial was Israel's prime minister). The British, however, refused to give Sharett a visa to Turkey and had arrested Brand on his way to Palestine in an attempt to meet Sharett there. Brand had been allowed to meet Sharett under British custody and supervision, but he had not been permitted to return to Hungary with an official answer for Eichmann.[53]

Tamir argued that the failure of Brand's mission was not accidental. As in the paratrooper affair Tamir placed all the blame on the Jewish leaders, who had allegedly preferred cooperation with the British authorities and had therefore handed Brand over to them. The paratroopers' failure, he argued, could no longer be attributed to the difficult circumstances in occupied Hungary, since the same thing had happened in Palestine. According to Tamir in both cases the failure could be explained by a certain mentality of deference to the authorities. In his closing arguments Tamir drew this analogy most vividly.

When I said cooperation here [in Palestine] and there [in Hungary] I meant that there is even an analogy in the mentality, in the cynical way in which they hid these acts. Menachem Bader has testified that it was Brand who decided to travel to the Land of Israel, adding: "we felt awe towards a man who came from the other side, that is why we decided to agree to his proposal to travel to the Land of Israel [to meet with Sharett], even though we were afraid that the British had set a trap." And when Kastner testifies that he left it to Palgi to decide whether to hand himself over to the Nazis he adds: "We left the decision to him because of the awe we felt for those messengers from the Land of Israel." Exactly the same expressions. In Istanbul awe for the messenger on the part of the murdered—go to prison! In Budapest—awe for the messenger from the Land of Israel—go to prison! They did not consult each other on this, your Honor, it is in their nature.[54]

The Brand affair was important to Tamir for another reason. In seeking to embarrass the political authorities, he needed to shift the public's attention from Kastner to the leaders of the Yishuv, and since Brand had met Sharett Tamir pressured the witnesses for the prosecution (Bader and Avriel) to admit that it was Sharett who had betrayed Brand to the British. The prosecution tried to refute these grave allegations by submitting a secret report on the Brand affair that Sharett had written and presented in London to the board of directors of the Jewish Agency on 27 June 1944. This was precisely the opportunity that Tamir had been waiting for. He objected to the report's being submitted without its author (Sharett) being summoned and cross-examined. The prosecution, determined to avoid subjecting the prime minister to cross-examination by Tamir, refused to summon him, and the judge accordingly refused to admit the report. Frustrated at being denied the forum of the court, one of the witnesses for the prosecution, Ehud Avriel, decided to publish the report in the newspaper *Maariv* (with the blessing of Sharett), thus violating the rules of sub judice. Infuriated by this act, judge Halevi announced that it amounted to contempt of the court.[55]

The Defense: "I Told the Truth"

It is ironic that the first political trial in Israel concerning events during the Holocaust took place in the framework of a libel trial, the very framework that became typical for what came to be known as "Holocaust denial trials" in the 1980s and 1990s.[56] In these latter cases the prosecution has to prove that the denials of the Holocaust are "false," and the courts often find themselves functioning as a tribunal burdened with determining the truth of the Holocaust according to legal conventions of proof and evidence. In the Kastner trial, however, this structure was reversed since it was the attorney for the defense, not the prosecution, who claimed that the state authorities were involved in an attempt to silence the truth about the Holocaust. Tamir drew an analogy between Kastner's alleged efforts in Budapest to conceal the truth about the destination of the trains to Auschwitz and what he saw as the concealment of information about the Holocaust by the Mapai leadership in Palestine. Tamir was convinced that the trial against Gruenwald was as an attempt to censor the truth about the Jewish leadership's part in the failure to stop the catastrophe.

The law usually tries to make a clear distinction between historical truth and legal truth, leaving the former to historians. Tamir could, of course, have based his defense on Gruenwald's lack of criminal intention (mens rea) in writing the pamphlet against Kastner. This option, however, would not have given Tamir the chance to present the "truth" as being on his side and to use it as political leverage. By adopting the "I told the truth" line of defense, Tamir forced the court to employ legal means to clarify complex and difficult historical issues. He promised to present "the naked truth" in the trial. But the truth in a trial is always the result of complex procedural rules, which involve additional considerations such as the finality of the legal proceedings, due process, legal precedents, and so on. In addition, Tamir cleverly used the procedural advantage afforded him as the attorney for the defense to make serious charges against Kastner and the Zionist leadership without fully substantiating them (e.g., the defense was exempt from proving its version beyond a reasonable doubt and did not have to present its charges at the beginning of the trial in order to allow for appropriate preparation of the prosecution).[57] In contrast, because Kastner's official status in the trial was that of a witness for the prosecution, he did not enjoy any of the procedural rights and protections that the adversarial system grants criminal defendants even though he was the de facto defendant. Although these procedural rules shaped the "truth" that was presented at the trial and tilted it in favor of Tamir's version, they were not apparent to the public, which was only concerned with the question of which version would receive the court's stamp of approval. Thus, the public was all too responsive to the "verdict" that acquitted Tamir's client without realizing the circumscribed character of the narrative frame of the trial. The complex and agonizing reality in which Kastner had acted was neatly trimmed to serve the purposes of a mythical story of heroism appropriated by one side of the Israeli political spectrum.

Conspiracy Theory

The only persons who were able to present a whole story without interruptions and outside the constraints of the question and answer framework were the attorneys in their closing arguments and the judge in his decision. In his closing argument, the prosecutor attempted to limit the wide range of facts presented in the trial in order to refocus attention on

Gruenwald's actions. Accordingly, he presented a legal analysis of the various sections of the law of libel. At one point, however, politics reentered his speech when he referred to the "collaboration" accusations against the Yishuv leaders, saying: "We are proud, your honor, that we collaborated with the British. The British and their allies were those who fought Hitler. And in time of war against such an enemy, the Jewish people had only one desire: to collaborate, to fight [with the British] with all the means of war."[58]

By contrast, the defense chose to concentrate on the factual aspects of the affair in order to reassemble them into a coherent story. Tamir wove all the elements of the narrative together in order to posit a conspiracy theory according to which the Jewish leadership in Budapest had allegedly worked together with Yishuv leaders in Palestine in order to mislead the Jews of Hungary. Tamir's version was consistent with popular conceptions of crime as represented in literature, where every single fact in the story serves to move the story forward. However, as noted by Alan Dershowitz, a law professor and well-known American criminal lawyer, real life is not a dramatic narrative and is full of irrelevant details and coincidences. In real life, a person who coughs a little in the evening isn't necessarily about to die and a gun revealed in Act I does not necessarily go off in Act III.[59]

The plausibility of the conspiracy story was enhanced by the structure of a criminal trial, which focuses the charges against a specific individual. Although the charges were de jure against Gruenwald, Tamir succeeded in turning Kastner into the de facto defendant. The individualistic nature of a criminal trial allowed him to disregard the broader historical background of the Holocaust and to present the public with a simplified version of the grave ethical dilemmas posed by the Nazi regime. Tamir redirected the blame onto the victims' leaders by accusing Kastner of having conspired with the Nazis to save his relatives and thus having facilitated the destruction of the Jews of Hungary. Since the charge was against one particular person, the Israeli public at large was absolved from the need for self-examination, and since the trial channeled all the blame onto Kastner (and the Mapai leadership) it offered an easy solution to the emerging sense of guilt of the Israeli public for not having done enough to rescue Jews during the Holocaust: convict Kastner and thus avoid confronting the past. Hence, although the formal charges were against Gruenwald, his acquittal by the judge was read as if it were a conviction against Kastner.[60] The

attorney general filed an appeal, but before the court reached its decision Kastner was murdered—the first political assassination to occur in
the State of Israel.[61] Even though the district court verdict was overturned, it was the trial court's sentence that created the political impact
for years to come.[62] Instead of facilitating a critical public debate, the
trial offered a simple answer to the troublesome question, "Like lambs
to the slaughter?"—an answer reiterated by witness after witness as in
a Greek chorus: "because our leaders betrayed us!"

Chapter 2

From Faust to Kastner
The Judge as Storyteller

Political trials signal points of rupture in the life of a state. This is especially apparent in "transitional trials" when a new regime takes the former regime to trial for its actions.[1] But such rupture is also present
when a fundamental challenge to the basic values of society as they are
embodied in its laws is raised by an oppositional group.[2] At such times
the parties to the debate (either the authorities or the opposition) are
tempted to bring their controversies to court since it offers a "known
practice—a stable format, and so a way of interpreting events in a
world temporarily become ambiguous."[3] The hope that the law will
supply clear rules to resolve the dispute proves to be futile in many
cases because in political trials the legitimacy of the laws themselves
often becomes the topic of contestation. Thus, it has been noted by
scholars of political trials that the courts' rhetoric stressing continuity in
the application of the law and strict adherence to the "rule of law" is
often a facade that masks the crucial way in which political trials differ
from ordinary ones. This rhetoric tries to hide the fact that in political
trials the "law" itself and the societal values that it embodies are being
radically challenged. Political trials can be described as an "identity
intersection" at which society has to decide its future course. Such
intersections call for a reflective judgment, for judging outside the
framework of predetermined rules. However, when these conflicts are
channeled into the courtroom, the transitional character of the law
tends to be obscured by the rhetoric of continuity and precedents.

These difficulties are multiplied when a political trial is also a historical trial, that is, a trial that is expected to illuminate the meaning of a
historical period, and are especially compounded when the period is
that of the Holocaust. Hannah Arendt, borrowing an expression from

Bertold Brecht, described that period as "dark times," by which she meant not only the monstrosity of the acts and the despair of the victims but the loss of the illuminating light of the public sphere, a loss that produced a crisis of understanding.[4] She links this epistemic crisis to a failure of existing modes of explanation (of the social sciences as well as canonical texts of religion and morality) to help us comprehend the events.[5] What is left, she argues, are the stories of individual persons who can kindle some light and illuminate the period.

The Kastner trial is a vivid demonstration of this crisis of comprehension that the Holocaust produced in law and morality. Judge Benjamin Halevi had to make sense of the new kind of collaboration that emerged under the Nazi regime. Existing legal categories such as "treason" or "complicity in murder" were ill fit to illuminate this phenomenon because both assume the actor's intention to produce harm, an intention that was entirely lacking in the Jewish leaders' acts of collaboration and cooperation with the Nazis. Since at the time of the trial new legal categories had yet to be developed, the judge had to try to comprehend Kastner's actions without clear guidelines from the law. Moreover, Kastner's actions also posed a problem for conventional morality since they had been guided by noble motives and yet seemed to have wrought more harm than if he had refrained from action altogether. It is not surprising, therefore, to find that the judge devoted his main intellectual efforts to weaving the facts of the affair into a coherent story about good and evil. He provided the Israeli public with a black and white narrative about the behavior of Jewish leaders during the Holocaust, a narrative that culminated in his damning statement that Kastner had sold his soul to the devil. Thus it came about that the subversive narrative of a defense lawyer, who cleverly turned a criminal trial against his client into a vehicle to embarrass the political authorities, encountered a sympathetic judge, who adopted this version of history and gave it the stamp of approval of a court of law. In this sense we can describe the Kastner trial as a political trial in which the risk to the authorities was fully realized, a phenomenon that signals a working democracy according to Kirschheimer's theory.[6] How this story was produced and how it was transformed into a paradigm of the evil of collaboration with the Nazis, which dominated the Israelis' perception of the Holocaust until the Eichmann trial, is the focus of my investigation in this chapter.

1. Case Number 124/53

The Kastner case (*Attorney General v. Gruenwald*) was brought before the district court in Jerusalem and was assigned to Judge Benjamin Halevi as a sole judge.[7] Halevi, a German Jew who had left Germany before the rise of nazism, had to confront the horrors produced by his country of birth and to give them a legal name and meaning. The issue was a most painful one for a Jewish court, since the trial focused not on the Nazis and their criminal acts or the world and its betrayal of the Jews but on the questionable behavior of certain Jewish leaders. In other words, the case forced the judge, and the Israeli public at large, to face the "evil within" and called for a legal judgment on the phenomenon of collaboration, which had emerged under the Nazi regime.

It is common to view legal judgments as consisting of two independent parts: facts and law. Most legal scholarship focuses on the latter component, in which questions about the interpretations of statutes and legal precedents are at issue. The determination of the facts has traditionally been perceived as unproblematic, the result of applying rules of evidence and proof to testimonies and documents. But this relative lack of interest in the narration of "facts" has changed in the last few years as legal scholars have discovered the relevance of narrative theory and studies of rhetoric. By invoking "truth" on behalf of his client, Tamir, the defense lawyer, impelled the judge to apply legal rules of proof and evidence to determining the historical truth about the Holocaust of Hungarian Jewry. The Kastner judgment, therefore, reflects an attempt to reorder the historical facts according to legal doctrines. The result of this effort is a coherent narrative, 239 pages long, written according to the conventions of a psychological detective story and a morality play.

The reordering of reality into legal categories is evident from the very beginning of the judgment, where Halevi reorganizes Gruenwald's confused pamphlet into a four-point indictment of Kastner.[8]

1. Collaboration with the Nazis
2. "Vicarious murder," or "paving the way for the murder," of Hungarian Jewry
3. Partnership with a Nazi war criminal [Kurt Becher] in acts of thievery
4. Saving a war criminal [Becher] from punishment after the war

The transformation of the pamphlet into a list of four allegations symbolizes the inversion that occurred during the trial whereby the defendant (Gruenwald) became the de facto accuser and the court had to
decide whether any of his claims against Kastner had merit.

I will focus on the first two accusations, which constitute the heart of
the court's judgment.[9] These allegations supplied a simple response to
the question that haunted the Israeli public at the time: what could
account for the "unheroic" deaths of millions of Jews during the Holocaust? Gruenwald's accusations against Kastner had the potential of
rehabilitating the masses of Jewish victims by attributing their deaths
to deception and betrayal by their leaders. Indeed, Judge Halevi studied the "bargain" between Kastner and Eichmann in the light of
Tamir's recurring question—did they go like lambs to the slaughter?

Addressing this tragic question required a story that would establish
a causal link between the diverse facts that were presented in the trial:
on the one hand, the lack of resistance on the part of the Jews of Cluj
(Kastner's hometown) to boarding the deportation trains, their misin-
formation about the destination of the trains and the fate awaiting
them, and the absence of any efforts to sabotage the trains or to escape
from the ghetto to the Romanian border; and, on the other hand, the
inclusion (and thereby salvation) of the Jewish leaders of Cluj and Kastner's relatives and friends in the "Bergen Belsen transport" to Switzerland. The judge found such a link by weaving a story that began with
the temptation of Kastner by the Nazis, continued with the subsequent
betrayal of his Jewish community, and culminated in his full collaboration with the Nazis. The essence of this judgment, which is related over
many pages, is expressed in a sentence that appears in the middle of the
decision when Judge Halevi breaks the flow of his account with a seemingly disconnected observation: "But—'timeo Danaos et dona ferentis' [I
fear the Greeks even when bringing presents]. In accepting this gift K.
sold his soul to the Devil."[10]

Halevi's sentence combines two archetypal stories: that of the Greek
victory over Troy and that of Satan's victory over Faust. It was the second allusion that was engraved in Israeli collective memory as a symbol of all the evils of Jewish collaboration with the Nazis. Years later,
reflecting on the political turmoil surrounding the trial that eventually
led to Kastner's assassination, Halevi said that his words had been
taken out of context and he regretted having added this unfortunate
remark to the judgment.[11] A close reading of the judgment reveals,

however, that this literary allusion could not be so easily erased, for it served as the glue that held the judgment together—a judgment that sought to establish Kastner's collaboration with the Nazis through an actual contract between Kastner and Eichmann.

The study of the court decision goes to the heart of the debate about the representation of the Holocaust in law and literature, which is commonly understood in terms of a comparison between the relative strengths and weaknesses of each field in providing a responsible memory of the past. The two fields are viewed as providing independent representations based on different rules for reordering reality into a coherent structure.[12] But this neat, "discrete" view is undermined by the first public confrontations with the Holocaust that occurred during the Kastner trial. The court's judgment reveals a complex interaction between the fields of law and literature. Literature provided stock stories that helped to attribute responsibility to recognizable individuals, while law provided a set of assumptions about human relations that made the messy reality fit the literary expectations.

In contrast to the view that unproblematically links a narrativist approach to sociological jurisprudence and contextual judgment,[13] I will argue that the Kastner judgment was supported by a formalist approach to contract law that allowed the judge to depict Kastner as Faust and to morally condemn him. It shows how literary tropes can support a formalist approach to law, maybe because both law and literature have their roots in the attempt to satisfy (in different ways) the human yearning for a coherent reality and mastery over chaos.[14] I suggest that Judge Halevi tried to understand the chaotic, arbitrary reality experienced by the victims of the Holocaust and establish a sense of control over it by adapting it to the abstract categories of human action and motivation offered by law and literature. The senseless deaths of the four hundred thousand Jews of Hungary, so close to the end of the war, was assigned its legal meaning by identifying the moment (the signing of the contract) at which the catastrophe could and should have been avoided. And since so much depended on this contract the judge resorted to the most formalist approach to contract law, assuming that behind every contract one can find equal, knowledgeable, and willing partners. This reliance on a system of cause and fault made the arbitrary predictable and comprehensible. And lacking legal precedents about the phenomenon of collaboration thus discovered the judge resorted to literary precedents and interpreted Kastner's actions in the light of literary tropes about evildoing from the Faust and the Trojan horse legends. This use of literature by the court supported the erasure of the historical circumstances from the judgment and helped to obscure the individuality of Kastner—one person facing horrific dilemmas with limited options. Instead Kastner was presented by Halevi as Dr. K—the symbol of the decay and corruption of Jewish leaders during the Holocaust.

2. The Contract with Satan

The very notion of selling one's soul to the devil presupposes the existence of a contract undertaken by rational and calculated choice. In this metaphor the judge emphasized what he took to be the main legal problematic of the Kastner affair—the contractual nature of Kastner's relationship with the Nazis.[15] Indeed establishing the existence of a contract between Kastner and the SS was crucial to proving Gruenwald's allegation that Kastner had collaborated with the Nazis. Judge Halevi had to decide when the contract was signed, what its content was, and whether it was valid.

In relating the historical facts Halevi adapted the 1944 reality of Hungarian Jewry to the Zionist ideology that was prevalent at the time of the trial. The judge, like Tamir, postulated that Kastner and his partners in the Aid and Rescue Committee had two mutually exclusive options: the path of resistance, rebellion, and attempts at mass escape to neighboring countries; and the path of negotiating an agreement with the Nazis that might save the Jews of Hungary.[16] Kastner chose negotiations and thus, according to Halevi, embarked on a path that inevitably led to full collaboration with the Nazis. The judgment describes this path from initial contacts, through a series of contractual offers and counteroffers, to an actual contract that allegedly was signed on 2 May 1944.

The first "offer" was made by a Nazi officer, Dieter Wisliceny, on the basis of a letter from Rabbi Weissmandel of Bratislava addressed to three individuals in Budapest urging them to continue the negotiations that he had begun with the SS about the Europa Plan, a plan to save the remaining Jews of Europe in exchange for large sums of money.[17] Wisliceny approached Fülop von Freudiger, leader of the Orthodox community in Budapest; Baroness Edith Weiss, an influential member of the richest and economically most important family in Hungary; and Rudolf Kastner, who represented the Zionist group. Thereafter, Kast-

ner and his partner Joel Brand seized the initiative and contacted Wisliceny with a counteroffer consisting of four obligations to be fulfilled
by the Nazis in exchange for the money, including a promise to abstain
from ghettoizing and expelling the Jews, to allow their emigration, and
to spare their lives.[18] The second "deal" that the judgment describes
was made with Eichmann, who approached Joel Brand with a proposal
to exchange a million Jews for ten thousand trucks. As we saw in chapter 1, Brand was asked to go to Istanbul and convey the proposal to representatives of the Jewish Agency and the Allies. Since this was the first
time the Nazis had agreed to the rescue of such numbers of Jews in
return for money and merchandise, Kastner and his committee were
anxious to test whether their intentions were serious. Kastner therefore
approached a Nazi officer, Kromey, with a proposal to allow the emigration of 600 Jews (a number that later grew to 1,685 through negotiations with Eichmann) as an indication of the seriousness of the Nazis'
intentions.[19] It was this contract, allegedly signed on 2 May 1944, that
became the focus of Halevi's decision. Kastner claimed that his initiative had not been intended to replace the main contract to rescue the
whole of Hungarian Jewry but had been proposed as a test of the Nazis'
intentions and in his view had remained such until the end. Tamir,
however, argued that all the negotiations boiled down to this contract,
which replaced all other initiatives. The judge preferred Tamir's interpretation and derived from this contract the main explanation for Kastner's subsequent betrayal of his people:

> The benefit that K. gained from the contract with the Nazis was the
> rescue of the "camp of prominent Jews" and the price that he had to
> pay for this was a complete surrender of any attempts at real rescue
> steps benefiting the "camp of the people." The price the Nazis paid
> for this was to waive the extermination of the "camp of prominent
> people." With this contract to save the prominent Jews, the head of
> the Aid and Rescue Committee made a "concession" with the exter-
> minator: in return for the rescue of the prominent Jews K. agreed to
> the extermination of the people and abandoned them to their fate.[20]

Halevi stressed that the Nazis had used this contract to "tempt" Kastner
and bind him to them, thus drawing him into full collaboration.[21] "In
accepting this gift" namely, the contract of 2 May 1944, "Kastner had
sold his soul to the Devil." The rescue transport had depended until the
very last moment on the goodwill of the Nazis, and that moment had

come long after the destruction of all the Jews in the towns of the periphery. In other words, according to Halevi, the promise of the transport to
Switzerland (which occurred only in December 1944) had contractually
bound Kastner to the Nazis, and this accounted for the absence of any
serious effort to rescue the Jews of Hungary as a whole.

As proven in the trial, the negotiations over Kastner's rescue train
were indeed contractual in nature, as the committee had to pay a certain amount of money for each person boarding the train. The problem
was that the judge saw this contract as a coverup for a more important
contract, which involved selling out the whole of Hungarian Jewry in
return for this rescue train. In other words, Halevi believed that the
Germans gained much more than money from this contract—they
received Kastner's silence and, as a consequence, the misleading of the
Jewish population. He also believed that this "price" was agreed on in
advance.[22] The application of contract law to Kastner's actions was
needed in order to overcome the legal problem of how to attribute a
criminal intention to a Jewish leader who had undertaken to rescue
Jews. The accusation of "assisting the Nazis in the mass murder of
Hungarian Jews" required proof that Kastner had known and intended
the results of his actions. By finding a valid contract between Kastner
and Nazi officials the judge could derive from it the needed criminal
intent since every contract presupposes choice based on appropriate
knowledge of the outcomes. Kastner's failure to inform the Jews of the
destination of the trains could thus be interpreted as the result of a prior
agreement between the parties.

Contract law doctrine addresses the issue of when we are allowed to
conclude from the specific actions and words of the parties that they are
bound by a contract. I propose to go in the opposite direction and ask
in what ways Judge Halevi's discovery of a contract shaped his conception of the protagonists' actions and the historical narrative. My
claim is that the lens of contract law allowed him to see a very restricted
portion of the lives of the people who were involved in the negotiations. It was precisely this narrow focus that generated the image of
Kastner as an omnipotent Faustian figure in a latter-day morality play.

3. The Language of Contracts

Halevi used the language of contracts not only to attribute legal responsibility but also to express his moral condemnation of Kastner's choice.

This language, ordinarily employed for commercial transactions, here frames the barter arrangement about the lives of Hungarian Jews, and this dissonance between subject matter and language was repeatedly emphasized by the judge. Halevi ignored the fact that Kastner had employed this grotesque language in his correspondence precisely to convey the tragic conditions of the Jews. Thus, Kastner wrote in one of his letters that "in the last several days new people were brought into the negotiations whose appearance can be viewed as *deus ex machina*. The new masters are probably responsible for the comprehensive solution of the Jewish question. They have no friendly intentions towards us, but it seems that they do appreciate fair partners to the negotiations."[23] The tragic irony in this letter was that of a slave forced to play a game of free choice; this nuance disappeared from Halevi's reformulation. The judge selectively quoted from Kastner's letter to deliver his moral condemnation in an ironic tone. Thus, Kastner's "behavior proves his level of loyalty as a 'fair partner' to the negotiations with the 'new masters' who comprehensively 'solved' the Jewish problem of Hungary by way of a 'final solution.'"[24]

Halevi condemned Kastner for using language that protects the speaker from acknowledging the full meaning of his actions. This was a common technique among the Nazis themselves, who employed it both for the sake of secrecy and as a means of distancing themselves from the harsh reality of their victims.[25] The historian Saul Friedlander calls this phenomenon "affect neutralization," which consists not only of using "clean language," as demonstrated in Kastner's letter, but of describing atrocities in day-to-day language without giving pause to the incongruity.[26] In his view, affect neutralization can also occur in cases when the speaker uses explicit language about the crimes committed but inserts them in the midst of familiar social conventions and moral norms. Friedlander demonstrates this technique by quoting from Heinrich Himmler's address of 4 October 1943 to the SS generals gathered in Posen.

> The wealth they [the Jews] had, we have taken. I gave strict orders—which SS Gruppenfuhrer Pohl has carried out—that this wealth be promptly transferred to the Reich. We have taken nothing. The few who have committed a crime will be punished according to the order I gave at the beginning. . . . We had the moral right, we had the duty to our people to annihilate the people who wanted to annihilate us.

But we do not have the right to enrich ourselves, no matter if it were only a fur, a watch, a mark, a cigarette, no matter what it might be.[27]

Friedlander explains: "Quite openly, Himmler talks to his audience about the annihilation of a people. . . . But at the same time he undertakes the neutralization of what he is going to say by linking the action he describes—the extermination of the Jewish people—to stable values, to rules everyone acknowledges, to the laws of everyday life."[28]

In light of this explanation Halevi's opinion can itself be seen as being implicated with the same errors for which he condemns Kastner. By adapting the events to the familiar order of contract doctrine, the judgment implies that the chaos and horror are, after all, coherent and explainable, that the familiar norms of contractual relations can be applied to the extraordinary circumstances of radical disparity of power, deceptions, threats, and uncertainty in which the negotiations were conducted.[29] It was only in the appeal that Justice Agranat undertook to expose the inadequacy of contract law to deal with these negotiations by citing the words of Eichmann to Kastner during one of their meetings: "You seem extremely tense, Kastner. I am sending you to Teresienstadt for recovery; or would you prefer Auschwitz?"[30]

4. The Protagonists (or Parties)

Contract law, which was so central in facilitating Halevi's moral condemnation of Kastner, posits a number of central premises—free-willed agents, self-interestedness, meetings of wills, formal equality of the parties to the contract, full disclosure, and strict responsibility for the outcomes. These premises were used to adapt the actions of the "parties" to the normative world of business transactions.

The language of contracts presented Kastner as a *self-interested, rational individual,* always scheming over how to best exploit the reality of occupation in Hungary to further his own interests.[31] Contract doctrine colored the negotiations in an individualistic light, obscuring the way in which a sense of responsibility toward his Jewish community shaped (and limited) Kastner's options.

A contract is based on the legal presumption of a *meeting of wills* between the parties. By finding that a contract had been signed between Kastner and Eichmann the judge created the impression that there was no abyss separating their worlds, although he granted that the motives of the parties for entering into the contract must have been very different. However, they have found the point of mutual benefit.

> Like every mutual agreement, the contract between K. and the leaders of the S.S. was made to the mutual benefit of both parties: each party got from the contract an agreed upon benefit and paid in return a carefully predefined price: the sum of benefits and the price for it were set in advance, all this according to the relative bargaining power of the two parties.[32]

The judge's willingness to find a valid contract at the root of the Kastner-Eichmann relationship lent a sense of formal equality to the two parties and obscured the radical inequality between them that resulted from the conditions of terror, deceit, and uncertainty in which Kastner and the rescue committee operated. The impression of equality was further reinforced by the judge's use throughout his opinion, of the initials K. and S.S. to refer to the parties to the contract. This use of the parties' initials, a common practice in legal documents, served to erase the human face of the parties and to depict them as symbols of their time, as archetypes: the Jewish leader and the Nazi.

Finally, the protagonists in Halevi's narrative were depicted as fully informed agents, and repeated reference was made to Kastner's boast that he was the best-informed person in all of Hungary.[33] This is important because, unlike torts or criminal law, both of which attribute individual responsibility according to the subjective intentions of the parties involved, contract law demands full disclosure at the outset and in turn assigns strict responsibility to the parties according to the objective consequences of the contract, even if these were not planned or intended. Halevi relied on this legal presumption to conclude that Kastner had all the information he had needed to come to a rational decision: "K. knew well the price from the very beginning of their contacts."[34] This approach facilitated the attribution of absolute responsibility to Kastner for the consequences of his actions—the death of approximately four hundred thousand Hungarian Jews.

5. Contract Time

The age-old construct of a contract also helped Halevi to represent the period of the Holocaust—a time of extreme uncertainty and helplessness for the victims—as one that was nonetheless logical, rational, and, most importantly, controllable. Hannah Arendt studied this need of human beings to control the passage of time with legal mechanisms. Faced with a past that cannot be erased and a future that cannot be controlled, human beings resort to legal mechanisms such as amnesties and contracts.[35] Halevi's attempt to impose a sense of order on the chaotic period is reflected in the structure of his narrative. The chapters of his judgment do not follow the chronological development of events but reorder them according to the logic of contract law. He begins by presenting the consequences of the contract ("The Holocaust of the Periphery Towns"), then moves back to the starting point ("The Contract between Kastner and the S.S."), and then considers the interpretation of the contract ("The Meaning of the Contract with the S.S.") and its main characteristics ("The Secrecy of the Contract with the S.S."). The judgment next focuses on Kastner's knowledge at the time of signing ("What Kastner Knew") and concludes with the attribution of strict responsibility to him. This construction of the facts is typical of a formalist approach to contract cases, but when it is applied to historical events it leads to anachronisms that obscure instead of clarifying the particular circumstances of the time.

By focusing on the moment of signing a supposed contract, the judge assumed the existence of a crossroad at which a clear choice between the path of "treason" and the path of "heroism" had been laid out. Kastner's decision to cooperate with the Nazis was presented as the easier choice, which had "foreseen consequences of saving only a well-defined and limited number of Jews" with a very high "price" of abandoning hundreds of thousands of Jews to their fate, as opposed to the more heroic (and riskier) path of resistance (exemplified in the behavior of the Warsaw ghetto rebels).[36] But in order to present such a clear-cut choice between two opposing paths the messiness of historical circumstances had to be expelled from the legal narrative. A chronological tale, such as the one later offered by the appellate court, was likely to limit Kastner's responsibility by highlighting not only the moment at which the contract was concluded but also the constant changes in the original plan, the conditions of terror, and the Jewish leaders' growing despair.[37] Contract law also gave the judge the freedom to move back and forth in time and to judge the events with *hindsight.* It allowed the judge to attribute later consequences to a prior plan and to hold Kastner responsible for these consequences. Implying that Kastner himself

had assumed responsibility for what would follow, he quoted Kastner's own words at the time: "[I]t is clear to me what lies in the balance
... [for] the loser in this game [of roulette] will also be called a traitor."[38]
Halevi completely missed the tragic implications of Kastner's words,
which evoke an arbitrary game of chance. Similarly, he rejected Kastner's description of the rescue of his friends and relatives as an "accidental success." The judge wrote that Kastner's description was accurate "apart from the word 'accidental'. . . for this success was never
'accidental' but promised."[39] The fact that Kastner had no certain
knowledge about the destination of the "Bergen Belsen transport" was
thus erased from the judgment, and the judge relied on our later knowledge that the occupants of this transport had been saved. Likewise, the
information that more than four hundred thousand Hungarian Jews
had eventually been murdered led the judge to overlook the constant
hope expressed in Kastner's reports that the negotiations would gain
the Jews some precious time and the war would end before the plan to
send them to their deaths was implemented.

6. The Literary Allusion to the Faustian Bargain

The use of contract doctrine to depict the protagonist as educated,
rational, and self-interested supports the allusion to the popular story
of Faust. The first reference to Faust in the judgment was a citation from
a report by Freudiger, a member of the Budapest Judenrat, describing
the (non-Jewish) Hungarian leaders who rose to power under Nazi rule
as "adventurers . . . whose sole purpose was to achieve power and who
would *sell their soul to the devil* in order to get this power."[40] Halevi
reapplied this description to Kastner without pausing to distinguish
the circumstances under which the Jewish leader had acted from those
of the Hungarian leaders.[41] The pact between Kastner and the Nazi
devil demonizes Kastner and provides a psychological motive for his
actions.

The Faust theme pervades many aspects of the narrative presented
in Halevi's judgment, even though the direct allusion occurs in only
one sentence. For example, by stressing Kastner's formal title of Doctor
(he had received his degree in law) throughout his judgment he evoked
the titles of both Christopher Marlowe's and Thomas Mann's version of
the legend.[42] He depicted Kastner as having superior knowledge, not
scholarly or artistic, as with the literary Faust, but political: according to

Halevi he knew of the pending destruction of European Jewry and, more specifically, about the destination of the Hungarian trains to the gas chambers in Auschwitz. The historical Faust, the sixteenth-century Johann Faustus, was known to be a magician and an alchemist. Kastner himself was merely a journalist and a political activist, but when he negotiated with Eichmann over the plan to exchange ten thousand trucks for the lives of a million Jews, which Eichmann presented as a way to transform "worthless Jews" into a source of wealth for the Nazis, the deal entered the realm of alchemy.[43]

The literature offers different answers to the motive underlying Faust's quest, such as knowledge, power, fame, wealth, and the pleasures of this world.[44] Even though Halevi acknowledged that Kastner's original aim was noble, he stressed elements that were more questionable. Kastner is depicted as a man from the provincial town of Cluj who sought to acquire power and influence in the Zionist circles of Budapest.[45] He acted in an opportunistic way, gradually gaining influence in the Aid and Rescue Committee and thereafter taking over the negotiations with the Nazis from the official Judenrat.[46] Halevi suggested that Kastner's fascination with power also explained his desire to help the important Jews in the community, since he viewed their rescue as his "Zionist and personal" success.[47] Halevi also stressed Kastner's self-interest in the rescue plan—out of the 1,685 passengers on Kastner's list, there were a few hundred from his hometown of Cluj and a few dozen of his relatives, including his mother, wife, and brother.[48]

Although the original aim of the negotiations could still potentially cast Kastner in a noble light, the progression of the events as described by the judge revealed that Kastner had undergone a process of moral degeneration, as though he were subject to a kind of "infection" that struck those who dared interact with the Nazi devil.[49] He had associated more and more with the Nazis, learned their ways (drinking and gambling), and gradually separated himself from his Jewish community (e.g., by choosing to reside in Nazi hotels rather than Jewish houses).[50] The language used by Kastner, from which the judge often quoted, also consisted of "incriminating" metaphors from the world of card games and gambling.[51]

Halevi hinted that Kastner had been motivated by more than a quest for power by relating the rumor about the money and jewelry taken from the Jews as ransom by the Nazis. The Nazi officer Kurt Becher had allegedly returned this "treasure" to Kastner and they had divided it among themselves. Although the judge concluded that this accusation against Kastner was not proved, his elaborate discussion of the affair created the impression of Kastner as a man driven by greed.[52] Kastner's character was also cast in a poor light by his refusal to meet with the mother of Hannah Senesh to help release the heroine from her Hungarian prison. Although this was not part of Gruenwald's accusations and was irrelevant to the libel trial, the judge nevertheless allowed testimonies and questioning on this issue and incorporated it into his judgment.[53]

Many of the Faust stories focus on the hubris of a man who purports to play God, transgressing the limits of human beings in scientific knowledge or creative powers. Indeed, Kastner aspired to go beyond the limits of human possibility in trying to save a million Jews where everybody else had failed. In Halevi's story, however, the element of "playing God" acquired a very literal meaning because it involved deciding who would die and who would live by boarding the special train (Kastner's list). Halevi argued that such a decision should never be taken by a human being and saw in this the heart of Kastner's moral failure.[54] Moreover, in the literary tradition part of playing God consists of Faust's visit to Hell accompanied by Mephistopheles. In Kastner's case this metaphor acquired a literal meaning toward the end of the war when Kastner traveled to the man-made hell of Nazi concentration camps together with a latter-day Mephistopheles (Kurt Becher) in order to prevent the murder of the remaining Jewish inmates. Ironically, instead of Faust's soul being saved at the last moment, in Halevi's version it is Kastner who saves the "soul" of his Mephistopheles from punishment by giving an affidavit on his behalf to the Nuremberg tribunal.[55]

The sense of time running out is another theme that links the Faust story to Kastner. The price that Faust has to pay for transcending the human condition is to agree on a time limit to his own life on earth (twenty-four years). This time limit resounds throughout the story like a ticking bomb that Faust tries to stop in vain. For Kastner and his friends on the Aid and Rescue Committee, the race against time also played a crucial role. As the war approached its end, they tried to use the bargaining process with the Nazis in order to "buy some time" and delay the murder of the rest of the Jewish community.[56] The time factor acquired a horrific urgency after Eichmann sent Brand to Istanbul under the threat that every day of delay in his return meant that twelve thousand more Jews would be sent to Auschwitz.[57] All of Kastner's affairs were dominated by the knowledge that there was not enough time to save the Jews, and the haunting question was who would win this game of time: Kastner (when the war ended) or Eichmann (when there were no more Jews left to kill).

7. A Moralistic Faust

These parallels with the story of Faust in the judge's narrative had the effect of moving the case from the realm of law to that of morality. Kastner was presented as the personification of evil, a selfish opportunist who had sold out his community to the Nazis. The analogy between Kastner and Faust suggested that the nature of evil under the Nazi regime was no different from the evil familiar to us from great works of literature. This sense of familiarity discourages any real inquiry into the uniqueness of the events and into the true nature of cooperation with a totalitarian regime. The gradual demonization of Kastner had a double effect. It portrayed Kastner as a modern Faust in isolation from the rest of the Jewish community, making it easier to blame him, but it also removed the story from the domain of human action, thus allowing the Israeli audience to avoid an honest confrontation with the choices of Jewish leaders throughout Europe.

The judge's choice of a simplistic moralistic version of Faust as a literary vehicle for understanding Jewish cooperation with the Nazis can perhaps be partly explained by the fact that he was a German Jew and thus had to confront a double betrayal: that of the Jewish leaders, including religious leaders, who chose to cooperate with the Nazis; and that of his homeland (Germany), the country of Goethe and Mozart and the embodiment of the ideals of humanity. Both betrayals demanded explanations, and the judge found them in the popular version of the legend, wherein Faust's sin condemns him to Hell. Halevi turned it into a story about the Nazi devil and the morally corrupt Kastner. Choosing this interpretation, the judge forwent an opportunity to rely on the rich literary tradition of Faust, which could have supplied clues to understanding the psychological origins of the phenomenon of collaboration as well as the cultural sources of Nazism in Germany. Indeed, the literary critic Alfred Hoelzel argues that the four major reformulations of the Faust story (Chapbook, Marlowe, Goethe, and Mann) should be read as attempts to understand the enigma of the relationship between good and evil.[58] If the judge succeeded in tracing lines of similarity between Faust and Kastner, he failed to unravel different threads from the Faustian tradition, which could have highlighted the ambiguities and contradictions in Kastner's actions.[59]

8. From Contract to Gift: The Trojan Horse

Halevi's striking observation—"But, '*timeo Danaos* et *dona ferentis*' [I fear the Greeks, even when bringing presents]. In accepting this gift K. sold his soul to the Devil."—brought together the story of Faust and that of the Trojan horse. If the literary allusion to Faust was mainly sustained through the language of contracts, the allusion to the Trojan horse introduced a very different logic to the judgment—the logic of gifts. More precisely, this is a story about a deceitful gift that was meant to assure victory over the enemy at minimum cost.[60] Contract and gift would seem to be opposites, but Halevi's words make them complementary: "In accepting this *gift* K. *sold* his soul to the Devil." How could Kastner have been both the well-informed agent of a contract and the victim of a deceitful gift? Judge Halevi's account had to solve this seeming contradiction in order to offer a coherent explanation.

The opinion gradually uncovers different layers of the contract and brings the reader to a surprising discovery. At the immediate level Halevi examined the visible contract between Kastner and Eichmann to exchange Jewish lives for two million dollars. This contract might be condemned for the very willingness to negotiate with the Nazis, but it still fell within the reasonable (though not heroic) realm of legitimate attempts to save Jews. The suspicion that there was something immoral in the contract arose when the initial contract intended to save the lives of all the Jews of Hungary shrank to one aimed at saving a small group of six hundred "privileged Jews." (As we recall, the judge rejected Kastner's contentions that this contract was merely meant to test the Nazis' real intentions.) The judge found the most sinister aspect of the deal with the Nazis in the "low price" that Kastner paid for adding another six hundred people to the original list: "The permission to emigrate was given to an additional 600 people without real payment, it was an extraordinary 'gift' in Nazi terms."[61] Questioning the authenticity of such a generous gift from the Nazis, the judge sought its real meaning in the ancient story of the Trojan horse.

Law treats the categories of gifts and contracts as distinct and even opposed to each other. A contract entails a reciprocal transfer (quid pro quo)—something is passed in return for something else from one party to another. A gift, by contrast, is understood as a unilateral transfer—I give you something for nothing. However, as Carol Rose demonstrates, the law is suspicious about the existence of "pure gifts." Different legal doctrines aim to expose what at first glance may appear to be a gift but in fact turns out to be a contract in disguise or (and this is more sinister) larceny based on fraud and deception.[62] Since only reciprocity indicates voluntarism, the gift transfer becomes something of an anomaly. It is "a leftover category with no easy scenario, because it seems to be voluntary without being reciprocal."[63] Legal doctrines for scrutinizing gifts have the effect of emptying the category, turning it into a contract or larceny.[64]

Judge Halevi shared the skepticism of the law toward the gift and therefore looked for the Nazis' real motivation for their sudden generosity. He explained that since the Nazis realized it would be extremely difficult to organize the destruction of the eight hundred thousand Jews of Hungary with Germany's diminishing resources, with the war approaching its end, and with the threat of another "Warsaw ghetto uprising," the "Kastner list" was constructed by Eichmann as a modern-day Trojan horse in order to make his task easier. By allowing a limited number of privileged Jews to be saved, Eichmann obtained the cooperation of the Jewish leaders and diverted their attention from their duty to warn their communities about the coming transfer to Auschwitz, channeling their energy into composing the list instead of organizing escape and resistance plans. Indeed, the judge concludes that the so-called gift had been very effective in paralyzing the Jewish leaders and in separating them from their communities. The extraordinary gift turned out to be fraudulent and dangerous. This interpretation, however, seems to exculpate the Jewish leaders from responsibility for accepting the gift (apart from their failure to see through the deception) unless we return to an older understanding of gifts. In the ancient world, a gift was understood to create an implicit obligation to the bestower of the gift. The very willingness to accept the gift from Eichmann placed moral blame on the recipients, just as the Trojans assumed partial responsibility by accepting the Greeks' gift.[65] The judge wrote that "the organizers of the destruction . . . allowed K. and the Judenrat in Budapest to save their kin and friends in the peripheral cities 'for free' in order to *'commit'* them to the Nazis."[66] Since the implicit contractual element of gifts is not obvious, the judge had to juxtapose the two narratives about Faust and the Trojan horse in one sentence, thus indicating that for Kastner the gift was actually a contract.[67]

The judge overlooked the important distinction between gift and contract that lies in their relation to time. Derrida reminds us that in a barter society the idea of gifts introduces into the relations among people the interval of time. While a barter contract demands immediate reciprocity, a gift gives time to the recipient before returning the (value of) the gift. The real element of gift in such a transaction, according to this interpretation, is time itself: "The gift is not a gift, the gift only gives to the extent it *gives time*."[68] Eichmann's proposal to Brand and Kastner about the exchange of "trucks for blood" returned them to a barter society. Since they did not have the trucks at their disposal, they could only hope to derive from this bargain the gift of time as a way of saving the Jews. As Kastner explains in his report, all of their bargaining was aimed at gaining time until the end of the war. Judge Halevi, however, missed the point of the bargaining by reducing it into a quid pro quo contractual transaction devoid of any "deferral" in time, that is, of any real gift.

This contractual interpretation of the supposed gift allowed the judge to reach his inculpating conclusion regarding Kastner's actions.

> I asked myself and K. how was it possible that at the same time that [his partner] Brand was trying to shock all the leaders of the free world and urge them to action, K. made ten phone calls to his father in law in [his hometown] Cluj and did not warn him about the destination of the trains? . . . The interest of K. in keeping the secret was not an accident. . . . The behavior of K. was systematic and logical indeed: to guarantee the rescue of the prominent people, including his relatives and friends, he was *bound* to keep silent.[69]

In other words, Kastner was working on behalf of the enemy and deliberately concealed from the Jewish leaders his knowledge that the list was a veritable Trojan horse. It was for this so-called gift that Kastner was willing to sell his soul to the devil. Moreover, since Kastner was selling much more than his soul, that is, the lives of the Jews of Hungary, the contract was finally exposed as a *conspiracy* between Kastner and the Nazis. This conspiracy, the judge suggested, was the key to understanding the difference between Kastner and other Jewish leaders.[70] While the Judenrat members in the provincial towns were in fact misled by the gift (Trojan horse), Kastner knew its real meaning all along and assumed responsibility for its consequences (Faust).[71] Halevi's judgment reads like a story within a story, uncovering a conspiracy between a Nazi and a Jewish leader eager to save his relatives and friends and willing to deliver the members of his community to the Nazis in exchange.[72]

We see than that literature may have the power to protect us from the collapse of our moral order, but it can also prevent us from recognizing a new kind of evil. Indeed, this is the greatest task presented to the judge in transformative political trials—the need to resist easy analogies and instead resort to reflective judgment in order to develop adequate legal categories. The question is whether it was the attempt to adapt reality to literary paradigms that blocked the possibility of reflective judgment in the Kastner trial. My short answer to this question is no. It is not literature as such but Halevi's kitsch version of Faust that is responsible for flattening out the existential dilemmas that are so salient in the literary tradition.

The problem of transferring insights from literature to the law may be attributed to inherent differences between the two fields. Literature as a medium is able to explore the ambiguities and gray areas of human actions, while law demands resolution and is inherently limited in this respect. I would suggest, however, that there might be another factor at work here. Halevi's judgment was the first encounter of an Israeli court with the Kastner affair, and it turned out to be only the first step in the reception of the Kastner story, which sparked a long process of coming to terms with Jewish behavior during the Holocaust. Thus, after the political assassination of Kastner, the story acquired a new formulation and meaning in the appellate judgment of the Israeli Supreme Court (which I will discuss subsequently). A much more subtle and complex version of the events was presented in the opinion of Justice Simon Agranat, who transformed the image of Kastner from villain to tragic figure. This suggests that it is not legal discourse as such that is responsible for simplifying the moral dilemma but rather the combination of a certain legal doctrine (contract law) and a specific jurisprudential approach (legal formalism) embedded in literary allusions.

9. The Appeal: The Judgment of Justice Agranat

Five justices were appointed to sit on appeal over the Kastner-Gruen-wald affair. The majority overturned Halevi's judgment, though it was too late for Kastner, who had been murdered ten months earlier. Each justice produced a well-reasoned opinion touching on various issues raised by the trial, such as the limits of legal procedure and the relationships between law and morality, law and history, and law and collective identity. However, Justice Simon Agranat was the only judge who attempted to provide a counterhistory to Halevi's version of the events—one that was designed to encourage a process of reflective judgment about the meaning of the Holocaust for Israeli identity and politics.

Agranat's opinion, long and methodical, reversed almost all of Halevi's legal findings. It revealed that the law as such does not necessitate a black and white understanding of evil and that it offers subtler tools than the ones used by Halevi to understand Kastner's decision to cooperate with the Nazis. A central change in the legal narrative occurred as a result of Agranat's firm rejection of contract law as irrelevant to deciding the case. In Agranat's opinion the so-called contract was illusory, because contract law requires some measure of equality between the parties and the exercise of free will, both of which were missing in the conditions of terror and deceit created in Hungary under Nazi rule.[73] This "factual" disagreement with the trial court discloses a more fundamental disagreement about legal jurisprudence: Judge Halevi employed the teaching of legal formalism to support his finding of a valid contract, while Justice Agranat relied on a more contextual approach to conclude that there was not enough evidence to support such a finding.[74] Thus, Agranat stressed that the psychological devices used by the Nazis, central among them their willingness to help family members of the people with whom they negotiated, undermined Kastner's contractual obligations.[75]

Justice Agranat replaced the framework of contract law with that of administrative law, moving from the language of contractual obligations to the language of *reasonable* actions and *balancing of interests*.[76] This move reveals how deep disagreements about matters of morality, about the duties and responsibilities of a leader, can be expressed through the employment of different legal doctrines. Whereas contract law painted Kastner in individualist and egoist colors, Agranat argued that he understood himself as a leader whose responsibility was to the community as a whole, not to each individual separately.[77] Administrative law, not contract law, better captures this aspect of Kastner's actions because it deals with the questions of how to balance the different interests of individual members of the community and how to reach a reasonable decision under conditions of uncertainty. Contract law, by contrast, perceives responsibility in terms of a personal obligation toward each member of the community individually on the basis of full disclosure and knowledge.

Contract law comes under the "private" side of the classical division between private and public law, while administrative law comes under the "public" side.[78] This fact partly accounts for the transformation in how Kastner's actions were perceived. Administrative law is collectively oriented since its emphasis is not on the private interests of the actor but on the leader's public duties toward his or her constituency. Moreover, unlike the absolutism of contract law (when interpreted according to a formalist approach), administrative law allows gradations and uncertainties to enter into the actor's calculations. In accordance with this change Agranat quoted a legal authority, saying that certainty itself is only a high probability.[79] Interestingly, this also allowed Agranat to undermine the moralistic tone of Halevi's decision. The discourse of probabilities common in administrative law translated Kastner's metaphor of gambling on the lives of the Jews into the acceptable legal terms of taking reasonable chances. This change was important because Halevi's judgment seemed to imply a seamless transition between the world of Kastner in occupied Budapest and that of Israel in the 1950s. It overlooked the fact that what would be considered virtuous in the radical conditions under which Kastner worked (forging documents, bribing government officials, lying in negotiations, etc.) was very different from what we value in a leader in ordinary times.[80] Agranat sought to correct this error by introducing a legal doctrine that could be adjusted to these different conditions, one that would be able to consider the need to gamble in human lives, to take risks and use trickery.[81] Administrative law, with its language of balancing of interests (Agranat actually used the verb *reconciling*), allowed him to break away from both the moral absolutism of Halevi's judgment and its binary worldview.[82] In sum, administrative law doctrine allowed the judge to depict Kastner as a responsible leader (instead of an omnipotent one), responsive to the needs of his community at large (rather than acting out of selfish considerations) and forced to make difficult decisions under impossible conditions of uncertainty, deceit, and time pressure.

Administrative law doctrine also helped Agranat to reorder the *time frame* of the narrative. We have seen how contract law erases historical time by focusing on two points in time—the signing of the contract and its ultimate outcome—while ignoring fluctuations in the circumstances, knowledge, and intentions of the parties between these moments. The contractual time frame allowed Halevi to judge with hindsight by attributing later (objective) results to the earlier (subjective) intentions of the parties. The reintroduction of time into the judgment forces us to listen to Kastner's own words at different points in time and to notice differences. Agranat argued that the main danger in Halevi's approach came from the failure of the judge to imagine himself in the place of the other. As a corrective he recommended that the judge should attempt to "put himself in the shoes of the participants themselves; evaluate the problems they faced as they might have done; take into consideration sufficiently the needs of time and place, where they lived their lives; understand life as they understood it."[83] In *Foregone Conclusions* Michael Bernstein connects the dangers of retrospective judgment (which he calls backshadowing) prevalent in literary and historical accounts of the Holocaust to the temporal framework that these writers impose on the events. Bernstein urges that backshadowing be replaced with "sideshadowing," an approach that allows the reader to remember the alternatives and possibilities that were present at the time the actors made their decisions: "The Shoah as a whole . . . can never be represented plausibly as a tragedy because the killing happened as part of an ongoing political and bureaucratic process. In the domain of history . . . there are always multiple paths and sideshadows, always moment-by-moment events, each of which is potentially significant in determining an individual's life, and each of which is a conjunction, unplottable and unpredictable in advance of its occurrence, of specific choices and accidents."[84] Agranat sought to achieve such sideshadowing by turning to administrative law doctrine, which does not fix our attention on one or two points in time but allows the judge to take into account the process of calculating probabilities on the basis of uncertain and partial knowledge, a process in which at each point in time the leader is expected to balance the risks and opportunities and act accordingly.

Agranat was careful to reintroduce historical time into the judgment by framing the legal discussion according to the chronology of events.[85] This move exploded the illusory sense of continuity with the practices of normal life that the application of contract law to the Nazi era created. In Agranat's opinion, the chaotic times provided the only framework in which we should interpret the meaning of the so-called contract between Kastner and Eichmann.[86] By drawing attention to the impact of historical development on Kastner's action (the approaching end of the war, the increasing number of trains to Auschwitz, the delay in the West's response, etc.) he undermined the possibility of producing a legal narrative with moral closure.[87] Instead, the justice's opinion reads like a chronology that leaves us with many open-ended moral questions and with legal answers that do not pertain to absolute knowledge and certainty.

Agranat's choice of legal doctrine not only affects the narration of the historical facts but also invites readers to consider Kastner the man as opposed to the archetypal figure of Dr. K. Kastner as a Zionist committed to the Enlightenment ideals of activism, self-help, and self-assertion. Indeed, unlike many Hungarian Jewish leaders who could not conceive of breaking the law, Kastner and his rescue committee assisted illegal Jewish refugees by providing them with forged passports and helping them settle in Hungary before the Nazi invasion.[88] Moreover, as a Zionist, Kastner did not see himself limited to conventional ways of action (which relied on the help of Hungarian authorities) and was willing to try radical action such as negotiations with the Nazis over fantastic plans such as the "blood for trucks" idea.[89] The aims of the rescue committee were indeed grand—to save a million Jews with the financial and material help of the Western Allies and Jewish funds all over the world (through the Jewish Agency). Kastner was not the passive sort who would sit and wait for the Nazis to approach him; rather, as we saw, he initiated many of the meetings and designed grandiose proposals for the Nazis.[90] Paradoxically, it was Kastner's very activism that attracted Eichmann's attention. The latter especially feared an uprising similar to the one that had occurred in the Warsaw ghetto and therefore directed his best efforts at deception to disarming Kastner and his committee.[91] In fact, Kastner's story could shed some light on the limits of action under a totalitarian regime. However, Judge Halevi preferred myth to the bleak reality, as when he attributed the failure of the Israeli paratroopers' mission to betrayal by Kastner, as though no other obstacles had stood in the way of this mission.[92] Justice Agranat, on the other hand, tried to learn from this incident the limits of "heroic action" given the historic conditions of the Jews at the time.[93] His judgment combines a legal doctrine more receptive to uncertainties and ambiguities, a sociological jurisprudence that insists on situating the actors in their sociohistorical circumstances, and a methodical chronological account open to sideshadowing and lacking narrative closure. In retelling Kastner's story Agranat also changed the tone from that of an ironic, omniscient narrator to that of an empathic one who explicitly acknowledges the limits of his knowledge and warns against taking his account as the "final arbiter" of truth about this affair.

Interestingly, Agranat's attempt to reintroduce the historical context that had been missing from the trial court's judgment was reinforced by his refusal to narrativize the drama of Kastner. His chronological, deliberately antinarrativist account emphasized distinctions and created a historical distance from the events so that a more nuanced judgment would become possible. In terms of our theory of political trials, Agranat attempted to replace the category of collective memory with that of historiography.[94] As we shall see in chapter 3, this approach could not serve as a counterstory that would capture the public's attention,[95] and only when it received a dramatic literary formulation in the hands of a national poet did it induce a process of public self-examination.[96]

In the three attempts that we have studied to narrate the Kastner affair in a court of law we have discovered three different views about the relation between the past events and the political situation in Israel at the time. Tamir, the defense lawyer, attempted to transform a historical past into a judiciary present by reenacting on the court's stage the painful dilemma of choosing who would board Kastner's rescue train. He skillfully used the binary structure of a trial in order to represent this dilemma according to the ideological construction of the "two paths" of collaboration versus resistance. In this way Tamir managed to shift the direction of the trial from an attempt to judge the past to an occasion for deciding the future actions of the Israeli polity with regard to its enemies (negotiations or military resistance). Judge Halevi firmly refocused the story on Kastner but used the judgment to universalize Kastner's actions and compare his negotiations with the Nazis to the contract between Faust and the devil. In Halevi's judgment the historical facts were replaced with literary myths, producing a clear sense of good and evil in the two political paths of resistance and collaboration. It is this background that explains Justice Agranat's attempt to reintroduce historical time into his judgment. Instead of transforming the past into a political present and judging it in accordance with ideological strictures, as Tamir had endeavored to do, Agranat called for the present to be set aside in order to avoid the error of judging with hindsight. In his view, judging the past fairly meant refraining from making misleading analogies and being mindful of the difference between us and the people whom we judge. It is only by remembering this difference that we can attempt to "visit in our imagination" the conditions under which the questionable actions were taken, and it is with this difference in mind that we should try to formulate our judgment.[97] Agranat's approach to legal drama is reminiscent of Bertolt Brecht's approach to theater. Brecht criticized traditional theater for relying on an attempt to arouse the audience's emotions so that its rational judgment remains clouded. Brecht developed the technique of the "alienation effect" as the core of a new type of theater (epic theater) by means of which the audience is constantly reminded of the difference separating the actor from the act and is thus encouraged to use critical faculties of judgment.[98] Agranat's judgment is so saturated with the Brechtian alienation effect that boredom overcomes the reader's interest in the human drama that is being recounted.

Chapter 3

The Poet's Countertrial

Émile Zola's public intervention on behalf of Alfred Dreyfus is held up as a model for the role of the intellectual in a political trial. Indeed, shortly after Judge Halevi handed down the verdict in which he stated that "K. sold his soul to the devil," Kastner published a press release in which he compared himself to Dreyfus and promised to clear himself of the unfounded judgment.[1] Even though the comparison was largely intended to alert the public to the injustice that Kastner had suffered, the nationally acclaimed poet Nathan Alterman seems to have taken it literally. He took upon himself the role of Zola by voicing a public challenge to the foundation of the verdict and the ideological conception of the Holocaust that supported it. In so doing Alterman mobilized art in an attempt to expose the injustices of the court decision.

Political trials have often served to awaken intellectuals from their "theoretical slumber" and forced them to enter the political realm of debate and contestation. Indeed, the very term *intellectual* was coined in France following Zola's intervention on behalf of Dreyfus.[2] The relationship that develops under such circumstances between the intellectual and the court is usually perceived in terms of a battle between the demands of justice and the demands of politics. I believe that this formulation is too simplistic for dealing with the complex phenomenon of political trials. By studying Alterman's intervention in the Kastner affair I intend to show that the real contribution of the intellectual in such trials lies in transforming them into political occasions in the original sense of politics, that is, occasions for the public to subject the most fundamental values of the common consensus to critical reflection. It is from this perspective that we can begin to understand how political trials contribute to the viability of a liberal political culture. The focus of this chapter will therefore be the element of plurality in political trials—how they encourage (or limit) the introduction of a competition of narratives over the fundamental values of society. In particular I am interested in exploring the way Alterman managed to translate the legal issues involved in the Kastner affair into matters of principle of vital interest to the Israeli public.

Law has the tendency to insulate its decisions from the public's criticism under a veil of professionalism. In order to authoritatively challenge the judgment of the court one has to show his or her "legal credentials." This, however, creates a dilemma for the artist as a social critic whose marginality in the legal domain can be offset only by his or her moral standing and power of expression in the public domain. Hence, the main concern of the social critic is how to make his or her criticism available to the public at large in clear and accessible language. But in so doing the critic seems to risk losing an important source of authority by inviting the same accusation that he or she is leveling against the law, namely, of betraying art for the sake of politics.

The vicious circle can only be broken if we distinguish between different meanings of the word *politics*. We have already seen how the defense attorney, Shmuel Tamir, played a central role in politicizing the Kastner trial. He turned the accusations against his client, Malchiel Gruenwald, into a legal case against Kastner, who was depicted as having betrayed the trust given to him by the Jews of Hungary. By pointing out Kastner's affiliation with Mapai, Tamir also succeeded in transforming the trial into a weapon in party politics. I argued that Tamir's success in politicizing the trial was largely due to his ability to connect the legal issues with the prevailing ideological conception of the Holocaust—the "two paths" conception of heroism and cowardice. I further suggested that this type of politicization did not require the public to seriously deliberate the relevance of the conception but merely, as it were, to switch boxes within the framework of that ideology, moving the leaders of Mapai from the New Jew to the Diaspora Jew box. Judge Halevi adopted Tamir's version of events and condemned Kastner's path of negotiations with the Nazis as a modern-day Faustian bargain. Having won the trial, Tamir could use the verdict as a political tool against his detractors, for his subversive version of history had won the court's stamp of approval. Since the court had sealed the Kastner affair with an authorized judgment, any criticism had to begin by deprofessionalizing the court's discourse and opening it up to public deliberation. An issue becomes political when it is contested across a range of different discursive arenas and among a range of different publics.[3] Accordingly, repoliticizing the Kastner judgment meant finding ways to transcend legal formalities and focus the debate on matters of principle. Unlike Tamir, who used the trial to strengthen the prevailing Zionist ideology, Alterman wanted to persuade the public to reflect critically about this ideology by raising questions about the plausibility of the two-paths conception of the Holocaust and the hegemonic narrative of national heroism.

Toward the end of the 1940s and the beginning of the 1950s Alterman enjoyed immense popularity in Israel.[4] Although his early poems had been lyrical and apolitical, the stormy days of the beginning of the state brought him closer to politics and he began to write political poetry, discussing the issues of the time in direct and simple language.[5] He published most of these poems in his weekly column "Ha-Tur ha-Shevii" (The Seventh Column) in the daily newspaper *Davar* in 1943–67.[6] Through this widely read platform for his views, Alterman gained increasing influence and popularity, especially among members of the younger generation who participated in the 1948 war of independence. He was admired and respected as a poet who articulated the Zionist ethos of heroism.[7]

Alterman was known for his ability to express in poetic form issues of principle and historical importance distilled from the mass of everyday occurrences. It is not surprising, therefore, that he was quick to identify the immense importance of the Kastner affair to the shaping of the collective identity of the young state. Alterman voiced his sharp criticism of the trial in a series of poems that were published during the trial, after the verdict was handed down, and following the assassination of Kastner. The pungency of Alterman's criticism stood in sharp contrast to his other political poems, which were generally written in a constructive and encouraging tone. The "poet of the consensus"[8] suddenly undertook to question the foundations of Israeli collective identity—the ethos of Zionist heroism that led to identification with the ghetto resistance fighters and the condemnation of the Judenrat path. Some have argued that Alterman did not really go against the political establishment and that he merely rallied to defend Mapai, which, as we have seen, was threatened by the affair.[9] His heightened interest in the trial might also have stemmed from his own guilt feelings for not having spoken out about the catastrophe during the Holocaust years.[10] However, it is now generally believed by Alterman scholars that, just as in previous instances he had demonstrated his ability to identify with marginalized groups that were considered "Others" in Israeli society (such as the Palestinians during the 1948 war and the Kufr Qassem trial), in the Kastner affair the poet was ahead of his time in identifying with the despised Judenrate members.[11] Whatever his motivation, what interests me here is the intense public controversy that Alterman's criticism aroused. I will explore the ways in which Alterman succeeded in initiating a profound and heated public debate about the fundamental values of the state, a debate that neither the verdict of the trial court nor its reversal by the appellate court instigated.

1. Entering the Debate

At the time of the Kastner trial Nathan Alterman was already engaged in an intense private examination of the behavior of Jewish leaders during the Holocaust. His interest in the period might have been raised by the publication of a monumental book on the struggle of the ghetto resistance fighters[12] and the emergence of ritualized memorial ceremonies in which the war of the ghettoes was exalted and the behavior of the Judenrate summarily condemned.[13] He devoted seven notebooks of his personal diary to exploring his views on this subject, which ran against the grain of the general perception of the Holocaust in Israel in the 1950s. In particular, he questioned the validity of the current ideological framework, which divided the behavior of the Jewish leaders into two diametrically opposed paths—what he refers to in his diaries as the "two-paths" conception of the Holocaust: the courageous path of the rebels (resistance) and the cowardly path of the Jewish Councils (collaboration). As we have seen, this ideological worldview was reinforced in the Kastner trial by Tamir's use of the binary structure of the trial to symbolize the two paths that the judge was called on to choose between. Alterman describes in his notebooks how he came to realize, through private conversations and a careful reading of survivors' testimonies, diaries, and the autobiographies of former ghetto fighters, that the two-paths conception, rather than illuminating the period, worked as an ideological blinder, preventing Israelis from understanding the period and its dilemmas.

These private notebooks were first published in 1989 accompanied by an explanatory essay by the Alterman scholar Dan Laor. According to Laor, the notebooks reveal that Alterman became obsessed with the need to discover the truth about Jewish behavior during the Holocaust.[14] However, the notebook that was devoted to the Kastner trial was not included in even this belated publication.[15] It is there that we find Alterman's unfiltered reaction to Halevi's judgment. Criticizing the judge for focusing on the events in Kastner's hometown, Cluj, in isolation from the historical context, he argues that in so doing the judge

> in no way helps the nation learn the necessary lesson. He makes no contribution at all to knowing and comprehending the reasons for the historical processes. . . . The cerebral and seemingly rational structure rests on a single chapter, thus distorting the content [of the whole] . . . and perhaps even distorting the chapter itself. In the many sections in which he treats the underlying personal motivations, the judgment reads like a psychological novel; and it is primarily on the basis of these chapters of psychology, which the judge serves to us on a platter, that the verdict is reached.

This comment demonstrates the profound sense of historical responsibility that Alterman attached to understanding the period and delivering accurate judgments of it. He realized that the main strength of a trial investigation—its tendency to examine an event in isolation from the wider historical circumstances—had produced in this case a distorted understanding of the historical period of the Holocaust as a whole. By concentrating on Kastner's actions, the trial presented him as the embodiment of the Judenrate, thus simplifying an enormously complex social phenomenon. However, being a careful reader of texts, Alterman noticed that there was a dissonance between the chaos of the period and the logical structures imposed on it by an excessively formal legal analysis. The formality of the law, Alterman wrote, distorted the historical events recounted by the judge and made them read like "a psychological novel."[16]

Alterman attributed the judge's main error to his attempt to adapt the complex reality revealed in the courtroom to the ideological preconception of the two paths. He wrote in his diary that the judge's conclusion that there had indeed existed a clear choice between two dichotomous paths resulted from the way he formulated the facts and was not based on the real life experiences of the survivors. Moreover, as soon as this conclusion became a judgment of the court it served to reinforce popular misconceptions about the two paths. Since Alterman was not a party to the trial and played no official role in it, he did not have to adapt his criticism to the strictures of procedure and evidence law. And since, unlike the appellate court (whose criticism of the judgment was similar to Alterman's), he was not obliged to focus on the Kastner affair in Hungary, he expanded his investigation to other places in Europe where the Judenrate and the Jewish underground had to decide how to respond to Nazi rule.

Like the Dreyfus trial for Zola, the Kastner trial proved to be an important factor in Alterman's decision to publicize his unconventional ideas about the Holocaust period.[17] He broke his silence in 1954, while the trial was still pending, and published a provocative poem that was carefully timed to appear on the "Holocaust and Resistance" day, which that year fell on 30 April. In the poem Alterman raised questions about the glorification of the partisans and ghetto rebels who chose the path of active struggle as the only resistance worth remembering. The poem, which was written in the form of a collective monologue by the ghetto rebels and resistance fighters themselves, was very provocative. They are depicted by Alterman as stepping down from their pedestal in order to give testimony about what had really happened, warning the Israeli public against the dangerous tendency to fictionalize history and judge it according to stereotypical conceptions of heroism. "And on Memorial Day said the fighters and rebels: / Don't put us on a pedestal to be distinguished from the Diaspora with a strong light. / In this hour of memory we leave the pedestal / to mingle again in darkness with the history of the people of Israel."[18] Both the content of the poem and the timing of the publication engendered intense public criticism in the press, to which Alterman responded with an essay entitled "The Resistance and Its Time" (published on 28 May 1954).[19]

The public debate was rekindled shortly after publication of the verdict that acquitted Gruenwald and sustained his accusations against Kastner as a collaborator. The verdict was handed down on 22 June 1955 in the midst of the election campaign to the third Knesset and immediately became a central issue of contestation in election speeches. Halevi's decision was celebrated among Herut members. The party's newspaper presented Kastner as Eichmann's partner and Tamir as "the main force to the discovery of the truth" and reminded its readers that it was Ze'ev Jabotinsky, the ideological father of Herut, who had demanded evacuation of all European Jews to Palestine, in contrast to the Mapai leaders who had supported selective immigration. Following the government's decision to appeal the verdict, Herut Knesset member Yochanan Bader submitted no-confidence motions, which subsequently led to the fall of the government and the formation of a new one based on a different coalition.[20] The verdict was also used by the left-wing parties, Mapam and Ahdut Ha-Avodah, which saw themselves as continuing the path of the resistance, claiming that most acts of rebellion had been conducted by people affiliated with them. In their election campaign they identified the Mapai leaders with Kastner and accused them of passivity, helplessness, and even neglect of the Jews during the Holocaust.[21]

Alterman published his response to the verdict in the form of four polemical poems devoted to the Kastner trial in his regular column in *Davar* in which he harshly criticized the verdict both for being anachronistic and for depicting Kastner as a stereotype of all the evils of the Judenrate.[22] In addition, Alterman warned against the tendency to judge according to absolute moral principles, advocating instead a more contextual judgment that would be attentive to the real experiences of people during the Holocaust. In particular, he argued that Israelis should make distinctions among the Judenrat members and refrain from condemning them en masse.

> Later we will consider and see whether absolute judgment and explanation can really be applied to the Judenrat affair, and whether its traits are so unambiguous and uniform. For it seems that if we warp this judgment, we shall warp the judgment of a great many who cannot speak. And by wrongly judging them, we shall find ourselves bending truth and the scales of justice itself.[23]

An unexpected epilogue was added to this series of poems in 1957 while Kastner's appeal was still pending in the Supreme Court. On 3 March, Kastner was shot while returning home from work late at night, and he subsequently died of his injuries. In April, Alterman published the poem "Thirty Days since Kastner's Murder,"[24] in which he adopted a more radical stance, urging that the question of Kastner's behavior be removed from the court of law altogether and left to the judgment of historians. The murder "orders us to go back to the affair and study it from the start. Maybe the courtroom was not the proper place to recount its history."

The Kastner trial helped the poet see more clearly the dangers posed by an ideological construction of reality. Israel in the 1950s was to a large extent a society trying to live up to its ideological (and literary) ideals about the virtuous life defined, among other ways, as pioneering work on the land, military heroism, self-help, and political activism.[25] As I noted, Alterman had been a central figure in articulating the Zionist ethos of heroism, and his earlier poems had contributed greatly to the ideological perception of the two paths. But during the trial the poet was faced with the injustice that can be done to people who lived through those times when they are judged according to a strict ideological model. In particular, he understood how his own literary creations could become larger than life and be used to silence the voices of real people who had tried—often in broken Hebrew and with great emotional difficulty—to give testimony about life under the Nazi regime. Alterman therefore began to criticize the plausibility of his own literary creations. As Laor comments:

> It is astonishing to see how Alterman—an admirer of the rebellion, who in the midst of the Warsaw ghetto uprising wrote poems like "A Hebrew Girl," a poet . . . who completely supports the path of military resistance in the poem "So Said the Sword of the Besieged," and who never concealed his own personal admiration for the heroes of the resistance—did not hesitate to destroy with his own hands the myth of heroism and resistance.[26]

The trial was an important learning experience for the poet, not only teaching him about the limits of literature but also providing him with a model that enabled him to give his counterstory a dramatic shape. Alterman decided to lend his voice to the voiceless Judenrat members. Being an outsider to the legal process he had only his literary credentials to rely on. In order for his counterstory to be heard, however, it was not enough to articulate the complaints of the Judenrat members, whose voices were missing from the public debate. After all, Kastner had also tried to explain and justify his actions in the courtroom, but his message had not been heard by those seeking black and white explanations. Realizing that to enable the public to listen to the repressed voices it was essential to dismantle the ideological framework that muted them, he cast his poems in the dramatic format of a courtroom investigation. In those poems, he put on trial the very conception of "heroism," which dominated the Israeli political discourse of the time.

2.   *The Poet Cross-Examines the Myth*

Alterman's poems about the Kastner trial are very different from all the other poems he published in "Ha-Tur Ha-Shevii."[27] He constantly mixes genres, moving between prose and poetry, between essayist writing and long citations from history books and from the personal accounts of resistance fighters, as though seeking a form that could adequately reflect the pain and doubt that he was experiencing. Unlike Judge Halevi, who tried to force the Kastner affair into the frameworks of familiar cultural idioms and legal doctrines, Alterman sought new ways to articulate his views, testing the limits of his poetry in order to find the proper dramatic form in which to express his criticism.

The dramatic form that Alterman chose for his poems was that of a trial. He may have been influenced by Tamir's dramatic cross-examination of the Israeli paratrooper Yoel Palgi, who, together with Peretz Goldstein and Hannah Senesh, had been sent to help organize the Jewish resistance in Hungary.[28] In his private notes Alterman wrote that in his view Palgi had spoken the truth in the courtroom and had had the courage to tell the Israeli public that the myth of heroism could not have saved the Jews of Hungary since they had deluded themselves about the Nazis' intentions until the last minute. In his poems Alterman adopted the format of cross-examination, using it to dismantle the myth of heroism presented by Tamir and expose the complex reality within which both the resistance and the Judenrate had acted.

The poems can be read as an imaginary trial in which the adversaries are the two paths of the rebels and the Judenrate. Alterman appointed himself as the attorney for the silenced members of the Judenrate (and by implication also for Kastner) and tried to "prove their case" by cross-examining the witnesses for the prosecution, that is, members of the Jewish resistance. Interestingly, he did not summon Judenrat members themselves to testify. Maybe he sensed that the public was not yet ready to hear them. Instead he tried to "prove" their innocence from the testimonies of their political adversaries, the resistance fighters.[29] For this purpose, Alterman quoted at length from the diaries of resistance fighters at the beginning of his poems and contrasted them with their more recent statements. This move is a familiar one in courtroom investigations. The law attributes more credibility to earlier statements than later ones, and the demonstration of inconsistencies between an earlier and a later statement is one of the prevailing legal techniques for discrediting an adversary. Thus, in order to undermine the condemnation of the Judenrate, Alterman quoted from the diary and notes of Mordechai Tenenbaum, the leader of the Jewish underground in the Bialystok ghetto, describing a meeting with the head of the local Judenrat, Ephraim Barash. Tenenbaum recorded in his diary that he had told his comrades:

> I say to those assembled that if the *Aktion* [German raid on the ghetto] takes place on this scale, there will be no response on our part. We'll sacrifice the 6,300 Jews in order to save the remaining 35,000. The situation at the front is such that a radical turnabout could come any day. If they want to broaden the *Aktion* or if during the *Aktion* they should force us by their behavior to take to the street, or if the street should rise spontaneously to defend itself, we will have no choice but to take the initiative ourselves.[30]

This and similar quotations from the writings of the Jewish fighters showed that the logic of sacrificing the few for the sake of the many was prevalent at the time among the resistance leaders themselves. Judge Halevi had condemned this type of cold calculation as a sign of the moral corruption of Kastner and the Judenrate in contrast to the heroism of the resistance fighters. Alterman's quotations, however, showed that in reality there had been no clear dividing line between the two paths. The pragmatic but tragic logic had stemmed from notions of collective responsibility that were shared by the Judenrate and resistance fighters alike. In another poem Alterman argued that the two-paths conception was a myth imposed on the historical events after the fact.[31] To support this view he summoned the testimony of Yitzhak (Antek) Zuckermann, one of the leaders of the Warsaw ghetto uprising. In a subsequent poem he again quoted Zuckermann as saying that the January revolt would never have begun if there had been enough time to consult with the leaders of the resistance, who probably would have decided to postpone it.[32] Again, Alterman claimed that the logic of "gaining some more time" had been shared by both the Judenrate and the resistance fighters. Alterman concluded that the judge's very attempt to present a moral dilemma with two mutually exclusive options was detrimental to the historical truth.

3. Cross-Examining the Poet

Alterman's public intervention caused turmoil at the time. Publicists and famous writers accused him of intentionally blurring the line between heroism and cowardice in order to acquit Kastner and the Judenrate. Yitzhak Zuckermann himself, who was cited by Alterman, insisted, in a speech during the election campaign of the left-wing party Ahdut Ha-Avodah that there had indeed been two very distinct paths and that he and his friends from the resistance had never advocated pleading with the Nazi authorities. He refused to be included in the same category as the Judenrat members, provocatively announcing that he and his friends had even executed some of them and demanding to be "judged by the people" for these actions.[33] Interestingly, most of the critics who responded in writing to Alterman also adopted a trial-like format in their essays that was very similar to the one presented by the poet. This time, however, it was Alterman himself who was summoned to the witness box for "cross-examination." Following Alterman's own method, they began their essays with quotations from his poems, contrasting his early poems with his current publications to reveal contradictions. At times they seemed to forget that these were literary creations and favored them over the living voice of the poet. They interpreted these contradictions as casting doubt on the purity of the poet's motivation, suggesting that it was political (the desire to defend Mapai) instead of an unyielding search for the truth.[34]

The impact of the Kastner trial can thus be seen not only in the form adopted by Alterman in his response to the verdict but also in the confrontation between Alterman and his critics, which imitated the format and logic of a courtroom examination and can be schematized in the following way. The two adversaries in this mock trial were the two paths which had figured so prominently in the Kastner trial. Alterman appointed himself as the attorney for the Judenrate, and his critics played the role of attorney for the resistance fighters. Trying to disprove each other's position, both parties engaged in "cross-examination": while Alterman "cross-examined" the resistance fighters, his critics "cross-examined" him.

As we saw in the previous chapters, the political significance of the Kastner trial lay in Tamir's success in linking the Mapai party with the path of "Kastnerism" as an ideology, through their common preference for negotiations with the ruler rather than military resistance. The trial produced an unlikely coalition of critics of Mapai's policies from both the right-wing Herut party and the left-wing parties (especially Ahdut Ha-Avodah). An interesting split occurred, though, during the public debate. While the criticism of Mapai was voiced both by the right-wing political attorney Tamir through the radical weekly *Ha-Olam Ha-Ze*[35] and by left-wing political leaders, the criticism of Alterman mainly came from people associated with left-wing parties to which many of the former resistance fighters belonged. This is not surprising since these were precisely the people whose position had been questioned in Alterman's poems. They attributed Alterman's defense of the Judenrate to his political association with Mapai, implying that in a sense Alterman had also *sold his soul* (in this case his poetic gift) in order to defend his party.[36] The publicist Meir Ben Gur contrasted Alterman's early poem "A Prayer of Retribution," which described the "courage of the fighters and defenders of the city," with his more recent poem "Around the Trial," written in reaction to the Kastner trial. Ben Gur wondered what effect these two poems, with contradictory messages but written by the same poet, might have on the education of the country's younger generation.[37] Another example of this courtroom technique was provided by David Kenaani, a writer and an expert on Alterman's literary work who became a harsh critic of his views about the Holocaust period. Kenaani published a reply to Alterman in which he pointed out the contradiction between Alterman's current questioning of the myth of Jewish heroism and his earlier poems, which had provided the young Israeli nation with its moral code of heroism and honor

> Nathan Alterman dedicated "Ha-Tur ha-Shevii" (30.4) to the "Day of Remembrance and the Resistance." And when you come across the words of a poet whom you respect and admire, and you sense that they are alien and strange, then you reread them to determine whether perhaps the fault lies not with the author but with yourself. . . . There is one book of Hebrew poetry that deserves the title "prophetic." In the early days of the War, before the extermination had begun, a Hebrew poet had a powerful vision of a war in which the few in numbers would face the many. . . . I am referring to "Simhat Aniim" [The Joy of the Poor] by Nathan Alterman, the greatest poem of our generation. Fear and wonder strikes the reader

of the prescient words of this *seer who transcends the bounds of time.*
Years before the Warsaw Ghetto Uprising he said:

The enemy bears scorn and death
Arise, for the foe is marching
Arise, hold fast your weapons
Prepare, for the time is near . . .

Far be it from me to suggest that Alterman is disavowing Simhat
Aniim. Far be it from me to imply that he intends to remove those
who realized his vision from their pedestal.[38]

Kenaani could detect a contradiction in Alterman's views only by
banishing the element of time. First, he presented the early writing of
Alterman as prophetic, that is, as transcending the limits of its own
time, and then he refused to acknowledge the possibility that the poet
might have changed his earlier views as a result of listening to survivors and learning about the period. Ironically, by choosing to erase
historical time from his account Kenaani repeated in his critique the
very mistake of hindsight that Alterman had warned against in his
response to the judgment in the Kastner trial.

Kenaani's criticism exemplifies the essence of the controversy
aroused by the Kastner trial: how the period of the Holocaust should be
presented to the Israeli public. The debate was between an approach
that insisted on concrete historical accounts as a means of understanding the complex reality in Europe and one that relied on the abstract
timelessness of myth to connect the traumatic events in Europe to the
new Jewish life being created in Israel. Alterman was deeply critical of
the common error of judging with hindsight (backshadowing). However, being a poet and a social critic, he was not content merely to discuss the period of the Holocaust with the meticulous precision of the
historian. Like Tamir, he understood that the only way to influence the
collective memory of the young country was to formulate his views in
a dramatic way that would arouse the public's interest. It is this constructive effort to produce counterimages about the heroism of Jewish
leaders who chose to cooperate with the Nazis that set him apart from
the justices of the Supreme Court.[39] Alterman thus sought a means of
reintroducing real historical time into the story of the Holocaust in
order to alert his readers to the need to view the events in their histori-

cal particularity. One of his solution was to personalize time in his poems and summon "time" itself to give testimony alongside the resistance fighters. Time remembers the Judenrate and rebels alike, refuses to provide the "moral" that its audience desires, and chooses instead to abandon the community that does not respect its history.[40] This rhetorical strategy is also found in his concluding poem, "Thirty Days since Kastner's Murder." Alterman presents time as refusing to accept its unfair exclusion from the judgment of the trial court and causing the judgment to disintegrate.

> And at that moment reappear the hellish days of this period
> To find their place among the paragraphs of the verdict
> And this verdict tears itself apart and its parts are carried away
>   like a storm
> Dispersed in the darkness and lost.[41]

As one who had contributed to the shaping of the Zionist ethos, Alterman understood that it was not enough simply to undermine the lesson of the two paths but that a new message should be articulated to replace it. Even though he refused to accept the dichotomy between resistance fighters and Judenrat members (arguing that the affinities between them, caused by the historical circumstances, exceeded their differences), he did offer a different distinction to be upheld as the "lesson" for the younger generation. He suggested that the Zionist dichotomy between Israel and the diaspora was the only division that could fairly explain different modes of behavior (military heroism versus passive collaboration) because only in an independent state could military resistance be expected to actually save the people from the enemy's attacks. This was the only lesson that Alterman was willing to distill from the Holocaust, the need to defend the continuing existence of a free and independent state of Israel.

3.   Conclusion

Our discussion of the Kastner trial as a political trial has exposed a complex relationship between art and law in judging the Holocaust. Judge Halevi used literary conventions in order to make the new phenomenon of Jewish leaders' collaboration with the Nazis fit his audience's cultural expectations about evil. In order to resist the totalizing power of the law, a strong oppositional voice was needed. Paradoxically, the one most fit to challenge the legitimacy of the judgment and call its bluff was the poet, who spoke in the name of art whose boundaries, he claimed, had been transgressed by the judgment of the court.

There is a tension that runs throughout Alterman's writings on the affair: on the one hand the poet was very critical of the attempt to morally judge Kastner with the inadequate tools of law, which reduced the complexities of the affair to the simplistic form of a psychological novel; and on the other hand he chose to formulate his own "poetic" critique in a pseudo-legal way (cross-examination). One explanation for this tension might be the court's immense influence on the public debate, a force that could only be countered by the adoption of quasi-legal discourse by the poet himself. Alterman came to realize (albeit reluctantly) that the law had the power to shape the way the Holocaust period would be perceived by the general public, how its collective memory would be constituted. In order to compete with the influence of the court he needed to produce a dramatic confrontation, and he did so by creating his own imaginary countertrial.

The judge and the poet took precisely opposite directions in dealing with the past. The judge estheticized the events in order to adapt them to literary precedents and form a clear-cut legal and moral judgment. The poet, on the other hand, resisted the illusions of literature and sought ways to highlight some of the gray shadings of the Jews' dark reality during the Holocaust without providing an artificial lesson.[42] It is interesting to note, however, a blind spot on Alterman's part. Even though he was intimately involved with the dilemma of whether "political poetry" should be considered art or the corruption of art, he did not recognize the possibility of a similar dilemma for the legal profession. In other words, he failed to perceive the dilemma confronting lawyers and judges of whether (and how) political trials can be made to conform with the demands of justice.[43] Instead Alterman resorted to the traditional solution of demanding the separation of law from the fields of morality, politics, and literature. In reviewing the Kastner affair in the previous chapters I have tried to expose its different threads and suggest that presenting the issue as a competition between justice and politics is misleading. By contrasting Judge Halevi's decision with Justice Agranat's, and Tamir's politics with those of Alterman, I sought to show that such trials cannot be separated from politics altogether but that we can begin to distinguish between different kinds of politics.

The elections to the third Knesset took place five weeks after the verdict was handed down and were conducted in its shadow. In these elections Mapai lost five mandates out of the forty-five it had held in the second Knesset. Prime Minister Moshe Sharett wrote in his diary about the effect of the verdict: "A new blow . . . a horrible nightmare, what did the judge take upon himself! Suffocating the party, stirring up disorder."[44] The reaction of the political establishment to the affair was very different from the one advocated by Alterman. It demonstrated little faith in deliberative democracy. As we saw, after Kastner's assassination the appellate court reached its decision and cleared him of most of Gruenwald's accusations. Justice Agranat relied on the same facts described by the trial court to produce a very different narrative. Instead of publishing the two decisions in the state's law reports, so that it would be left to the public (and historical research) to decide which version of the events was more convincing, only the appellate court's decision was published. In other words, a subversive telling of Zionist history was met with an attempt at silencing. It was only in 1965, after the Eichmann trial had been concluded, that Halevi's decision (239 pages long) was finally published in the state's law reports.[45] By that time, however, Israeli public attention was firmly focused on the devil (Adolf Eichmann) and his victims and was no longer interested in contemplating the devastating dilemmas of the Jewish Councils.

The Eichmann Trial

Chapter 4

A Tale of Two Narratives

1. Between the Kastner and Eichmann Trials

Unlike the Kastner trial of the 1950s, the Eichmann trial was intended to be a celebrated educational affair. Great efforts were made to make it more accessible to the public. The court sessions were broadcast on the radio (there was no television in Israel until 1967) and special permission was given to record the proceedings. The trial was cast as historic, one in which the entire Jewish nation (represented by Israel) stood in judgment of one of its worst oppressors, Adolf Eichmann, and by implication nazism itself. The very structure of the trial symbolically inverted the past by transforming the persecuted victims into the prosecutors. This was to become a "transformative trial" for Israeli society by reenacting on a public stage both the return of the rule of law (bringing Eichmann to trial) and the transformation of a nation of persecuted people into a sovereign state with a respected legal system.

The state's case against Adolf Eichmann was brought to trial in Jerusalem in 1961 and was concluded with the judgment of the court, which convicted Eichmann and sentenced him to death.[1] The judgment was pronounced unanimously, and the court spoke with one voice in providing the official (hi)story.[2] Judges, however, are not the only storytellers in trials. Lawyers have their own share in the storytelling. The kind of story they tell depends on their choice of legal framework for the trial's narrative and their decision as to who will tell it. Lawyers also provide contrasting (uninterrupted) narratives in their opening and closing statements. Gideon Hausner, the attorney general and the chief prosecutor in the Eichmann trial, took upon himself the role of master storyteller. He claimed to speak with the voice of six million victims, six million accusers.

As I stand before you, judges of Israel, to lead the prosecution of
Adolf Eichmann, I am not standing alone. With me are six million
accusers. But they cannot rise to their feet to point an accusing finger
toward the glass booth and cry out at the man sitting there, "I
accuse." For their ashes are piled up on the hills of Auschwitz and
the fields of Treblinka, washed by the rivers of Poland, and their
graves are scattered the length and breadth of Europe. Their blood
cries out, but their voices cannot be heard. I, therefore, will be their
spokesman and will pronounce, in their names, their awesome
indictment.[3]

Hannah Arendt was also a storyteller at the Eichmann trial, although
not an official actor in the legal drama. At the time of the trial she was
already a prominent writer in the fields of history and philosophy and
was particularly well-known for her pathbreaking book *The Origins of
Totalitarianism* (1951). Seeing the trial as an opportunity to closely
observe one of the main agents of a totalitarian state, she asked the editors of the *New Yorker* to appoint her to cover it. As she wrote to her
friend the philosopher Karl Jaspers, since she had not attended the
Nuremberg trials, she felt that coming to the Eichmann trial was a debt
she owed to herself and her past as a Jewish refugee from Nazi Germany.[4] Arendt took it upon herself to provide a counternarrative, the
story that was not told but in her opinion should have been told in the
courtroom. Her critical reports of the trial were widely read in the
United States, both because of the magazine's standing and because of
her own prestige, but they reached only a limited audience in Israel.[5]
Eichmann in Jerusalem, the book she published on the basis of the
reports, was translated into Hebrew only forty years after the trial, in
2000. Hence, the "competition of storytellers" took place offstage without direct impact on the trial's reception within Israel. It was a competition between the prosecution's view of the trial's role in Jewish history
and Arendt's view of the trial's role in human history—a view that generated a great deal of controversy, especially among the American Jewish community, but failed to gain serious public attention in Israel until
recently.

In *Eichmann in Jerusalem* Arendt criticized Hausner's decisions time
and again. She rewrote his accusations, challenged his choice of witnesses, objected to the direction in which he led the trial, reinterpreted

the crime, and finally even produced her own judgment.[6] Hausner, for his part, mentioned Arendt only once in *Justice in Jerusalem*, his own book on the trial. He quoted from an article that criticized "Miss Arendt" and added in a footnote that since her book had been refuted by many reviewers it did not warrant further discussion by him.[7] In their zeal to produce the "correct" story—that is, the master story that would determine the temporal and spatial framework of the trial, the choice of protagonists, the question of voice, and so forth—both at times forgot the limits of storytelling and, deeply aware of the impact the trial's narrative would have on all subsequent stories about the Holocaust, sought to occupy the position of sole author.

Studying the controversy can teach us something about the positions of the parties, but more importantly it can illuminate the way in which the trial was used as a way to change the Israeli collective memory and identity. Choosing to approach the trial via a sidetrack, via Arendt's attempts to report a story that was never told in the courtroom, may shed light on the deep tensions and conflicts inherent in political trials. Conflict between worldviews characterizes every political trial, but it is only in political trials within democratic regimes that such conflict is allowed to surface, thereby introducing an element of uncertainty into the trial.[8] It may be an irony of history that by criticizing the Eichmann trial and its tendency to become a "show trial" in the hands of the prosecution Arendt contributed to making it a real political trial for her readers. Her counternarrative forces them to contemplate the most serious jurisprudential, moral, and historical dilemmas that were raised by the trial but often hidden from the public eye.

The Missing Chapter

Since political trials are always an embarrassment to liberals, each political trial is depicted as an exception or a pathology in need of justification. Even scholars who are willing to defend the divergence from the rule of law in some trials, such as during a society's transition to a more democratic regime, are quick to limit their defense to these special circumstances. The literature on political trials therefore tends to view each trial in isolation from preceding and following ones. This "episodic" approach, however, obscures the intricate relations that often exist between political trials within a given society over a span of

time and therefore fails to illuminate the question of changes in collective identity and memory. For this reason my discussion of the Eichmann trial begins with an exploration of its roots in the Kastner trial.

In his memoirs Gideon Hausner comments: "After fifty sessions, we
reached the chapter on Hungarian Jewry. . . . The shadow of another
trial now fell over our courtroom."[9] Many intricate threads, political,
legal, and personal, connected the Eichmann trial to the Kastner trial,
but they were mostly suppressed. There are several reasons that can
explain this approach: some were legal, such as the reluctance to supply the defense with materials about Jewish cooperation with the Nazis
that could undermine the prosecution's case; some were political, such
as the need to clear the name of the Mapai party of the accusations lev-
eled against it during the Kastner trial;[10] and some were humanist, such
as the desire to change the status of Holocaust survivors in Israeli society and its judgmental attitude toward them. Whatever the reasons, the
policy of suppressing discussion of the Kastner affair in the Eichmann
trial turned the affair into a taboo subject, thus precluding the possibility of conducting an honest public discussion about the wisdom or
desirability of this approach.

Notwithstanding the prosecution's efforts, it could not keep the
shadows of the Kastner trial completely at bay. Three main sources of
tension introduced the element of risk to the trial: subversive questions
by Judge Halevi; witnesses who resisted the official line of the prosecution; and an outside attorney, Tamir, who attempted to join the trial.

The first source of tension was Judge Benjamin Halevi, who had
served as sole judge at the Kastner trial. At the time of Eichmann's capture, he was president of the Jerusalem District Court and as such had
the authority to decide the composition of the panel that would sit in
judgment over Eichmann.[11] Halevi's famous verdict that Kastner had
"sold his soul to the devil" had made it clear how he viewed Eichmann.
For this reason, the president of the Supreme Court, Yitzhak Olshan,
tried to dissuade him from appointing himself to the case. Halevi
refused to comply.[12] Further pressure on Halevi by the justice minister
was also to no avail. In an interview several years later Halevi disclosed
that he suspected that these efforts had political rather than legal
motives, since the government feared that he might probe too closely
into the behavior of Jewish leaders (such as Kastner) during the Holocaust.[13] Halevi's speculation may be supported by the fact that the
Israeli authorities, rather than resorting to the regular legal procedure

of disqualifying prejudicial judges, proposed a special law that would transfer the authority to decide the composition of the Eichmann panel to the president of the Supreme Court.[14] The government cloaked the maneuver in the argument that in cases involving the death penalty the highest standard of judgment had to be ensured.[15] During the Knesset debate opposition members criticized the fact that this was an "in personem" law against Halevi, constituting a reprehensible practice that allowed the government to disqualify a particular judge from sitting on a case.[16] After the passage of this law, Justice Moshe Landau of the Supreme Court was appointed to preside over the Eichmann case. Nonetheless, in the end Halevi did appoint himself to the panel alongside Justice Landau.[17] Indeed, as we shall see, several times during the trial Halevi acted the part of a "Trojan horse," taking an active role in questioning the Jewish leaders and Eichmann himself about their cooperation with the Nazis and keeping the Kastner controversy never very far from public consciousness.

The witnesses for the prosecution presented Hausner with further difficulties. One important group of witnesses were former members of the Jewish resistance. Hausner fought hard during the trial to establish their relevance by arguing that their testimonies (about Jewish acts of heroism) shed light on the annihilation process and were therefore relevant to proving Eichmann's guilt.[18] Politically, they represented the heroic side of the Zionist ethos and were therefore crucial to Hausner's narrative with its stress on active resistance to Nazi persecution. However, as had become apparent during the Kastner controversy, the resistance fighters had often found themselves in conflict with the Judenrat leaders and had greatly contributed to the wide acceptance of the "two-paths" conception of the Holocaust in Israel, which Alterman had so poignantly criticized during the Kastner affair. It was only to be expected that the resistance fighters would want the Eichmann trial to endorse their tactics and not those of the Judenrate. Indeed, Hausner recalls that the issue of the Judenrate was raised by Yitzhak Zukerman and Zivia Lubetkin, two of the leaders of the Jewish resistance in the Warsaw ghetto, during one of Hausner's consultations with them in preparation for the trial.

> "What will you say about the Jewish Councils?" Yitzhak asked me.
> . . . "This is going to be the trial of the murderer, not of his victims," I replied. "But you will not be able to avoid the issue," Zivia said.

... "No," I replied, "and what we shall bring forth will be the truth. No embellishments." "That is good," said Yitzhak. "The whole truth must be told."[19]

Hausner, however, did not keep his promise. This may well be because in the early 1960s Israeli society was only beginning to mature beyond the painful stage of blaming the victims for their own disaster and slowly shifting the full blame to the perpetrators.[20]

The third and most difficult obstacle came from the Hungarian group of witnesses. It originated in Hausner's decision to base the case of the prosecution on the live testimonies of approximately one hundred Holocaust survivors in addition to written documents. I will return later to the reasons that led to this decision, but at this stage I would like to point out the difficulties that it created for separating the two trials. Among the Holocaust survivors, the most important witnesses for the prosecution were those who had negotiated personally with Eichmann, particularly those who were connected in one way or another to the Kastner affair. Among them were Hansi and Joel Brand, Kastner's partners on the Aid and Rescue Committee (whom Eichmann himself mentioned in his testimony), and Pinchas Freudiger, the leader of the Orthodox community in Budapest and a member of the Judenrat. Hausner approached the witnesses from among the Hungarian community in advance and asked them, for the sake of national unity, not to drag the bitter controversy over the Kastner affair into the trial of Eichmann. In his memoirs Hausner recalls: "I had appealed to everyone to abstain from internal reckoning, since this was the trial of the exterminator and not of his victims."[21] He describes how carefully the prosecution handled the "Hungarian chapter," deciding not to call any witness who would use the platform for a pro- or anti-Kastner demonstration.[22] Thus, the witnesses who were most relevant to proving the case of the prosecution were also the most risky for the historical narrative it sought to promote in the trial.[23] By contrast, the witnesses who had the least relevance for establishing the legal case against Eichmann (the resistance fighters) were crucial for the educational message of the trial. This tension between legalistic and pedagogical concerns came to characterize the whole trial.[24]

Another obstacle to insulating *Eichmann* from the Kastner trial came from outside. Attorney Shmuel Tamir, who understood the importance of the Eichmann trial as a public stage for mounting his counterstory about the Kastner affair, made every effort to join the trial. He expressed his wish to be appointed the chief prosecutor, or at least part of the prosecution team,[25] and also tried to interrogate Eichmann in his prison cell about his connections to Kastner and to reopen the case of his client Gruenwald on the basis of the new information revealed in the trial.[26] He even attempted to join the trial as a civil party.[27] All of these attempts failed, and Tamir's voice did not become part of the Eichmann trial.

Despite Hausner's efforts to keep the trial free of the influences of the past, traces of the Kastner controversy filtered in and prevented the prosecution from presenting its official narrative undisturbed. Judge Halevi, as the political authorities had feared, succeeded in resurrecting the painful issue of the Jewish leaders' cooperation with the Nazis. During the testimony of Kastner's partner, Hansi Brand, Halevi asked her whether the Aid and Rescue Committee had ever considered the possibility of assassinating Eichmann. In her response Brand rejected the implicit accusation in the judge's question (why didn't you rebel?) and answered as follows.

> We were a rescue committee and none of us was a hero. Our goal was to try and save these people. We did not know if killing Eichmann would bring relief. . . . [W]e were sure . . . that someone else would replace him and the system would keep on moving, maybe even faster.[28]

This answer recalled the public controversy that had erupted in Kastner's trial about the legitimacy of negotiating with the Nazis. It echoed even louder during Halevi's questioning of Pinchas Freudiger, which led to one of the few emotional outbursts during the trial. A member of the audience stood up and shouted at the witness in Hungarian: "You soothed us so that we should not run away while you were saving your families."[29]

Even though defense attorney Robert Servatius did not adopt a political line, he managed to raise the subject of the Kastner affair on several occasions. During Joel Brand's testimony Hausner produced documents from the private archive of the former president of Israel, Chaim Weizmann, showing how seriously leaders of the Jewish Agency had taken Brand's mission and the strong pressures for action that Weizmann had exerted on the British.[30] We have seen how Tamir managed to exclude these documents from the Kastner trial by insisting that the prime minister, Moshe Sharett, who authored most of them, would be available for cross-examination.[31] Servatius, in contrast, had no interest in opposing the admission of these documents since they could be used to reduce Eichmann's responsibility. He attempted to use them to shift some of the responsibility for the failure of the "trucks for blood deal" (which he described in a businesslike manner), and the subsequent murder of a large part of the Hungarian Jewish community, to the British.[32] When questioning Joel Brand about whether the British had viewed the possibility of admitting a million Jewish refugees as an "overload," he cited Brand's book, where he had written that things might have been different if the British had agreed to inform the Nazis that their deal was being considered.[33] Likewise, during his cross-examination of Hansi Brand Servatius asked: "You said that Eichmann did not keep his promise, but were the conditions upon which his promise was based fulfilled?"[34] He also noted the continuous relations of Joel Brand and Rudolph Kastner with Kurt Becher after the war.

Kastner's affidavit in support of Becher was the only part of Gruenwald's accusation that the Supreme Court had sustained. Aware of the sensitivity of the issue, Hausner decided not to summon a member of the rescue committee, Andre Biss, who might otherwise have been beneficial to the prosecution, because he promised to clear Becher's name. Becher's own testimony was taken in Germany and became the subject of a fierce battle between the prosecution and the defense.[35] Hausner was interested in Becher's testimony about Eichmann's attempts at the end of 1944 to sabotage Himmler's order to stop killing the Jews of Hungary. This testimony could have undermined Eichmann's main line of defense of "obeying superior orders." Servatius, however, tried to disqualify the entire testimony on the basis that the German judge had provided Becher with the questions of cross-examination in advance.[36] He wanted to summon Becher to be cross-examined in person in Jerusalem. Hausner refused to promise Becher immunity from prosecution, thereby preventing his appearance. Had Becher testified, he surely would have kindled harsh public debate and reopened the Kastner controversy.[37]

The disturbances provided by Judge Halevi, Tamir, and some of the witnesses ensured that the prosecution's story was not the only available narrative. According to Kirschheimer, such "disturbances" are crucial in preventing a political trial from becoming a show trial and ensure that it "remains a contest, rather than a unilateral reaffirmation of unassailable power positions."[38] The relative independence of the judiciary, alongside the ability of defense lawyers to exploit rules of procedure and the space for maneuver allowed by the law, introduces an element of uncertainty even if the contest is not one between equals. However, the disturbances in the Eichmann trial fell short of posing a real challenge to the prosecution's narrative, and it was only Arendt's book that provided a comprehensive framework for introducing a counterstory questioning the values that the trial promoted.

Although all of the "incidents" mentioned above remained as mere footnotes to the trial, Arendt immediately discerned the staged silence over the Kastner affair. What was erased from the official transcript quickly found its way into her report. Indeed, she devoted twenty-two of the most controversial pages of her book to the cooperation of Kastner in particular and to the cooperation of the Jewish leadership (Judenrate) with the Nazis, even though the issue was never directly discussed during the trial.[39] Her harsh judgment of the Jewish leaders was reminiscent of the accusations made by the defense at the Kastner trial.[40] While Judge Halevi and defense attorney Servatius managed to highlight some issues that were embarrassing to the Israeli government, only Arendt, an outsider to the trial, succeeded in weaving these threads together into a coherent counternarrative. In doing so, she turned a spotlight on the relations between law and politics in the Eichmann trial. Thus, the social critic and the Israeli prosecution embarked on a path of collision in the form of competing stories.

The Competition of Storytellers

The clash between Arendt and Hausner is informed by two opposing views of historiography, justice, and politics. The storytellers' respective stories have two aspects: the framework of the narrative and the voice of the narrative. The framework has both temporal and spatial boundaries. With respect to temporal boundaries, Hausner's story embraces the whole of Jewish history while Arendt begins her story in the nineteenth century. With respect to spatial boundaries, Hausner's story focuses on the Jewish people while Arendt addresses humankind as a whole. These different temporal and spatial boundaries produce two competing histories of the Holocaust. The second aspect relates to

Arendt's and Hausner's disagreement over the question of *how* to tell
the story, that is, whether the story should be told through written documents or the oral testimonies of survivors. This discussion will lead to
an examination of the two conceptions of justice that informed the different ways in which Hausner and Arendt responded to one of the key
questions in the Eichmann trial: what role should be given to the victims in the trial of their victimizer?

Truth and Politics

At the time of the publication of her report, Arendt was harshly criticized for including the issue of Jewish cooperation.[41] This controversy
took place mainly in the pages of American journals. Arendt chose not
to answer her many critics directly. Instead, as she wrote to her friend
the writer Mary McCarthy in a letter of October 1963, she undertook to
write an essay on "Truth and Politics" as an implicit answer to her critics.[42] This essay, published in the *New Yorker* in February 1967, will
serve as a basis for the discussion of Arendt's views about the role of
the trial and her reasons for raising the issue of the Judenrate in her
book.

In *Eichmann in Jerusalem* Arendt presents the courtroom drama as a
struggle between the two age-old antagonists, politics and justice, personified by Gideon Hausner, the prosecutor, and Justice Moshe Landau.[43] She argued that justice demanded that the trial concentrated on
proving the acts of Adolf Eichmann the accused, while politics called
for providing a stage for survivors' testimonies about the "suffering of
the Jewish people."[44] Politics called for emotions while justice
demanded detachment. Arendt herself did not remain an impartial
spectator but claimed to take the side of justice. She therefore criticized
Hausner's digressions from the narrow framework of a criminal trial—
his constant attempts to "draw the big picture" of the Jewish tragedy—
as signs of his political agenda.[45] However, she herself failed to obey
the "dictates of justice" when she decided to "enlarge the picture" of
the trial and discuss Jewish cooperation with the Nazis. In her report on
the trial, she offers an entirely different explanation for bringing up this
issue.

I have dwelt on this chapter of the story, which the Jerusalem trial
failed to put before the eyes of the world in its true dimensions,

because it offers the most striking insight into the totality of the moral collapse the Nazis caused in respectable European society— not only in Germany but in almost all countries, not only among the persecutors but also among the victims.[46]

This explanation has nothing to do with the simple demand of justice to concentrate on the acts of Eichmann. It may be argued that Arendt thought that understanding the background to the Jewish leaders' cooperation with the Nazis could better serve justice because it would show that traditional legal doctrines about criminal responsibility had to be rethought in the context of a totalitarian state that blurs the line between victim and perpetrator. However, Arendt's book reveals that her interest in the moral collapse under the Nazi totalitarian regime went beyond the issue of assigning legal responsibility. Fearing a recurrence of this phenomenon in the future, she sought to comprehend its historical origins. If this was indeed her main concern, then the controversy between Arendt and Hausner was not about justice and politics but about which "big picture" to draw or the proper historical framework for the trial's story. Aware that Eichmann's trial could not be contained within the scope of narrow legalistic considerations, both Arendt and Hausner tried to supply a historical narrative as the basis for judging his acts. The trial was important for both of them because they understood that it occupied what Arendt has called "the gap between past and future," a place where human beings are called to reflect on their common past, try to comprehend it, and use this comprehension to shape their common future.[47] In short, the conflict between Arendt and Hausner may be better understood as a dispute over what kind of politics *Eichmann*, as a transformative trial, should promote.

The Politics of the Trial

Both Hausner and Arendt tried to hide their political vision of the trial by insisting that their demands were dictated by the law. Therefore, in order to evaluate their conceptions of the trial one should first uncover their political purposes and assess their compatibility with liberal criteria. Once politics is admitted into the discussion of trials, a substantive criterion for distinguishing between different types of political trials must be developed. Judith Shklar has pointed out that according to

liberal theory, which assumes that law and politics are mutually exclusive, a trial's adherence to the law is the only criterion for evaluating
its compatibility with liberal principles. In contrast to this legalistic
view, Shklar suggests that the crucial question is which type of politics
a trial can legitimately promote in facilitating a transition to democracy while still remaining true to liberal principles of a criminal defendant's right to a fair trial.[48] She offers two complementary criteria for
evaluating political trials. One deals with the fairness of the legal procedure to the individual (which will be considered in chapter 5). The
second is substantive, examining how the trial contributes to the formation of a liberal-democratic system of government: "political trials
may actually serve liberal ends, [in cases] where they promote legalistic values in such a way as to contribute to constitutional politics and
to a decent legal system."[49] Assessing this criterion requires an understanding of the specific historical and political context in which the
trial was conducted and of the audience to which it was directed. In
our case, Shklar's test requires determining to what extent the different historical narratives offered by Hausner and Arendt were suited to
promoting liberal values of pluralism and tolerance in the State of
Israel. This approach is particularly useful for our purposes because it
directs us to the metalegal choices of the Israeli prosecution and in particular to the impact of its historical narrative on the political culture of
Israel.

What kind of politics did the Eichmann trial advance, and could it be
justified according to liberal principles? Shklar argued against assessing the trial solely in terms of its adherence to international law: "Eichmann, alas, was always a Jewish problem. Once he landed in Jerusalem
his trial became an issue of Jewish politics and interests, both in Israel
and in other Jewish communities."[50] However, she did not offer a comprehensive critique of the trial. Recently, Mark Osiel applied Shklar's
test to the Eichmann trial and concluded that it was a failure from a liberal perspective because it advanced a communitarian worldview. His
conclusion is based mainly on the definition of the offense as one committed against a particular ethno-religious community (crimes against
the Jewish people) and on the historical narrative that Hausner
advanced in the trial about the persecution of the Jewish community as
demonstrating the limits of liberalism in protecting minority groups.[51]
This evaluation, however, does not capture the full complexities of the
politics of the Eichmann trial. It is true that on the spectrum between

communitarism and liberalism Hausner is closer to the communitarian end. However, Shklar herself clarifies that for the purposes of her book she endorses a very "thin" version of liberalism, one that is focused on society's tolerance for plurality.[52] From this perspective Hausner's approach can also be seen as an attempt to promote liberal values. Indeed, he was deeply concerned about Israeli society's attitude toward Holocaust survivors in the 1950s. Providing the survivors, about a quarter of the Jewish population in Israel at the time, with a public stage on which to tell their stories was a crucial step toward developing a more tolerant society in Israel.[53] Arendt's approach, however, seems to accord more easily with basic liberal demands since she cast the crime in universal terms and offered a historical narrative that she believed would be more conducive to the development of a pluralist-liberal society in Israel—in particular toward Arab Israelis.

Applying Shklar's criteria to the two competing narratives therefore yields ambiguous results. Both visions of the trial had the power to enhance Israeli society's tolerance toward groups that had previously been excluded and silenced—but these were not the same groups. Arendt was concerned that the us-them rhetoric of Hausner, which placed anti-Semitism at the center of the trial, left no room for seeing nazism as a universal example of the persecution of any minority group within any nation. However, her own more universal narrative about crimes against humanity ignored the need to enable Holocaust survivors to overcome their silence and be heard and understood by Israeli society. It seems that at the time of the trial these two visions could not be reconciled.[54]

2. The Historical Narrative

In trying to understand the relationship among history, narrative, and law, the historian Hayden White came to a surprising conclusion:

> We cannot but be struck by the frequency with which narrativity . . . presupposes the existence of a legal system against which the typical agents of a narrative account militate. . . . The more historically self-conscious the writer of any form of historiography, the more the question of the social system and the law which sustains it, the authority of this law and its justification and threats to the law occupy his attention.[55]

This insight presents the thorniest problems for the storyteller, the historian, and the judge when dealing with the Nazi regime. They all had to grapple with a reality of discontinuity—the unbridgeable abyss between the pre-Nazi and Nazi realities. However, while the storyteller and the historian are free to define the rules of their narratives, the judge is constrained by preexisting rules, rules that in this case existed both before and after the Nazi regime. In particular, traditional criminal law concepts available to jurists in the wake of the Holocaust were ill fitted to illuminate the nature of this discontinuity and did not offer legal tools that could protect society from the recurrence of such crimes in the future. Addressing this discontinuity in the courtroom was a great challenge, but it also indicated a possible solution. A trial forces its participants to judge a past event and to reflect on the precedent it sets for the future. In transformative trials the participants have to formulate a whole new historical narrative on which judgment is to be based. Arendt, who was preoccupied with these questions, wrote in a letter to Karl Jaspers that "It seems to me to be in the nature of this case that we have no tools except the legal ones with which we have to judge and pass sentence on something that cannot even be adequately represented within legal terms or in political terms. That is precisely what makes the process itself, namely the trial, so exciting."[56] Arendt realized that traditional frameworks of judgment, social narratives, and historical accounts were missing in the case of judging the Holocaust. But Eichmann's trial also offered the lawyer and the historian a great opportunity precisely because it functioned as a meeting place where the need to tell the story, the need to judge the criminal, and the need to relate the history all coincided. Let us now examine how Arendt and Hausner confronted this challenge of judging the past in order to continue into the future.

Two Competing Historical Narratives

Hausner sought to bridge the abyss between past and future with the tools of traditional Jewish historiography. His framework was based on a structure of repetition: Jews have always been persecuted for anti-Semitic reasons and every generation has its own Pharaoh and Haman.[57] For this purpose Hausner linked the Holocaust to present enemies by seeking to prove the links between the mufti of Jerusalem, Haj Amin Al-Husseini, and Eichmann.[58] The framework of the story was the long history of victimization and persecution of the Jews throughout the ages, and it was intended to illuminate the Jewish story that had been missing from the Nuremberg trials.[59] Accordingly, the prosecution chose to focus its case on the legal category of "crimes against the Jewish people."[60] Hausner's clear-cut distinction between victims and victimizers left no room for dwelling on the murky category of Jewish cooperation with the Nazis, the phenomenon of the Judenrate, which could illuminate the danger that Eichmann embodied not just to the Jews but to humanity as a whole.

Arendt criticized this historical narrative as

bad history and cheap rhetoric; worse, it was clearly at cross-purposes with putting Eichmann on trial, suggesting that perhaps he was only an innocent executor of some mysteriously foreordained destiny, or, for that matter, even of anti-Semitism, which perhaps was necessary to blaze the trail of "the bloodstained road traveled by this people" to fulfill its destiny.[61]

Arendt disagreed that traditional Jewish historiography could account for the new phenomenon because it sought present-day analogies to the old story of anti-Semitism. Instead, she wanted to understand Eichmann's actions using the tools of modern historiography in terms of the immediate historical circumstances. She suggested locating the modern catastrophe within the European context of the rise of the totalitarian state. Her tools were not analogies but *distinctions*. She was careful to distinguish Eichmann the man from the mythical figures of Pharaoh and Haman and to depict him as the product of his own age—the age of bureaucracy, science, and ideology. The totalitarian state conducted a systematic attack on civil society and by crushing it turned all members of society, even the targeted groups of victims, into participants in their own destruction. Arendt's decision to devote part of her historical narrative to the cooperation of the Jewish victims with their victimizers should therefore be seen as reinforcing her argument about the unique nature of totalitarian crimes.

Arendt's historical narrative highlighted the lack of historical precedents for Auschwitz. She replaced the thesis of unique Jewish victimhood with the proposition that "the physical extermination of the Jewish people was a crime against humanity, perpetrated upon the body of the Jewish people."[62] She rebutted Hausner's narrative of continuity and repetition by noting that "only the choice of victims, not the nature of the crime, could be derived from the long history of Jew-hatred and anti-Semitism."[63] In confronting the future, Arendt sought to construct a legal precedent that would be adequate to deal with the very real possibility that such crimes would be repeated in the future "against other people and in other places."[64]

The different legal categories adopted by Hausner and Arendt engender disparate historical narratives within which the same "facts" have very different implications. It is only in Hausner's legal framework ("crimes against the Jewish people") that including the issue of the behavior of the Jewish leadership, as suggested by Arendt, might be seen as blaming the victims. Since the legal framework of crimes against the Jewish people did not call for comparisons with the behavior of other people under Nazi rule, discussing the cooperation of Jewish leaders with the Nazis would tend to reflect on the *nature* of the Jewish people instead of on the circumstances under the Nazi regime. In contrast, Arendt's choice of the legal category "crimes against humanity" placed the behavior of Jewish leaders in context by showing what she interpreted as the totality of the moral collapse throughout occupied Europe. She wrote that the "deliberate attempt at the trial to tell only the Jewish side of the story distorted the truth, *even the Jewish truth.*"[65] Her legal framework emphasized the need of the nation-state to guarantee the rights of minority groups and to nurture the development of a pluralistic society. Thus, she attempted to draw from the Holocaust general implications for international law. In particular, her story exposed the weakness of an international legal system based on the protection of individual rights without providing real protection to minority groups.

Convicting Eichmann could serve as a closure to both Hausner's and Arendt's historical accounts, but the meaning of this closure depended on the narrative that would be offered to uphold the verdict. If Arendt and Hausner are both storytellers of sorts, whose story should be preferred as more "true"? Both shied away from confronting the problem of narrative authority. Hausner relied on legal tools to endow his account with "objectivity."[66] Arendt, an outsider, relied on her position as a "reporter" to minimize her presence as the narrator of facts. Indeed, this stance can explain her choice of subtitle of the book, *A Report on the Banality of Evil.*[67]

This circumvention of the problem of narrative authority later proved to be unsatisfying to Arendt, and she returned to it in her essay "Truth and Politics." This time, she presented her general views on historiography as narration, arguing for the need to respect the facts while acknowledging the importance of ordering them into a narrative form. She viewed facts as functioning as limits to our historical narrations, as the "ground on which we stand" and the "sky that stretches above us."[68] She explains that "Even if we admit that every generation has the right to write its own history, we admit no more than that it has the right to rearrange the facts in accordance with its own perspective; we don't admit the right to touch the factual matter itself."[69] This subtler formulation, however, is not of much help for our purposes because the controversy in the Eichmann trial was precisely over how to rearrange the facts, in which framework, and from what perspective. Arendt and Hausner did not offer their reasons for preferring one narrative framework to the other. Indeed, they stressed their position as "fact finders" and minimized their role as narrators. In order to evaluate their choices as storytellers, their reasons for choosing their respective historical frameworks need to be reconstructed. Arendt and Hausner's views on how the trial related the past to the future, or, more simply, their views on the political role of Eichmann's trial, must be examined if we are to understand their choices.

The Politics of Reconciliation

With very different stories, both Arendt and Hausner hoped that the trial would bring about reconciliation. Hausner writes that "only through knowledge could understanding and *reconciliation with the past* be achieved."[70] And Arendt explains that "To the extent that the teller of factual truth is also a storyteller, he brings about that *"reconciliation with reality."*[71] Thus, reconciliation can be achieved only when the facts are ordered into a humanly comprehensible narrative.[72] She argues that reconciliation with reality through storytelling also provides a solid basis for judgment: "The political function of the storyteller—historian or novelist—is to teach acceptance of things as they are. Out of this acceptance, which can also be called truthfulness, arises the *faculty of judgment*."[73] Hausner and Arendt strongly disagreed, however, over the way in which this reconciliation should take place.

Hausner's choice of historical framework can be understood in the light of the Kastner and Nuremberg trials. Neither the Kastner trial, which was a form of self-castigation by survivors, nor the Nuremberg trials, which advanced the agenda of the victorious Allies, could be seen as providing the kind of reconciliation with the past needed by Israeli society. As we have seen, the Kastner trial had produced a public narrative divided by political affiliations. It was like a traumatic repetition of the past, a reopening of the wound, which could not bring about reconciliation. Also the Kastner trial was little known in the world at large and therefore could not serve as the yardstick for evaluating the Eichmann trial or its historical narration of the period. The Nuremberg trials were looked to as a model. In many respects Hausner needed to rely on the Nuremberg precedent in order to legitimize the various deviations of the prosecution's case from strict adherence to the rule of law.[74] However, Hausner also needed to discard the historical narrative of World War II, which Nuremberg had promoted, in order to replace it with a historical narrative about the Jewish Holocaust.[75] The jurisdiction of the International Military Tribunal at Nuremberg (the result of a political compromise between the Allies) had been limited to crimes committed in furtherance of the "planning, preparation, initiation or waging of a war of aggression," which excluded crimes against particular groups of civilians.[76] This restrictive interpretation had helped overcome problems of retroactivity and concerns about states' sovereignty and had suited the Allies' own objectives for the trial. Accordingly, the interpretation that the tribunal had come to uphold was that the Holocaust had been the horrific consequence of a war of aggression.[77] Likewise, the decision of the Nuremberg prosecution to rely primarily on documents guaranteed the objectivity of the court but at the same time distorted the Jewish story since those documents told it in the language of the perpetrators and from their point of view. Nuremberg had for the most part excluded the victims' voices and their human stories of suffering and humiliation. This may have been one of the factors that convinced Ben-Gurion that Eichmann's trial must be conducted in Israel if it was to tell the missing story of the Jewish victims of the Nazi regime. One of the purposes of the Eichmann trial was therefore to draw a very clear line between victims and perpetrators. Former political divisions were to be set aside when confronting the common enemy, and a collective identity was sought by way of demarcating the differences from an Other.

For this purpose it was not enough simply to put Eichmann on trial (as Hausner sometimes implied), but rather there was a need to base

the trial on the Israeli Law of Punishment of Nazis and Their Collaborators, which was able to shape the jurisdiction of the court in a way
that promoted the telling of the Jewish story. Specifically, the Israeli
law extended the temporal framework of the court's investigation
(1933–45) and allowed the prosecution to put the category of crimes
against the Jewish people at the center.[78] Thus, the Eichmann trial was
never a simple continuation of the Nuremberg precedent because it
was intended to facilitate the very different political goals that
informed the Israeli prosecution.[79] Reconciliation with the past was to
be achieved by focusing on the Jewish people and by presenting the
very act of judgment by an Israeli court as a resolution to that painful
past. An Israeli court represented the sovereignty of the victims, of the
Jewish people, who were now empowered to conduct their own trial.
Hausner commented that "now it was the Jews themselves who could
decide what was best for their position. They could do so because they
had their own machinery of justice, their own prosecutors and their
own policemen. *The trial was thus, in itself, an overwhelming manifestation
of the revolution in the position of the Jewish people* that has taken place in
this generation."[80]

Arendt sought to bring about reconciliation with the past in a very
different way. She was disturbed by the omission of the Judenrate story
in Eichmann's trial. She was well aware that her report did not expose
any facts that were previously unknown to the Israeli public. She
acknowledged that "these issues . . . are discussed quite openly and
with astonishing frankness in Israeli schoolbooks."[81] But this was precisely why the omissions in the trial seemed all the more dangerous to
her. As she explained in "Truth and Politics," even though these facts
were known, "yet the same public that knows them can successfully,
and often spontaneously, taboo their public discussion and treat them
as though they were what they are not—namely, secrets."[82] In other
words, it was Arendt's awareness of the dynamics of collective memory that made her fear that the omissions in Eichmann's trial would
produce dangerous gaps in the Israeli collective memory, could undermine the development of a deliberative democracy and might even
lead to a recurrence of such tragedies in the future. As she noted in
"Truth and Politics," factual truth in trials "is established by witnesses
and depends upon testimony; *it exists only to the extent that it is spoken
about.*"[83] Only by openly discussing the issues of Jewish cooperation
and by honestly confronting the painful questions it raised could Israeli

society become truly reconciled with its past and avoid moving in circles of blame and counterblame.

Arendt's concept of human *natality,* the possibility of beginning anew, sheds further light on her concern with the danger of repressing uncomfortable facts as the main obstacle in achieving social reconciliation. In "Truth and Politics," she writes: "Not the past—and all factual truth, of course, concerns the past—or the present, insofar as it is the outcome of the past, but the future is open for action."[84] Arendt's narrative of the Eichmann trial, with its insistence on including the chapter on the Jewish Judenrate, was thus based on her conviction that the only hope for learning and changing is to confront the past as it was, without defense mechanisms but with an understanding that the future is still open for change: "If the past and present are treated as parts of the future—that is, changed back into their former state of potentiality—the political realm is deprived not only of its main stabilizing force but of *the starting point from which to change, to begin something new.*"[85]

From this perspective it becomes clear that Arendt was not intent on "blaming the victims," as many of her critics mistook her words, but was rather attempting to create the grounds for change in the future. However, the meaning of her complex arguments was lost in the charged public atmosphere surrounding the trial. In any case, Hausner's frame of reference was the trial, and he did not think that the Judenrate's behavior was in any way relevant to trying Eichmann. He later argued that the Eichmann trial allowed for a more balanced judgment of the Judenrate than the Kastner trial had because of the larger perspective it provided on the Holocaust as a whole. He therefore urged adopting a nonjudgmental attitude toward Holocaust survivors ("who are we to judge them?") and denounced Arendt for her harsh criticism.[86]

We are thus offered two different forms of reconciliation with the past. Hausner advocated splitting the story in two and focusing on the suffering of the victims. Arendt saw this as intentional collective oblivion that condemned a society to be caught in the past. She advocated telling the whole story (with all its ambiguities) of how Jews and others had been led to cooperate with the Nazi system so that this painful experience would become part of the nation's history. These differences in approach are connected to a larger view of history. According to Hausner's deterministic approach, the persecution of Jews throughout the ages was a historical constant that could be changed only with the establishment of a Jewish state. The lesson he drew from the Holocaust was therefore particularistic: the need to empower the Jews by protecting their state. For Arendt, however, the persecution of the Jews was a warning sign to humanity at large against the dangers of the totalitarian state, from which no nations are protected in advance. All could cooperate to create international tools to avoid such holocausts in the future.

3. The Role of the Victims in Eichmann's Trial

Arendt's and Hausner's positions on the proper legal and historical framework for Eichmann's trial were both shaped, to a large degree, by the shadow of the Kastner trial. Yet another crucial question remained to be decided—who was to tell the story? The most important legacy of the Eichmann trial was Hausner's decision to base the prosecution's case on the testimonies of around a hundred Holocaust survivors about their experiences and sufferings under Nazi rule. These testimonies were largely responsible for creating the consciousness of the Holocaust in Israel and throughout the world. In doing so Hausner radically diverged from the precedent set by the Nuremberg trials of relying on documents to prove the actions of the accused.

For the purposes of a trial, documents do seem to provide a more reliable source. There is no need to depend on the retentive memory of witnesses many years after the event. A document speaks in a steady voice that cannot be silenced or interrupted. Most important, documents produced by the defendants during the war cannot be charged with bias, prejudice, or perjury.[87] The Nuremberg trial, however, shows that the presentation of documents in a trial tends to become tedious. They "fail[ed] to reach the hearts of men."[88] Arendt feared that oral testimonies by survivors would open the door to the suffering of the victims—a suffering that had no measure and could not be comprehended. She came to Eichmann's trial with the hope that the law would provide some measure of understanding.[89] The only hope of achieving such understanding, she wrote, was to concentrate on the acts of the accused, not on the immeasurable suffering of the victims.[90]

The Lawyer as a Facilitator of Speech

The background to Hausner's decision was the silence of Holocaust survivors during the 1950s. Initially the case that the police prepared for the prosecution team was based mainly on documents with a list of some fifty potential witnesses (several of whom were suggested as alternatives) to support these documents.[91] Hausner reversed this order and placed the testimonies of the Holocaust survivors at the center. He explained his choice as stemming from the need to "shake the hearts" of the audience and to provide a live reconstruction of the national disaster.[92] But the central role given to the victims in the Eichmann trial was not the result of one man's idea, as is commonly assumed. Rather, as recently demonstrated, it was a grassroots process in which pressure from survivors gradually convinced Hausner to take the innovative and risky step of opening the stage to the victims.[93]

In his opening address, as we have seen, Hausner declared himself to be a spokesman for the six million dead. The writer and Holocaust survivor Primo Levi captured the ambiguities inherent in such a position in his account of his first attempt to describe his experience in Auschwitz, with the help of a lawyer, shortly after his release from the camp.

Perhaps I was the first dressed in "zebra" clothes to appear in that place called Trzebinia; I immediately found myself in the center of a dense group of curious people, who interrogated me volubly in Polish. I replied as best I could in German; and in the middle of the group of workers and peasants a bourgeois appeared, with a felt hat, glasses and a leather briefcase in his hand—a lawyer.

He was Polish, he spoke French and German well, he was an extremely courteous and benevolent person; in short, he possessed all the requisites enabling me finally, after the long year of slavery and silence, to recognize in him the messenger, the spokesman of the civilized world, the first that I had met.

I had a torrent of urgent things to tell the civilized world: not my things, but everyone's, things of blood, things which (it seemed to me) ought to shake every conscience to its very foundations. In truth, the lawyer was courteous and benevolent: he questioned me, and I spoke at dizzy speed of those so recent experiences of mine, of Auschwitz nearby, yet, it seemed unknown to all, of the hecatomb from which I alone had escaped, of everything. The lawyer translated into Polish for the public. Now, I do not know Polish, but I know how one says "Jew" and how one says "political"; and I soon realized that the translation of my account, although sympathetic, was not faithful to it. The lawyer described me to the public not as an Italian Jew, but as an Italian political prisoner.

I had dreamed, we had always dreamed, of something like this, in the nights of Auschwitz: of speaking and not being listened to, of finding liberty and remaining alone. After a while I remained alone with the lawyer; a few minutes later he also left me, urbanely excusing himself.[94]

The key word in Levi's story is *translation*, in the literal sense of translating his words from German into Polish but also in the broader sense of connecting between cultures, between the world of the peasants and the world of the city, between the civilized world of lawfulness and the barbarity of Auschwitz. The lawyer seems to posses all the necessary qualities for this act of translation: expertise, courtesy, benevolence and sympathy.[95] Yet the very act of translation from the living experience of the survivor to the categories of law actually does violence to his experience, effacing its important part. Here the agenda of the lawyer, often in conflict with that of the victim in political trials, is exposed. Levi is presented by the lawyer as a "political prisoner." The true meaning of the Nazi crimes—that he was enslaved and punished merely for being a Jew—is lost in translation. The betrayal of language and law leaves Levi with a deep sense of failure to communicate, of remaining alone. Legal translation is an unfulfilled promise and raises the question of what is lost in translation in a political trial.

In order to remedy worries of translation in the Nuremberg trials, Hausner opened the Eichmann trial to the victims' voices, but this decision presented its own difficulties. Hausner was well aware that by relying on the oral testimonies of survivors, who were not always regarded as reliable, he risked weakening the prosecution's position.[96] Moreover, while preparing the witnesses to give testimony in the trial he confronted the difficulties they had in telling a coherent story with a beginning, middle, and end. He faced the phenomenon that Lawrence Langer calls "deep memory," a moment when the trauma surfaces and engulfs one.[97] Hausner wrote:

At a pretrial conference they would sometimes stop conveying facts in an intelligible manner and begin speaking as if through a fog. The narrative, which had been precise and lucid up to this point, became detached and obscured. They found it difficult to describe in concrete terms phenomena from a different world.[98]

This, indeed, was the case in one of the most famous testimonies in the trial, that of Yehiel Dinur (a writer who used the pen name K-Zetnik, i.e., a concentration camp inmate), who lapsed into incoherence before collapsing on the witness stand.[99] Nonetheless, Hausner was convinced that the story of the Jewish Holocaust could only be told through the testimonies of survivors. To enable their testimonies he relaxed the ordinary framework of questions and answers of a courtroom investigation and allowed them to tell an almost undisturbed narrative.[100] Arendt harshly criticized this divergence from trial procedure. The prosecution "simply refused to guide its witnesses . . . the witnesses behaved as though they were speakers at a meeting chaired by the Attorney General, who introduced them to the audience before they took the floor."[101] Another important decision in this respect was to allow oral testimony only on the part of the prosecution, while the defense was effectively prevented from summoning witnesses to testify on Eichmann's behalf (apart from Eichmann himself), since Hausner would not guarantee them legal immunity.[102] These decisions empowered the victims while weakening the position of the defendant, thus strengthening the impression of an illegitimate political trial.

Representing the Victims

Although the victims were provided with a public stage, this stage was not innocent of political considerations, which served to limit their empowerment. The witnesses were not a homogeneous group. They were divided in their political affiliations and came from different countries and various backgrounds; some had belonged to the resistance and others to the Judenrate; some had been in labor camps, others in concentration camps; some had known Eichmann personally, others had only heard his name. Tensions among these groups of survivors were never far from the surface so that the issue of who was authorized to represent the victims at the trial had immense significance. Two questions were implied in this: whether *Israel* had the right to represent the victims as a group and whether it had the *exclusive* right to do so.

The structure of criminal law proceedings implied that the state as a collectivity was suing Eichmann since his acts had injured not only individual victims but the community at large.[103] What distinguished this case from ordinary criminal trials was that Hausner, as the representative of the State of Israel, claimed to speak in the name of six million dead victims. This might have been a rhetorical gesture on Hausner's part, but it also pointed to his awareness of the problem of representation. In whose name and on whose authority was he speaking? Since the crimes that Eichmann committed had occurred outside the territory of the State of Israel and before its establishment, Hausner could not speak in the name of the state alone. By inverting the ordinary hierarchy and putting the victim before the state, Hausner's opening statement implied that he was authorized to speak in the name of the Jewish victims. His words also emphasized the moral justification for the existence of the State of Israel as the heir and representative of European Jewry.[104]

In order to create a transformative trial with a clear message—one in which the State of Israel judged Eichmann in the name of Jews everywhere—it was crucial to ensure the state's exclusivity of representation. Lawyers who wished to represent living survivors alongside Hausner were unwelcome. Unlike the Holocaust trials that took place later, such as the Auschwitz trials in Germany (1963) or the Klaus Barbie trial in France (1987), in which civil parties joined the state prosecution, Hausner retained a monopoly over the trial's narrative. Although Israel's Law of Procedure now follows the common law in excluding civil parties in criminal prosecutions, this was not true at the time of Eichmann's trial. The state prosecution's exclusive right of representation in criminal proceedings actually required an amendment of section 43 of the 1936 Criminal Code. This section gave the victim of the offense the right to become a civil party to a criminal suit alongside the state prosecutor. This practice not only would have opened the Eichmann trial to a multiplicity of voices but it might even have permitted the attorney Tamir to join the trial and present his (Kastnerized) version of the story. As one member of the Knesset argued during the heated debate over the amendment, the state's exclusivity in such a "historical trial" was essential.

Who knows how many people there are in the world, Jews and non-Jews, who will try to bring civil actions against the oppressor. Then, instead of one law suit being promoted by the Jewish people, represented by the state of Israel, against the terrible evil of the Nazi regime, there will appear many suits that will swallow up the one large historical suit of the Jewish people, represented by its state, through the office of the general prosecutor.[105]

Although the specific reasons for the proposal of the amendment remain unclear,[106] the legal struggle reveals a deep ambivalence about the proper role of the survivors in what was known as the survivors' trial. On the one hand, in order to justify the jurisdiction of the Israeli court over Eichmann, the prosecution emphasized the fact that many of the survivors lived in Israel and played an important role in the trial. On the other hand, in order to enhance the Zionist moral of the trial it was crucial to assure the state prosecution's exclusivity (through the amendment of the law).[107]

Giving Voice to the Victims

Every seasoned practitioner knows that trials are rarely an accurate representation of the past. More often they reenact past events in a concentrated and dramatized form. The theatrical aspects of a trial help reveal a truth about the past that might otherwise remain obscured, but they also contribute to the symbolic reenactment of the original crime within the courtroom, thereby causing victims to relive the trauma.[108]

Hausner understood that the role of the Eichmann trial was not merely to tell the untold story of the Jewish Holocaust. The novelty of the Nazis' crimes lay not only in their plan to "eliminate" an entire human group (what Arendt called crimes against the human status of diversity), but also in their attempt to produce a crime without a witness.[109] For this purpose an elaborate system of distancing and concealment had been erected, from walls and fences to the use of euphemisms.[110] In her book Arendt referred to this aspect of the crime as "the holes of oblivion" that the perpetrators intended to bring about.[111] She was one of the first to expose this aspect of the concentration camps when she pointed out that they were not just death factories but were meant to supply living "proofs" of the Nazi ideology that some people were subhuman. This was accomplished by starving and torturing the prisoners until they lost not only the capacity for action but even the ability to speak of their suffering.[112] Paradoxically, her insistence that the court establish the truth through the more objective tools of documents could have served to repeat the silencing intended by the Nazis—the erasure of the human voice as a reliable witness. If Hausner had chosen to rely solely on documents and pictures, he would have denied the victims a voice once again.[113] In this sense, providing a stage for victims' testimonies carried the ethical message of "giving voice." Hausner was willing to take the legal risks involved in this decision in order to transform the victims from statistical figures into human beings. It was as a result of this decision that the Eichmann trial "created" the Holocaust in the consciousness of the world.

The victims' voices reliving the horrors had a profound effect on the audience. Israeli poet Haim Gouri, who reported on the trial for an Israeli newspaper, admitted: "I did not know that there were people like these in this country. Now I know."[114] The abstract knowledge about the Holocaust was made real through the authentic voices of the survivors. History turned into collective memory.

> "When this material was brought to the prosecution's desk and became part of the indictment, when these documents broke out of the silence of the archives, they seemed to be speaking now for the first time, and that [previous] knowledge was very different from this knowledge. They underwent the same change that things undergo when they pass from potentiality to reality and this process released the enormous energy of "now I understand, now I get it."[115]

Clearly, the survivors felt a strong moral obligation to bear witness, and believed that their testimonies needed to be given a public stage. The difficult question is whether the courtroom was the proper forum for such an endeavor. What is the added value of a courtroom to the testimony of survivors and does it justify the risks of turning the trial into a show trial, risks that Arendt was so careful to expose? There is no general answer to this question that is applicable to all trials. Rather, the answer should combine an understanding both of the structural characteristics of a trial and of the specific historical and social context in which it unfolds. Hence, any reflections about the value of the courtroom testimonies of Holocaust survivors should be limited to the circumstances surrounding the Eichmann trial. This trial played a central role in conferring authority on the testimonies of Holocaust survivors and in making them reliable witnesses for the purposes of forming a legal judgment as well as for the writing of history. Although survivors' memoirs, which described the Holocaust from the victims' point of view, already existed at the time, historians were quite reluctant to use them, regarding the perpetrators' documents as a more reliable source.[116] This was evident in the Nuremberg decision to rely solely on documents. Thus, law affected history by privileging a certain kind of evidence and then creating a "hierarchy" of sources in which the perpetrators' point of view enjoyed a higher status. Hausner's choice, therefore, was novel not only in the legal sense but also in the historical sense. Indeed, a link can be made between the change in the perception of the victims following the Eichmann trial and the shift to history writing based on victims' testimonies.[117] Although Hausner also used documents, a sharp contrast was apparent between his presentation, based mainly on survivors' testimonies, and the s case of the defense, which relied mainly on documents and affidavits, with only one oral testimony, that of the defendant. This contrast, rather than promoting the integration of the sources, demonstrated the huge and unbridgeable gap between them.[118]

The Eichmann trial provided a public stage for survivors' testimonies that was qualitatively different from films and books. A trial weaves the private story into the web of communal stories, which are then authorized by the judgment of the court. As we have seen, this was especially important in the Eichmann trial given the prevailing attitude toward Holocaust survivors in Israel during the 1950s.[119] In order to begin to listen to what the survivors had to tell, the entire conceptual framework in which they were viewed as somehow blameworthy had to be changed. The Eichmann trial, with its well-defined roles of accuser and accused, could facilitate such a change far more effectively than the media or political forums alone because for the first time the survivors were unambiguously linked to the accusing party (witnesses for the prosecution) and not the accused. Moreover, this was the first time that the survivors stood as part of Israeli society against a common enemy—Adolf Eichmann. Hausner's opening statement exemplified this change. However, there was still tension, as the meta-narrative of the trial was designed to enhance a heroic memory of the Holocaust, drawing a line of continuity between the fight of the Jewish resistance and the heroism of Israeli soldiers. As one writer argued recently, the way to overcome this tension was to transform the very act of bearing witness in trial into an act of resistance.[120] Such an attempt was apparent in the testimony of the writer Abba Kovner, leader of the Jewish resistance in Vilna. Kovner was known in Israel as the one who had coined the scornful expression "like lambs to the slaughter" in order to describe the Jews' behavior during the Holocaust.[121] During his testimony, he protested against the way his words had been misinterpreted in order to condemn the victims: "[T]here's a question floating in the air in this courtroom: "how is it that they didn't rebel?" As a fighting Jew, my whole being protests against this question if it has an accusatory tone."[122]

The historical narrative of the Holocaust (in terms of chronology and geography) presented by the prosecution enabled the individual victims to better understand the meaning of their personal experiences.[123] By basing the case of the prosecution on the testimonies of survivors the trial presented the victims as reliable witnesses and conferred authority to their words. The structure of the trial helped contain the chaos and strong emotions that arose during the proceedings and threatened to overwhelm speakers and listeners alike. Gouri noted the power of the legal process in this context: "In the bright cruelty of the law machine you find a noble display of the ability to organize out of chaos, which restores meaning to the stubborn facts, and releases, through its special procedure, the energy of the truth that is revealed."[124] The Eichmann trial thus offered a double gesture of imputing *responsibility* to the perpetrator by *responding* to the words of the victims.

4. Conclusion

What kind of a political trial was the Eichmann trial? The prominent role given to victims' testimonies undoubtedly undermined the defendant's right to a trial that would concentrate on proving his own specific actions and not make him a symbol for the crimes of the Nazi regime as a whole. The needs of collective memory, Osiel argues, should not compromise the rights of the defendant in political trials. In his view, if the two cannot be reconciled the rights of the defendant should have the upper hand. In the last decade, however, we have witnessed a growing understanding of the need to balance the rights of the defendant with those of the victims.[125] Hausner's decision seems to have presaged this jurisprudential development. By deciding to prove Eichmann's guilt through the testimonies of Holocaust survivors,

Hausner offered a unique interpretation of the meaning of justice, an interpretation that not only insists on telling the untold story but also acknowledges the importance of who tells it. This may be the lasting contribution of Eichmann's trial to the development of international and criminal law. The role given to the Jewish victim in the trial carried a universal message about society's commitment to restore the dignity of the victims of the crime through the legal process. The theoretical questions raised by the issue of "giving voice to victims" in trials are only now beginning to be addressed. One of the most important questions, I believe, is how to rethink the role of a courtroom in enhancing the "recognition" of silenced groups, such as victims of atrocities, as part of the process of "doing justice."[126]

Arendt herself began to change her mind with respect to the role of victims' testimonies while she was still reporting on Eichmann's trial, and it might well be that this change was induced by Hausner's procedural decision.[127] Deeply moved by the testimony of Zindel Grynszpan, she wrote, contrary to all her previous warnings, that "everybody should have his day in court," meaning every victim.[128] Arendt here inverts the basic principle of criminal procedure—that every defendant should be given his or her day in court. I believe that at this point Arendt suddenly realized the deeper significance of the Eichmann trial as a public forum where human action was given a name and a story. At this point she seems to have abandoned the legalistic framework into which she had tried to fit the trial and was reminded of her own ethics of storytelling.

The dangers posed by "holes of oblivion" to our historical understanding were exposed by Arendt in her work on Nazi concentration camps. She later extended her analysis to warn against a different type: holes of oblivion that are self-imposed by society and affect its collective memory. Hence, Arendt opposed the historical framework that Hausner advanced in the trial because it excluded the chapter on Kastner and the Judenrate. However, her more comprehensive framework could not serve to encourage the testimony of survivors. In relation to the question of who should tell the story, it was Hausner who insisted on giving voice to the victims precisely because of his awareness of the continuing effects of their silence on the Israeli collective memory of the Holocaust. Hausner's decision to omit the chapter on Kastner from Eichmann's trial was thus an essential step in enabling the testimonies of survivors to be heard. Arendt was wrong to think that only Hausner was guilty of silencing. Had the Kastner affair become a central chapter in the Eichmann trial, the result might have been the continued silencing of Holocaust survivors. As an outsider to Israeli society Arendt enjoyed a perspective that allowed her to develop a counternarrative, but she failed to understand the complex attitudes of Israeli society to the Holocaust and the deep way in which they shaped Hausner's procedural decisions. Arendt's conclusion to her chapter "Evidence and Witnesses" seems to acknowledge the effect that Hausner's decision had on her, almost against her will.

> The holes of oblivion do not exist. Nothing human is that perfect, and there are simply too many people in the world to make oblivion possible. One man will always be left alive to tell the story.[129]

I would add that at least two people were needed to tell this story—with different frameworks and distinct voices. The two frameworks allowed us to see (and hear) different things that are basically incompatible: in order to understand the meaning of "crimes against humanity" we needed to hear about the way in which a totalitarian regime could make its victims cooperate in their own destruction. In order to understand the meaning of the Holocaust as crimes against the Jewish people the stage had to be opened to the testimonies of the victims, and for this the issue of Jewish cooperation had to be put aside. At the time these two frameworks could not be reconciled and each storyteller had to constantly deny the validity of the other's narrative. The meaning of the Holocaust and a final judgment of Eichmann can be found neither in Hausner's narrative nor in Arendt's. Instead of choosing between them we should recognize that it is precisely the contest of narratives that is crucial to the possibility of judgment in the wake of the Holocaust. This leads to the surprising conclusion that we should not attempt to choose sides in evaluating the politics of the trial, nor can we easily reconcile the two views.[130] Both Hausner and Arendt promoted narratives that needed different and often contradictory frameworks in order to be heard. It is only by paying attention to the tension between the two approaches that we can understand how the political trial contributes to establishing a democratic society by exposing the need to learn to live with oppositions and therefore to value the voice of the law as providing a civilizing platform in which to address radical differences in worldviews.

Chapter 5

Reflective Judgment and the Spectacle of Justice

Transitional trials proceed on two levels. On one level, the judges ascertain the guilt of the defendant as in ordinary criminal trials. But on the other level their judgment is also a performative act through which society's collective identity is formed in opposition to an Other (the defendant) whose values are contrasted with the fundamental values of society. Eichmann's trial presented the Jerusalem court with special difficulties in this respect because the two levels seemed to pull in opposite directions. Nazi law had broken every fundamental precept of liberalism: it had treated people differently according to their ethnicity, it had established special courts ("people's courts") to prosecute groups that were persecuted by the regime, it had sent people to labor and concentration camps without a trial, it had not respected the prohibition against retroactive and extraterritorial application of the law, and so forth. In judging Eichmann it was not enough to ascertain his guilt and define his crimes; the court was also expected to do this in a way that would demonstrate Israeli society's commitment to liberal principles of the rule of law in contradistinction to Nazi law. This, however, created difficulties since not only was the decision to prosecute the Nazi crimes based on the innovative precedent of the recent Nuremberg trial but the crimes themselves could not be easily subsumed under the ordinary rules and precedents of domestic criminal law. Moreover, since the crimes had occurred outside Israel and many years before the trial, ordinary rules of jurisdiction and procedure were inadequate. In order to judge Eichmann according to the immensity of his crimes the court had to diverge from strict legality, but such divergences threatened to blur the distinction between Israeli law and the troubling legacy of Nazi law. This brought the dilemma of political trials to the doorstep of the Israeli court.

117

One of the fundamental principles of liberalism is the right to a public trial (principle of publicity). Constitutionally, open proceedings are viewed as a safeguard to fair trials for defendants.[1] The exposure of the trial to the public also endows the courts with special legitimacy because "justice is being seen." Thus, every criminal trial in a liberal society has to be a theater of sorts since it unfolds in front of an audience. The principle of publicity gains special importance in political trials, where the authorities are suspected of prosecuting the defendant for political reasons. Opening the proceedings to the public is meant to serve as a check on the political pressures of the government. However, this very publicity poses the danger that the authorities (and sometimes the defense) will attempt to use the theatrical aspects of the trial to advance their political message. Paradoxically, the principle of publicity that is considered by liberal theory as fundamental to guaranteeing a fair trial is also what threatens to turn the trial into the worse miscarriage of justice—a "show trial." It is for this reason that the ambivalent relation between law and the theater metaphor is intensified when we deal with political trials.

The need to guard the line between a show trial and a just trial constitutes the initial framework for Arendt's report.[2] In her polemics she accused the prosecution of trying to turn the trial into a show trial, seeing Prime Minister Ben-Gurion as the "stage manager" who pulled the strings behind the scenes.[3] However, Arendt was also well aware of the legitimate theatrical elements of a trial. She wrote that a trial is similar to a theater play in one fundamental issue: "both begin and end with the doer, not with the victim."[4] In Eichmann's trial this issue created the danger that in judging the "doer" (i.e., the perpetrator) the trial would turn him into the "hero" once more, thus undermining the attempt to shift the focus to the victims.[5] This is no small danger, particularly in situations of "transitional justice" when the victims of a previous regime undertake to judge their former oppressors. This may partly explain the recent development of alternatives to trials in such situations, like the Truth and Reconciliation Commissions in South Africa, which offer separate "stages" to victims and perpetrators.[6] As we saw in the previous chapter, Gideon Hausner, who had to conduct Eichmann's trial in the ordinary setting of a domestic criminal trial, tried to circumvent the problem by changing the status of the victims in the trial and giving their testimonies the full stage. Arendt rejected this solution as undermining the possibility of providing Eichmann with a fair trial. She advised the judges to refrain from enlarging the scope of the trial in this way and recommended that they focus on the defendant and concentrate on the questions of what he had done and how he had done it.[7]

Arendt's main dispute with the judges, however, was different. It involved their ability to resist the pressures of the past, of legal precedents and doctrines that were rendered irrelevant by the Nazi crimes. Interestingly, by demanding that the judges express their independence not only from the political branch but also in relation to legal precedents Arendt seemed to push the court in the direction of politics of a different sort, since politics is concerned with the particular and unprecedented event while law always tends to concentrate on continuity, regularity, and precedents. Shklar articulated this difficulty in relation to the Nuremberg trial.

> What tends to distinguish all political trials, even those most similar to ordinary criminal cases, is the difficulty of blending them into a continuous process by which one case can be more or less assimilated into a pattern of similar cases. The sense of regularity which comes from merely adding one decision to a host of apparently identical ones cannot be maintained, for what can be ignored in cases of murder and theft is unavoidably clear in political crimes. Each one is unique, because political interests, actions, and circumstances, and especially attitudes toward them, change rapidly and are subject to greater conflict of opinion than are cases involving acts that are and have almost always been regarded with fear and outrage, such as private murder.[8]

While the executive branch is expected to respond to the particularities of the new situation in real time, the courts are always expected to respond retrospectively within a given framework of general laws and precedents. In transitional situations, when the court has to respond to novel crimes without adequate legal concepts any attempt to judge outside the given framework risks turning the court itself into a political actor, thus raising the specter of a show trial. Hence, one of the crucial challenges for a theory of legitimate political trials is to set limits to "novel judgments" by defining the criteria that can legitimate them.

It has been noted by others that the Eichmann trial posed the question of judgment to Arendt in all its urgency for our modern age.[9] She later called the act of judgment that is required when the court confront facts that cannot be subsumed under the body of existing laws and precedents *reflective judgment*. Although the theory of judgment that she later elaborated in her lectures on Kant remained unarticulated in *Eichmann in Jerusalem*, I suggest that her report contained the seeds of a much needed theory about political trials. In this chapter, I therefore examine the Eichmann trial in the light of that later theory of judgment, tracing its sources in the answers she gave to the specific problems presented by the trial and through the critical dialogue that she conducted in her report with the Jerusalem court.

1. A New Theory of Judgment

In Arendt's treatment of the prosecution she seems completely committed to the traditional liberal approach, which sees no legitimate role for political trials. However a different reading of Arendt's treatment of the issue in *Eichmann in Jerusalem* uncovers a theoretical framework for evaluating the legitimacy of the use of political trials within democratic regimes. For this purpose we should shift our attention from Arendt's criticism of the prosecution to her much more balanced treatment of the conduct of Eichmann's judges. She acknowledged the dilemmas that they had to face in the trial, praised some of their decisions and criticized others. She no longer invoked the rigid dichotomy of law and politics but seems to have developed her own criteria informed by her general philosophy of political action. Even though Arendt did not give her observations about the trial a theoretical formulation at this stage, it seems that the philosophy she developed prior to writing the Eichmann book provided her with the necessary tools for approaching the dilemmas of political trials and devising original solutions. In the postscript of her book she mentioned some of these dilemmas: how to justify the retroactive and extraterritorial application of the law, how to adapt the traditional criminal law notion of mens rea to a bureaucratic mass murderer, how to interpret "crimes against humanity" in a way that would reflect the nature of these new crimes, and how to adapt the doctrine of disobeying a manifestly illegal order to the context of a totalitarian regime. All these issues illuminated the dilemmas of transformative political trials and pointed to the urgent need to formulate a new theory of judgment that would provide guidance. Below I examine

Arendt's book through this lens, first describing the failure of traditional conceptions of judgment (determinative judgment) to illuminate the kind of judgment needed in transformative political trials. I demonstrate the limits of this conception through specific examples from the Eichmann trial. Thereafter I turn to Arendt's theory of reflective judgment and show how it solves some of the problems we identified while creating new kinds of problems for judges in a court of law. In the final section I suggest ways in which the process of reflective judgment can impose meaningful constraints on the judges and allow them to navigate their way between the pressures of the past and the pressures of the future in a transformative trial.

The Failure of Determinative Judgment

One of the cornerstones of criminal law in a democratic society is the rule *nullum crimen, nulla poena sine lege* (no punishment without law).[10] The principle of legality dictates that judges are required to apply existing rules of law to the alleged acts of the accused. Indeed, the efforts of the judges in Jerusalem to fit Eichmann's acts into existing legal categories and to give the impression that they were acting on the solid ground of legal precedent stemmed from this obligation. This aspect of judgment was studied by Kant in his "First Critique," wherein he examined the problem of bridging the gap between the universal (abstract categories) and the sense data (the "facts") and called the act of combining the two determinative judgment. According to Kant, judgment cannot be reduced to a mechanical operation because it requires the help of the imagination.[11] A similar problem is raised by the use of judges' discretion in reaching a legal decision, which has been a major issue considered by liberal legal theory.[12] Arendt could not find the answer to the problem of natality in Kant's First Critique. Instead, she turned to his Third Critique (the Critique of Judgment) in search of an answer to the thorny question of how we judge the "particular qua particular" without relying on existing rules and concepts and how we elaborate a new framework for judgment when old standards betray us. In his words:

> Judgment in general is the faculty of thinking the particular as being contained in the universal. If the universal (the rule, the principle,

the law) is given, then judgment which subsumes the particular under it . . . is *determinant*. If, however, the particular is given, to which judgment is to find the universal, then it is merely *reflective*.[13]

The aesthetic experience of judging something as beautiful, of finding harmony without rules by relying on our faculty of taste, suggested the solution for her. It pointed to the ability of judgment to transcend a given conceptual system and arrive at "fresh" judgments.[14] In particular, Arendt was intrigued by the process of what she terms "enlarged mentality," which accompanies the act of reflective judgment and can ensure its validity.[15] Two features of reflective judgment in particular captured her attention. First, since judgment of the beautiful can only occur within a human community, a community is a constitutive condition for judgment.[16] Arendt therefore focused on the attempts of totalitarian regimes to destroy the basic condition of a human community—the condition of human plurality. Second, reflective judgment relates to the particular qua particular since it does not have to rely on a pregiven rule to decide that "this flower is beautiful." Understanding the connection between the two elements of community and particularity opened a way to grapple with the question of how to judge the novel crimes of the Nazis.

The Banality of Evil

The term coined by Arendt, *the banality of evil,* has generated volumes of theoretical reflections. My purpose here is not to engage in the familiar debate but to illuminate the process of judgment that drew Arendt's attention to this phenomenon.

Reflective judgment begins with the particular (act, event, person) by distinguishing it from what is more familiar and noticing its newness. In Eichmann's case this meant putting aside moral theories about evildoing (that men do evil because they are evil), as well as the prosecution's grand narrative of Jewish history as a long tale of recurring persecution and divine rescue (Eichmann as a modern Pharaoh).[17] Instead, Arendt presented what can be called a phenomenology of human action. Rather than digging beneath Eichmann's answers to discover his lies, she decided to entertain the possibility that "what we see is what we have" and take his cliches and "winged words" seriously. In so doing, she discovered a man capable of easily replacing one language code with another because he used language not to communicate but to block out reality.[18] In Michael Denneny's words:

> Certainly Eichmann was not insane. He could function and apply the rules of conduct given him well enough; he was able to exercise what Kant would call determinative judgment, the ability to subsume the particular under a general concept or rule. What he was incapable of was Kant's reflective judgment. . . . *Eichmann's problem, or rather our problem with Eichmann, comes from the fact that he judged according to the rule only too well . . . he never looked at the particular case in front of him and tried to judge it without a rule.*[19]

Confronted with Eichmann's failure of reflective judgment, Arendt offered her own judgment of the man and his deeds, a judgment summed up in the phrase "the banality of evil."[20] Arendt used this provocative phrase to alert her readers to the disjunction between banal motive and horrific deed that was produced by the Nazi bureaucracy and to a new type of criminal—the bureaucratic criminal. Eichmann's motivation, she argued, was not hatred of Jews, wickedness, ideological conviction, or pathology but rather the job holder's concern with success, promotion, the esteem of his coworkers and the praise of his superiors.[21] Arendt saw Eichmann's evildoing, therefore, as a superficial phenomenon in the sense that it did not have "deep roots" in monstrous feelings or a sadistic personality. Her judgment is a reflective one because her explanation frustrates traditional expectations that evildoing is rooted in an evil nature. In Arendt's opinion, the banality of evil only makes it a more dangerous phenomenon because it can spread "like a fungus" among normal people in a totalitarian system.[22] Addressing the phenomenon of the banality of evil engendered by a state bureaucracy that performs mass murder requires a revision of the fundamental notions of liberal criminal law about individual responsibility. Arendt called this extreme situation "rule by nobody" to emphasize the difficulty that traditional notions of the "rule of law" (such as the requirement of proving the mental state of the individual perpetrator) have in dealing adequately with it.[23]

Arendt argued that Eichmann's use of cliches, his "empty talk," was not a means of hiding his fanatical hatred of Jews but a symptom of his inability to think independently, which led to a profound failure of judgment. At one point, when Eichmann did not succeed in explaining to the judges an expression that he had used, he apologized, saying that "officialese" was his only language. Arendt suggested that a more accurate description would be the reverse, that "officialese became his language *because* he was genuinely incapable of uttering a single sentence that was not a cliche."[24] For Eichmann language was not a means of communication with other people but a means of blocking out the reality of his interlocutor: "The longer one listened to him, the more obvious it became that his inability to speak was closely connected with an inability to *think*, namely, to think from the standpoint of somebody else. No communication was possible with him, not because he lied, but because he was surrounded by the most reliable of all safeguards against the words and the presence of others, and hence against reality as such."[25] Here she makes a clear link between the failure of communication and the failure of judgment.

The connection between Eichmann's failure of judgment and his perverted use of language (language as a tool of discommunication with others)[26] becomes clear when we examine the three examples that Arendt provided to demonstrate his inability to look at anything from another point of view. When Eichmann described his activities in Vienna in organizing the forced emigration of the Jews, he used the expression "pulling together" to describe his work with the Jewish representatives as though there had been a real commonality of interests between the two sides. This inability to understand the other's viewpoint became all the more apparent when Eichmann described his encounter with one of the Jewish functionaries, Mr. Storfer, with whom he had worked and who had been caught and sent to Auschwitz while attempting to escape. Eichmann recounted their meeting in Auschwitz in similar terms: "With Storfer afterward, well, it was normal and human, we had a normal human encounter. He told me all his grief and sorrow: I said: 'Well, my dear old friend (Ja, mein lieber guter Storfer), we certainly got it! What rotten luck!' And I also said: 'Look, I really cannot help you. . . . I hear you made a mistake, that you went into hiding or wanted to bolt, which after all *you* did not need to do.' . . . And then I asked him how he was."[27] This "horror comedy" as Arendt described Eichmann's testimony, reached its height in his taped police interrogation, which was conducted by a police officer, Captain Less, a Jewish survivor from Germany to whom Eichmann told his biography as a sympathy-seeking "hard luck story."[28] Eichmann tried to gain Less's sympathy for his failure to be promoted within the ranks of the

SS, to which Arendt responded: "The presence of Captain Less, a Jew from Germany and unlikely in any case to think that members of the S.S. advanced in their careers through the exercise of high moral qualities, did not for a moment throw this mechanism [his hard luck story] out of gear."[29]

Concluding from these examples that Eichmann had completely blocked out the reality of his victims, Arendt, unlike the judges, was not surprised to discover that he could not remember the important dates in the development of the "final solution." In the isolated world created by his clichés, the only dates that Eichmann could remember were those that really mattered to him, that is, the turning points in his own career.[30] Arendt often used the term *comedy* to describe Eichmann's deficient use of language, a term that caused many readers to see her as lacking sensitivity to the victims. In fact, she saw it as the key to understanding his failure of moral judgment. Eichmann's banality was not primarily the result of his obedience to his superiors; on the contrary, he was shown to have used his discretion and creativity in applying their orders. Rather, he had been able to play a central part in the final solution precisely because his victims' reality had no place in his mental world. Enclosed in a world of clichés he was unable to hear his victims or understand their pain. She argued that it was this "sterile" language, disconnected from living experience, that had prevented Nazi functionaries such as Eichmann from equating the crimes made legal under that regime with what they had previously known to be murder and lies.[31] Studying Eichmann's language helped Arendt identify the connection between his inability to communicate with his victims and his total lack of "internal critical dialogue." The language he used provided him with the best shield against the basic human need to judge our actions according to moral standards by imagining the world from the point of view of the Other.[32]

Arendt was not the only reporter who was struck by Eichmann's manifest lack of representative thinking. The Israeli poet Haim Gouri, whose reports on the trial were published in the Israeli press, noted the same phenomenon in Eichmann's testimony about his negotiations with Joel Brand over the "trucks for blood" deal.[33] Brand related the conversation to the court, noting bitterly "this was a terrible proposition, it destroyed my life. On my conscience were the lives of a million Jews." In response, Eichmann drew an artificial symmetry between Brand's sorrow and his own sorrow over the failure of the deal.

If other countries obstructed this deal, it caused me much grief at the time and I permit myself to say that I can well understand Joel Brand's anger and pain, and I hope that, for his part, Joel Brand, in light of the documents that now prove to him that I was not the one responsible for the extermination, will also understand my own anger and pain.[34]

Indeed, his misuse of language allowed Eichmann to conceptualize the whole encounter as an ordinary business transaction that had failed due to the intervention of a third party to the dismay of all involved.[35] Even in the courtroom, where Eichmann was confronted with his victims and forced to listen to them, Brand's sorrow could not penetrate his mental wall. The glass booth built to protect him in the courtroom became a symbol of his own failure of judgment.

Judging Eichmann

Eichmann and the system he represented were the impetus behind Arendt's criticism of the limitations of the court's judgment. She found many of the court's judgments conventional and therefore inadequate to confront the novelty of Nazi crimes. *Eichmann in Jerusalem* directs our attention to limitations of determinative judgment. While legal theories admit the dynamics of occasional modifications in legal categories in order to adjust them to new fact situations, Arendt identified a line beyond which any such modification would actually inhibit the judge from reaching a just solution. Thus, in Eichmann's trial the prosecution's efforts to subsume his crimes under traditional legal categories (murder, aiding and abetting a crime, and obeying a manifestly illegal order) only obscured the novelty of his crimes and the nature of the criminal. It is this neglected aspect of judgment, the failure of determinative judgment when it is most needed, that Arendt undertook to examine.[36] Although the judges indeed rejected many of the prosecution's efforts to urge them toward a determinative judgment, and at some points moved beyond traditional criminal law categories, they were restricted by the pressures of liberal jurisprudence. Arendt undertook to expose the limitations of this jurisprudence and demanded that the court exercise what she later termed reflective judgment in order to deal adequately with the novel crimes it was called upon to judge. This confrontation between two jurisprudential worldviews is revealed in the following examples.

MASS ADMINISTRATIVE MURDER

What should judges do when they are asked to judge new crimes? Since determinative judgment requires particular acts to be subsumed under a general legal category, Eichmann's acts were placed under the rubric of murder, which was the available legal category, and were seen as constituting murder writ large. However, within this framework Eichmann's contention that "I never killed a Jew or, for that matter, I never killed a non-Jew" sounded preposterous, for how can we make sense of a mass murderer who insists that he never killed with his own hands?[37] According to the traditional conception of criminal law, responsibility increases the closer one comes to the actual act of killing.[38] For this reason, the prosecution tried to prove individual murders committed by Eichmann in order to move him from the legal rubric of "aiding and abetting" to the core category of killing.[39]

Arendt argued that the prosecution's effort to apply traditional conceptions of criminal law to Eichmann's actions threatened to divert the court from understanding the nature of his crimes. In order to understand individual responsibility under a totalitarian regime it was necessary to restructure the legal imagination and invert ordinary assumptions about responsibility and guilt. Despite the arguments of the prosecution, the judges rejected the notion of criminal law that responsibility increases the closer one is to the actual killing. The court explained that in the Nazi regime the opposite was true, for "the degree of responsibility increases as we draw further away from the man who uses the fatal instrument with his own hands."[40] Paradoxically, only by refraining from determinative judgment were the judges able to attribute responsibility to Eichmann in proportion to the magnitude of his crimes.

CRIMES AGAINST THE JEWISH PEOPLE

The Nuremberg tribunal tried to overcome the difficulty of attributing individual responsibility to the architects of the final solution by relying on the law of criminal conspiracy (a conspiracy to wage an aggressive war). This solution was criticized by scholars, who claimed that the nature of conspiracy law contradicts core principles of liberalism because it allows the court to hold a person guilty of crimes which he or she did not individually commit simply by having acted in unison to promote a criminal plan.[41] Indeed, the law of conspiracy acquired its bad reputation because of its frequent use in political trials designed to suppress a political adversary.[42] Moreover, the historian Michael Marrus argues that the conspiracy charge in Nuremberg created a distorted historiography of the Nazi regime.[43]

The attorney general in Eichmann's trial argued that the Jerusalem court should also view the final solution as a criminal conspiracy to commit innumerable criminal acts in order to annihilate the Jews and should attribute responsibility to Eichmann for participating in this conspiracy.[44] The court rejected this argument because such an analogy contradicted the spirit of liberal criminal law based on individual responsibility for one's actions.[45] Instead, the court was ready to recognize the unique and novel nature of the Nazi crimes that constituted the "final solution of the Jewish problem." It viewed all the acts implemented in the furtherance of the 'final solution' as being of one piece since the crime had been directed not against many individual victims as individuals but against the Jewish people as a whole.[46] The implementation of the crime had extended over several years and required the participation of many individuals and the operation of a complex bureaucracy. The court concluded, therefore, that Eichmann was not responsible as a fellow conspirator but as a principal agent. This was a clear example of the use of reflective judgment by the court. It is interesting that Arendt did not praise the court for its ability to overcome the tendency to rely on determinative judgment (applying the law of conspiracy) by attempting to develop a new category to respond to the novelty of the final solution. One reason might be that the court's innovative approach was based on the category of "crimes against the Jewish people" rather than the category she recommended of "crimes against humanity."[47]

OBEYING A MANIFESTLY ILLEGAL ORDER

Whereas the court demonstrated its ability to go beyond the confines of determinative judgment with regard to the issue of mass murder, it failed to do so with regard to the issue of "superiors' orders." This failure led the court to efface what Arendt considered to be the central moral dilemma posed by Eichmann's case, namely, the relation between conscience and law:

> There remains . . . one fundamental problem, which was implicitly present in all these postwar trials and which must be mentioned here because it touches upon one of the central moral questions of all time, namely upon the nature and function of human judgment. What we have demanded in these trials, where the defendants had committed "legal" crimes, is that human beings be capable of telling right from wrong even when all they have to guide them is their own judgment, which moreover, happens to be completely at odds with what they must regard as the unanimous opinion of all those around them.[48]

Arendt's report examined what happens to conscience under a totalitarian system where there are no "voices" from the outside to give direction to the isolated individual. One of Eichmann's central contentions was that he was a "law-abiding citizen." The court considered two alternative ways to tackle this contention: either Eichmann was lying or he was telling the truth but nevertheless had failed his legal duty to disobey a manifestly illegal order. Arendt argued that both ways led the court away from confronting the central dilemma that the trial posed for legal theory.

Was Eichmann lying? The prosecution tried to undermine his contention that he was a law-abiding citizen with evidence about his behavior toward the end of the war when his superior Heinrich Himmler, faced with the certainty of defeat, had tried to save himself by ordering an end to the deportations to Auschwitz. Yet Eichmann had disobeyed the orders and relentlessly continued to march Jews to their deaths. The judges took this as proof of his fanaticism and hatred of Jews and concluded that he was indeed lying (an interpretation that coincided with traditional assumptions about the base motivation behind criminal acts).[49] Yet Arendt, listening carefully to Eichmann's contentions and studying his conduct in court, arrived at a different explanation (alas, one that frustrated traditional conceptions of criminal conduct). She explained that, whereas the judges regarded the actual orders given to Eichmann by his superior Himmler as "acts performed on superior orders," he claimed adherence to the law not just to a superior order. This distinction was crucial in the context of a legal system in which the spoken word of the Führer constituted the supreme law of the land. In other words, Eichmann had known that Himmler's orders ran directly counter to the Führer's words and intentions. As Arendt explains, "it was not an order but a law which had turned them all into criminals."[50] Paradoxically, in the Third Reich Eichmann's refusal to obey Himmler's order fulfilled in his eyes a duty to disobey a manifestly illegal order. In this inverted world, "The sad and very uncomfortable truth of the matter probably was that it was not his fanaticism but his very conscience that prompted Eichmann to adopt his uncompromising attitude during the last year of the war."[51]

Can the legal precedents regarding a duty to disobey a manifestly illegal order apply to Eichmann's actions? The court thought it could and relied on an Israeli precedent known as the Kufr Qassem Massacre, a case that bases the duty to disobey an illegal order on the strictures of universal morality.[52] The difficulty, Arendt explained, was that the duty to disobey presupposes the existence of a functioning legal system in which a manifestly illegal order can be distinguished by being an exception to the rule.[53] However, in the Third Reich, where the general rule was "Thou shalt kill," the situation was exactly the opposite. Evil in the Third Reich lost the quality by which most people recognize it— the quality of temptation—because it was enacted into the laws of the land.[54] Arendt commented that Eichmann "did not need to 'close his ears to the voice of conscience,' as the judgment has it, not because he had none, but because his conscience spoke with a 'respectable voice,' with the voice of respected society around him."[55] Instead of attributing Eichmann's failure to his lack of conscience, she argued, the court should have tried to understand how a totalitarian system silences the "voice of conscience" by making reality disappear behind a wall of clichés. For this task, however, determinative judgment, which attempts to explain unfamiliar crimes by analogizing them to more familiar ones, is ill fitted. The judges were faced with the need to engage in a different type of judging—to arrive at a judgment without reference to existing concepts of criminal law.[56]

CRIMES AGAINST HUMANITY

Arendt's observations about the banality of evil led her to realize the urgent need to create adequate legal rules to confront the new type of criminal and the new crimes he produced in order to prevent their future recurrence.[57] This approach, however, placed her in opposition to two powerful stories that pulled the court in the other direction. As actors in the legal system who were bound by its categories and distinctions, the judges tried to advance the story that Eichmann's crimes could be adapted to existing legal precedents. As spectators at the trial, listening to the testimonies of Holocaust survivors, the judges also responded to the victims' need to maintain the uniqueness of the Holocaust. These opposite tendencies converged in the court's interpretation of "crimes against humanity." The court broadened the legal category to encompass different acts, some new and some old, so that it could apply legal precedents to Eichmann's case. At the same time, it interpreted crimes against humanity as "inhuman acts" and attributed their uniqueness to the demonic motivation behind them.[58] Arendt was critical of the court's interpretation on both scores. She saw in crimes against humanity the opening chapter of a new story (of totalitarian crimes), not the last chapter in a long history of anti-Semitism as the prosecution presented it, and therefore sought to offer her own innovative interpretation of the crimes that would take into account their unprecedented nature. In Arendt's view, what was unprecedented about Eichmann's crimes was the fact that they had been directed against a fundamental condition of human existence, against what she called the condition of human plurality.

This presents a link between her theories of human action and human judgment. Plurality in action is based on the multiple perspectives of participants and spectators who occupy different standpoints yet are reciprocally connected. "Crime against Humanity,", in Arendt's view, unlike any other crime, is an attack on this condition of human plurality.

> It was when the Nazi Regime declared that the German people not only were unwilling to have any Jews in Germany but wished to make the entire Jewish people disappear from the face of the earth that the new crime, the crime against humanity—in the sense of a crime "against the human status," or against the very nature of mankind appeared . . . [it is] an attack upon human diversity as such.[59]

In this formulation crimes against humanity are not just "inhuman acts," as the court had it, nor are they similar to more familiar crimes such as mass murder. Rather, they threaten the very possibility of humanity (what she calls the "human status") even though they are perpetrated against particular nations (Jews, Gypsies, etc.).[60] An attempt to annihilate one group should be understood as an attack on human plurality and therefore on humanity as such. It was on this point that Arendt differed from the court. While the district court was willing to acknowledge the unique nature of the crime as crimes against the Jewish people, Arendt saw the particular crime as an instance of a universal crime against humanity that could be perpetrated against other groups in the future. This interpretation of crimes against humanity echoed Arendt's earlier formulation of the prepolitical role of law in *The Human Condition*, where she suggested that one of the central roles of law is to guarantee a protected space in which human plurality can flourish.[61]

THE PROBLEM OF RETROACTIVITY

Arendt's interpretation of crimes against humanity was offered from the standpoint of the spectator, that is, one who was an outsider to the legal game and hence did not have to abide by its rules. The Israeli judges, in contrast, were actors in the legal system. If they had attempted the kind of reflective judgment that Arendt recommended, they would have been accused of jeopardizing one of the fundamental rules of their legal system, the rule against retroactivity.[62] At the same time, neglecting to practice reflective judgment (facing the unprecedented with new categories and concepts), they might fail their equally important obligation to set the right precedent (for which they also have to play the role of historian and spectator).[63] This is but another variation on the dilemma of political trials that I presented in the beginning. Given the judges' uneasy position of being both actors in a legal system and spectators of history, either route seems to undermine their power of judgment.

Can it be, then, that only a spectator, like Arendt, is able to render a just judgment in Eichmann's case? Arendt's answer to this question would be a firm no. She was well aware of this dilemma, but by offering her interpretation of the rule against retroactivity she sought to show that there was no real conflict between the two roles of judges. Only when we think of legal judgment as limited to determinative judgment are we caught in this conflict. Arendt argued that the rule against retroactivity was based on the assumption that the act under consideration had been known to the legislator and he had decided against forbidding it. It helps protect individuals by giving them a clear indication of the scope of their freedom to act. This assumption does not apply, however, to unprecedented crimes. When a completely new crime such as genocide is introduced into the world, justice demands that the criminal will not be able to rely on the rule against retroactivity to ensure his or her impunity.[64] Arendt suggested, therefore, that the rule against retroactivity should apply only to acts known to the legislator in advance. This innovative theory presupposes that reflective judgment can be practiced equally well by spectators and actors in order to justify the punishment of an agent by ex post facto laws.[65]

THE PROBLEM OF JURISDICTION

Arendt's novel interpretation of crimes against humanity extended also to her interpretation of the law of jurisdiction. The defense argued that since the crimes had been committed outside Israel and prior to the establishment of the state Israel lacked jurisdiction. The court based its extraterritorial jurisdiction on the doctrine of passive personality, according to which a state acquires jurisdiction over crimes committed outside its territory when it can show special relations to the victim.[66] Normally this requires that the victim be a citizen, but since Israel had not existed at the time the court saw this special link in the fact that the victims were Jewish. Due to the difficulties that such an ethno-religious categorization raised, the appellate court offered the doctrine of "universal jurisdiction" as an alternative basis for the jurisdiction of the court.[67] According to this doctrine, by undertaking to prosecute and judge Eichmann for his crimes against humanity Israel was acting as the delegate of the international community, thus fulfilling its role as a loyal member of the family of nations.[68] Arendt rejected both approaches as unsatisfactory. The doctrine of passive personality, she argued, was not compatible with the foundations of modern criminal law because it stressed the injury to the individual victims as the reason for the legal process and not the injury to the community at large.[69] She was also dissatisfied with the principle of universal jurisdiction since it was based on an unfounded analogy to the law of piracy. A pirate, Arendt wrote, is an outlaw who has no flag and acts in the high seas outside the territorial jurisdiction of any state. Far from being an outlaw, Eichmann had been a loyal member of his state and had acted in its name. In other words, the problem with nazism was not the actions of outlaw individuals but the actions of an outlaw state.[70]

Although Arendt dismissed both doctrines of international law for extending territorial jurisdiction, she nonetheless upheld the Israeli court's jurisdiction over Eichmann.[71] Instead of focusing on the exceptions (the doctrines of passive personality and universal jurisdiction) she chose to examine the rule (the territoriality principle) as the basis for jurisdiction over Eichmann. Since her interpretation is so novel it is worth quoting it in full.

> Israel could easily have claimed territorial jurisdiction if she had only explained that "territory," as the law understands it, is a political and a legal concept, and not merely a geographical term. It relates not so much and not primarily to a piece of land as to the space between individuals in a group whose members are bound to, and at the same time separated and protected from, each other by all kinds of relationships, based on a common language, religion, a common history, customs, and laws. Such relationships become spatially manifest insofar as they themselves constitute the space wherein the different members of a group relate to and have intercourse with each other.[72]

On the basis of this cultural interpretation of territory Arendt justified Israeli jurisdiction for crimes against humanity since they had been intended to exterminate the Jewish people. She explained that Jews throughout the ages had kept their territory as a community and that after the Holocaust Israel had inherited this cultural space.[73] The Nazis' very attempt to destroy the special territory that bound the Jews together throughout the ages made their crime unique, that is, different in quality from an attempt to murder Jews as individuals (even on a massive scale). The state of Israel, which was created after the Holocaust as a result of the world's recognition of what had happened to the Jewish communities, therefore had a special justification for trying Eichmann. This is not to say that Arendt adopted an ethnic interpretation of the law of jurisdiction because she would not have justified Israel's jurisdiction over any crime committed against Jews but only over those crimes that were directed against the continual existence of the Jewish nation.[74] Thus, with the help of radically new interpretations of the principles of nonretroactivity and territorial jurisdiction, Arendt demonstrated how our ability to notice the new yields the ability to formulate new interpretations of the laws to ensure that the perpetrator will be judged according to his crimes in a court acting under the rule of law.

2. Toward a Theory of Reflective Judgment

Reflective judgment in political trials will remain arbitrary and subjective in the absence of a theory of judgment capable of constraining the discretion of the court and adapting it to the demands of a liberal democracy. Such a theory, however, is still missing from the Eichmann report. It is only in the Kant lectures that Arendt elaborates the process of forming valid judgments that enables actors and spectators to arrive at intersubjectively valid judgments, terming it "enlarged mentality."[75] As I described in the introduction to this book, reflective judgment requires the presence of three features, *natality* (developing new concepts to judge the new), *plurality* (engaging the different point of views of the participants), and *narrativity* (articulating a story with exemplary validity), which can provide the criteria for evaluating the conduct of the court in political trials under the rule of law. None of these features of reflective judgment is in itself capable of ensuring the compatibility of the court's judgment with liberal values, but together they constitute a system of "checks and balances" that constrain and guide the court's discretion in accordance with the needs of a liberal democracy.

Natality: Judging the Particular qua Particular

Before writing *Eichmann in Jerusalem* Arendt had considered the problem of how to judge the unprecedented in her discussion of human action, ascribing a term coined by Augustine, *natality*, to the human capacity for beginning, rooted in the fact of human birth.[76] Human beings, she explains, have the ability to initiate actions and to begin a new route, and human history provides examples of unprecedented actions.[77] The dark side of this insight is the realization that human beings can bring into the world terrible and unprecedented horrors such as the Nazi concentrations camps.[78] It also means that we can expect judgment (itself a human action) to confront new crimes, perceive their novelty, and create the conceptual tools with which to address them.[79] Arendt's report of the Eichmann trial was motivated by this desire to comprehend the new and face the unprecedented. For this purpose she rendered her own "fresh judgment" but did not yet give it a name or elaborate its process. Only later, in her Kant lectures, did she attempt to give her act of judgment a more theoretical formulation and explain what we do when we judge without rules. As demonstrated in the examples we discussed so far the judges in the Eichmann trial were on the verge of developing new categories by which to judge a crime not previously imagined by the law. But they failed to achieve the natality Arendt would argue is necessary for a true reflective judgment. They may have feared that a "judge-made law" would lay them open to the accusation of conducting a political show trial. This fear might explain why they did not consider the larger implications that state bureaucracy's involvement in annihilating the Jews had for the individualist and voluntarist conceptions of criminal law. Nonetheless, Arendt's willingness to go further in formulating new legal concepts with which to judge Nazi crimes in itself presents serious problems to judges who are bound to the rule of law. Even if we are satisfied with Arendt's solutions to the problems of retroactivity and jurisdiction on a theoretical level, there remains the problem of how to distinguish reflective judgment from the Nazi legacy of the total collapse of the rule of law. After all, Hitler's judges were notorious for their innovative judgments (it could be said that natality played a role in their judgments).[80] In her later lectures Arendt returned to this issue by articulating the process of representative thinking necessary for attaining a valid reflective judgment. I believe that these theoretical ideas can be imported into the context of legal judgment and can further our understanding of a legitimate political trial.

Plurality: The Process of Enlarged Mentality

Arendt argued that before forming a judgment one should enter a process of deliberation in which one gradually distances oneself from one's particular circumstances and familiarizes oneself with the standpoints of other people: "To think with enlarged mentality means that one trains one's imagination to go visiting."[81] The judging subject engages in such an exercise through communication with others and by relying on his or her faculty of imagination to conceive how the world would have looked from another's person's position. This procedure is described in Arendt's essay "Truth and Politics."

> Political thought is representative. I form an opinion by considering a given issue from different viewpoints, by making present to my mind the standpoint of those who are absent; that is, I represent them. This process of representation does not blindly adopt the actual views of those who stand somewhere else, and hence look upon the world from a different perspective; this is a question neither of empathy, as though I tried to be or feel like somebody else, nor of counting noses and joining a majority but of being and thinking in my own identity where actually I am not. The more people's standpoints I have present in my mind while I am pondering the issue, and the better I can imagine how I would feel and think if I where in their place, the stronger will be my capacity for representative thinking and the more valid my final conclusions, my opinion.[82]

In articulating the process of reflective judgment, Arendt diverges from Kant in some respects in order to accommodate her ideas about the conditions of human action. In her hands reflective judgment becomes a situated judgment that takes place within human time and is inscribed with human perspective. It consists of noticing the particular, engaging in representative thinking (enlarged mentality), and offering the community a new narrative with exemplary validity. Thus, the process of enlarged mentality is no longer a formal procedure devoid of the specific history and tradition of a concrete community, as Kant meant it to be, nor can it guarantee that judgment will be universally valid.[83]

An important difference between the innovative judgments of Hitler's judges and the type of reflective judgment that Arendt recommends depends on this dialogic process of representative thinking. In Nazi Germany the judges actively blocked themselves from the people they judged. Arendt, in contrast, urged the Israeli judges to do the opposite, to try and engage Eichmann's viewpoint, to see the world from his perspective in judging him. For this purpose Arendt used the narrative strategy of citing Eichmann in the first person and letting his voice be heard in the report. This process, as the passage quoted from "Truth and Politics" indicates, is not to be confused with empathy.

Reflective judgment does not mean seeking complete identification with the other, since that would merely be to trade one's subjective viewpoint (and prejudices) for another's. Rather, it requires rising above one's private inclinations and interests and learning to entertain a plurality of perspectives simultaneously: "the more people's standpoints I have in my mind . . . the more valid my final conclusion." This is the meaning that Arendt attributes to impartiality in judgment. Impartiality is not the attempt to occupy an objective viewpoint detached from particular human interests but the ability to entertain a plurality of perspectives simultaneously.

Even though neither Arendt nor Kant developed their insights on the process of enlarged mentality with reference to a court deliberation, it seems that they are applicable to judicial decision making.[84] As others have noted, the courtroom presentation invites the decision maker to play the case over in his or her mind from the standpoint of the plaintiff or the prosecutor, the defendant, judges who have decided similar cases in the past, and reasonable people in general, thereby ultimately reaching a valid judgment. Arendt's explanation of enlarged mentality—"doing and thinking in my own identity where I am not"—is suggestive of the position of a judge in a trial who is expected to interpret the story of an event from an unfamiliar standpoint before forming a judgment. The conditions of the courtroom presentation, such as oral testimonies, the symmetrical roles allotted to prosecution and defense, the cross-examination of each testimony, the publicity of the proceedings, and so on, can all be viewed as aiming to facilitate such an enlarged mentality. According to this approach, it was not legalistic issues such as the law against retroactivity or the law of jurisdiction that should have been the center of the discussion on the legitimacy of Eichmann's trial but issues pertaining to the process of enlarged mentality.

For example, the condition of plurality shows how the testimonies of survivors can contribute to personalizing and particularizing the Holocaust so that it ceases to be an ideological abstraction and becomes a human experience capable of being confronted and judged. However, it also shows how the structure of the trial created a manifest asymmetry in this respect, since the witnesses for the defense (who, as noted, had not been guaranteed immunity from prosecution) did not testify in the open court, so that their words tended to become an abstraction. Moreover, due to differences between the Israeli and German legal systems, while the German defense lawyer Servatius submitted documents without reading them out loud (the continental approach), the prosecution read out loud most of the documents that it submitted (the common law approach). Thus, Eichmann's testimony remained the main direct means for trying to understand the circumstances of action under the Nazi regime and for evaluating the options that had been open to him.[85] Simultaneous translation is an indispensable tool for facilitating this process of enlarged mentality, and this may well be the reason why Arendt decided to open her book with comments on the translation and, later in her report, to praise the Israeli judges for speaking to Eichmann directly in their common mother tongue, German.[86] As we have seen, however, Eichmann's own language undermined any attempt at real communication.

Arendt's report on the trial can be read as an exercise in enlarged mentality. Arendt reacted to Eichmann's manifest lack of judgment by attempting to "enter his shoes" in order to understand the cause of this failure before rendering her judgment.[87] As we have suggested, this attempt should not be confused with empathy.[88] It may explain her harsh criticism of the philosopher Martin Buber's assertion that he felt no obligation to understand someone with whom he shared a common humanity only in a formal sense. For Arendt, Eichmann's judges were not allowed to entertain such an attitude since the law presupposes that we share a common humanity with those whom we accuse, judge, and condemn.[89] This is also why, according to Arendt, we do not try the insane, with whom communication is no longer possible.[90] It is this foundation of criminal law on the assumption of common humanity that the extremity of Eichmann's actions threatened to undermine. However, Arendt herself failed in two respects. First, she failed to practice enlarged mentality in relation to the Jewish victims. On guard against the flood of emotions that their testimonies might produce in the spectators, she failed to understand the importance of oral testimonies in general and victims' narratives in particular to the process of enlarged mentality. Second, anxious to render an "objective" judgment, she seemed to forget her own role as an actor in the Jewish community.[91] Arendt's choice of the term *banal,* her condemnation of any effort to focus the trial on the victims' sufferings, and her refusal to draw a clearer line between perpetrators and victims all indicated a failure to "go visiting" her own people. These failures can account for some of the controversy that the book raised in the Jewish community.

The question of how the trial can facilitate enlarged mentality raises another question, that of whose judgment a political trial should aim to facilitate in the first place. As one commentator suggests, we can view every trial as encompassing two distinct plays: "the small play, the advocate's production of his client's case (played primarily to the judge), and the larger play, the trial as a whole (played before the public audience at large)."[92] Accordingly, the political trial has to fulfill the double role of "enlarging the minds" both of the judges and of the general public. Judges can later balance their unmediated impressions from the oral testimonies with the trial's protocol and the documents submitted to the court. In contrast, the judgment of the public is based mainly on the oral testimonies heard in the trial and on the reports in the media. For example, in Eichmann's trial the court based its judgment mainly on documents produced by Nazi perpetrators and not on the oral testimonies of survivors, which appeared in the judgment only when they could be corroborated by the documents. Moreover, as Arendt noticed, the court shifted the emphasis from Eastern Europe (where the extermination process had taken place) to Central and Western Europe, where "transportation" to the death camps had been organized.[93] But for the public at large the trial remained equated with the survivors' testimonies so that their ability to engage in reflective judgment was much more limited.

3. Narrativity: When Actor Meets Spectator

The third feature of human action, according to Arendt, in addition to natality and plurality, is its narrativity: action produces stories and is rendered meaningful through stories. This is also the modality that Arendt chooses for reflective judgments (such as her judgment of Eichmann). The narrative mode constitutes, therefore, the third link between action and judgment.

Scholars have noted that the ordinary ratio between law and narrative is changed in political trials. While in the ordinary trial the focus is on the interpretation of the rule, political trials are remembered, and can contribute to the rule of law, mainly through their narrative function. As one scholar notes, political trials "shape our thinking about the dilemmas of law, influence our sense of justice, and change our morality. . . . They provide society with a crucible for defining and refining its identity."[94] It is for this reason that the court's opinion tends to be remembered less than the trial proceedings in which competing narratives are offered and contested. Moreover, while the ordinary trial presupposes a fair degree of homogeneity and agreement in the interpretation of the laws arising from a central ethos, in political trials, where this ethos is no longer taken for granted, the contest of narratives becomes paramount.[95] In the absence of agreement on the basic rules of the game, the stories presented by the various parties are the only means of persuasion they have left.

Well aware of the power of narrative in political trials, the Israeli prosecution provided Holocaust survivors with the opportunity to testify about their personal experiences. These testimonies, which were here heard in public for the first time, were meant to initiate the long process of pondering on what had happened and to give a human face to the abstract notions of crimes against the Jewish people and crimes against humanity. On another level, the attorney general used the trial to present a metanarrative about the relationship between the Holocaust and the establishment of the State of Israel in an effort to include the Holocaust survivors in the constitutive narrative of the Israeli collective identity. The case of the prosecution was thus literally built on a chain of human stories.

Although Arendt criticized the prosecution's heavy reliance on survivor testimonies rather than written documents, the "alternative" that she offered in her own report also adopted the narrative mode. The report consists of a narrative framework in which the first and final chapters discuss the conduct of the trial, with the intervening chapters following the story of Eichmann and the destruction of the Jewish communities. Arendt rarely offers abstract arguments or statistics but proceeds by relating stories that could throw some light on the meaning of Eichmann's crimes. In this respect, *Eichmann in Jerusalem* resembles her previous work, *The Origins of Totalitarianism*.[96] Arendt's choice of a narrative voice has been attributed to her deep suspicion of the scientific model of historiography and social science, as well as to her attempt to confront the moral crisis in the wake of the Holocaust through stories intimately connected to the human experience from which they sprang.[97]

In the context of the courtroom—maybe the last public space in our modern society where stories in general, and oral stories in particular, are still considered to be the privileged way of arriving at the truth—it seems that Arendt, a great advocate of the narrative mode, turned suddenly against it. When confronting the tensions and contradictions of a political trial under the rule of law, she found herself at war with herself. As noted earlier, this internal conflict was particularly apparent in her reaction to Zindel Gryszpan's testimony. On the one hand, his testimony confirmed her belief that even in the darkest of times stories could still serve to offer some illumination. But on the other hand she also realized the immense difficulty of telling such a story and that survivors' testimonies might lead the trial away from the main task of rendering judgment on Eichmann's crimes.[98] Nonetheless, when it came to articulating the meaning of crimes against humanity and of the totalitarian system of destruction, Arendt herself turned to live testimony. She rendered her own judgment of Eichmann not on the basis of written documents but on the sole basis of his testimony, which she viewed as revealing a very deep truth about the meaning of the new criminal produced by the age of totalitarianism. Moreover, her judgment of Eichmann was offered in the narrative voice. Her catchphrase, "the banality of evil," encapsulated her complex arguments in a condensed narrative with an exemplary validity.[99] But unlike the narratives about Socrates or Achilles, which were offered by the storytellers of antiquity as exemplars of what it meant to practice critical thinking or act courageously, in the hope that they would serve humanity as a model for imitation, Arendt's narrative about Eichmann's banality of evil was offered as exemplary of something negative—a failure of judgment—which came with a stern warning, "not to be repeated!"

An important advantage of the narrative mode, according to Arendt, is that it remains open to interpretation and retelling and can thus set in motion a process of narration in which a plurality of voices and perspectives is visited. By refusing to rush into general categorization and by proceeding piecemeal by way of narratives, Arendt celebrates the possibilities of the "in-between" (on both levels, between individuals in a community and between the particular and the concept). In other words, the narrative mode can best accommodate the condition of human natality and human plurality. Moreover, it enables the reader to reenact the process of enlarged mentality while reading the text and in this way to remain critical of the judgments offered. Walter Benjamin captures this quality of narratives in his essay on storytelling.

It is half the "art" of storytelling to keep a story from explanation as one reproduces it. . . . The most extraordinary things, marvelous things, are related with the greatest accuracy, but the psychological connection of the events is not forced on the reader. It is left up to him to interpret things the way he understands them, and thus the narrative achieves an amplitude that information lacks.[100]

Arendt echoes this insight when she describes the work of the historian as "setting [a] process of narration in motion, and involving us in it" rather than mastering the events once and for all.[101]

This approach might help us understand Arendt's choice of the narrative mode in Eichmann's case. It might also explain some of the misunderstanding that her judgment caused, since her critics understood the book as aiming to render a "final judgment." This could not have been further from Arendt's intentions. In her view, judgment should not be equated with the court decision or her own report of it. Rather, judgment is an act of narration, an act of participation in the public realm informed by a sense of individual responsibility to the community.[102] Such was indeed the purpose of Arendt's book. It was not meant to produce consensus but to set in motion a process of deliberation and public debate.

4. Conclusion

The Eichmann trial offers not only a fascinating story about judgment but a model for the relations between actor and spectator that are created in a political trial. The institutional setting endows the judges with the dual role of actor and spectator. As actors they learn to exercise determinative judgment, going back and forth between the facts and the legal categories in order to bridge the gap between them. As spectators, they are trained to remain open to the newness of each case and to entertain the perspectives of all parties before reaching a decision.[103] Although the need to judge someone when we were not in his or her place demands an immense effort of communication and reflection (as Eichmann's case demonstrates), this does not mean that we should renounce judging altogether. The common humanity that is assumed in every trial is based on our ability to occupy the roles of both actor and spectator, that is, our ability to "go visit." This human potential can be realized even in the difficult situation of a political trial if the trial respects the conditions of natality, plurality, and narrativity as elaborated in this chapter.

Studying a political trial through the prism of reflective judgment enables us to evaluate to what extent the Eichmann trial succeeded in overcoming the central dilemma of political trials, the simultaneous need to judge the defendant according to pregiven rules while noticing the new in his or her actions and finding ways to develop new legal concepts. We have seen that the Israeli court was able to practice natality in confronting the new crimes of the Nazi regime, in particular, by interpreting the final solution as a crime committed by members of a state bureaucracy. In doing so it overcame traditional criminal law doctrines of accessory and criminal conspiracy that unduly limited the court's understanding of Eichmann's crimes. Nonetheless, as Arendt noted, the court was unable to grasp the full meaning of the new crimes because it failed to give due respect to the element of plurality. Finally, the element of narrativity generated the greatest controversy between Arendt and the Israeli prosecution. While the prosecution's narrative was based on the testimonies of Holocaust survivors, Arendt's counternarrative, focused on Eichmann's testimony, depicted the extermination machine as a tool of a totalitarian bureaucracy whose "ideal" perpetrator was Eichmann. In this narrative she pointed to the phenomenon she dubbed the "banality of evil" and urged jurists to develop legal concepts that could extend legal responsibility to a state bureaucracy engaged in mass murder. These narratives competed and continue to compete in our collective memory of the trial and the Holocaust. The court itself refrained from choosing between them by, on the one hand, allowing the testimonies of survivors, while on the other hand basing its judgment mainly on perpetrators' documents. I argued that the imbalance between the elements of natality, plurality, and narrativity impaired the ability of the Eichmann trial to become a just political trial. Nonetheless, a political trial should be evaluated not only in the context of the courtroom proceedings but also with regard to its potential to foster a deliberative democracy. Chapter 6 will therefore examine the public debate that the Eichmann trial kindled in Israel and the United States—a debate that raised the complex issues of how collective identity and memory are formed in the shadow of a controversial political trial—and the role of the social critic in framing the debate.

Chapter 6

Social Criticism in the Shadow of a Transformative Trial

Hannah Arendt was faced with a difficult dilemma while reporting on the Eichmann trial for the *New Yorker*. As a German Jew, she had to negotiate between her solidarity with a particular national group and her universalistic commitment to justice.[1] How could she express her criticism about the trial without her views being appropriated by anti-Semites and without being seen as a "disloyal daughter" of the Jewish people? The intense emotions aroused by her report and its overwhelming denunciation by American Jews, as well as by the few Israelis who had access to it, demonstrate how difficult it is to occupy the role of social critic in such times. As we have seen in the previous chapters, the trial was not only an attempt to bring the Holocaust to the consciousness of the world but also an important vehicle through which the young Israeli nation sought to overcome the bitter political debates regarding the behavior of the Jewish leadership during the Holocaust, as exemplified by the Kastner affair. At this moment of crucial importance for the articulation of the Israeli national identity, Arendt intervened to question the very goals the trial was designed to achieve.

This chapter is about Arendt's criticism of the terms of the Israeli collective identity that the trial was enhancing and about the controversy that it initiated. It also compares the critique of Arendt, a German Jew but still an outsider in Israeli society, with that of the Israeli poet Haim Gouri, who reported on the trial to an Israeli audience.[2] Finally, it examines the similarities between the *Arendt controversy*, which took place mainly on the pages of American magazines, to the *Alterman controversy* during the Kastner trial, which was conducted in Israeli newspapers. This comparison will provide a framework for examining the ways in which political trials can influence the collective memory of a national group against the backdrop of social criticism from outside the trial. While most of Arendt's book is devoted to elaborating an alternative history of Eichmann's role in the Nazi bureaucracy, she also discerned the trial's impact on the formation of Israel's political culture, in particular with regard to the focus on victimhood and anti-Semitism. It was, however, only many decades later, after the publication of the book in Hebrew in 2000, that her vision became part of the political discourse in Israel. Nonetheless, juxtaposing Arendt's critique with Alterman's earlier critique can shed light on the dynamics of social criticism in the context of a political trial.

1. Arendt as Critic

The proper attitude of the social critic vis-à-vis her people was a central concern of the famous exchange of letters between Arendt and the prominent scholar of Jewish Kabbalah Gershom Scholem.[3] Following the publication of her report, Scholem set the terms of the debate by highlighting the contrast between the detached and the connected critic (a loving member of the community), criticizing Arendt for adopting the former position.

> In the Jewish tradition there is a concept, hard to define and yet concrete enough, which we know as Ahabath Israel: "Love of the Jewish people." . . . In you, dear Hannah, as in so many intellectuals who came from the German Left, I find little trace of this.[4]

In her reply Arendt rejected the notion that love of the people was the proper stance of the social critic and insisted on the need to judge (and possibility of judging) critically for the sake of the community's own good. In this way she transformed her book from a specific critique of the trial to a principled position about the importance of disagreement and a plurality of voices for the existence of a deliberative democracy.

The Philosopher Contests the Terms of the Israeli Collective Identity

One focus of Arendt's criticism was the decision to prosecute Eichmann under the legal category "crimes against the Jewish people."[5] This choice, she explained, went hand in hand with the belief that "only a

Jewish court could render justice to Jews, and that it was the business of Jews to sit in judgment on their enemies."[6] She was alarmed by the ethnic categorization implicit in the choice of legal category, notwithstanding the prosecutor's insistence that he would also prosecute Eichmann for crimes against non-Jews because "we make no ethnic distinctions."[7] In fact, Arendt asserted that Israeli law did make ethnic distinctions, particularly in its personal status laws. For example, by conferring jurisdiction on matters of marriage and divorce of Jewish citizens to rabbinical courts, Israeli law sanctioned a situation in which a Jew could not marry a non-Jew in the State of Israel. She was alarmed by the apparent consensus between secular and religious Jews in Israel about the desirability of such a law, viewing this as one of the reasons for Israel's lack of a written constitution in which it would have to spell out this abridgment of individual freedom in the name of ethno-religious solidarity.[8] She did not fail to note the irony of this situation in a trial intended to condemn the murderous trail of Nazism that had begun with the exclusionary Nuremberg laws of 1935.

But Arendt's main concern was not the existence of historical ironies. By connecting the choice of legal category (crimes against the Jewish people) to Israel's policy of religious distinctions, she pointed to the trial's much broader implications. She realized early on that the trial had the power to shape not only the way in which Israelis understood the nature of Eichmann's crimes but also the way in which they understood themselves. To put it differently, she understood that the legal result was not the only factor to consider in such a trial. The way in which the verdict was reached was of equal importance. Eichmann could have been indicted under any one of several legal categories, but each would have had different implications for the way in which Israelis perceived themselves and would act in the future.[9] Taking the particularistic road of crimes against the Jewish people emphasized the problem of anti-Semitism and the Jews' image as the eternal victim. In this regard Arendt warned against the us-them (Jews-Gentiles) logic inherent in the category of crimes against the Jewish people, which undermined the ability of Israeli society to embrace plurality (within Israel and in relation to other nations) and practice normal politics. Indeed, the prosecutor, Gideon Hausner, depicted Eichmann as the incarnation of the persecutors of old, presenting the history of the Jews as a long history of persecution and victimization by the Gentiles.[10] Arendt insisted that a "change in this mentality is actually one of the indispensable prerequisites for Israeli statehood . . . depending now on a *plurality* which no longer permits the age-old, and unfortunately, religiously anchored *dichotomy of Jews and Gentiles.*"[11] Arendt was particularly disturbed by the symbolic connection that the trial created between enemies of old (Nazis) and present enemies (the Arabs) through its focus on the relations between the Palestinian leader Haj Amin Al-Husseini, the former mufti of Jerusalem, and Eichmann.[12] The national conflict between Israelis and Arabs was thus reinterpreted in the trial according to a binary scheme in which Israelis were portrayed as falling squarely in the category of victims and the Arabs were portrayed as allies of the worst enemies of the Jews. This framework left no conceptual space for recognizing the victimization of Arabs by Israelis.[13]

Arendt's second focus of criticism was the Zionist lesson, which contrasted "Israeli heroism" with "Jewish submissiveness," as expressed in the prosecution's repeated question to the witnesses: "Why did you not rebel?"[14] She thought that this question was not relevant to proving Eichmann's guilt but expressed the tendency in Israeli society to blame the victim for lack of resistance. In fact, by uttering the question out loud and forcing his witnesses to answer it, Hausner hoped to change this attitude. Thus, when he presented the question to Dr. Moshe Beiski (later to become a Supreme Court justice) the shocked witness hardly found the words to answer it. After a few stuttering sentences Beiski asked to be seated and tried to describe the fear experienced by the Nazis' victims, a fear that was almost never discussed in public at that time.

> This sense of fear, when I stand here today in front of you, your honors, no longer exists, and I do not believe it can be conveyed to anyone. In short, it is sheer terror. When you stand in front of a machine gun . . . you're not left with any ability to react. . . . The conditions of those times cannot be conveyed to the court. It's not that I think that this won't be understood. It's just that even I can't feel it again, and I experienced it in my own flesh. So perhaps this question can be asked dialectically, but the conditions that existed then are impossible to describe.[15]

This and similar testimonies by other survivors made a profound impact on the Israeli public. Haim Gouri, for example, noted that the tendency to blame the victim, which had caused such injustice to the survivors, was the result of an attempt to avoid confronting the horrors of the Holocaust: "At least, after this trial they [the Israeli public] will stop dealing with the behavior of the Jews there, stop accusing them. They [the survivors] have told us everything. One day we ourselves will have to start talking. I am afraid."[16]

As we have seen, Arendt opposed the prosecution's reliance on survivors' testimonies whose main purpose was to describe their sufferings, since she thought that sufferings, which had no measure, could not be dealt with by means of legal tools. She took issue in particular with the testimony of Yehiel Dinur (a writer who used the pen name Ka-Zetnik) for describing the Holocaust as having taken place on "another planet." Arendt's approach was the opposite: she wanted her readers to understand that the Holocaust was a human possibility in their own world that had to be confronted with the rational tools of law, historiography, and philosophy. Dinur's confused testimony and his subsequent collapse on the witness stand became one of the most memorable symbols of the trial and as such personified a victim's suffering for the audience.[17] Arendt failed to see the testimony in this light and sarcastically described Dinur's collapse as the response of someone who had been insulted by having his story unduly interrupted by the court.[18]

Arendt was far more affected by another witness, Zindel Grynszpan, who testified about what it meant to become a refugee.[19] Zindel was the father of Herschel Grynszpan, who on 7 November 1938 shot to death the third secretary of the German Embassy in Paris in reaction to Germany's anti-Jewish policies, an event that was used by the Nazis as the pretext for the Kristallnacht (Crystal Night) pogrom.[20] Arendt did not focus on the son but on the seemingly nonheroic story of his father, Zindel, whom she described in the following terms: "He was an old man, wearing the traditional Jewish skullcap, small very frail, with sparse white hair and beard, holding himself quite erect. . . . Now he had come to tell his story, carefully answering questions put to him by the prosecutor; he spoke clearly and firmly, without embroidery, using a minimum of words."[21] In her view, this testimony was the exact opposite to Dinur's. Grynszpan's account of what it meant to lose one's home and be deported from one's country was related without any sentimentality and with a matter-of-fact precision. It might well be that Arendt chose his testimony as exemplary precisely because of its lack of saintly or heroic pathos, which enabled her to discuss the Holocaust free of the ideological lens that was imposed on it.

Arendt, too, was a refugee from Germany who had had the good fortune to leave in time. This experience may have enabled her to identify with the human experiences recounted by Grynszpan more than with the stories of immense suffering in the concentration camps related by other witnesses. In her account of the trial she tried to dismantle the Zionist construct of the "submissive survivor" in a more subtle and personal way. Criticizing the trial's educative goals, designed to present the younger generation with a particular story of the Holocaust, she told her readers that the courtroom "was filled with survivors, with middle-aged and elderly people, immigrants from Europe, *like myself*"[22] She identified herself as a survivor but one who refused to obey the code of behavior expected of her. Instead, she presented her criticism of the prosecution in a strong and direct voice, frustrating the image of the passive survivor through her own textual resistance.[23] She thus rejected the idea that the ideological lenses of the prosecution could encompass the whole range of Holocaust experiences and insisted on exposing the plurality of voices among the survivors. In particular, she refused to choose sides between being a passive victim or a heroic resister.

Arendt also sought to dismantle the other side of the dichotomy— the testimonies to heroism. In legal terms, she thought they were irrelevant to the prosecution's case. On the contrary, a good defense lawyer could easily use them to strengthen his or her own case since they depicted the fight of the Nazis against the Jews in military terms.[24] She recognized that the main purpose of the testimonies of resistance fighters and Jewish partisans was political—to portray the Zionists of that time as heroes and to link their heroism with that of the State of Israel. Although she harshly criticized this political agenda, she was willing to admit that these testimonies were important in other ways since they allowed some hope to enter the courtroom.

Instead of the victim-hero dichotomy Arendt drew her readers' attention to the painful issue of Jewish cooperation with the Nazis, which the prosecution had tried so hard to exclude from the trial, writing: "But the question the prosecutor regularly addressed to each witness except the resistance fighters, which sounded so very natural to those who knew nothing of the factual background of the trial, the question 'why did you not rebel?' actually served as a smoke screen for the question that was not asked."[25] She formulated her counterquestion as follows: "Why did you cooperate in the destruction of your own people and, eventually, in your own ruin?"[26] According to Arendt, it was the omission of the Judenrat issue that enabled the prosecution to establish the clear polarity between Nazi monsters and Jewish martyrs.[27] If a totalitarian regime achieves control over the population by blurring the line between perpetrator and victim, in order to judge such regimes there is a need to develop the tools to understand the gray area of cooperation and collaboration that is radically different from the available legal notion of treason.[28] As we have seen, in dealing with this painful subject, Arendt focused on the figure of Rudolf Kastner, and since he was a Zionist affiliated with Mapai her discussion undermined the Israeli heroism/Jewish submissiveness dichotomy that had been so carefully constructed by the prosecution.

The Poet's Critique of the Israeli Collective Identity

Haim Gouri, who also reported on the trial, was much admired by the younger generation of Israelis as embodying in his work and life story the ethos of the new nation. He also criticized Hausner's provocative question to his witnesses. Like Arendt he thought that it concealed another, much more important question that was not raised during the trial, but the question Gouri had in mind was very different from hers.

> So why didn't you get rid of Eichmann? And why, why didn't you run away. . . ? etc. etc. These questions come back to us like a smashing wounding boomerang. Why didn't we tell? Why didn't we cry out? Why didn't we demonstrate? Why didn't we fast? Why didn't we drive the world crazy? What shall we reply to these questions— can we say that we did everything we could have done to help at that time?[29]

Gouri thought that more attention should have been given in the trial to the Yishuv's reaction to the reports of the Holocaust during the war. We have already noted that during Joel Brand's testimony the prosecution submitted documents showing the Yishuv leaders' effort to convince the British and Americans to facilitate the negotiations with the Nazis and to take direct military action to rescue the remaining Jews. These documents were meant to shift the blame from Kastner and

Mapai to the British and the Americans, who had refused to heed these warnings and requests. Gouri, however, sought to probe more deeply.

> They knew more. That's true. But we also knew. In May 1943 we knew that Jewish Warsaw no longer existed. We heard the broadcast on London radio. Even before that we knew that the Jewish tribe in Europe was dying out day by day. We went to fight the Nazis. Thousands joined up. They marched on the battle fields. But at the same time life continued here. . . . How are we to make this personal reckoning today? I don't know. But at the same time I realize that such a reckoning cannot be avoided. . . . The more I reflect the greater the fear that wells within me. These questions are too cruel to be run away from and too dangerous to be talked about today. But they will always beset us.[30]

Gouri was concerned with the reactions of Jewish civil society in Mandatory Palestine to the events in Europe, with the failure of the Yishuv to do more to rescue the Jews there. He refrained from directing all the blame at the leaders, thus forcing the Israeli public to address its own behavior and begin the process of reckoning. This passage may also shed some light on the very different responses to Arendt's and Gouri's reports in Israel. Although Gouri's criticism potentially presented a more painful challenge to Israeli society than Arendt's, it was favorably received. This may have been because Gouri spoke as a member of the collectivity and included himself in the circle of blame while Arendt directed all the blame outside—to the Jewish leaders.[31] Moreover, the tone they used was very different. While Arendt's was confident, critical, and at times sarcastic, Gouri was much more hesitant and ambivalent, willing to admit his fears and doubts in public. (Arendt disclosed them only to her closest friends.) He acknowledged that the circumstances of the Yishuv—its lack of sovereignty, its efforts to deal with Arab hostility and British restrictions—had made any action difficult, while the tendency to continue one's normal life was all too human (as manifested in other Jewish communities such as those in the United States and Britain). Although both were critical of the prevailing tendency in Israel to blame the victims, only Gouri went even further, questioning the tendency to blame the leaders instead of taking personal responsibility. Arendt's criticism of the Judenrate was part of her wider criticism of the conduct of the prosecution, while Gouri limited his criticism to this one point and praised the prosecution's choices as a whole. Finally, Gouri admitted that this might not have been the proper time or place to raise these issues, while Arendt insisted that it was crucial to discuss these painful points right there and then. All these differences can explain why Arendt's report generated a much fiercer and more emotional response in the Jewish world.

2. The Controversy

While Gouri's criticism was addressed, in Hebrew, to a domestic Israeli audience, Arendt criticized the Jewish leaders on the pages of an American magazine. The heated public debate kindled by her articles therefore was mostly conducted among intellectuals on the pages of the American press (a fact that led to the additional accusation of "airing dirty linen" in public about internal Jewish matters).[32] The critics focused on two issues—the inclusion of the chapter on the Judenrate and Arendt's thesis on the banality of evil—which, they argued, obscured the distinction between victims and perpetrators.[33] In some reviews Arendt was even accused of providing a "legal defense" for Eichmann.[34] Here, I shall limit myself to considering one aspect of the controversy that has not been studied so far and suggests parallels with Alterman's role during the Kastner trial: the difficulties of articulating a critical view that competes with the judgment of the court. On what authority does the critic offer an alternative to the court's decision? What is the role of the critic's identity in articulating and authorizing his or her positions? Studying these questions will reveal structural affinities in the positions of the participants in the controversies and will also highlight some important differences between the criticism directed at Arendt and that directed at Alterman a decade before.

The Question of Judgment

Arendt's focus on the Judenrate and her determination to judge them were the focus of Scholem's critique of Arendt's report of the Eichmann trial. He pointed out that:

> There were among them [the Jewish leaders] also many people in no way different from ourselves, who were compelled to make terrible decisions in circumstances that we cannot even begin to reproduce

or reconstruct. I do not know whether they were right or wrong. Nor do I presume to judge. I was not there.[35]

Arendt, however, refused to refrain from judging the issue of Jewish cooperation.

> This [the behavior of the Jews] constitutes our part of the so called "unmastered past," and although you may be right that it is too early for a "balanced judgment" (though I doubt this), I do believe that we shall only come to terms with this past if we begin to judge and to be frank about it.[36]

Interesting parallels can be discerned between the controversy over Arendt's report and the Alterman controversy of the 1950s discussed in chapter 3. Arendt and Alterman appear to have held opposing views regarding the need to judge the Judenrate. While Alterman called for a deferral of judgment, Arendt insisted on judging them immediately at any cost. Both, however, opposed the position taken by the court. Alterman was critical of the court's judgmental treatment of Kastner, while Arendt defied the prosecution's attempts to circumvent the issue of the Judenrate in Eichmann's trial. Arendt was condemned by Scholem for her willingness to judge the Judenrate, while Alterman was harshly criticized precisely for his reluctance to judge them.[37] Indeed David Kenaani, one of Alterman's fiercest critics in the 1950s, accused him of lack of ideological clarity:

> Doubly strange is the blurring of the boundary between the rebels and the "the elders of the Jews." . . . The rebels in their lives and deaths erected this wall—a wall of honor, of wisdom, of historical account . . . for the "time that has no analogy" corrupted the Jewish leaders and turned them into tools of destruction of their Jewish brethren. . . . Under these extreme circumstances such different paths cannot be reconciled. . . . We should inherit our values from only one of the two paths. Only one path can become the symbol of the time and its struggles.[38]

Alterman had answered Kenaani by restating his reservations about the sweeping condemnation of the Judenrate, based on the two-paths conception, and called for an approach that would allow for hesitations and uncertainties.[39] We see, then, that Alterman's idiosyncratic views of the 1950s had become the conventional wisdom that Scholem advocated in the 1960s. Arendt seems to have been swimming against the current, for her subversive views about Eichmann's trial were reminiscent of Israeli popular sentiment in the 1950s.

Arendt's criticism, however, had an entirely different motivation. She raised this issue not in order to endorse the ideological condemnation of the survivors ("Why did you not rebel?") but rather to oppose the new ideological order that was being advanced in the Eichmann trial and, in particular, to disrupt the clear-cut binarism of devilish murderer and passive victims. She criticized the Judenrate not because they had not subscribed to the Zionist code of military heroism but because they had not adopted a position of civil disobedience.[40] She was also careful to distinguish between the leaders and the Jewish people as a whole as well as between the different stages of the destruction of European Jewry. Consequently, she limited her criticism to the actions of the Jewish Councils in the early stages of ghettoization when civil disobedience may still have been possible.

Judgment and Identity

Although Arendt and Alterman seem to hold opposite views about the Judenrate's behavior, they both strive to demythologize them and stress their human agency. While Alterman explores their actions as a different type of resistance, Arendt criticizes their lack of civil disobedience. It is significant that both writers invoked their own identities to support their dissident judgments. Expressing his views on the Judenrate, Alterman resorted to the personal voice.

> I have said it already to several of the ghetto rebels and I repeat it here: I do not know in whose faith I would have lived and died if I had been there—in the faith of the rebellion or in the faith of those who resisted it. And David Kenaani, does he know with certainty with whom he would have sided? Is he certain of this?[41]

The invocation of the personal voice during such a debate is peculiar. Objective judgment and personal voice are generally regarded as opposites. The conflation of the two voices by Alterman calls for explanation. His published reply to Kenaani was a milder version of the views he actually held on the subject, as demonstrated by a private conversation he had with the former resistance fighter, the writer Abba Kovner, which took place around 1947 in Alterman's apartment and was later reported by Kovner. Kovner writes that Alterman questioned him about the ghetto, taking notes and listening carefully.

> Later we went outside again. I think it was at the end of Ben-Ami street that he said: "Had I been in the Ghetto—I would have been with the Judenrate members."
> I stopped walking. Seeing that I had stopped, he stopped as well. A gap opened between us. A woman pushing a stroller with a baby entered the gap. She recognized Alterman and smiled at him, he did not smile back.
> And I said: "But Nathan, I read *Simchat Aniim* [Alterman's book of poems glorifying Jewish heroism]—how can you—?"
> That was here—he answered sharply—that after all was here![42]

In this passage, Alterman is described as trying to imagine himself in the shoes of the Jewish victims and concluding that had he been there he would have joined the Judenrate. Kovner's shocked response was due to the discordance between this statement and Alterman's public image of heroism and defiance. When Alterman was confronted with the concrete situation in the ghetto, he rejected his own ideals of military heroism and identified with the Judenrat members—so despised by Israeli society. It was this act of personal exposure, more than the content of his judgment, that could help to fracture the ideological lens through which the Holocaust was judged at the time.

Kovner's report of this conversation introduces another element into the controversy: that of gender. The two men (Kovner and Alterman) represent in their words the two paths: resistance (New Jew, Israeli) and compliance (Old Jew, Diaspora Jew). The woman appears in this paragraph as an interruption. She seems unable to integrate into the symbolic order of the two exclusive paths so that her entrance induces a shift from the symbolic to the real. She enters the rift that opens between the disputing men with a baby stroller and a smile. As a literary artifice, her appearance underlines the dramatic confrontation between the men; it also signals, however, an implicit opposition between men's contemplative preoccupation with the past and women's worldly activities of raising the next generation. In his description, Kovner does not allow the woman to blur the ideological line between the two men.

In recent years several writers have shown that the Zionist contra-position of New and Old Jew accords with the binary approach to male and female behavior.[43] The figure of the Diaspora Jew is linked with characteristics traditionally associated with women, such as passivity and pragmatism, as opposed to the New Jew, whose characteristics of activism and military heroism are considered male. This perspective can help illuminate a covert gender dimension in the two controversies. First, it can explain some of the shock created by Alterman's identification with the Judenrat members, since his rhetorical move can be seen as representing a crossing of both national and gender identities. By identifying with the Judenrate, Alterman crosses not only a national line (from Israeli to Diaspora Jew) but also an implicit gender line (identifying with the "feminine" figure of the Diaspora Jew).

Similarly, Jennifer Ring has suggested that the volume and heat of the reactions to Arendt's report should be explained in terms of its gen-der subtext.

> Had a man written *Eichmann in Jerusalem,* there would have been two volatile sides to the issue, just as there had been to the major Jewish issues of the previous two decades: negotiation with the Nazis or not? Armed resistance or survival tactics? Those battles were fierce and hard fought, but there was a "critical mass" of opin-ion on both sides.[44]

To substantiate this claim, Ring compares the reactions to Arendt with the more balanced and respectful criticism received by the historian Raul Hilberg, who held similar views about the Judenrate and upon whose work Arendt relied heavily in her report. Although the more moderate reactions to Hilberg's work can be explained equally well by other factors,[45] it seems that gender categories can still be illuminating if we consider the way they were constructed and contested by Arendt and Alterman respectively.

Both Alterman and Arendt employed an act of cross-gendering to undermine the use of Zionist identity categories (New versus Diaspora Jew) that the Israeli public regarded as self-evident and to reveal their constructed nature. Alterman refused to uphold the militant "male" identity expected of him and adopted the "female" identity of the Diaspora Jew. Likewise, Arendt refused to act according to the traditional feminine image of the Diaspora Jew (passive and compliant). Instead, she adopted a male identity of defiance, condemning the "womanly" behavior of the Jewish leaders. They produced a shock effect by skillfully playing out the discrepancy between their real and assumed identities. I suggest that this move can account for the intensity of the reactions in both cases.

3. The Politics of Love

This point can be elaborated by taking a closer look at the way in which Arendt disrupted the ideological binarism advanced in the Eichmann trial. Let us return to Scholem's accusations that Arendt's very willingness to judge the Judenrate demonstrated her lack of love for her people. In her reply, Arendt acknowledged, "You are quite right—I am not moved by any 'love' of this sort. . . . I have never in my life 'loved' any people or collective. . . . I indeed love 'only' my friends and the only kind of love I know of and believe in is the love of persons." Scholem attributed Arendt's "heartless" treatment of the Jews to her association with intellectuals from the German Left: "In you, dear Hannah, as in so many intellectuals who came from the German Left, I find little trace of this [love of the Jewish People]." Nevertheless, Scholem hastened to add, "I regard you wholly as a daughter of our people, and in no other way."[46] Notwithstanding *his* confidence in Arendt's belonging, the implication of Scholem's words was that the only way for Arendt to show her loyalty as "a daughter of our people" to the public at large was to uphold love over judgment. Thus, love became a means of judging Arendt's misbehavior.

Arendt was quick to notice the disciplinary aspects of the politics of love. She disputed Scholem's insinuation that her report amounted to a repudiation of her Jewish identity: "I have never pretended to be anything else [other than Jewish] or to be in any way other than I am, and I have never even felt tempted in that direction. It would have been like saying that I was a man and not a woman—that is to say, kind of insane." Interestingly, this is the only time in the debate that Arendt invoked her identity as a woman.[47] This statement should be read as a rhetorical move on the part of Arendt. It indicated that what really disturbed Scholem (and other Zionist critics) was the "masculine" position that Arendt adopted, betraying the traditional role reserved for women on such occasions.[48]

Arendt, however, went beyond rhetoric to dispute the terms of the debate that Scholem imposed on her. She argued that we should distinguish between repudiating one's group identity and guarding one's independence ("the trouble is that I am independent. . . . I do not belong to any organization and always speak only for myself").[49] And, as for the alleged lack of love in her treatment of the Jews, Arendt unveiled the politics behind this statement, saying, "You know as well as I how often those who merely report certain unpleasant facts are accused of lack of soul, lack of heart, or lack of what you call *Herzenstakt*. We both know, in other words, how often these emotions are used in order to conceal factual truth."[50] In other words, in the name of solidarity, abuses and injuries are covered up and women (referred to as sisters or daughters) are urged not to report them lest they be seen as repudiating their group identity or betraying their community.

Having exposed the underlying "politics of love" in Scholem's response, Arendt then examined whether judgment really stood in opposition to loyalty and solidarity with one's group. Patriotism, she urged, should not be confused with love. Indeed, Arendt argued that patriotism was not only compatible with but even necessitated criticism.[51] In her view, the viability of a people depends on constant criticism even more than on love. Thus, when judging the behavior of the Jewish leaders during the Holocaust she was inspired by this kind of critical patriotism. Adopting an internal group perspective, she wrote: "To a Jew this role of the Jewish leaders in the destruction of their own people is undoubtedly the darkest chapter of the whole dark story."[52] Similarly, in her reply to Scholem she justified her criticism of the Judenrate by admitting that "wrong done by my own people naturally grieves me more than wrong done by other people."[53] In other words, taking one's group affiliation seriously (as Scholem demanded) can lead one to be more critical of (and saddened by) the wrongs conducted by one's own people than judging them from a detached standpoint.[54]

4. *The Kastner and Eichmann Controversies Reconsidered*

Social criticism in the shadow of a transformative political trial may have the advantage of capturing the public's attention through high visibility and dramatic confrontation, but it also suffers from significant disadvantages. Two such impediments have been the focus of our discussion in this chapter. First, how is it possible to develop a counterjudgment to that of a court of law, given the exclusivity and the finality of a court's judgment? And, second, how can one disrupt the "collective identity" categories that are uncritically endorsed by the legal judgment while avoiding the accusation of betraying one's community? A consideration of these questions reveals common features in the strategies of criticism that were used by Alterman in the 1950s and Arendt in the 1960s.

With regard to the first question, both writers criticized the court for transgressing the proper limits of a legal judgment by entering the domains of literature and historiography. The fact that both writers enjoyed considerable reputations in the realms of literature and historiography allowed them to depict their criticism as guarding the borders of proper legal discourse. Alterman exposed the mythical narrative implicit in Judge Halevi's judgment and accused him of producing a psychological novel instead of a proper legal judgment. Likewise, Arendt pointed out the prosecutor's incursions into the field of history, painting the big picture about the Jewish Holocaust instead of concentrating on Eichmann's actions. Moreover, both writers chose to cast their counternarratives in quasi-legal terms, imitating the discourse of a court of law. Alterman delivered his criticism in the form of a crossexamination, appointing himself defense attorney for the silent Judenrat members. Arendt developed what was (wrongly) perceived to be an alternative line of defense for Eichmann by raising questions about the omission of the issue of Jewish cooperation with the Nazis from the trial. Both writers criticized the judgment of the court and sought to supplement it if not to replace it altogether. Alterman gave his criticism a literary form and described in a poem how time in its rage tore apart the court's judgment.[55] Arendt, for her part, endorsed the court's decision but remained critical of its reluctance to admit the central (and justifiable) role that feelings of "vengeance" played in the Eichmann trial.[56] To correct the court's omission of this rationale she offered her own alternative verdict, which stressed the element of retribution.

[J]ust as you supported and carried out a policy of not wanting to share the earth with the Jewish people and the people of a number of other nations . . . we find that no one, that is, no member of the human race, can be expected to want to share the earth with you. This is the reason, and the only reason, you must hang.[57]

In one important respect, however, the controversy diverged from the procedures of a court of law. While an attorney in a courtroom remains a professional whose own character is not the subject of investigation, both Alterman and Arendt were put on the witness stand by their critics and subjected to public scrutiny. Interestingly, in both cases, the technique for discrediting the writers was similar: their current controversial views were contrasted with their previous works. Alterman's current defense of the Judenrate was opposed to his earlier praise for the heroism of the Jewish fighters in works such as *Simchat Aniim*. Likewise, Arendt's harsh condemnation of Jewish leaders' cooperation with the Nazis was compared with her views in *The Origins of Totalitarianism*, where she described the difficulties of resisting a totalitarian state.[58] In both cases, these inconsistencies were attributed to the writer's current political agenda and not to fundamental changes in his or her knowledge and understanding of the Holocaust. Haim Gouri's reports, in contrast, did not encounter such condemnation, despite his criticism of the Yishuv, because he supplied his readers with a language in which they could begin to relate to the Holocaust as something connected to their own world.[59] Instead of placing himself in "competition" with the court, he adopted the more modest course of supplementing and clarifying the proceedings.

The personal attacks against Alterman and Arendt were intended to undermine the writers' credibility. In response, the two writers sought a way to turn a vicious attack into a constructive tool of criticism. They each used the strategy of acting in opposition to their own public image in order to undermine the rigidity of ideological categories such as New Jew, Old Jew, resistance fighter, and Holocaust survivor. They thus exposed the constructed nature of these identity labels and the disciplinary practices that upheld them. The intense debate that greeted their interventions suggests that the purpose of social criticism may be best served not by calm deliberation but rather by the ability of the critic to anger, shock, and challenge the conventional wisdom—in short, by his or her introduction of *agonistic politics* based on conflict and disagreement.[60] This attitude is based on the idea that a democracy can survive only by virtue of the critical intervention of people who are as suspicious as they are combative. Arendt called this attitude "loyal opposition" and saw it as crucial to the development of a healthy democracy in Israel.[61] Both understood that the importance of the transformative trial goes beyond the attribution of individual responsibility, since it provides an occasion for developing a critical perspective on the collective identities advanced by the political authorities and for promoting an ethos of independent thought and action.

The first two major political trials that took place in Israel point to the need to recognize the value of a "competition of stories" and the political implications of the impulse to suppress dissenting narratives. The Kastner affair began as a criminal libel trial directed against the subversive voice of Gruenwald for defaming a public figure. Likewise, the attorney general in the Eichmann trial sought to ensure that internal controversies over the role of the Jewish Councils would not surface in the trial so that the State of Israel's "official story" about the Holocaust would go unchallenged. The fear of the counterstory continued even after the conclusion of the trials. Judge Halevi's condemnation of Kastner for "selling his soul to the Devil" was followed by an appeal to the Supreme Court, where the decision was reversed on most counts. While the appeal was pending, Kastner was assassinated. Significantly, only the rehabilitative judgment of the appellate court was published. The trial court judgment was published only ten years later, accompanied by a note to the reader that later the judgment had been reversed by the Supreme Court.[62] Thus, instead of allowing the two judgments to compete for recognition by the public, the Israeli authorities suppressed the controversy and prevented honest confrontation with the painful issues raised by the Kastner trial. We saw a similar approach in the Eichmann trial, in which the Kastner affair and the issue of Jewish cooperation were avoided. Arendt insisted on discussing these issues because she was convinced that their suppression would impede the development of a democratic political culture in Israel. However, the fate of Arendt's report was similar to that of Halevi's judgment. Her book was not translated into Hebrew until recently, when it sparked a renewed controversy, which I will consider briefly in the next section.[63] In contrast, Jacob Robinson's book, refuting Arendt's arguments, was immediately published in Hebrew.[64] It seems that in both cases the Israeli authorities, when threatened by a counterstory, preferred to silence the voices of opposition instead of encouraging a culture of contestation.

5. In Favor of Agonistic Politics

What, then, is the unique contribution of the social critic to the political trial and in what way can he or she help transform it into a means of developing a liberal-democratic culture? In discussing the first two major political trials in Israel I have stressed the importance of ensuring the possibility of a competition of stories. A competition of stories is generally encouraged by the structure of a trial in the common law tradition, with its emphasis on ensuring the symmetry between the parties and on various procedural rules that enhances the dramaturgical effect of the trial. This competition was apparent in the Kastner trial between the defense team (led by Shmuel Tamir) and the prosecution team (led by Haim Cohn). Nonetheless, this competition took a pathological turn because the formal adversary structure of the trial was used to reinforce the ideological binary discourse about the Holocaust prevailing at the time in Israeli politics. Since it is in the nature of the legal process to create a polar picture of black and white, when the legalistic worldview is imposed on political debates the political culture is threatened. The "legalistic" transformation of the political field forces the public to divide its loyalties in absolute ways between two exclusive options and discourages it from perceiving intermediate possibilities. It is against this background that we can understand the unique contribution of the social critic to the kind of competition of stories that developed in the trials. On the simplest level Arendt and Alterman undermined the polarity of the positions by adding another story, which offered a new perspective on the facts and challenged what was than considered the "commonsense" understanding of events. But this could also have been achieved by a sensitive lawyer or a more perceptive judge.[65] The contribution of social critics does not, however, amount merely to the addition of another narrative or viewpoint. Rather, their narratives undermined the polarity of the discourse by revealing that the two poles were not monolithic but were comprised of a range of views and behavior. Alterman challenged the two-paths conception of heroism and betrayal by pointing out that the Judenrat members were far from being a homogeneous group and had displayed very different kinds of behavior in response to the tragic choices they faced. Likewise, he resisted the tendency to turn the resistance fighters' heroism into an ideological symbol. He instead gave human faces to the symbol, highlighting their dilemmas and doubts about the right response, as well as their decisions, at times, to cooperate with the Judenrate. His poems and essays thus encouraged the public to perceive the prejudices created by the ideological discourse and to realize that one should judge only after listening carefully to each story in its particular context.

Arendt also thought that the main danger that the Eichmann trial posed to Israeli political culture lay in its reinforcement of a binary worldview, only she concentrated on the opposition between holy victims and monstrous perpetrators. This polar picture might have been needed to enable a legal judgment, but it was destructive to the political sphere, especially when the trial itself was an integral part of a political endeavor to reshape the Israeli collective identity and memory. She urged that distinctions should be made within the group of victims, in particular between the leaders and the mass of the population, and criticized the former for their policy of cooperation. She also drew attention to different types of resistance, noting that while an armed revolt had not been a feasible option in most cases civil disobedience or inaction, which did not depend on resources or organization, had been possible (at least in the early stages) as well as "textual resistance" by men and women of letters. She refused to see Eichmann as a monster, beyond human comprehension, because such a view tended to judge him outside the context of the Nazi administration as a whole and encouraged the public to avoid dealing with the larger phenomenon. While Alterman demanded that the public start viewing the Judenrat members as individuals with individual responses to tragic situations, Arendt's intervention was much more painful since she demanded that the Israeli public see Eichmann—the ultimate Other of the Jewish collectivity—as a human being, that is, as not essentially "different." Moreover, she intervened in a trial that also functioned as a collective process of mourning, a process that requires empathizing with the victims and setting aside all criticism and judgmental tendencies toward them. For this reason, I believe that her contribution could only be understood by later generations. By offering a subversive text that undermined any tendency to mythologize she enabled later generations to think about the trial in more nuanced terms.

The implications for Israeli politics of the missed opportunity to promote democracy through the trial are shown by the controversy about Arendt's book that erupted over three decades later. In this respect, it is fascinating to read the responses in the Israeli press to the recent Hebrew translation of her *Eichmann in Jerusalem,* which in many ways replayed the controversy of the 1960s in an entirely new context. Interestingly, this time the controversy took the form of an intergenerational struggle and became interwoven with a very different debate that has emerged in Israel in recent years over the critical interpretations of Israeli history by a new generation of scholars known as the "new historians" (or "post-Zionists").[66] But once again the two sides adopted an ideologically inspired binary approach. Thus, for example, Israel Gutman, a historian of the older generation, cited historical studies about nazism that refuted some of Arendt's arguments, accusing Arendt's supporters of an ahistorical attitude, while ignoring developments in Israeli society and politics that bear out Arendt's perceptive and prophetic analyses of over thirty years ago. On the other side, younger scholars leapt to Arendt's defense, completely unwilling to admit such shortcomings of her report as her blindness to the important role the trial played in bringing the Holocaust to the consciousness of the world and in rehabilitating the image of the survivors.

In conclusion, the main deficiency we identified in the Eichmann trial was its lack of plurality—the suppression of dissident voices in order to achieve a certain educative goal—and it was precisely this feature that Arendt, the public critic, was driven to correct. Such plurality might be limited for good reasons within a trial, but when the whole public debate is reduced to a courtlike format, and when the voices of criticism do not become part of the collective memory of the trial, the development of a democratic culture is damaged. As Arendt herself foresaw, suppressed issues have a way of returning to haunt a society, albeit in different forms. It is therefore not surprising that the controversy has erupted again in a pathological manner, addressed to a different audience but revealing the same unresolved tensions.

The Kufr Qassem Trial

Chapter 7

Between Ordinary Politics and Transformative Politics

As we saw in chapter 5, Adolf Eichmann contended that in all his actions he had merely fulfilled his duty as a soldier to obey superior orders and therefore was legally exculpated. The court rejected this line of defense, relying on the precedent set by the Nuremberg trials that the duty to obey orders cannot be used as a defense against the charge of committing war crimes.[1] However, alongside this famous precedent from international law, the Israeli court also relied on an Israeli precedent that had been determined in *Military Prosecutor v. Major Melinki*, better known as the Kufr Qassem trial.[2]

The Kufr Qassem trial opened on 15 January 1957 in the military district court in Jerusalem. On the bench sat three judges: Col. Benjamin Halevi, Lt. Col. Yitzhak Dibon, and Maj. Yehuda Cohen.[3] The events leading to this extraordinary trial took place on 29 October 1956 on the eve of the Sinai war. A battalion of the Israeli Border Police was ordered to enforce an unusually early curfew that had been imposed on the Arab villages of the so-called little triangle near the border with Jordan. The battalion commander, Maj. Shmuel Melinki, in accordance with an order higher up the hierarchy, instructed his soldiers to kill anyone who remained outside in violation of the curfew, despite the fact that many inhabitants who worked outside their villages would not know about it. In one of the villages, Kufr Qassem, a massacre occurred. Upon their return home, in the hour between 5:00 P.M. and 6:00 P.M., forty-nine villagers, including men, women, elderly people, and children, were killed in cold blood.[4] Many others were wounded. Eleven soldiers of the border police belonging to the unit posted in Kufr Kassem were charged with obeying a murderous order, and Melinki was charged with giving the order that had led to the massacre. Col. Yisaschar Shadmi, the Israeli Defense Forces (IDF) brigade commander with whom the order to shoot anyone caught breaking the curfew had originated, was not among the accused.[5] In his verdict the presiding judge, Benjamin Halevi, found the defendants guilty of murder as a result of obeying a manifestly illegal order. The Kufr Qassem massacre became a symbol of blind obedience to a large extent because of one memorable passage in the decision, which came to be known as the "black flag" test.

> The hallmark of manifest illegality is that it must wave like a black flag over the given order, a warning that says: "forbidden!" Not formal illegality, obscure or partially obscure, not illegality that can be discerned only by legal scholars, is important here, but rather, the clear and obvious violation of law. . . . Illegality that pierces the eye and revolts the heart, if the eye is not blind and the heart is not impenetrable or corrupt—this is the measure of manifest illegality needed to override the soldier's duty to obey and to impose on him criminal liability for his action.[6]

Judge Halevi, who at the time was the president of the district court in Jerusalem, was especially drafted into the army to preside over this trial.[7] As we recall, he was the judge at the Gruenwald trial who had written the controversial sentence that Kastner had "sold his soul to the Devil" by negotiating with Eichmann over the lives of Hungarian Jewry. We also saw that Halevi was later the cause of an unusual amendment to the Nazi and Nazi Collaborators (Punishment) Law, in an attempt by the government to prevent him from presiding over the Eichmann trial as well.[8] However, the thread connecting the three trials ran much deeper than this, for each constitutes an important chapter in the struggle to determine the content of the Israeli collective memory and identity. The Kufr Qassem trial was a key moment in this process, since here for the first time the court was called on to recognize the immanent dangers posed to the young Israeli democracy by the lack of a legal and civilian mechanism that could integrate Arab Israelis into the collective. However, as we shall see, the trial was also a very fragile moment, immediately threatened by an attempt of the Israeli political authorities to reverse its results. In this chapter I examine how the Kufr Qassem trial contributed to opening the possibility of a more inclusive Israeli citizenship and why this opening was so narrow. More specifically, I explore the role played by the testimonies of the Arab victims in the transformation of the Israeli collective identity and ask what kind of political trial it was, what power it had, and what its limits were. My focus is on the transformative aspects of the Kufr Qassem trial. As we shall see, the danger in such a trial is that the transformative rhetoric of the court may remain a dead letter and not be translated into social change. When this happens, even a very harsh verdict can be used by the political authorities to legitimize existing policy without having to undertake any real change.

1.   The Legitimization Effect

The legitimization effect of political trials has become a focal point for legal scholarship since the 1980s. However, twenty years earlier Otto Kirschheimer had already pointed to this effect. He defined political trials as instances in which "court action is called upon to exert influence on the distribution of political power,"[9] arguing that political trials are inevitable not only under totalitarian regimes but also under democratic ones. The novelty of his theory lay in identifying the dual function of political trials: the political repression of an adversary and the legitimization effect on public opinion. The latter can explain why the authorities turn to the court instead of using more direct means of oppression. They seek to benefit from the trial without increasing the risk to their political causes. However, they find themselves in a bind, being obliged to relinquish complete control over the trial, since any interference on their part in order to ensure favorable results would undermine the legitimization effect. Hence the political authorities are induced to guarantee the courts some degree of independence despite the risk involved. It is this dual function of the political trial that creates leeway for the court and the defendant and introduces an element of uncertainty as to the outcome of the trial.

During the 1980s, writers associated with the Critical Legal Studies (CLS) movement took this idea a step further and argued that every trial is a political trial. In their view, the very attempt of liberals to define a special category for political trials works to conceal the politics reflected in "ordinary" trials.[10] Challenging the liberal myth of the separation between law and politics, they examined areas of law that were traditionally considered apolitical, such as private law and low-profile litigation, and exposed the various ways in which the dominant ideology shaped them. An important observation that emerged from these writings is the thesis about the relative autonomy of law. Legal historian Robert Gordon explains that

> since the legal system must at least appear universal, it must operate to some extent independently (or with "relative autonomy," as the saying goes) from concrete economic interests or social classes. And this need for legitimacy is what makes it possible for other classes to use the system against itself, to try to entrap it and force it to make good on its utopian promises. Such promises may therefore become rallying points for organization, so that the state and law become not merely instruments of class domination but "arenas of class struggle."[11]

The relative autonomy thesis goes beyond merely exposing the politics of law to inquire how the legitimization mechanism works to benefit the courts themselves and how the courts can both consistently support the rulers and maintain their image of independence. One observer sharpened the dilemma by formulating it as a paradox: "If courts are autonomous, what ensures that they will support those in power? And if they consistently support the rulers, how do they maintain their own legitimacy?"[12] This is precisely what makes those rare occasions when courts decide to rule against the political authorities—as happened in the Kufr Qassem trial—such interesting cases for studying the legitimization effect.

The scholarship thus provides two main conceptualizations of political trials either as a special category (liberal) or as infiltrating every area of law (CLS). In this chapter I suggest a third way of conceptualizing this, by distinguishing between *ordinary* and *transformative* political trials,[13] in order to clarify the special features of the transformative trial that have not been sufficiently addressed in the existing literature. Transformative court decisions offer legal narratives designed to change the terms of the collective memory and the hegemonic narratives of identity. As such, they perform a special function in a democratic society and should therefore be studied as a separate category. These trials function as junctures in which the imaginary boundaries of the collective identity are exposed through a confrontation with an Other, who is effectively excluded from the society's dominant narrative of membership. If the court responds to such a challenge by developing a new constitutive narrative, the trial can mark a symbolic turning point and can therefore be seen as transformative. Of course, the court can refuse to do so and instead undertake to enhance the dominant understanding of who is included in the collective. Nonetheless, many transformative decisions are celebrated as manifestations of the court's independence and the strength of the democratic system, even though their actual effect remains symbolic and is not accompanied by any material changes.[14] This should come as no surprise, given the legitimization mechanism inherent in political trials. Toward the end of this chapter I shall consider factors that determine whether a transformative court decision will have a lasting material effect or merely remain a symbolic statement.

The high-profile Kufr Qassem trial took place in the context of numerous low-profile trials in the 1950s known as the Arab infiltrators' trials. I shall compare the Kufr Qassem trial with one such low-profile case—the Hassin trial.[15] Although I view them both as political trials their politics were very different: the Kufr Qassem decision was transformative in its attempt to redefine the boundaries of the Israeli collective identity by describing the atrocities committed by Israeli soldiers against innocent Arab citizens, even though it ultimately failed to bring about a real transformation in the relationship between Arabs and Jews in Israel. The Hassin judgment, on the other hand, was conservative, perpetuating the dominant suspicious attitude toward the Arab population in Israel.

2. Infiltrators' Trials during the 1950s

On the eve of the 1948 war the population in Mandatory Palestine consisted of 1,300,000 Arabs and 670,000 Jews. During the war the proportions between the populations were inverted and the Arabs became a minority in the State of Israel.[16] The war redrew the territorial borders of the young state, but the newly established borders remained unstable, especially during the 1950s, and were defined mostly by their violation from both sides. "Infiltration" was used as a generic name covering various categories of attempts by Palestinian refugees to enter Israel illegally during 1949–56. The majority of these attempts were socially and economically rather then politically motivated, but they sometimes involved attacks on Jews that resulted in bodily injuries and even deaths.[17] Those who committed the more organized terrorist attacks were called *Fedayeen*.[18] In order to stop the infiltrators the authorities adopted several means, including the establishment of the Border Police, which applied a tough policy of "free shooting" against suspects and a routine of searches and deportations of infiltrators who were caught. This activity was accompanied by retaliatory military raids across the borders by special units of the IDF.[19]

The infiltrators were perceived by the Israeli government as threatening the stability of the borders of the newborn state, as many of them wanted to resettle in the villages they had left during the war. The issue arrived on the doorstep of the Supreme Court in several instances when infiltrators who had been caught petitioned the court to forbid their deportation and instruct the authorities to issue them Israeli identity cards. The court reacted by creating new legal classifications that simplified the complex reality by consolidating the various subgroups under a unified image of the infiltrator as terrorist.[20] Most petitions were decided according to legal classification into two distinct categories on the basis of the precedent established in the *Hassin* case which I discuss in the next section: deportation by force and emigration of one's own free will. Only those petitioners whose departure from the country in 1948 could be defined as "forced deportation" were entitled to the court's intervention on their behalf. The majority of the petitions were classified as free will emigration and rejected by the court. This group included people who had fled in fear of war, students and workers who had left for study or work before or during the war, former fighters who had escaped after the defeat, and many others. In other words, narrowing the category of forced deportation and expanding the category of voluntary emigration determined the results of most petitions in favor of the government.[21] Those rare cases in which the court intervened and changed the decision of the government rested on firm legal grounds and therefore had the additional effect of strengthening the independent image of the Supreme Court, thus legitimizing the majority of rejected petitions as apolitical decisions.[22]

Muhammad Ali Hassin v. Minister of Interior

In the case I consider here several petitioners, inhabitants of Majd-El-Kurum, an Arab village in northern Israel, petitioned the Supreme Court in July 1951 for a restraining order against their deportation by the minister of interior. The petitioners claimed that they had left their village after an act of retaliation committed by an IDF unit subsequent to the conquest of their village by the Israeli army on 30 October 1949.[23] Later they had reentered Israel illegally, were caught by the Border Police, and, under threat of deportation, petitioned the court. The Israeli Supreme Court had to decide between two opposing factual versions, that of the army and that of the petitioners. The petitioners claimed that several days after the surrender of the village the IDF had entered it, rounded up the inhabitants, shot and killed several of them, and demolished several houses. As a consequence they had fled the country to Lebanon and subsequently reentered Israel illegally. The army claimed that the petitioners had not been in their village on the day of the conquest and denied that any act of retaliation had been committed by the IDF in Majd-El-Kurum.

The *Hassin* trial occurred at a time when the Supreme Court of Israel had existed only for three years and touched on a very sensitive issue with significant demographic implications. Nevertheless, the court demonstrated a certain degree of independence. It refused to attribute much reliability to the army's version of the events since it was based on anonymous sources and attributed a high degree of credibility to the testimony of the *mukhtar* (village leader), accepting his version as true. At the end of the day, the petitioners' version of the facts of the matter was preferred, though the court played down its significance by describing what had happened as "an ordinary act of retaliation."[24] Historian Benny Morris, however, concludes that a massacre did indeed take place, in which a few unarmed people were killed and as a result dozens of families had left for Lebanon.[25] As we shall see, the different names given to the same event turned out to be crucial.

Contrary to what we might have expected, the court's acceptance of the petitioners' version of the events did not determine the outcome of the case.[26] In order to decide the legal issues, the court drew a distinction between forcible expulsion from Israel during the war and voluntary departure from the country and determined that only the former would justify the intervention of the Supreme Court in favor of petitioners. Since in the *Hassin* case no one argued that there had been forced deportation from the village, but only that people had left as a consequence of the "act of retaliation," the court rejected the petition and refused to issue a restraining order. With this double move—accepting the factual basis of the petition while rejecting it on the merits—the court was able to retain its image of independence vis-à-vis the political and military authorities and at the same time legitimize their policy by creating a legal classification on the basis of which most future petitions would be rejected.[27]

From a legal perspective, the court could have ended its opinion at this point, having rejected the petitioners' claim on the basis of a legal classification. However, in an exceptional move Justice Shneur Z. Cheshin, speaking on behalf of the court, added a moral justification to the legal one in the form of a short narrative that reveals the ideology that shaped the judgment, an ideology that is not apparent until this part of the decision.

> During days of danger to the state, when it was surrounded by hostile nations that had fought it relentlessly and viciously and were still harassing it and determined to swallow it alive—in those chaotic days, people desert the country and move over to the enemy camp. Later they return, claiming to be its loyal citizens, and have the presumption to demand equal rights with all its other citizens."
>
> This court asserts that a man who journeys of his own accord, and without permit, from the defense lines of the state to the offense lines of the enemy, does not deserve this Court's help and assistance in the struggle that the army authorities are waging against him and his like in defense of the state and its citizens.[28]

Until this point the court has been satisfied with a formal legal explanation for rejecting the petition, without any moralizing, but here the court suddenly resorts to a rhetoric of "blaming the victims" for their misfortune. They are described as abandoning their country in a time of hardship, joining the enemy camp, and later pretending to be its loyal citizens, as having the audacity to claim their rights in the Supreme Court. At first glance, this type of narrative seems odd. After all, even if the petitioners were not entitled to a remedy they could not be equated with those who "chose" to join the enemy. To describe the petitioners as people who had "abandoned" the country or "journeyed" of their own free will is plausible only if we ignore the moral meaning of the act of "retaliation" that preceded their departure. Thus, the court's short narrative fulfills an important function: to retell the events so that Arab Israelis will fall neatly into one of two categories: loyal citizens or enemies. As a consequence, the petitioners who entered the court as infiltrators leave it as impostors, as people who pretend to be loyal citizens but are revealed as belonging to the enemy. This short legal narrative leaves no place for fuzzy categories, for the ambivalent feelings the Arab Israelis might have about the new state, or for their complex situation within Israel. In other words, the legal narrative draws the boundaries of the Israeli collective, placing the infiltrators (except those who had been forcibly deported) firmly behind enemy lines. The *Hassin* decision thus provided the legal justification for the policy of preventing most refugees from reentering Israel.[29] Hence it cannot be considered transformative in our terms since its rhetoric was meant to reinforce the prevailing understanding in Israel that the Arabs who had fled the country had preferred to join the enemy and therefore were responsible for their own fate.[30]

3. The Kufr Qassem Decision as a Border Case

The Majd-El-Kurum incident discussed in the *Hassin* judgment attracted little attention at the time and did not become part of Israeli collective memory. The Kufr Qassem massacre, however, resulted in a prominent trial and entered the Israeli collective memory as a symbol of the limits of military obedience. If you were to stop an Israeli on the street and ask him or her about that event, you are likely to be given the very short answer that it was a massacre of several dozens of Israeli-Arab citizens who were returning home from work, in violation of a curfew about which they had not received prior warning. You might also be told that the murder of the Arab citizens constituted a manifestly illegal order, an order described by the court as a black flag. More detailed questions such as why the curfew was imposed on the village in the first place or in what way the people were killed (all together, in small groups, by a firing squad?) are not likely to receive a coherent response. What can these points of collective amnesia teach us about the Israeli perception of the Kufr Qassem massacre and in what way did the trial contribute to its constructed memory?

The legal scholarship on the subject has mainly dealt with the question of the duty to obey a superior's order, thus ignoring almost completely the long narrative presented by the presiding judge, Benjamin Halevi, which, I believe, contains the key to understanding the novelty in the court's decision.[31] This narrative constitutes the first attempt by an Israeli court to confront an atrocity committed by Israeli soldiers and to comprehend the suffering it caused the Arab victims. For this purpose, the judge had to overcome the legal impulse to see the events through the narrow prism of formal legal categories, which often obscured the problematic reality that had been the fertile ground for this massacre.[32] Instead, the court had to learn to listen to the testimonies of the Arab victims who for the first time were given a public forum on which to recount their traumatic experience. Through this narrative, I shall explore the ways in which the court attempted to redraw the boundaries of Israeli collective identity to include the Arab citizens of Israel.

Although the Declaration of Independence defines Israel as a Jewish state committed to respecting the equal rights of its citizens, the two paragraphs that refer to the status of the Arabs as equal citizens reveal the tension between granting universal citizenship and acknowledging the complex status of Arabs in the Jewish state[33]

> The State of Israel will be open to Jewish immigration and for the Ingathering of the Exiles; it will foster the development of the country for the benefit of all its inhabitants; it will be based on the principles of liberty, justice and peace as conceived by the prophets of Israel; it will ensure complete equality of social and political rights to all its inhabitants irrespective of religion, race or sex; it will guarantee freedom of religion, conscience, language, education, and culture. It will safeguard the Holy Places of all religions; and it will be faithful to the principles of the Charter of the United Nations.
>
> We Appeal—in the very midst of the onslaught launched against us now for months—to the Arab inhabitants of the State of Israel to preserve the peace and participate in the development of the State on the basis of full and equal citizenship and due representation in all its provisional and permanent institutions.

Notwithstanding this promise of equality, the legal status of the Arabs in Israel remained problematic. They became citizens, but many of them had to fulfill certain conditions before that status was conferred on them.[34] Although their right to vote and to be elected to the Knesset was guaranteed, until 1966 they lived under military rule, which undermined such basic civil rights as the freedom of movement and expression.[35] The Kufr Qassem massacre prompted the court to address some of these contradictions.

The massacre took place in a border zone, a place of political ambiguity. The Arab villages of the so-called little triangle, which was

located close to the Israeli-Jordanian border, lived under a nightly curfew that usually began at nine in the evening. On the day of the massacre, the curfew had been imposed earlier in the evening, a few hours
before the IDF offensive in the Sinai began.[36] In the period preceding
the offensive, Israel had tried to create a misleading impression of its
intentions by concentrating forces along its borders with Jordan. This
ambiguity penetrated the army forces, and on 29 October 1956 it was
unclear to the lower ranks whether there was a plan to open a front
with the Jordanians as well. The aim of the unusually early curfew on
that day was not clear either. Two explanations were given in the trial:
the need to protect those villages from accidentally being attacked by
the army forces and the fear that in case of war the Arab population,
which ever since the 1948 war had been suspected of being a "fifth column," would cooperate with the enemy.[37] A unit of the Border Police
that was annexed for the duration of the war to the army was charged
with keeping the curfew. The Border Police, which had been established to fight the wave of infiltrators, was trained to identify Arab
civilians as potential enemies.[38]

The frontier is characterized by ambiguous identities. As we have
seen in the *Hassin* case, this ambiguity requires the court to draw clear
lines, but it also opens up a space for judicial discretion over how and
where to draw the line of permissible action. The court could have tried
to locate the Kufr Qassem massacre in the context of the Sinai war, the
struggle against the infiltrators, the military rule and to see all these factors as "mitigating circumstances." After all, there had been previous
cases of alleged massacres committed by Israeli units during the 1948
war, as in the village of Deir Yassin near Jerusalem, and later during an
act of retaliation across the Jordanian border in Kibye in 1953, which
had never reached the courts because of the implicit understanding
that such military actions fell outside their jurisdiction.[39] This time the
political authorities brought the case to court (albeit after public pressure), and the court, refusing to view the events in Kufr Qassem as
related to the Sinai war, applied the ordinary norms of criminal and
administrative law. Indeed, it is my contention that it was the legal narrative advanced by Judge Halevi that was largely responsible for the
fact that the Kufr Qassem massacre is remembered as a massacre of
peaceful Arab citizens who were shot through no fault of their own. In
contrast to the *Hassin* narrative, which enhanced the prevailing suspicious attitude toward Arab Israelis, the Kufr Qassem narrative endeav-

ored to change these beliefs. In particular it sought to transform the perception that they were a fifth column or "semi-enemies" into their recognition as full-fledged citizens.[40]

4. Obstacles on the Way to Court

It was no simple task to make the Kufr Qassem massacre known. Not only were the Arab villages under curfew and isolated from the Jewish population by military rule, but at that time the Arab population had little access to the Israeli media. The dead were buried in a mass grave by the army, and the injured were taken to hospital and placed under police guard. The military forces first tried to cover up the incident. But when news of the massacre reached Prime Minister and Minister of Defense Ben-Gurion, he ordered an internal inquiry. Censorship kept the affair out of the newspapers, but a group of Israeli intellectuals, both Arabs and Jews, and a Communist party member of the Knesset, Tawfiq Tubi, found ways to publicize the incident.[41] On 12 December 1956 Ben-Gurion addressed the Knesset, condemning the massacre as a "dreadful atrocity," and the ban on publication was lifted. The prime minister described the various actions he was taking to investigate the affair and bring the guilty to justice and expressed his repulsion at the atrocity, which undermined the very foundations of human morality. He then went on to say that "The command not to murder is the ultimate command given us on Mount Sinai. And there is no people in the world that respects human life more than the Jewish people, without distinction of sex, race, religion and nationality."[42] Even after the decision to conduct a trial was made, publicity was not guaranteed, as the army demanded that the sessions be conducted behind closed doors. Eventually a compromise was reached, and the court retained the discretion to decide which sessions would be closed for security reasons. This promised that most of the trial (about two-thirds of its sessions) would be open to the public. Thus, since the Israeli authorities did not have to use direct censorship, the legitimacy of the trial was further enhanced.[43]

5. Obstacles in the Court

The Kufr Qassem trial was the first time that Arab victims of Israeli army brutality were invited to give testimony in a court of law, and the court made every effort to ensure that this would be a respectable forum, treated them with empathy, and attributed very high credibility to their testimonies. Judge Halevi often asked the Arab survivors-witnesses about their injuries and their medical and mental condition. This attitude is also apparent in his judgment.

> The survivors who took the stand, some of them wounded, invalids or bereaved due to the discussed events, gave a detailed and impressive testimony, each witness about the particular events he had seen, and all the parts came together to constitute one big devastating picture of a continuous and systematic massacre. The honorable defense counsels . . . did their best to fulfill their professional duty in a murder trial and harshly cross-examined each and every eyewitness, but for the most part their attempt failed.[44]

Nonetheless, the stage was not at all symmetrical. On one side stood the Arab victims and eyewitnesses, alone in the witness box, testifying in simple Arabic or broken Hebrew, injured and traumatized by the events. Since this was a military criminal trial the victims were not represented by their own lawyers but by the military prosecutor, who had a separate agenda. The prosecutor wanted to narrow down the charge to the Border Police unit involved and to absolve the rest of the army in order to protect the ethos of "purity of arms."[45] Thus, in his opening statement the prosecutor commented that "the Army and the Border Police that guard the borders without fear or rest, had no part [in the massacre]."[46] This focus contradicted the intent of those who had exposed the affair, hoping that the trial would include the IDF commander with whom the order had originated and would investigate the broad issue of military forces' attitude toward Arab Israelis. In the dock stood the eleven defendants as a unified group, wearing their uniforms, enjoying the support of most of the public and the Hebrew press, and represented by a whole battery of lawyers. This structure tended to create a symbolic reenactment of the situation in which the massacre had taken place: the Arab survivors stood isolated, surrounded by people in uniform, who attacked them, this time verbally. This was not an empowering reenactment. Even though the Arab witnesses were treated with respect and empathy by the court, they underwent harsh cross-examinations by the defense attorneys who accused them of running away and thus bringing the shooting upon themselves (a contention that the court rejected as a blatant lie in its judgment).[47] The defense relied on the assumption that if it could prove that the victims had run away before the order to fire was given, thus by implication arousing the soldiers' suspicions, then the killing could be justified as a reasonable response to the violation of the curfew. For this reason the defense attorneys concentrated their interrogations on whether the victims had been afraid of the soldiers, which could explain their attempts to run away. This line of investigation created a surreal situation in which the Arab victims of the massacre repeatedly had to testify about their great trust in the Israeli army and their complete lack of fear. Thus, for example, Ismail Aqeb Badir answered the defense lawyer's accusation that he had been afraid by saying: "I was not afraid, what had I to be afraid of? I saw soldiers in front of me." Sallah Halil Issa also testified: "I was not afraid. We were used to it, a policeman, or the military police comes and asks for permits. . . . I did not believe. There is an Arabic saying that a man who is afraid should go to the police or to the authorities, and there he will not be frightened anymore."[48] During one of these cross-examinations, a survivor of the massacre, Abdallah Samir Badir, when asked why he had not escaped or shouted that he was from Kufr Qassem, burst out angrily: "What? Don't they know? Are we from Germany? Where can we be from?"[49]

In considering the limitations of the courtroom as a consciousness-transforming vehicle, it is interesting to compare the Kufr Qassem trial with the very unique forum of the Eichmann trial. I do not suggest, of course, a comparison between the Holocaust as a historical event and the limited and contained massacre of Kufr Qassem. My focus is not the historical similarities between the events but rather the structural dissimilarities of the forum provided by a court in two dramatic trials that had educational purposes beyond the legal ones. As we have seen in chapter 4, the Israeli prosecution had placed the victims' stories at the center of the Eichmann trial in order to use it as an educational and consciousness-raising event. The aim of the survivors' testimonies was not only (or mainly) to prove Eichmann's guilt but to tell the story of the Jewish Holocaust on a public stage for the first time. In contrast, the prosecution in Kufr Qassem perceived its role more traditionally and therefore treated the testimonies of survivors primarily as a means of proving the guilt of the defendants and only incidentally as a means of describing the massacre to the Israeli public. Indeed both the prosecution and the defense in the Eichmann trial allowed the witnesses to tell their stories with very few interruptions, while in Kufr Qassem they were expected to answer very focused questions.[50] These structural differences also had an important effect on the ability of witnesses in the two trials to tell their traumatic stories. In the Eichmann trial the survivors who testified were mostly Israeli Jews, represented by an Israeli prosecutor and testifying before Israeli judges, in a trial that was conducted in Hebrew. In Kufr Qassem, the witnesses were Arab survivors, testifying in a military court and represented by an Israeli military prosecutor in a trial conducted in Hebrew. The court allowed the witnesses to testify on request in Arabic and supplied translators. Moreover, one of the judges, Yehuda Cohen, who was fluent in Arabic, often intervened in the translation to make it more accurate.[51] Nevertheless, they had to testify before judges wearing army uniforms and against defendants who were all soldiers in uniform. They found it difficult to confront Israeli soldiers and were also reluctant to blame them in court.[52] Thus, while in the Eichmann trial it was the defendant and his lawyer, Robert Servatius, who were perceived as the Other in Israeli society (that is, "classical political trial"), in the Kufr Qassem trial, conducted in an Israeli military court, it was the Arab witnesses who were perceived by the Israeli public as the Other.[53]

6.   The Language of Dehumanization

Language played a central role in the Kufr Qassem trial in exposing the dehumanization of the Arab victims by Israeli soldiers. The prosecution tried to prove the guilt of the defendants through their choice of words, in particular the command *tiktzor!* (harvest), which was used as an order to open fire and indicated that the shooting was not accidental but premeditated. For this purpose it brought witnesses, many of whom spoke broken Hebrew, to testify about the last word they had heard before the soldiers opened fire on them. Their cross-examination often turned into a grotesque "Hebrew lesson." In order to prove that the shooting had occurred as a result of the attempt of the Arab victims to run away from the soldiers, it became crucial to prove that the word *tiktzor* had not been used by the soldiers. By showing that the Arab witnesses did not understand the meaning of *tiktzor*, the defense tried to undermine their credibility and suggest that the word had probably been "planted" in them by Arab Knesset member Tuwfiq Tubi, who had come to the village to question them after the massacre.[54] Thus, for example, Judge Halevi tried to clarify this contention by questioning the witness Ismail A'qb Badir.

Q: Do you know the meaning of *liktzor*, "to harvest"?

A: I don't know.

Q [*turning to the translator*]: Translate for the witness the meaning of the word *liktzor*: "to harvest, to cut the corn, etc."

(The translator translates the meaning of the word *liktzor*)

A: "Short, shorten, to harvest." [In Hebrew the verb *harvest* comes from the same root as *shorten*.]

Q: Did you ever ask what the meaning of the word *liktzor* is?

A: No.

Q: This was the last word you heard before the soldiers opened fire, weren't you curious afterward to understand this word?

A: Now I know what *liktzor* is.

Q: Wasn't it important for you to know it before?

A: You know I went straight from there to the hospital, I didn't walk around the village, I suffered from pains all the time, and only two weeks ago I returned home, and I still have constant pain.

Q: Until now what did you think the meaning of the word was approximately? How did you guess?

A: I thought *tiktzor* means "shoot," and he shot us, so that is what *tiktzor* means. He did not use the word as a metaphor. He said *tiktzor* and then came the shootings.[55]

Another grotesque moment occurred in the cross-examination of Asad Salim Issa by the attorney Shweig, when the witness was asked to decline the verb in the masculine and feminine singular and plural and in the different tenses. The frustrated witness asked the lawyer "are you giving me a test in Hebrew?"[56] Even if unintended, the effect was to reenact the differential treatment given to Arabs in the law of citizenship, which stipulated that they, unlike Jewish immigrants, were expected to prove their knowledge of Hebrew as a condition for citizenship.[57] Moreover, in this theater of the absurd it was the Arab witnesses who were expected to explain to the court the soldiers' perverted use of the Hebrew language instead of the soldiers being examined about their own dehumanizing language.[58] The acclaimed Palestinian poet Mahmoud Darwish captured the horrific gap that opened up during the trial between the ordinary use of language (harvesting the fields, nature, harmony) and its corrupt and dehumanizing use by the soldiers

> Kufr Qassem
> A village dreaming about wheat and violets
> And the wedding of handsome boys
> Cut them down
> Cut down
> . . .
> . . .
> They were harvested
> . . .
> Ah, ears of corn in the midst of the fields,
> Singing to you shall say
> I wish I knew the secret of the tree
> I wish I had buried all the dead words
> I wish I had the strength of the graves' silence
> Woe to the hand that plays music,
> Woe to the shame, fifty strings.
> I wish I had written my story with a scythe.[59]

In a surprising reversal of the general trend in the trial the Israeli soldiers were questioned about their own understanding of the Arabic expression "Allah yerahmo" (God have mercy on them), which was allegedly used by Colonel Shadmi to indicate that those who violated the curfew would be shot.[60] It was a particularly cynical way of using the Arabic language to bring about the death of innocent Arab civilians. It revealed that in the army, learning the language of the Arab/Other (which often became army slang) did not create new channels of communication but channels of violence and degradation.[61]

Judge Halevi sought to show the connection between the commanders' choice of language and the soldiers' deficient moral judgment. He saw the source of evil in the priority given to the instrumental rationality of means and ends, as reflected in the soldiers' language, to the exclusion of all moral considerations. Within this distorted logic, the most "efficient" way of keeping the curfew was to rely on the extreme method of killing anyone caught outside the home. The soldiers described the killing as a "task" to be completed and as an "efficient method" of achieving the goal of keeping the curfew, a neutral language devoid of the moral significance of such actions. Judge Halevi remarked that "these orders stated that for the 'task' of keeping the curfew a single 'method' is to be employed: shoot in order to kill anyone found outside home." He added cynically: "It can't be denied that this too is a 'method'—although an inhuman and illegal method—of accomplishing the task. Indeed, if anyone found outside home is shot and killed, the curfew will be strictly kept and the task will be fully and radically accomplished: a total curfew will prevail in the villages, without leaving a single living soul outside."[62]

The judge went on to criticize Major Melinki's distorted interpretation of the concept of murder, according to which only killing those who stayed at home was to be regarded as murder, while killing those who were caught outside (including women, children, and people who were on their way home not even aware of the curfew) should be interpreted as obeying an order, maintaining discipline, and a necessary evil.[63] Halevi remarked that "It was Melinki's order that created the *arbitrary difference* between the murder of people at home and the allegedly legal killing of all those outside home, a false theory which was given extreme expression in Gabriel Dahan's order to his soldiers,[64] prevented them from distinguishing right from wrong, and stiffened their hearts so that they could commit abominable murder, on the pretext of keeping 'law and order.'"[65]

7. Language and Morality

Judge Halevi, in undertaking to write a consciousness-transforming judgment, faced a difficult task. The horrifying testimonies had probably convinced him that Israeli society was in need of a bitter medicine. In order to begin to change the Israeli perception of the massacre it was not enough to recount its horrific details publicly or to expose the corruption of language as it was revealed in court. The judgment also had to restore language to its human task of communication and respect for other human beings.

As noted above, during the 1950s the main obstacle to developing an Israeli civil discourse inclusive of Arab citizens was the phenomenon of infiltrators, which constantly undermined the stability of Israel's borders. There were reports of about a thousand incidents of infiltration a month, and although only a small percentage of them were terrorist attacks they created a constant fear among the Jewish inhabitants. This contributed to the general feeling shared by Jews and Arabs that the 1948 war was not the last round of violence and that a second decisive round was to be expected.[66] Indeed, some scholars believe that the Sinai war of 1956 was this second round and that in demonstrating the superiority of Israeli military power it constituted a turning point in the reconciliation of Arab Israelis to the borders of Israel.[67] It might be that the sense of security brought about by the Sinai war also contributed to Halevi's decision to condemn the Kufr Qassem massacre in very strong words and to insist on a change of attitude toward Arab Israelis. In any case, the decision reveals how much the hybrid category of "the infiltrator" had blurred the line between enemy and citizen and prepared the ground for the massacre. Here we can discern an unexpected link between the infiltrators' petitions to the High Court in the early 1950s and the Kufr Qassem decision.[68] In their testimonies the defendants cited the difficulty of distinguishing between an Arab citizen and an Arab infiltrator as an excuse for their willingness to shoot civilians returning from work. Major Melinki testified that he had conveyed to Colonel Shadmi that he was "ready to kill a Fedayeen" but had inquired "what about the citizen returning to his village without knowing about the curfew?" Colonel Shadmi's response has become part of Israeli collective memory ever since the trial: "*I don't want any sentiments, I don't want any arrests, Allah yerahmo.*"[69] The moral twilight became apparent when in his cross-examination Melinki tried to justify the murder of women by invoking the fear of infiltrators: "And if I see someone returning to the village, who says he is not a fedayeen, who can guarantee that every woman is really a woman, and that every woman with a belly is pregnant and not a fedayeen who is carrying something?"[70] Judge Halevi was well aware that Dahan (the commander of the unit) was at the time mainly occupied with fighting infiltrators.[71] The fact that the defense repeatedly resorted to this type of explanation must have convinced the judge that he must clearly draw the boundaries of Israeli citizenship so as to include Arab Israelis. Accordingly, the rhetoric of the judgment reflected an unusual awareness of the deep connection between language and citizenship. Throughout the judgment Halevi meticulously "translated" all references to "Arabs" in the quotations from the soldier's affidavits into "Arab citizens."[72] At one point he drew attention to the moral implications of using the word "Arab": "In these three confessions they [the soldiers] refer simply to Arabs, without explaining that most victims were women; none of the defendants was interested in emphasizing this shameful and aggravating circumstance."[73]

In addition to changing the terms of the debate (from Arabs to Arab citizens), the judge wrote a narrative that gave the victims a name and a story.[74] Instead of the traditional method of progressing rapidly to the legal issues, Halevi adopted a rhetorical strategy of delay, describing the massacre in great detail and at great length (83 out of 132 pages). His narrative broke down a massacre that lasted about an hour into small episodes, which were described minutely in chronological order. The plot advanced from the random shooting at vehicles to the removal of the victims from the vehicles, the act of lining them up and executing them by firing squad, and finally the individual shooting of the injured in order to "assure" that they were dead.[75] This description created a sense of horror that intensified as the events unfolded. Moreover, at the end of each shooting episode the judge listed the names of the victims killed, one after the other, as if the judgment should also serve as a memorial. The judge gave the dry factual description a human face by inserting within every shooting episode brief exchanges that took place between victim and perpetrator. For example: "Ismail, who saw nearby the bodies of those who had been killed in the previous incident, and could already sense the murderous intention of Dahan and his soldiers, approached Dahan saying, "*dehilkum* [the Arabic equivalent of 'come on'], why do you want to shoot us?" Dahan answered: 'shut up!' and gave the order to fire and shot the three with the Uzi in his hand."[76] The judge contrasted the hair-raising descriptions of the survivors with the way in which the defendants chose to describe the events in their own statements, demonstrating how language itself had become part of the dehumanizing process that had led to the killing. Thus, for example, he quotes from the statement of one of the soldiers as follows.

> Later . . . came a truck with about 7–8 Arabs on it. I stopped it in order to get them into the village. . . . I told them "follow me" but they began to run, I opened fire and killed them. After that came another car, with about 7–8 Arabs, and it was the same again. After that came a horse and wagon with 5 Arabs in it, and the same happened.[77]

The judge rejected the soldiers' contention that the victims had attempted to run away as a blatant lie. Instead he pointed to the routine explanation that the soldiers provided, "and the same happened," as throwing light on the way in which human beings could be reduced to statistical numbers and murdered in cold blood (Melinki reported "4 down," "15 down," and "many down").[78]

As this was the first time that soldiers from the Israeli army had been put on trial for obeying an illegal order that had resulted in a massacre of Arab civilians, the Kufr Qassem trial marked the first attempt to set limits on the soldiers' hitherto unbounded duty to obey orders.[79] For this purpose, the court was faced with the challenge of integrating the victimization of Arab Israelis by Israeli soldiers into the Israeli collective memory. It was a moment of recognition of the immanent dangers of the abuse of power by Israeli security forces. Legal historian Kim Lane Scheppele explains that many societies tell themselves such "narratives of horror" in order to refrain from taking such a route in the future. These narratives can often be found in constitutive documents in societies in transition from a military or authoritative regime to a democratic one.[80] As we have seen, this moment of recognition was undermined later, in the Eichmann trial, when the court referred to the mufti of Jerusalem as having supported the Nazis, thus strengthening the perception of the Palestinians as (potential) victimizers of the Jews in Israel.

Halevi's narrative was constructed so as to change the attitude toward Arab Israelis. He rejected the army's perception of them as potential enemies and treated them as equal citizens who enjoyed the equal protection of the law. For this purpose the judgment had to redefine the boundaries of legitimate army actions. Halevi squarely rejected the defense's attempt to apply the laws of war to the situation and insisted on judging the events as falling under the jurisdiction of the norms of criminal and administrative law. To emphasize this position he repeated the word *law* over and over again, as if to perform rhetorically the moment of imposing the rule of law.

> No one, not even a policeman or a soldier, is entitled to kill, or to order to kill a human being, except *in the exceptional cases defined by law* . . . [for] not a single *law* in the world permits killing "curfew breakers" just like that, not to mention people on their way back [home] who find themselves under curfew with no intention of breaking it. *The Law* permits those who are keeping a curfew imposed by *law* to use the necessary amount of power to prevent the breaking of the *law*, that is—the breaking of a *legal* curfew.[81]

Another theme that arose from the long and carefully constructed narrative was the insistence that security needs could be reconciled with the rule of law and that both were indispensable for a democratic society. This was no easy task because of the common belief that the functioning of the army depended on strict hierarchy and discipline, which would be undermined by any attempt by the court to place limits on the duty to obey orders. The judgment therefore sought to stress the horrific results of blind obedience. In particular, it showed how the vague words of a high officer ("Allah yerahmo") were transmitted down the line of command and transformed on the way into a detailed order to systematically kill innocent civilians.

8. *Bridging the Gap between Past and Future*

The judge had to walk the thin line between setting a limit on the duty to obey and explaining why his decision did not undermine the whole logic of army discipline. Halevi's solution was to avoid highly technical legal doctrine and appeal to fundamental, even intuitive, moral sentiments. Against the inhuman order of Colonel Shadmi to kill "without sentiments" the judge posited the "human heart" as the moral guide that could tell the soldier where to draw the line beyond which obedience should not be given absolute priority.[82] In order to absolve Melinki, the defense cited the fact that in seven of the eight villages of the little triangle soldiers who had received Melinki's order had found ways of preventing a massacre. It claimed that it was these soldiers who had understood his order in the spirit in which it was given. Judge Halevi not only rejected this claim but saw the behavior of the other soldiers as actually aggravating the defendants' compliance with an immoral order. His narrative stressed the important role that moral sentiments and conscience played in guiding the soldiers' discretion.[83] The judge quoted at length from the testimony of soldiers who had disobeyed the order in an effort to understand their motives: "When we received the order in the room, it seemed logical, but when we were out there it was not easy at all. . . . When I saw it with *my eyes*, to see such a thing with *your own eyes*—maybe I am *sentimental*, I don't know, but it was too hard for me to do."[84] Halevi also quoted at length from the testimony of a soldier, explaining in detail the doubts that had led him to disobey the order twice: "This honest testimony shows that his [the soldier's] decision to allow the boy and the old man to live were not the result of using ordinary discretion in obeying an order, but the result of *inner restraints and human emotions in his heart* that clashed with the order of the Major to kill anyone found outside his home" (emphasis added). These quotations are echoed in Halevi's black flag paragraph: "Illegality that pierces the eye and revolts the heart, if the eye is not blind and the heart is not impenetrable or corrupt." They serve as the basis for his distinction between an "illegal order" that must be obeyed and a "manifestly illegal order" that should be disobeyed.[85]

Halevi's narrative depicts the soldiers' conduct in black and white, as in a morality play. The figure of the heartless soldier who blindly obeys a cruel and inhuman order (Melinki, Dahan, Ofer) is opposed to the figure of the good soldier who questions the order, and then finds ways to disobey it. His moralistic narrative was criticized by the dissenting judge, who offered an alternative depiction of the events in which contingent circumstances in each of the villages played a central role in determining who would comply with the order and who would not.[86] But it was precisely Halevi's willful blindness to historical contingencies and his tendency to portray figures larger than life, the same approach as in his famous Kastner decision, where he had portrayed Dr. Kastner as a modern Faust, that helped him create a consciousness-transforming narrative. He instrumentalized the testimonies given in the court in order to construct a didactic narrative with a straightforward moral. The court decision can be seen as symbolizing an imaginative threshold: the Arabs entered the court as suspects (of being infiltrators, a fifth column) and left it as full-fledged citizens of the State of Israel. The army entered the court with unbounded powers (security considerations, emergency rule) and left it subjected to and limited by the rule of law. Rhetorically the decision attempted to transform the terms of public discourse from an ethnic categorization of Jews and Arabs into a civic categorization of Israeli and non-Israeli citizens.

In addition to its ordinary task of determining guilt, the judgment thus fulfilled the educative function of transforming the military discourse of security risks that knows no limits into a civil discourse that is well defined under the law. This might also explain the extraordinary decision to publish the decision in the civil law annals of court decisions, which stood in sharp contrast to the decision not to publish (in either military or civil law annals) the later decision given in Colonel Shadmi's trial, in which the court exonerated him from any responsibility for the massacre, finding him accountable only for exceeding his authority in giving the curfew order.[87] In terms of the "legitimization effect," the publication of the Kufr Qassem decision presented Israeli democracy in a positive light—as a country in which the army is fully accountable for its crimes.

9.   The Limits of a Political Trial as a Vehicle for Social Change

Despite the differences between the two political trials we have examined in this chapter—*Hassin* and Kufr Qassem, both were cases in which the Israeli court was not content to decide the matter on its merits but also sought to advance an educational message with the help of a legal narrative. Examining these narratives helped us to identify the political aspects of the judgment. However, the two cases demonstrated two very different types of politics. The *Hassin* narrative divided the Arab inhabitants of Israel into two mutually exclusive categories: loyal citizens and vicious enemies, thus legitimizing the policy of deporting Arab refugees who infiltrated into Israel. This categorization, however, was not a stable one, and the Arab citizens of Israel, who had lived under military rule since 1948, continued to be perceived with suspicion. The politics underlying Halevi's narrative in the Kufr Qassem trial was meant to address this situation and to provide a counternarrative to the prevailing perception of Israeli Arabs as suspect citizens not easily differentiated from the many infiltrators entering the country from Jordan and Egypt. The judgment was designed to give a concrete content to the abstract notion of Israeli citizenship conferred on the Arab inhabitants of the State of Israel and to close the gap between the physical borders and the human borders of the Israeli collective by making it inclusive of the Arab citizens of Israel. One can only guess what induced this change. As suggested earlier, the military victory in the Sinai war, which helped change the general atmosphere of insecurity that characterized the early 1950s, together with the realization of the horrible consequences of unlimited military power, may have prompted Halevi to take a first step toward this transformation.

In both cases the hypothesis about the relative independence of the court in political trials was found helpful. In the *Hassin* case the court's relative independence manifested itself mainly in its procedural rulings (attributing more reliability to the testimonies of the Arab villagers than to that of the army authorities) but without this changing the substantive results of the decision. In the Kufr Qassem trial, the court demonstrated a higher degree of independence on both the procedural and substantive levels. The testimonies of the Arab victims were consistently preferred to the testimonies of the soldiers, which the court called "blatant lies." Moreover, the procedural decisions led to a strong moral condemnation by the court, accompanied by severe sentences, between seven and seventeen years in prison. The clash between the court and the political authorities was revealed by certain decisions taken by the court, including its refusal to conduct a trial behind closed doors, as the army requested,[88] and its insistence on giving the horror a name, a story, and a human face. The efforts of Judge Halevi succeeded in imprinting on the public the fact that this had been the cold-blooded murder of Israeli citizens. Nonetheless, they did not induce a collective reckoning about the causes of this massacre and the fragile status of Arabs in Israel.[89] What can explain this failure?

One explanation points to the relations between the court and the political authorities. As we saw at the beginning, government officials, and particularly Ben-Gurion, were at first reluctant to publicize the affair. Confronted with the efforts of several Arab and Jewish public figures to investigate and publicize the massacre, the political authorities agreed to a trial. But the prevailing attitude was that the trial was a purifying ritual in which the entire society was cleansing its hands.[90] The trial was also a way of appeasing international public opinion. Ben-Gurion, concerned that the affair would tarnish the good image of the Israeli army, insisted upon drawing a sharp distinction between the Border Police unit that had committed the massacre, which was to be condemned, and the rest of the army, whose ethos of "purity of arms" must remain untarnished.[91] Halevi made this distinction the cornerstone of his judgment, even though his judgment can also be seen as undermining this distinction, since it forced the political authorities to bring to trial Colonel Shadmi from the IDF, from whom the order had issued.[92] But at this later trial he was convicted only of a "technical" failure (of ordering a curfew in excess of his authority) and not of the subsequent massacre. For this "technical breach" of the law he was given a symbolic fine of one *grush* (cent), a sentence that the Arab public saw as an enormous insult.[93] In addition, a double standard developed regarding the soldiers who had committed the massacre: although publicly condemned, they were privately seen as having sacrificed themselves for the sake of the country.[94] Accordingly, immediately after their verdicts were announced, several steps were taken to ensure that the punishment would not be carried out. After their appeal was accepted and their punishments mitigated, the chief of staff used his authority to reduce their punishment, and all were released from jail after serving three years at the most. Moreover, many of the soldiers who were found guilty were not banned from public service but were even given important civil positions or promoted within the security forces.[95] These developments can help explain why it was not Halevi's narrative about the massacre but rather "Shadmi's cent" that became a symbol of the Kufr Qassem trials for the Arab citizens of Israel. More than anything, they saw it as expressing the low value of Arab lives in Israel and the contempt and disrespect with which they were treated by the army authorities and Israeli courts alike.[96] We should also bear in mind that there are limits to the transformative power of a legal narrative when it is not backed up with actual social change. Although the judgment recognized Arab Israelis as full citizens, this recognition was only de jure and not de facto. In 1956 military rule was still in force and every effort to abolish it was met with strong opposition from Ben-Gurion and his Mapai party.

Another explanation of why the Kufr Qassem judgment failed to induce a change in Israeli collective identity is connected to the limits of the liberal legal ideology as a mechanism for social change. We have seen that Judge Halevi tried to use his judgment as an "entrance card" for Arab citizens to the Israeli collective. The sordid facts of the massacre demonstrated that the formal citizenship conferred on Israeli Arabs was an important step toward their inclusion but far from enough. It did not prevent their exclusion and de facto separation created by the military rule, and it did not change the Jewish public's suspicious attitude toward them. It certainly did not prevent the development of dehumanizing attitudes among the security forces toward Arab Israelis. We have seen that Halevi used the trial as an attempt to change these attitudes, in particular by employing a language that respected the Arab witnesses as human beings and Israeli citizens whose right to life and dignity should be protected by the courts. For this purpose, the judge had to willingly blind himself to the reality of the military rule and the ongoing fight against infiltrators, which undermined Israelis' ability to see the Arabs as full and equal citizens. The concept of citizenship implied in his judgment was passive (negative liberty) and minimal (respect for life and human dignity). Years later, the same liberal approach toward Arab citizens became the basis for a desegregation decision by the Israeli court, forbidding the policy of excluding *individual* Arabs from purchasing houses in a Jewish village in the Galillee.[97] However, just as in the Kufr Qassem decision, and in many other decisions given throughout the years by the Israeli Supreme Court, the recognition was limited to Arab citizens as individuals, without recognition of their collective group rights.[98] Judge Halevi was also willing to limit the scope of his criticism of the army and confined his moral condemnation to individuals in the Border Police unit who had deviated from the norm, thus keeping intact the "purity of the arms" ethos of the Israeli army (although these constraints may partly be explained by the nature of the criminal trial, which is meant to focus the blame on recognizable individuals). These constraints on the legal narrative all had their effect on the collective memory of the affair. It was remembered as a cold-blooded murder of Arab citizens, while the historical context of the Sinai war, military rule, the fight of the Border Police against the infiltrators, and the racism revealed in the language and testimonies of the soldiers were forgotten.

The judge's attempt to develop a civil discourse and impose the limits of the rule of law on the army was undermined from the outset. As the trial took place in a military court, there was constant tension between the civil rhetoric of the court and the actual appearance of judges and lawyers in army uniform. Moreover, the efforts to treat the trial as an ordinary criminal case could not disguise the fact that it was a military court in which the independence of the judges was curbed.[99] Almost immediately after the publication of the decision the public's attention began to be diverted from the moral issues to the legalistic points of the Kufr Qassem affair. Instead of dealing with the serious issues of the social and political conditions that had enabled such a massacre to occur, a long and pedantic discussion began in the press and the law journals about the proper limits of the duty to obey orders and whether the legal distinction advanced by Halevi (between an illegal order and a manifestly illegal order) was capable of dealing with the needs of the army.[100]

The dangers of deflecting the public debate in this direction were noted by the poet Nathan Alterman in his political column in the newspaper *Davar*. Just a week after the massacre, on 7 November 1956, he published a poem, "The Triangle Zone," in which he harshly criticized the government's attempts to conceal the event from the public. Two years later, his poem "About the Verdict" criticized the fact that almost all the responses to the verdict were concerned with the nature of the military orders instead of with the moral issues, ignoring the real problem: that Israeli soldiers could have committed such atrocities. The main question, he insisted, was not the subordination of soldiers to their commanders but their subordination to the murderous impulse to kill. In this case, as in the Kastner affair, Alterman was ahead of his time. Until the 1990s the Kufr Qassem massacre was not taught in Israeli schools but only in military courses during discussions on the limitations of obeying an illegal order.[101] On 22 October 1992, Sheikh Abdallah Nimmer Darwish, the leader of the Islamic movement in Israel, sent a "peace letter" to Prime Minister Yitzhak Rabin, in which he demanded that the Israeli government show its serious concern with the Kufr Qassem affair by establishing a public committee of investigation and including the massacre in the school curriculum. It was only in 1999 that Minister of Education Yossi Sarid initiated this process by deciding to include the subject in the curriculum, which immediately kindled a public debate.[102] Sarid was able to begin this process of recognizing the wrong done to Arabs by the Israeli army in the Kufr Qassem affair only because he could rely on a legal judgment that had determined the sordid facts of the massacre without varnish.[103]

10. Conclusion: A Divided Memory

I began this chapter with the contention that law cannot be completely separated from politics and that as liberals we have to learn to accept the existence of political trials and draw distinctions between their different types. I argued that one of the most important functions of political trials is their legitimization function. The degree of legitimization, however, is related to the degree of independence enjoyed by the courts, which creates a leeway for activist judges and political lawyers to expand the space of judicial freedom and to begin a process of transformation. I also suggested that we should look for the politics of the decision in the narrative advanced by the court. In the *Hassin* judgment, since the independence of the court was confined to the procedural level, the judgment could legitimize both the court's decision and the government's policy while consolidating the hegemonic ideology about infiltrators with a moralistic narrative. Thus, we can identify the legitimization effect of the judgment in the gap between the procedural and the substantive levels of the decision. This dialectic between legitimization and criticism was even more apparent in the Kufr Qassem decision. This time the political function of the legal narrative was revealed to have a greater transformative potential, offering a new reading of Israeli citizenship that included the Arab citizens more fully. For this purpose the court had to confront the army in a more direct way and to constrain its power both on the symbolic level (subjecting it to the jurisdiction of the court) and on a material level (imposing severe prison sentences on the defendants). However, here, too, the court was unable to go all the way, and the judgment had the legitimization effect of maintaining the purity of arms ethos of the Israeli army. Indeed, both the symbolic and the material aspects of the decision were subsequently undermined when the political authorities overrode the court's sentence by mitigating the defendants' punishments and promoting some of the convicted soldiers to sensitive public positions. We can, however, view this issue from another perspective and see the limitations accepted by Halevi as enabling him to advance a transformative narrative of Israeli society. Adopting the distinction between the Border Police and the army allowed him to keep the moral image of the army intact. This helped both the public and the political authorities to "digest" the judgment, especially as the Border Police mostly consisted of Mizrahim (Jews from Muslim countries) and non-Jews (Druze or Bedouin), groups that were held in low social esteem at the time.[104] It was maybe because Halevi realized the inherent limitations of a trial in transforming the status of Arabs in Israel that he later took the unprecedented step of leaving the Supreme Court and entering politics. He was elected in 1969 to the Knesset as a member of the right-wing Herut party. In his position as a member of the Knesset Law Committee and the head of the Subcommittee for Basic Laws, he made every effort to promote the legislation of a Basic Law for human and civil rights.[105]

Interestingly, the division of the legal process into two separate trials (of the Border Police and Colonel Shadmi from the IDF) resulted not in a "collective memory" of the event but in a divided memory. Israeli Jews remember the affair with the image of the black flag and judge Halevi's harsh sentence, symbolizing the superiority of the rule of law over the rule of power. The Arab minority remembers Shadmi's cent, representing the disregard for the lives of Arab citizens and the army's superiority over the law. Our return to the forgotten narrative of Halevi's judgment is a belated attempt to bring these two opposing memories closer together by recalling the transformative potential of the judgment, which was not fulfilled for so many reasons.

The Yigal Amir Trial

Chapter 8

"A Jewish and Democratic State" Reconsidered

We saw the need to stress that the trial conducted before us was not a "political trial" but an ordinary criminal one . . . The one and only question that was submitted for our decision—and decide we did—was whether the defendant had committed the crime of murder as defined in the penal law. . . . We answered this question in the affirmative.

(Judge Edmond Levy, *State of Israel v. Yigal Amir*)

The trial was conducted according to the rules of the ritual. However, it missed the most important issue. There was no consideration of the reasons that brought me to do the deed. It was not an ordinary murder trial, no matter how many times you'll say that. This is a trial about the existence of the State of Israel. This issue was not addressed. They did exactly what the media wanted. It was a public trial from beginning to end. May God help you.

(Amir's last statement to the district court)

On Saturday evening, 4 November 1995, Prime Minister Yitzhak Rabin addressed a mass rally in support of the Oslo peace process in the large square by Tel Aviv municipality. The rally concluded with the "Song of Peace," a popular Israeli song that over the years had become a symbol of the struggle for peace. The prime minister participated in the singing from the speakers' stage. Upon returning to his car, escorted by two bodyguards, he was shot in his back and died from his wounds a short while afterward. The assassin was identified as a young religious Jew, a law student, named Yigal (which means in Hebrew "he will redeem") Amir.

The trial of Yigal Amir opened on 19 December 1995 in the Tel Aviv District Court and concluded on 27 March 1996, around five months after the assassination. The court convicted the defendant of murdering the prime minister of Israel, Yitzhak Rabin. From a legal standpoint,

Rabin's murder was an "easy" case to prove, since there was plenty of evidence to tie Yigal Amir to the assassination, including a videotape of the murder,[1] and because the mental element required for a conviction could easily be established from the defendant's statements and testimony. The difficulty of the case lay in its political repercussions, which posed an implicit challenge to the court's legitimacy. Amir attempted to use the trial as a political platform to explain his ideological motivation and cited a passage from Jewish religious law (Halakhah), as opposed to Israeli criminal law, to provide him with a "legal" justification for his act.[2] In so doing he challenged the legitimacy of the court and exposed the need to clarify the relations between Jewish and secular law in the State of Israel. The court was thus faced with a difficult dilemma. On the one hand, presenting the case as an ordinary murder case and ignoring any defense not recognized by state law would reinforce the court's legitimacy. On the other hand, ignoring Amir's political defense would make the court appear to be avoiding the hardest challenge posed by the murder: what value should prevail when the "Jewish" seems to contradict the "democratic" and what is the hierarchy of secular law and Jewish law in the State of Israel?

As I shall show, the court adopted a dual solution to this dilemma: it endeavored to remove politics from the judgment, but it also presented an implicit "political" answer to Amir. In its decision the court presented the case as an ordinary murder case, resorted to formalistic legal reasoning, and resisted all attempts by the defendant to politicize the trial. The sentence, by contrast, was politicized from its very first word. It stressed the extraordinary nature of the trial and the specific identity of the victim, resorting to an unusual kind of rhetoric, which drew on poetry, literary allusions, and quotations from the Bible to convey the pain and trauma induced by the murder. This part of the judgment, I argue, is not, however, merely a eulogy to Rabin but reveals an attempt by the court to reconstitute the terms of the Israeli collective identity by rejecting the divisive message proclaimed by the assassin. Speaking in the name of the community, the court expelled the murderer from the community both materially (by sentencing him to a lifetime in prison) and symbolically (describing him as an outcast) and by offering its own mythological narrative of the murder, connecting Amir's deed with the most traumatic moments in the Jewish collective memory and warning against the existential dangers it harbored for the community.

In terms of the theory of political trials we can say that the court

responded to the "symbolic threat" implicit in Amir's act and words—
the debunking of the foundational myth of Israel—by defending the
basic values of the community. However, out of the two competing
narratives of identity found in the previous political trials examined in
this book—the civic-universalist and Jewish-particularist—the court, as
we shall see, chose to endorse the latter, describing the community that
was hurt by Amir's act in ethnic-national terms. As a result, Rabin's
message of peace and democratization was reduced to a message of
peace, ignoring its far-reaching implications for the physical and internal borders of Israeli society. The discussion will be divided into three
parts. The first retraces the ways in which Amir's political challenge
was repressed and ignored in the court's judgment. The second
describes the ways in which the court implicitly responded to Amir's
challenge in the sentencing portion of the judgment. The third examines an alternative approach to the problem of political murder, which
was not taken by the court, and discusses the implications of the court's
choice of path for Israeli politics.

1.   Amir's Challenge

Traces of a Political Defense

Amir's story, the ideology he drew on in a bid to justify his deed, is not
presented coherently in the judgment, since the court's basic position
was that the trial should not become a political platform for the assassin. Nevertheless, a glimpse of the political defense presented by Amir
in the trial can be discerned in the court's discussion of procedural
questions: whether Amir should be sent for a psychological examination, whether he should be appointed a lawyer by the court, and
whether he should be allowed to develop his own line of defense in
opposition to the one chosen by his attorney. It is at these junctures that
the judgment reveals Amir's refusal to act according to what is
expected of an ordinary criminal defendant.

When Amir's lawyers raised various procedural contentions regarding the admissibility of the statement of confession taken from him by
the police, Amir thwarted their intention by testifying as follows.

It's not true that this statement was extracted from me involuntarily.
I had no intention of being represented by lawyers. It doesn't matter

to me if there's a life sentence or not. I executed the deed whole-heartedly. The media interpreted the things the way it wanted. I was depicted as a criminal murderer who goes around killing people all the time. I want to make certain points clear. As regards the prose-cution witnesses—they do not contradict what I've said. I don't understand why they have to be brought. Apparently, they [the prosecution] didn't understand me. I would like the world to be told the truth. I didn't commit the act because I'm a criminal, but from an ideological standpoint.[3]

Amir hastened to confirm (in contradiction to the defense line pro-moted by his attorneys) that he was warned about his rights prior to giving his confession. It was evidently important for him to have the statement admitted, even though it would harm his chances of winning the case, since it contained an explicit explanation of his political moti-vations. To this end, he had to overcome the intermediaries (lawyers, psychologists, rabbis, etc.), the experts who did not share his political worldview and therefore could not faithfully represent his convictions. Indeed, contrary to a regular criminal, Amir was not at all interested in the best legal defense but aspired to represent himself and speak in his own voice as much as possible.[4] Thus, being a law student, he used his legal knowledge to intervene in his lawyers' questioning of the prose-cution witnesses in order to conduct his own examination.[5] Although from a narrow legal perspective these interventions harmed his legal defense, from his point of view they served the overriding aim of enabling him to underline his political defense. For example, after his attorney had completed his interrogation of police officer Avi Cohen, he intervened and asked the witness whether Amir (referring to him-self in the third person) had shown any signs of remorse or emotional upheaval during the investigation. The witness answered that Amir had been "as cold as a fish."[6] Although in legal terms this answer destroyed the possibility of mitigating the charge of premeditated mur-der on the basis of extenuating circumstances such as provocation, it served Amir's political defense admirably, since it established that his deed was not a "crime of passion" but had been rationally calculated. As a result of such subversive conduct one of his attorneys asked the court to be released from his representation, while the other expressed his difficulties to the court: "I bear a heavy responsibility in this matter. This is the trial of the defendant, this is his day in court and I cannot stop him from asking questions. I cannot agree or disagree to his questions. I am being placed in a difficult situation and I cannot protest."[7] The court responded by appointing another attorney out of concern that Amir was not receiving a proper defense.[8]

The tension between the legal and the political emerged several times in the course of the trial: every time Amir sought to present the political motives that had led him to the murder, the judges cut him short.[9] On one occasion, the presiding judge, Edmond Levy, reportedly interrupted Amir and asked him not to "give speeches." To this Amir responded: "What do you want, that I should say I killed him because I felt like it?"[10] From a legal standpoint, all that is required for a murder conviction is proof of the intent to kill, whereas the larger political motive is irrelevant.[11] However, for Amir it was precisely the political motive—the determination to stop by any means available the Oslo accords, which he viewed as leading the people to disaster—and not his legal intent—the willingness to kill Rabin in order to achieve this political goal—that should be the main issue discussed in the trial.

The tension between the legalistic defense sought by Amir's lawyers and the political defense advanced by Amir emerged in the court's decision to send Amir for psychological evaluation (after the trial had begun) in order to ensure him a fair trial.[12] Unlike ordinary defendants, who usually request a psychological evaluation in order to prove their legal incompetence (insanity defense) and reduce their sentences, Amir was interested that his sanity be attested by the experts. Indeed, he explained to the court that one of the reasons that had impelled him to commit the murder as soon as possible was the fear that an insane person might murder the prime minister first and thus undermine the ideological message. "From the beginning of the first Oslo accord, the idea was to do it, that somebody had to do it, but not that I should do it. The situation deteriorated slowly, and seeing that no one was doing it, I decided to do it before a lunatic did, which would have left an impression and impact that would not serve to stop the so-called peace process."[13] The court pointed out that:

> The defendant described himself as one who, the moment his consciousness and emotion reach a certain conclusion, ceases having any qualms about executing the deed or achieving the goal he has striven for. It appears that it was important for him to stress that the killing of the Prime Minister was not done out of a lust for revenge

or murder, for fear that the act he had committed would be labeled as criminal. According to his view, there could be only one solution to removing the deceased from the state's leadership, since according to the defendant's view, the acts of the deceased posed a very real existential danger to the state.[14]

The psychological evaluation established that the defendant was sane and fit to stand trial. At the same time, the opinion noted that the defendant "tends to see the world in terms of black and white and believes with all his heart in the justice of his way and the correctness of his views."[15] By relying on the psychological evaluation the court attempted to confront one of the most difficult dilemmas of political trials. To judge the defendant meant to address the political views that led to the murder, but if his views were allowed to become the center of the trial the courtroom was liable to be transformed into another platform for the political assassin. The psychological evaluation provided a way out. Amir's ideological worldview was cited in the judgment as part of the psychologist's opinion, which, while giving the readers an insight into his radical world outlook, did not obligate the court to deal directly with the substance of his political contentions. The court's response to his political challenge was thus delayed until the sentencing.

Reconstructing Amir's Subversive Narrative

The judgment shows only glimpses of Amir's political defense since the court was determined not to allow his narrative to dominate the decision. Nevertheless, a close reading enables us to reconstruct Amir's subversive narrative from the various brief quotations interspersed throughout the judgment and thus understand the counternarrative presented in the court's sentence. Amir's narrative can be broken down into four themes that were woven together in his testimony: an alternative history, an alternative system of justice, a religious justification for the murder, and competition with the sovereign.

At one point the judgment quotes Amir's response to the police interrogator, who had asked whether he thought it was right to kill Rabin and whether he regretted his act. Amir had vehemently denied any remorse.

A Jew who murdered fourteen Jews that were aboard the ship *Altalena*, a Jew whose entire rise through the ranks of the army was due to party connections, even though he fled the bloody convoy battle, even though he collapsed during the Six Day War and didn't function. But all that doesn't matter, because my aim was not to avenge. God will avenge that. My aim was to prevent the further deterioration in public morale, which Rabin was incapable of stopping by himself. He would have ultimately led us to a second version of the Yom Kippur War. It was also for his persecution of everything sacred to Judaism, for ordering the use of violence in demonstrations held by the true pioneers of Israel, and for the general brainwashing in the media and statements of this kind *that Rabin was executed.*[16]

This quotation, which refers to crucial events in Israel's past, contains a synopsis of an *alternative history*—a subversive narrative competing with that version advanced by the media. The Israeli media depicted Rabin's life as the story of the ultimate Sabra: a young warrior in the 1948 war of Independence; Israel's chief of staff during the Six-Day War of 1967, who turned a war of survival into a spectacular victory; and then minister of defense during the first Palestinian uprising (Intifada) in 1987–88, who subsequently came to recognize the right of the Palestinian people to an independent state alongside Israel, realizing that there was no military solution to the conflict.[17]

Amir gives each of these constitutive events a subversive interpretation. From the 1948 war he refers to Rabin's role in the attack on the *Altalena,* a boat smuggling weapons to the right-wing National Military Organization (Etzel) to assist in the 1948 war against the Arabs.[18] This event, which was part of Ben-Gurian's attempt to disband the right-wing militias and unite the military forces under his government, was a traumatic moment in Israel's early history since it brought the young state to the brink of civil war in its very first year of existence. From the 1967 war, Amir undermines Rabin's image as the great war hero by citing his mental state in the very first days of the war. On reaching the Oslo accords, the cause of enormous controversy and political upheaval in Israel, Amir depicts the agreements from the point of view of the extreme right-wing opposition, as a process leading not to peace but to war and catastrophe. According to Amir, the Oslo accords signaled a watershed in Israeli politics that transformed previous political adversaries into potential enemies. Amir depicts politics in terms of a war over the future of the Land of Israel and, by implication, over the identity of Israel as a "Jewish" state. He returned to this point many times during the trial (though none of this enters the judgment). As he explained it:

> After the second Oslo accord I understood that something had happened. For the first time in the history of the Jewish people a Jewish leader was willing to give up the Land of Israel. . . . When I saw the announcement about the "peace" rally I understood that there was dancing and rejoicing. This is the point of no return. Until now it was understood that we give up the land only out of no choice. If it is done like that, it is all right. But it is a completely different thing to be glad about it. From my point of view, this was the point that if someone did not get up and do something about it, the results of this rejoicing, the results of this sin would impact the people for generations to come.[19]

Interestingly, while Amir was driven to act because of the "rejoicing" of the Left, it was Amir's own smile that became the center of public and media attention throughout the trial, culminating in a surrealist court session in which an expert witness in psychology was asked to explain Amir's smile to the court.[20]

In order to transform the act of ending a human life from an abominable act of murder into a heroic act of self-sacrifice for the sake of the people, Amir resorted to a justifying rhetoric. The political assassin often attempts to legitimate his act by appealing to *an alternative system of justice* by which he ought to be judged.[21] Since the act of the assassin is directed at challenging an existing system of law (or some parts of it), the justification often assumes a quasi-legal form. However, as one author explains, "decisions to assassinate are typically not the result of a fair legal procedure based on 'due process.' "[22] An interesting case in point is the assassination of Kastner, which we discussed in chapter 1. Unlike other cases of political murder, Kastner's assassination was preceded by a lengthy and traumatic legal proceeding. As a result, the public discourse about the legitimacy of his actions in Hungary was couched in legal terms. In contrast, all attempts to bring the question of the legitimacy of the Oslo accords to the court before Rabin's assassination failed.[23] Indeed, at one point during the trial Amir told the court: "If the courts had done their job in the last three years I would not have had to kill."[24]

Nonetheless, Amir himself relied on a quasi-legal rhetoric to justify

Rabin's murder. The paragraph quoted earlier in effect constitutes an "alternative bill of indictment" against the prime minister. Rabin is put on trial by Amir for "murder" allegedly committed as a result of the attack on the *Altalena*, for persecuting the Jewish religion, and for the violence used by the police, on his orders, against demonstrators. But, above all, Amir presents the assassination as a preemptive act, an act intended to prevent another war, not as a vengeful act of murder. "The intention was to impair Yitzhak Rabin's functioning as Prime Minister. I make a distinction between what I'm saying and the word 'murder.' I'm saying that if I could have paralyzed him, that would have been enough. When I said that my intention was to stop Rabin, I meant that my object was not Rabin himself, but rather to stop his political activity."[25] He tries to make the distinction between wanting to stop Rabin politically and wanting to kill him as a person. Only the latter, in his view, should be considered murder. Amir also imitates the rhetoric of judges by distancing his act from vengeance and presenting his "sentence" as having been arrived at after due deliberation (including a "character testimonial" on Rabin's malfunctioning as chief of staff) and consideration of all the alternatives.[26] With the aid of this severe "bill of indictment" he depicts his deed as an "execution" not a murder. Needless to say, Amir's quasi trial of Rabin is a far cry from the due process of an orderly legal system. According to his form of lynch law, he plays simultaneously the roles of plaintiff, judge, and executor of the sentence—and the accused has no right to defend himself or to appeal.

A major theme in Amir's testimony is his appeal to the Halakhah. It is this part of his challenge that seems most threatening to the court, and it is this part alone that receives a direct answer from the court in the judgment itself (as opposed to the sentence). In Israel the authority to judge according to Halakhic law is restricted to the rabbinical courts, which have sole jurisdiction only in matters of the marriage and divorce of Jews.[27] Hence Amir's insistence that, in matters involving the state's continued existence as a Jewish state, the authority of the Halakhah overrode that of the secular court had ominous implications since it implied that the "Jewish" and "democratic" definitions of the state were fundamentally irreconcilable.

Amir predicates his defense on Din Rodef (Law of the Persecutor), which he interpreted as establishing that "whoever delivers Israel into the hands of the gentiles . . . is punishable by death. Look at the Hellenists, the Hellenists also killed Jews."[28] The invocation of Din Rodef played a dual role in Amir's testimony. First, it contributed to delegit-imizing the victim by identifying Rabin with the "persecutor" and "traitor," that is, one who betrays his people and collaborates with the enemy. Second, it provided a quasi-legal facade, since this Halakhic term, which was not familiar to most of the public, sounds like legal parlance. Amir took pains to present Din Rodef as requiring the exhaustion of all other alternatives before resorting to violence and bloodshed, thus portraying himself as one who had made every attempt to avoid using the most extreme means.[29]

> The decision was that he [Rabin] fits the category of Din Rodef. . . . I reached the conclusion that the peace process threatens the people with an existential danger. . . . I began with passive participation in demonstrations. Then I began to sign people up on protests. Then I participated in hunger strikes in Bar Ilan university, and when I saw that the public remained indifferent I tried to make it empathize by organizing Sabbaths [bringing people to spend the weekend in set-tlements in the occupied territories].[30]

The legal deliberation in court concentrated on whether any rabbini-cal authority had given Amir permission to kill Rabin according to Din Rodef, even though Amir insisted that he had not needed rabbinical approval since he himself was capable of interpreting the Halakhah (another example of his arrogant assumption of the right to bypass institutional intermediaries). "According to Halakhah, the moment a Jew delivers his people and land into the hands of the enemy, he must be killed. No one taught me this Halakhic law. All my life I've been studying Gemara [part of the Talmud] and I have all the informa-tion."[31] Moreover, he explained that Din Rodef should not be confused with a "rabbinical ruling" since it is a preemptive act, equivalent to "self-defense," which is left to the discretion of the individual commit-ting it. Interestingly, Amir also claimed that the only question that required an "expert" opinion was whether Rabin indeed threatened the existence of Israel, and this could only be answered by an army com-mander.[32] Amir's personal history—his military service had followed the road taken by many Orthodox Jews, partly studying in a yeshiva and partly serving in one of the combat units—had made him, in his eyes, the perfect candidate for answering this question. This conflation of Jewish law and security considerations is a potentially explosive subject in Israeli society (as indicated by the heated debate about the right of religious soldiers to disobey an eventual order to evacuate settlements in the occupied territories), which may be the reason why the court did not include this part of Amir's testimony in the judgment.

Despite Amir's appeal to Din Rodef, the judgment is largely devoted to placing his deed firmly within the framework of murder law doctrine and justifying the conviction pursuant to Israeli Penal Law. Nonetheless, the court evidently realized that Amir's position could not be contended with only from within the secular legal system. Accordingly, the last part of the judgment sought to answer the deepest challenge that Amir raised: whether it is conceivable that a parallel normative system (in this case Jewish religious law) can be used by individuals in society to justify breaking the law. In other words, *who is the sovereign power* in the State of Israel?

The Italian philosopher Giorgio Agamben, adopting Carl Schmitt's definition that sovereignty is the power to declare the exception to the rule, has written that the ultimate privilege of the sovereign is the power to determine who is excluded from protection by the law (and who therefore can be killed without that killing being considered murder). This power, he believes, is also revealed in the original meaning of the term *homo sacer*—an individual whose life has been turned into "bare life," that is, life that can be taken with impunity by any person.[33] Amir's understanding of Rabin as subject to Din Rodef can be viewed as an attempt to turn him into a homo sacer, an outcast, no longer afforded protection by the Halakhah.[34] Thus, the threat posed by Amir was not merely that he vested himself with the power to murder Rabin—for this alone would not suffice to threaten the state's sovereignty—but that he took upon himself the power to define who was to be cast outside the protection of the law (definition of the exception) and hence to determine that killing such a person should not be considered murder. This is the prerogative of the sovereign. Thus, by assuming the power to decide that Din Rodef applied to Rabin, Amir placed himself in direct competition with the sovereign.

The presiding judge, Edmond Levy, who was also a religious Jew, took it upon himself to solve this dilemma by answering the defendant from within his own world, according to the Halakhah. His response attempted to restore the hierarchy between state law (democratic) and Halakhic law (Jewish) in Israel. We can describe such a response as an endeavor to restore the bridge between the rule of law and the Halakhah in order to allow their peaceful coexistence.[35] Judge Levy maintained that according to the Halakhah the rabbis of our time had lost the authority to determine whether Din Rodef applied or not, since the authorized Halakhic body that could rule on this issue (the Sanhedrin) no longer existed.[36] The judge also argued that even if the Halakhah was applied to the case of Rabin, Jewish law required proceeding gradually and resorting to violence only when there was no other alternative. Despite Amir's attempt to prove that he had tried every other possible means prior to killing Rabin, he had failed to take into consideration the democratic nature of the state. Judge Levy maintained that a correct interpretation of Din Rodef entailed exhausting all the democratic means that made it possible to replace the government. In other words, there could be no contradiction between the two normative systems because Jewish law subordinates itself to the law of the state.[37] The judge thus showed that the Halakhah could be reconciled with secular law from an intra-Halakhic view and that the contradiction between the two as presented by Amir was chimerical. He therefore concluded that the "attempt to give Rabin's assassination Halakhic sanction is misplaced and constitutes a cynical and blatant exploitation of the Halakhah for aims that are foreign to Judaism."[38]

2.   The Court's Sentence

The transition from the decision to the sentence is abrupt. Since the sentencing stage of the judgment is not dictated by rigid rules and patterns, the judges are able to give expression to their feelings of pain, loss, and fear. Accordingly, the opening words of the sentence in *Amir* are not ordinary legal prose but the last stanza of the poem "After My Death" by Haim Nachman Bialik, who is regarded as Israel's national poet.

> Great is the pain, very great!
> There was a man—and behold, he is no more.
> His life's song was stopped in the middle
> He had one more psalm
> And now the psalm is lost forever,
> Lost forever.[39]

This stanza returns the readers to the night of the murder, when Rabin, the prime minister, who was known to be a very shy and private person, had joined in singing the "Song of Peace" along with other speakers at the mass rally in support of the Oslo accords. In this context the words "his life's song was stopped in the middle" have a horrific literal meaning, as well as serving as a metaphor for the Oslo peace process, which was cut short before it was completed. Thus, the last line of the poem might be read as expressing the fear that not only a leader had been lost but also his unfinished mission of bringing peace to his people. By choosing to quote from this poem the court moves the readers from the realm of law to that of myth, in which people can have an afterlife. While Bialik was trying to envision his own eulogy, Judge Levy concludes the first paragraph of the sentence, saying that, since Rabin's final thoughts can never be known, "we ask to be his mouthpiece."[40]

The sentence thus offers the court latitude to relate its judgment to disturbing questions that remained outside the legal part of the decision. What threshold did Israeli society cross with the assassination of its prime minister? How could it reconstitute itself after this terrible rupture? In the sentence the judges speak as members of the Israeli community facing a serious crisis of identity. The sentence, therefore, does not constitute an ordinary supplement to the decision but can be called a "dangerous supplement," which threatens to invert the hierarchy between law and politics that the decision so carefully constructed.[41] Whereas the decision made every effort to stress that the trial was like any other murder trial, in the sentence the court was prepared to bring the political facet of Amir's deed—the very facet that makes it unlike any other murder case—to center stage.

> We chose to open with the words of the national poet because they serve to underscore the cardinal point in this trial—the loss of a leader, caused by one who cast himself as judge of the land.[42]

While the decision concentrated on the defendant's deeds, the sentence shifted the focus to the victim, his family, and his community, thus emphasizing the singularity of a trial that concerns the murder, not just of any person but of a leader.

> The present bill of indictment is one of the most serious ever submitted to a court in Israel. The decision to murder the Prime Minister,

taken with cold calculation and a clear mind, is not just an "ordinary" crime, which in itself should not be taken lightly, but one that
was carried out, *at least according to the defendant's version*, against a
political backdrop, which heretofore we thought was the lot of others but not ours."[43]

Even at this stage, after Amir's legal responsibility has been established, the court shows reluctance to face the political background of
the assassination by attributing the political definition of the crime to
the defendant. However, as we shall see, the sentence—in substance
and form—is designed precisely to contend with the political aspects of
the murder. Politics for the court is not sectarian politics (taking sides
between Right and Left, secular and religious, etc.) but a willingness to
address the painful issue that the murder exposed—the fragile coexistence of Israel's two fundamental values as a Jewish and democratic
state. This recognition leads the court, within the framework of its
short, eight-page sentence, to delve into the realm of collective memory, history, and myth in an attempt to re-create solidarity in a deeply
divided society. In the following sections we will discuss three components that characterize the political aspects of the court's response to
Amir's challenge: (1) the sentence as a critical discourse event, (2) the
appeal to civil religion, and (3) the attempt to create a new constitutive
myth. Finally, I will consider how the court's response was shaped by
an attempt to deny its politics and what alternative narrative of identity
was neglected by the court's decision.

A Critical Discourse Event

The court's unusual choice of rhetoric in the sentence inverts all the
conventions of legal writing: the resort to poetry instead of prose,
expression of personal feelings instead of neutral and detached speech,
the preponderance of quotes from extralegal as opposed to legal
sources, flowery metaphorical language, and so on. According to James
Boyd White law should be seen as a branch of rhetoric, which is a central art by which culture and community are established, maintained,
and transformed.[44] This aspect of the law, which is usually overlooked,
is exposed in times of crisis such as the one experienced in the aftermath of Rabin's assassination. Israeli society was facing what can be
described as a liminal moment, a situation of intense communal emo-

tion in which "society looks at itself and asks not just what it is, but what it should become."[45] The distinction between the law's role as "world preserving" and its role as "world building" can also explain the sudden change of discourse in the sentence part of the judgment.[46] Amir's judges can be seen as resorting here to the world-building role of law, using this part of the judgment not only to conduct a ritual of collective mourning over the lost leader but also to offer a new constitutive myth for society upon whose basis the belief in the rule of law could be restored.

The extraordinary use of rhetoric by the court can be better understood if we compare it with the media discourse following the assassination. Yoram Peri has defined the media's reports on Rabin's murder as a "critical discourse event," that is, a "significant social event in which a public debate ensues about issues fundamental to society, with various interpretive groups competing to bestow symbolic meaning on them."[47] However, instead of providing an arena for competing interpretations and critical debate, the national media enhanced one dominant narrative to the exclusion of all others in a bid to reconstitute the collective identity threatened by Rabin's murder. As if to seal the rift that had been exposed in the nation, all the television channels broadcast the same materials, mixing different genres, such as news reporting, with an ornate and lofty rhetoric infused with a quasi-religious tone. Many of these characteristics can also be found in the court's rhetoric, even though the sentence was handed down around five months after the assassination. The overlapping of genres is especially striking in the sentence, as the law is usually strict in observing its own rules of discourse (prose interspersed with legal references and legal clauses). Contrary to what is commonly accepted, the sentence contains numerous quotes from the most prominent Hebrew poets (such as Bialik, Leah Goldberg, Nathan Yonatan, and Rachel). Alongside references to legal sources, there are quotes from the Bible and the Halakhah. This commingling of literary genres— prose and poetry, holy and secular, everyday language and legal parlance, history and myth—suggests an effort to unite the multiple voices of Israeli society vis-à-vis the divisive message of Amir.[48] Thus, ironically, while Amir's rhetoric imitated formal legal discourse to achieve authority the court broke the boundaries of formal legal discourse in order to express the trauma it shared with the rest of the community.

The rhetoric of the sentence is collectivist, using the first person plural ("We have chosen to open with the words of . . ."). This use of *we* implies that the judge is speaking in the name of the court, but a few lines further it emerges that the real collective behind *we* is the national collective—the people of Israel: "*We as a people* have received a resounding slap in the face."[49] Rabin "was killed by bullets fired from an unexpected direction, not from a stranger or an enemy, but from one of our own."[50] The judges relinquish any pretence of detachment; their rhetoric posits them as members of the community injured by Amir's deed. But what is this community? How does the court imagine its boundaries? A first clue can be found in the composition of the panel of judges. Each judge represented a different part of the Jewish community: the religious-Mizrahi (oriental) sector (Edmond Levy, the presiding judge), the military-security sector (Oded Mudrik, a former chief army prosecutor), and women (Savyona Rotlevi, a former delinquent juvenile judge). Together their different voices were supposed to blend to form a united community condemning Yigal Amir and placing him beyond the pale. Significantly, there was no Arab-Israeli judge on the panel, and, as we shall see, this absence helped the court to present the assassination as concerning primarily the Jewish community in Israel.[51]

Civil Religion in the Israeli Court

BETWEEN THE SACRED AND THE SECULAR

The collective trauma caused by Rabin's assassination can explain the extraordinary rhetoric used by the court, but it fails to explain why two judges of the panel relied so heavily on religious concepts. Legal discourse in Israel is usually secular. In Amir's sentence, by contrast, there is a constant tendency to slip into the domain of the sacred, with the legal system of concepts being translated into a corresponding religious system. This rhetorical choice is surprising, since Amir's willingness to transgress the dictates of positive law arose from his inability to distinguish between the boundaries of Israeli law and those of the Halakhah. The court may have felt that only a legal discourse that deviated from the legalism of positive law and promoted a kind of "civil religion" was capable of providing a suitable response to Amir's challenge. Thus, the resort to religious parlance can be seen as an attempt to promote the commitment to democracy.

Israeli society, including all its strata, has been guilty time and again of the sin of senseless hatred and shown little brotherly love. In a democratic regime, it is allowed, and at times even desirable, to disagree with the government's view or with the political line it follows. But everyone must internalize the idea that a people that wishes to live does not replace its leadership by means of an assassin's bullets, and that the one and only means of doing so is by free and democratic elections or a no-confidence vote in the Knesset.[52]

In the world of religion there are no offenses, only sins. The court identifies the root of the problem, the soil on which Amir's horrific act sprouted, in terms of a collective sin, "the *sin* of senseless hatred and . . . little brotherly love." Religion sees the community in familial terms (brethren) and seeks to regulate also the realms of love and hate. The sentence is based on these concepts, as opposed to the discourse of positive law, which purports to distance itself from these domains and to make do with defining the legal and illegal.[53] Religion is predicated not on laws but on precepts that must be learned and committed to memory. The court mentions the "command to treat a leader with respect" and notes that political leaders "are bidden to recite to themselves every morning and evening 'wise men, take heed of your words!' " The prohibitions Amir transgressed are presented as sacred: "There is no greater desecration of God than this act, as the defendant tried to find in the Torah facets it does not have in order to justify his terrible deed."[54] The root of the Hebrew word meaning "holy" (*kadosh*) appears in different variations throughout the sentence. The transition from profane to holy also dictates a change in the function of the judge, who appears not only as an adjudicator but also as an educator and a prophet of wrath.

This subtle, though important, change can be better understood by comparing the rhetoric found in Amir's sentence with that used in the 1948 Declaration of Independence, whose opening sentence proclaims:

Eretz-Israel [the Land of Israel] was the birthplace of the Jewish people. Here their spiritual, religious and political identity was shaped. Here they first attained statehood, created cultural values of national and universal significance and gave the world the eternal Book of Books.

In Amir's sentence we find another assertion.

Life was sanctified already at the birth of the nation, when we were commanded at the revelation of Mt. Sinai (Horev)—"thou shalt not kill." This commandment should beat in the heart of every civilized person and all the more so in the heart of a Jew who has taken upon himself voluntarily to observe the 613 precepts. The degree of importance attached to this commandment caused our sages to add to it one tier after another, to fortify its standing and accord it further validity.[55]

At first glance the two paragraphs convey a similar message. They deal with the origins of the Jewish people, constituting them as distinct people through their association with the Bible. There is, however, a crucial difference between them. The sentence, especially the part written by the presiding judge, generally refers not to the Book of Books but to the Ten Commandments and the "613 precepts" observed by Orthodox Jews. This emphasis on an Orthodox Jewish identity is reinforced by references to the Talmud and the Poskim (literature of rabbinical scholars on Halakhic questions) throughout the sentence, sources that were deliberately ignored by the Declaration of Independence, which opted to promote a Zionist secular identity rather than a Jewish-religious one.[56] It could be argued that in the sentence the court sought to respond to a religious defendant from the perspective of his own worldview.[57] At a deeper level, the court can be seen as undertaking the much more difficult task of re-creating the bridge that the declaration had endeavored to build between the secular and religious sectors of society by reaffirming the basic commitments of both camps to the rule of law.

THE SACRIFICE OF ISAAC

This oscillation between the sacred and the secular in the sentence reaches a climax with the discussion of the *korban* (victim or sacrifice), a term that refers both to the realm of the profane (the victim of an offense) and the realm of the sacred (the ritual sacrifice to God).[58] Usually there is no tension between the two meanings of the word, as they occur in completely different contexts. The judgment, however, in aiming to overcome the fault line between the Jewish religion and democratic law that Amir had tried to delineate with his act, revealed the potential of conflict within the term *korban*. The sentence opens by depicting Rabin as a murder victim in the secular sense of the term ("with the bullets he dispatched toward his victim [*korban*], he tore the life out of the late prime minister"),[59] but later the court resorts to the ritual sense of the word, combining secular and sacred language: "The acts of the defendant are not just his personal failure and it is not with him alone that we are settling accounts today but with all those . . . [who] allowed him to understand that it is permissible *to sacrifice the life of an individual on the altar of the 'Moloch'* [a Semitic deity to whom parents sacrificed their children] *of any ideology.*"[60] Finally, the court repudiates Yigal Amir's contention that he had sacrificed himself for the sake of the people, saying that "the aura the defendant wishes to wrap himself in, *as one who has sacrificed himself on the altar of his faith*, is false."[61] Once again we find an allusion to the way Amir sought to create direct competition between himself and the sovereign (in the image of Rabin)—this time with regard to who the true victim/sacrifice was.[62]

Symbolically, even the victim's name, Yitzhak (Isaac), suggests the dangerous duality hidden in the encounter between the sacred and profane in the same Hebrew word.[63] The name alludes to the biblical Isaac, the most famous victim/sacrifice in Judaism, and indirectly to Abraham, the father of the nation, who was prepared to murder his son to perform what he perceived to be the supreme act of faith. The human sacrifice was finally replaced, following divine intervention, by the sacrifice of a ram. The philosopher Søren Kierkegaard devoted his book *Fear and Trembling* to examining the significance of the "binding of Isaac," analyzing in particular the great fear revealed in the confrontation between the religious and the ethical, when there is no possibility of interception between them. According to Kierkegaard, the story arouses the fear that someone who hears it may wish to emulate Abraham's deed. He asks whether such a person should be called a "murderer of his own son" or a "knight of faith," in other words, how fraud and sin can be distinguished from a pure act of faith. If there is no way of differentiating between them, Kierkegaard wonders whether it would not be better to repress the story and its memory on account of the potential threat it poses to law and order in society.[64] He writes:

> If faith cannot make it a holy act to be willing to murder his son, then let the same judgment be passed on Abraham as on anyone else. If a

person lacks the courage to think his thought all the way through and say that Abraham was a murderer, then it is certainly better to attain this courage then to waste time on unmerited eulogies. The ethical expression for what Abraham did is that he meant to murder Isaac; the religious expression is that he meant to sacrifice Isaac—but precisely in this contradiction is the anxiety that can make a person sleepless, and yet without this anxiety Abraham is not who he is.[65]

This is precisely the source of the great anxiety experienced by the court when trying to remove the mask of "religious faith" from Amir's face in order to expose him as having committed the most ignominious of crimes.[66] All the judges articulated this consternation by attempting to discern between appearance and reality. Thus, Judge Levy determined that "The defendant standing before us and those of his ilk are the nightmare of any seeker of democracy . . . the aura the defendant seeks to wrap himself in, as one who has sacrificed himself on the altar of his faith, is false."[67] Judge Rotlevi quoted Albert Camus: "If Man wants to become God . . . he is a sub-man himself and not God, but the ignoble servant of death."[68] And finally, Judge Mudrik wrote: "From deep within the walls of prison, the sign of Cain will stand out eternally on the defendant's forehead, marking him as a villain and trouble-maker to his people, as the violator of the covenant who trampled the basic universal commandment—'thou shalt not kill!' "[69] All the judges relied on the human capacity to see through the mask and reveal the murderer behind it. The court's need to remove the mask points to the particular fear engendered by Amir's act—not on account of his being an "Other" in Israeli society but precisely on account of his being all too familiar, a person whose biography until then seemed to reflect the ideals on which the Zionist movement had been established.[70]

THE DILEMMA OF RELIGIOUS ZIONISM

The image of the Sabra that emerges from between the lines of the Declaration of Independence is that of the pioneer who clings staunchly to his homeland, makes the desert bloom, revives the Hebrew language, defends himself, and provides for all his needs. The attributes of this "New Jew" are practicality, initiative, military prowess combined with humanitarianism, and the aspiration to justice, liberty, and peace.[71] The declaration notes that while the Jews of the diaspora "never ceased to pray and hope" for the return to the land, the Zionists (New Jews) turned to action in order to realize these hopes. The Sabra-diaspora contrast is portrayed both in terms of geography (the Land of Israel versus the lands of dispersion) and in terms of time (the ancient past of national independence prior to expulsion from the land and the modern-day return of the people of Israel to the promised land versus two thousand years of exile culminating in the Holocaust). Less noticeable is the fact that this opposition is based also on the contrast between the secular and the Orthodox Jew. Zionism was the sons' and daughters' path of rebellion against their parents, who for the most part lived religious lives in the diaspora.[72] It is no wonder that the Orthodox religious Jew is not mentioned in the Declaration of Independence, even though all other parts of the community—the pioneer, refugee, Arab, and indirectly also the woman—are referred to.[73] The Sabra-diaspora dichotomy implies a negation not only of the diaspora as a physical domicile but also of the spiritual characteristics of diaspora behavior as manifested by the Orthodox religious lifestyle. The solution promoted by Zionism was essentially one of nationalism, the transformation of the Jews into "a nation like all other nations,"the secularization of the Jew. The ideal of the Sabra can be seen as an emulation of the Gentile ideal of virility—the active individual, a man of the earth, a military man in the Land of Israel.[74]

The ideal of the Zionist Sabra posed a serious dilemma for religious Zionists, for it confronted them with the negation on which their movement was built.[75] The development of the right-wing settlement movement Gush Emunim (Bloc of the Faithful) within the religious Zionist camp, following the teachings of Rabbi Kook,[76] was in essence an extreme case of assimilation to the Sabra ideal of virility. Gush Emunim, the settlements, and the combination of yeshiva study with military service fostered by the National-Religious party express the adoption of the Sabra ideal of settlement, militarism, and activism (the negation of diaspora passivity) as articulated in the Declaration of Independence but without the concomitant relinquishment of religious faith.[77]

This perspective sheds light on an interesting rhetorical inversion that emerges from Amir's statements. He endeavors to delegitimize the peace process by replicating the negation of the diaspora discourse of classical Zionism but directing the negation against the very embodiment of the ideal New Jew: Yitzhak Rabin. Amir describes Rabin's conduct as "the way of the diaspora" since he preferred peace negotiations to the course of military heroism and an unflinching stand against the enemy. This approach echoes slogans at demonstrations against the Oslo process prior to the assassination that compared Rabin's course to "Kastnerism" or "Judenratism."[78] Those terms represent in the collective memory the passive strategies of Jewish survival in the diaspora and the preference for negotiations over resolute fighting, which had led to the cooperation of some Jewish leaders with the Nazis during the Holocaust in an attempt to save their communities. As we saw in chapters 1–3, this was the path that was contrasted in the Israeli ethos with the way of the resistance fighters and Jewish partisans. Opponents of the Oslo accords were in fact contending that Rabin was betraying fundamental Zionist values and returning to the passive ways of Diaspora Jews that the independent State of Israel was supposed to replace. Amir depicted himself and his group as representing the authentic New Jew, who sought to remind the larger public of the ideals on which the State of Israel had been established.[79] This same logic of constructing a Zionist identity by way of contrast with the diasporic Other had made it possible to delegitimize an elected Israeli leadership by linking its actions to the traumatic collective memory of the Holocaust.

The court, and particularly Judge Levy, seemed to be alert to the danger hidden in the contrast between the New Jew and Old Jew in the Zionist narrative and hence endeavored to construct a new constitutive narrative that could overcome this dichotomy. Judge Levy presented an image of a national hero based not solely on militarism but primarily on a shared commitment to the rule of law, thus attempting to move away from the ideal of the "people of the land" and return to the ideal of the "people of the book." However, this new constitutive narrative preserved, and even reinforced, another opposition—that between the Jew (both secular and religious) and the Other—this time the Arab-Israeli citizen, who remained outside the judicial narrative.[80]

The Seeds of a New Constitutive Myth

In the eyes of many in Israel, Rabin had embodied the New Jew, the blue-eyed soldier boy with the shock of golden hair who would restore independence and honor after generations of massacres and humiliations.[81] His assassination led to the emergence of a new national myth in which Rabin's life came to symbolize the annals of the Israeli nation.

As one writer put it: "With the emergence of Yitzhak Rabin as a major Israeli leader, history conspired with personality to create a mythical biography that converged with the key stations of the odyssey of an entire nation."[82]

A myth, as the term will be used here, is a dramatic narrative that deals with the past of a group, expresses its values and beliefs, and at the same time reinforces them. Its primary political role lies in elucidating reality to the group and being a guide to its future conduct.[83] Accordingly, Rabin's death was transformed by the court from the passive death of an innocent victim into the death of a heroic soldier: "A leader of a state and a nation, who bore the burden of public service for several decades, first as a soldier, and then as a statesman. His course throughout his life was beset by many dangers, all of which he managed to escape. But at the height of his activity he was felled by bullets fired from an unexpected direction—not from a stranger or an enemy, but from one of our own."[84] The sacrifice described is no longer a religious rite but one made to fit the rite of Israeli civil religion—the sacrifice of the soldier's life for the sake of the people. Judge Mudrik invoked the image of the fallen soldier when he described the assassination: "At the conclusion of the Sabbath, Nov. 4, 1995, the Prime Minister was assassinated. The murderer lay in ambush from behind and smote him with a gunshot. Yitzhak Rabin *fell*, his hands unshackled and his feet unfettered."[85]

The hero's image in itself would not provide an answer to Amir's deeper challenge, which depicted Rabin as the hero of "Hellenist Jews" (i.e., Jews who were willing to betray all that was sacred in their traditions to find favor in the eyes of non-Jews), who did not represent large groups in Israeli society. A new unifying myth was needed to bridge the harsh political conflicts within Israeli society that had led to the assassination. Accordingly, an effort was made (chiefly in the sentence authored by the presiding judge) to redraw the boundaries of the collective identity so that Rabin could be regarded as a national hero above all political controversies. This attempt can be discerned in certain idioms and expressions scattered throughout the sentence that seek to blend the familiar secular image of Rabin with that of another kind of national hero—taken not from the customary pantheon of Zionist heroes (Bar Kochba, Judah the Maccabee, Joseph Trumpeldor, and so on) but from the world of religious Jewish society.[86] This is the figure of Moses, who takes us back to a very early moment in the history of the

Jewish people that is not mentioned in the Declaration of Independence: the giving of the Torah on Mount Sinai.[87] The immediate pretext for referring to Mt. Sinai is the commandment "Thou shalt not kill," which the Jewish people took on themselves on that occasion. At a deeper level, this was a constitutive moment in the life of the nation, when an aggregate of individuals and families was transformed into a people through their shared commitment to a divine book of laws. The judge creates a bond between the divine and the human systems of law by blending the images of Moses and Rabin into a single mythological figure around which a collective identity can be forged.[88] The various references to the story of Moses serves to create a composite image out of the two national leaders around which the various factions among the people could unify. Recognizing the divisive nature of the ideal of the Sabra based on a negation of the Diaspora and religiosity, the new narrative stresses continuity and commonality between secular Zionism and religious Judaism.

The court's attempt to reunite the people around a new myth had, however, an entirely Jewish focus. Two of the three judges on the panel chose to promote a national-particularistic discourse that assimilated the murder to the images of Jewish collective memory, rooted in the realms of myth and legend, according to which fraternal hatred was the source of all the catastrophes that had befallen the Jewish people. This tendency is particularly striking in the sentence of Judge Mudrik, who drew a direct line between Rabin's assassination, Cain's murder of his brother Abel, and the fight between Kamtza and Bar Kamtza, which, according to the Jewish tradition, had led to the destruction of the Second Temple and the expulsion from the Land of Israel in 70 A.D. The primary lesson drawn from these historical allusions is that unity and solidarity among Jews in Israel are the paramount value: "extending a brotherly hand is the need of the hour and place."[89]

Can the different groups in Israeli society be reconciled without uniting them around the notion that "the world is against us"? Hannah Arendt had observed during the Eichmann trial that it was this notion that

> produced the dangerous inability of the Jews to distinguish between friend and foe . . . a change in this mentality is actually one of the indispensable prerequisites for Israeli statehood, which by definition

has made of the Jews a people among peoples, a nation among nations, a state among states, depending now on a plurality which no longer permits the age-old and, unfortunately, religiously anchored dichotomy of Jews and Gentiles.[90]

There is a certain irony in the court's response to Amir because, despite the court's attempt to steer clear of Amir's political message, it opts to advance a collective identity that blurs the difference between the Jewish nation and the Israeli state. There is almost no allusion in the sentence to the transformation that Rabin tried to bring about in the fundamental terms of this identity by entering into a process of reconciliation with the Palestinians, defining the borders of the state, and integrating Arab Israelis as active citizens in Israeli democracy. The possibility of adopting a civic-universalistic discourse to counterbalance Amir's nationalistic-religious rhetoric is hinted at only in the short judgment of Judge Savyona Rotlevi: "The words of the writer and philosopher Albert Camus express the essence of my view that if man wants to become God, he arrogates to himself the power of life or death over others. Manufacturer of corpses and of sub-men, he is a sub-man himself and not a God, but the ignoble servant of Death."[91] With a short quotation from Camus's *The Rebel*, Rotlevi offered an alternative framework of reference for understanding the meaning of Rabin's assassination. Instead of citing the traditional Jewish warning against the perils of intra-Jewish conflicts, the judge invoked the rise of fascist and racist movements in the twentieth century. By placing the assassination in a context outside the specific Jewish-Israeli tradition, she implied that Jews, too, were not immune to these dangers and that it was these dangers that the murder of Rabin compelled Israeli society to address.

The majority judgment ignored the lessons of the rise of racist ideologies in Europe in the twentieth century and the way they had infiltrated the extremist right-wing groups in Israel. Its simplistic message of the need for tolerance among Jews forgoes a more critical examination of the foundations of the Israeli democracy: whether a commitment to democracy expressed in narrow ethno-national terms can serve as a solid basis for solidarity between the various national groups in Israeli society, Jews and Arabs; what would happen when "the people's unity" clashed with the "peace process" without the possibility of reconciling between them; and whether the commitment to Israeli democracy really necessitated protecting the people's unity above all other values. It is these implications of the court's judgment that I will consider in the following section.

3. Memory, Responsibility, and Politics in the Court of Law

The murder of Israel's prime minister Yitzhak Rabin, was a political assassination. It was brought to trial because a murder had been committed, but it raised fundamental questions for Israeli society because of its political nature. The way in which the trial court chose to answer Amir brings us back to the question that has accompanied us throughout this book: how can a political trial serve as a consciousness-transforming forum? By insisting on presenting the case as a simple murder case, the court missed an opportunity to discuss the fundamental challenge to Israeli democracy presented by Amir's radical act—the need to draw the limits of civil disobedience in a democratic state. The court also failed to acknowledge the political significance of its own attempts to reconstitute the terms of the Israeli collective identity in ethnonational terms. The judgment thus contributed to eliding the specific historical context in which the murder took place, which was an integral part of the struggle between Jews and Arabs over the future of the land and the borders of the state. In resorting to a mythological memory (a Jew never murders another Jew) the court was also oblivious to the history of harsh political struggles that had led to several political murders in Israel, as we have seen in the Kastner affair. This deliberate amnesia did not enhance the separation of politics from law but rather produced a very distorted kind of political trial that missed an important opportunity to play a role in reinforcing the ideal of full democracy within Israeli society. In the following sections I will suggest an alternative route that could have been taken by the court. First, I consider in what sense the period preceding the murder can be described as a transitional time in Israeli politics. Subsequently, I explore the special dilemmas that such a transition creates for the courts and suggest that the rich scholarship on "transitional justice" can be usefully applied with some modifications to political trials in national courts. In this my approach diverges from the view that transitional justice theory should be applied only to emerging democracies.[92] Finally, I return to Amir's judgment to outline a possible response the court could have made in order to address the difficult questions of transitional justice raised by this trial.

Oslo as a Transitional Period

Any murder is a violation of a basic norm of human society—"Thou shalt not kill"—which enables members of a group to exist in peace. In an ordinary murder case the defendant uses the various lines of defense provided by positive law,[93] without disputing the authority of the legal system to define the act as murder and to adjudicate it accordingly. By contrast, in the case of a political murder the defendant, seeking to advance the ideology in whose name he committed the murder, has no desire to rely primarily on formal legal arguments or on defenses that indicate an impairment of his legal competence. As the Amir case shows, such a defendant prefers to challenge the very legal system that defines his acts as murder and assumes the authority to judge him. In other words, instead of viewing the case as internal to the system, that is, subject to the usual rules of the game, the defendant seeks to present it as external to the system, as challenging the very definition of the rules of the game. In the case of murder, the defendant competes with the sovereign over a fundamental norm: who has the right to define what "murder" is, and what constitutes "self-defense" for a society confronting existential dangers.

Although every society is predicated on the basic norm of "Thou shalt not kill," it also justifies taking an individual's life in certain circumstances according to certain criteria. Thus, in every normative system certain acts of killing are sanctioned as a defense against an enemy that threatens its continued existence. The law thus conveys a dual message of both prohibiting and encouraging violence.[94] It is between the image of the "murderer" and that of the "courageous soldier" that the collective identity of society is forged. The murderer acts against the fundamental norm that enables the community's peaceful existence, while the soldier is prepared to endanger his life to protect the community's continued existence.

In Schmitt's view, the application of the norm "Thou shalt not kill" hinges on the more fundamental and prior definition of who is a friend and who is a foe. In order to define an act as murder we first have to know how the political community defines its boundaries with respect to the Other—the foe.[95] Changes in the collective identity result in shifts in the definition of friend and foe within the community. The political murderer relies on this ambiguity of the basic norm "Thou shalt not kill" to challenge the generally accepted identification of the murder victim as a friend (community member). Therefore, in such cases the defendant often resorts to the argument that the murder victim was in fact an enemy, or a traitor who aided and abetted the enemy, thereby putting the community in jeopardy.

As we have seen, Rabin's assassination had been preceded by a long process of delegitimization on the part of the political opposition to the Oslo peace process and its "directors." Posters displayed at mass demonstrations against the government's policy depicted Rabin wearing SS uniform or an Arab kaffiyeh and identified him as a traitor to Zionist values through his willingness to negotiate with the enemy.[96] Such insinuations revived the traumatic memory of the Kastner trial. It was but a short road from questioning the legitimacy of the Oslo agreement to contesting the legitimacy of the ruling government as a whole and presenting its head as one who had joined forces with the nation's enemies. The step from there to political murder proved equally short.[97] Amir chose to justify his deed in court in these terms, saying, "There is a commandment more important than 'thou shalt not kill'— that to 'save a life.' In this case, one saves lives even when one kills in war. It is a negative act, but its goal is lofty, hence it is permitted to do this."[98]

In times of transition, when there is a shift in the community's boundaries, the application of the basic norm "Thou shalt not kill" is especially problematic. At such moments, an act regarded only yesterday as treason (meeting with the enemy, passing on information, signing agreements) becomes a matter of daily, run of the mill politics (peace negotiations). In such situations there is a greater likelihood that opponents of the change, who cling to the former definitions of friend and foe, will resort to political murder.[99] The initial negotiations over the Oslo accords were one such point of ambiguity. On the one hand, the official ban on meetings with the Palestine Liberation Organization (PLO) and its representatives was still in force,[100] and Abie Nathan, regarded in Israel as a symbol of the peace struggle, was still serving a prison sentence for holding such meetings. On the other hand, the elected leadership was itself meeting clandestinely with PLO representatives to devise a peace agreement. This sudden, completely unexpected shift in the definitions of *friend* and *foe* deepened the ideological rifts within the Jewish population in Israel, creating fears that the process could undermine the basic solidarity of that society.

Although the Oslo accords were intended to move Israel from a state of conflict with the Palestinians to a state of peace, it has been argued that they should be viewed in broader terms as initiating a process of democratization in Israeli society.[101] The attempt to define the external borders of the state was paralleled by a process of redefining the internal boundaries, particularly with regard to the civil status of the Arabs and the status of the Jewish religion in the state. In chapter 7 I discussed the tension between granting formal citizenship to the Arab residents of Israel and the military rule imposed on them in 1948 and revoked only in 1966. We saw that Judge Benjamin Halevi, who tried to give more significant substance to the citizenship of Israel's Arab residents, made do with a passive interpretation of citizenship (protection of the Arabs' right to life and dignity as individuals in Israeli society). This conception of citizenship was still a long way from the active inclusion of Arab citizens as equal partners in the decision-making process in Israeli politics. Indeed, from 1948 to 1992, notwithstanding the Arabs' right to elect and be elected to the Knesset, there was a prevalent taboo that prevented the inclusion of the Arab parties and Arab members of the Knesset in the government coalition. The Oslo accords marked the beginning of a change in this approach. As a result of the 1992 elections, the five members from the Arab parties became crucial to the government's majority in the Knesset. The opposition fiercely criticized Rabin for his willingness to rely on the Arab members to preserve his government, especially when so fundamental an issue as the delineation of the state's borders was on the agenda.[102] Rabin, for his part, staunchly defended his decision, stating that to deny the legitimacy of support from the Arab factions in the Knesset was a racist attitude that endangered democracy. This position led to the campaign to delegitimize the Rabin government.[103]

Rabin's assassination highlighted another tension peculiar to Israeli society: As we have noted previously, the legal system in Israel comprises two normative systems that are supposed to complement each other. In matters of personal law, jurisdiction is given to religious courts that adjudicate in accordance with their religious laws—Jewish law, Islamic law, and so on. On matters of constitutional law, the definition of the state as Jewish means that several issues, such as the decision on who is entitled to enjoy the benefits of the Law of Return, are decided in accordance with the dictates of Jewish law.[104] The two normative systems can coexist because each has developed different doctrines intended to mitigate areas of conflict and tension. Hence, a change in one system necessitates a readjustment in the relationship between the two normative systems. At such moments the delicate balance between the systems is liable to turn into a head-on confrontation between "Jewish" and "democratic" values.[105] Some warned that this was precisely the danger posed by the decision of the elected representatives of the state to negotiate a peace agreement in return for withdrawal from occupied territories when the Halakhah, according to the interpretation of certain circles, regards the sanctity of the Land of Israel as a supreme principle so that relinquishing any part of the land is a violation of religious law. Thus, the effort to resolve the conflict with the Palestinians served to highlight the issues of the status of Jewish religion within the state and the civil equality of Arab Israelis.[106] The issue of external borders (Israel-Palestine) was intertwined with the issue of internal borders (secular-religious), as well as with the profound controversy about the meaning of the state's identity as a Jewish and democratic state.[107]

At this critical time, radicals strove to intensify this tension in a variety of ways. An initial point of friction centered on the question of the duty to obey a potential future order to evacuate Jewish settlements in the occupied territories. Indeed, the plan of Rabin's government to evacuate Jews from the Tel Rumeida settlement in Hebron brought about a dramatic response from several prominent rabbis, who issued Halakhic rulings that categorically prohibited the evacuation of Jewish settlements and proclaimed that such orders were illegal and must be disobeyed by the soldiers.[108] These rulings ostensibly prevented the invocation of one of the principal means of defusing the tension between the two systems of law—the Halakhic rule of subordinating itself to the laws of the land in political matters.[109]

Dilemmas of Transitional Justice in National Courts

Regardless of whether the Oslo agreements are considered in broad terms as a process conducive to maintaining a democratic society in Israel or more narrowly as one that redefined the boundaries of the Israeli political community, it was a moment of transition—a twilight zone between the rules of the previous political game and the new one. Judgment of transitional processes poses a difficult problem for any legal system, a problem that Hannah Arendt dubbed "the riddle of foundation."[110] She contended that any normative system is in effect "suspended in a void" because it is built on a moment of alegality, often manifested by a violent revolution or war, which falls between two normative systems, the previous and the new. The new is usually justified only retroactively, in light of the political answer to the question of whether the revolution succeeded or not. The moment of transition itself seems to fall outside the law. The philosopher Jacques Derrida returns to this issue in his article "Force of Law," to point out the difficulty in judging an alegal and atemporal moment such as this.

> This moment always takes place and never takes place in a presence. It is the moment in which the foundation of law remains suspended in the void or over the abyss, suspended by a pure performative act that would not have to answer to or before anyone. The supposed subject of this pure performative would no longer be before the law, or rather he would be before a law not yet determined, before the law as before a law not yet existing, a law yet to come.[111]

In the Israeli context, the opponents of the peace process tried to compel the court to address the ostensible illegality of the government's deeds at the moment of transition. Among others, in a petition to the High Court of Justice the court was asked to pronounce the negotiations over the transfer of territories an act of treason pursuant to section 97(B) of the Penal Law.[112] The court rejected the petition, stating that there was nothing in criminal law to restrict the government's authority to conduct negotiations insofar as it deemed this "its authority and duty."[113] In other words, the petition attempted to subject the sovereign power to the ordinary law applicable to individuals within the state and the court declined to do so, determining that the sovereign retained the power to determine the community's boundaries.

The distinction between foundational and ordinary politics can also be useful in this context.[114] The petitioners in effect asked the court to recognize that Rabin had overstepped his authority in the realm of foundational politics by attempting to alter the state's borders without appealing to a special process of authorization by the Knesset or a referendum. If this question had been brought before the court in a petition regarding the majority required for approval of the Oslo accords in the Knesset, the court might indeed have felt obligated to address the difficult constitutional issues involved. However, since the petitioners sought to subject Rabin to the criminal law of treason, it was perceived by the court as a symbolic political protest and not as raising a real legal problem.

Although the Knesset has both constitutive and ordinary legislative authority, the question of the special conditions for invoking constitutive authority has so far arisen only with respect to the legislation of basic laws and never with regard to the issue of determining the state's borders.[115] Political scientists who view the entire Oslo process as one of a transition to democracy attribute part of the violence that erupted to this legal void.[116] The process occurred in the absence of agreed-upon democratic rules for deciding such fundamental issues. In principle, the "riddle of foundation" requires addressing the question of how the people can decide democratically who precisely constitutes "we the people" for the sake of determining the permanent borders of the state.[117] Rabin's problem was that he had instituted a peace process with the Palestinians that was meant to redefine the borders of the state, even though the rules of such foundational politics were still indeterminate. In so doing he had also challenged the tacit agreement among the political parties in Israel not to include the elected representatives of Arab citizens of Israel in the crucial decision-making process of determining the state's borders—a consensus that had been perceived as democratic and legitimate in the framework of the previous rules of the game.[118]

This particular Israeli quandary raises the general question of how the court should respond to controversies created by such fundamental political transitions when brought before it for judgment. Does the court in fact possess the tools to deal with foundational politics, and is it the proper forum for determining the rules of the game of foundational politics in the absence of political agreement? The difficulty facing the court in such situations is that any decision on the rules of the game necessarily shapes the outcome of the political dispute. In our matter, preserving the de facto situation of excluding Arab parties from crucial political decisions would have deprived the Israeli government of the majority it needed to bring about a change. On the other hand, invoking the de jure right of Arabs to be elected to the Knesset, and therefore to become part of a government coalition would have changed the old rules of the democratic game in Israel and tipped the scales in favor of altering the borders, with profound implications for the Israeli collective identity. In other words, when a critical controversial issue of transitional politics is brought to the court's doorstep, it cannot keep politics at bay anymore. By ruling on such issues, the court assumes the power to define the very rules of the political game under which it is adjudicating the dispute. This is what transformative politics means when it enters a national court.

A similar question was raised in Canada regarding the constitutionality of unilateral secession by Quebec. The Canadian court decided that even though the question had political implications the court was under the obligation to answer it because it raised important constitutional questions. However, the court limited its decision to "the aspects of the legal framework in which this democratic decision is to be taken." The court thus acquired jurisdiction precisely by framing the question as one concerning the democratic rules of the game. It refused to take the easy way out by treating the issue as nonjusticiable and instead was willing to decide the case according to the fundamental principles of Canada.[119]

If we return now to our particular case, in the period under discussion Yitzhak Rabin was engaged in transformative politics, which purported to redefine the rules of the political game: who was a legitimate partner for negotiations and who could take part in deciding that question, who could take part in determining the state's borders, who could be authorized to define the demos, and so forth. As we have seen, the petition that was brought before the court in an attempt to stop the peace negotiations was formulated in such a way that the court was in fact able to steer clear of this explosive issue. A different formulation would have confronted the court with the basic question that has concerned us throughout this book: what legal rules apply to transformative trials and whether they should differ from the rules that apply to ordinary trials. The decision of the High Court of Justice to dismiss the petition may be construed as determining that the entire matter was not justiciable, meaning that the ball should be returned to the political field for the Knesset to decide, as the American legal scholar Alexander Bickel suggested many years ago.[120] Nonetheless, as we have seen in previous chapters, in the end this question cannot be avoided, especially since it is now being brought to the attention of the Israeli court in criminal suits discussing the limits of freedom of speech (the differ-

ence between incitement and protest),[121] the limits of civil disobedience, and possibly even the invocation of "self-defense" and "necessity" as justification for committing illegal acts of violent protest and
resistance.[122] Although many of these questions were hovering in the
air before Rabin's assassination, they had not been addressed by the
court in an orderly fashion. The assassination returned these questions
to the court, and this time it had to confront them under the difficult
conditions of national trauma engendered by the assassination of a
political leader.

Amir's Judgment: The Road Not Taken

The court's decision to promote a new constitutive narrative predicated
on the mythical memory of internecine warring that had led to the temple's destruction and the people's exile from the land blocked the possibility of addressing other explanations for the prime minister's assassination. The court created the impression that providing the "correct"
religious interpretation of Din Rodef could solve the difficult political
questions raised by the assassination. The court thus eschewed the
opportunity to contribute to building a collective identity on an alternative basis (civic, for instance). This decision had two major implications: it established an ahistorical approach to political murder among
Jews and an apolitical approach to the Jewish-Palestinian dispute.[123]
The "chosen people" discourse fostered by the court reinforced the perception that the political murder committed by Yigal Amir was exceptional. The sentence depicted the people of Israel as always resolving
political disputes through rational dialogue, not through political violence, thus ignoring previous political murders such as those of Haim
Arlosoroff, Rudolf Kastner, or, more recently, Emil Grunzweig during
a peace demonstration in 1983.[124] Rabin's assassination could be
described as an anomaly only if historical precedents were consigned
to oblivion. This mythological approach reveals a reluctance to address
the historical processes that had led to previous political murders in the
Jewish community in Israel. Although there had never been a murder
of such a high-level Jewish political leader by another Jew in the modern age, a certain pattern can be discerned. Thus, for instance, the
course of negotiations advocated by the various murder victims had
been depicted as collaboration with the enemy, whence it was but a
short step to accusing them of betraying their people.[125] Similarly, the

rhetoric justifying the political murder voiced by radical opposition groups in the previous affairs had also borne a quasi-legal nature. This disregard of modern history and similarities with these previous political murders is odd in view of the court's great effort to find parallels between Rabin's assassination and precedents from the nation's ancient tradition.

This supplanting of historical memory by mythological memory also had implications for understanding the Jewish-Palestinian dispute. Although the assassination required the court to address the relations within the Jewish community that had led to this murder, the court refrained from dealing with the origins of the violence in the context of the Israeli-Palestinian conflict in an effort to avoid all political controversy. In effect, the sentence created a virtual space consisting only of Jews. Even though Rabin's assassination took place against the backdrop of a deep dispute regarding the settlement of geographical borders between Israel and the Palestinians, and indirectly the boundaries of the collective identity, in essence the sentence isolated the intra-Jewish discourse from the Jewish-Palestinian discourse. This compartmentalization did not leave any room for drawing comparisons with cases of intercommunal murder, such as Baruch Goldstein's massacre of Palestinians in the Machpela Cave in Hebron—also in response to the peace process—even though Amir himself invoked this comparison several times during the trial.[126] This conceptual separation between murders committed between Arab and Jews and those committed inside the Jewish community precluded an understanding of the political pressures at work.[127]

Amir himself used his legal defense to expose the double standard prevailing in Israel: when asked what had made him think that assassinating Rabin would stop the peace process, Amir pointed to the longstanding policy of so-called target killings carried out by the Israeli Mossad and General Security Service against suspected Palestinian terrorists. Indeed, about a week before his assassination, Rabin had ordered the killing of the Islamic Jihad leader Fatkhi Shkaki. In other words, Amir pointed to the power of the sovereign to determine the outcast (whose killing will not be considered murder) and placed himself in direct competition with it.[128]

Rabin's murder, then, marks the ease with which events in the Jewish-Palestinian sphere could spill over into the intra-Jewish sphere. All that was needed to justify Rabin's murder was to mark him as an Other (traitor, persecutor) to the Jewish collective. Amir's deed shattered the illusion that it was possible to maintain concurrently the "rule of law" within the pre-1967 borders and the "rule of force" in the occupied territories. However, by embracing in its sentence a particularistic discourse about Jews as the chosen people the court engaged in the same practice of concealing the interrelation between the two spheres. This rhetoric prevented the court from contending with the dual messages that Israel's citizens, Jews and Arabs alike, are given with regard to the rule of law and with the substantive dangers that this situation engenders for the possibility of maintaining a democratic regime in Israel.

As we saw, the sentence contains a different voice—that of Judge Savyona Rotlevi—which subtly subverts the retreat to Jewish memory and to the particularistic identity of "a nation that shall dwell alone" as a response to the murderer. The dispute between the two approaches is not merely a scholarly debate. The question of collective memory embodies an ethical choice concerning which historical patterns are to be used to comprehend the collective lesson that should be drawn from the case at hand. This choice shapes a community's relationship with its past and future and with the groups with which it shares a common space. By choosing the tradition of Jewish memory, Rabin's murder was dissociated from the Jewish-Palestinian dispute and turned into a purely internal Jewish matter. Against the backdrop of these processes of collective amnesia, Rotlevi's short verdict stands out as a warning sign. By linking Rabin's assassination to the history of European totalitarianism and fascism, she refused to detach the Jewish nation from general history, rejecting the particularistic approach that served to obscure the disturbing processes at work in Israeli society in this time of transformation.

Conclusion
Between Transformative Trials
and Truth Commissions

This book has explored the various ways in which a transformative trial can be used to enhance a society's commitment to democracy. The problems raised by transformative trials can in many ways be compared to those that truth and reconciliation commissions (TRC) are designed to overcome. Indeed, in the context of societies engaged in a transition from a nondemocratic to a democratic regime there has been a growing movement to replace criminal trials with TRCs that relinquish the punitive aspect of criminal justice in order to secure the stability of the new regime while insisting on exposing the truth about the previous regime's crimes.[1] This truth becomes part of the new society's collective memory. The recovery of a more accurate past is seen as an integral part of democratization. In South Africa and elsewhere, victims of the previous regime were allowed to testify before these commissions about the injuries and injustices they had suffered. Separating the role of punishment from the role of relating history allowed a deviation from the rules of evidence so that the victims' testimonies of their traumatic experiences did not violate the defendants' right to a fair trial.

As I argued in the introduction to the book many of the dilemmas of political trials to which liberal theory does not provide an answer are engaged seriously and creatively in the debate about TRC. In particular, three dilemmas that arose in each of the trials discussed in this book have received new theoretical elaboration in the literature on transitional justice. What role should be given to the personal testimonies of survivors? Where should the line be drawn between the rule of law and the desire to advance "external" goals such as a responsible representation of the past and the promotion of collective memory in a divided society? How can the trial be used as a vehicle of reconciliation between the victims and civil society, and what role does the social critic play in such a process? These questions are illuminated at moments of transition, but, as this book has demonstrated, they are also prevalent in transformative trials. By reading the four Israeli trials as interacting with each other and by treating the legal questions as shaped and influenced by several centers of gravity—politics, historical consciousness, and social and cultural criticism—I aimed to show the alternative approaches to conducting criminal trials that were advocated, and rejected, at the time of the trials as real possibilities. However, working with real cases, I could not open a broad enough door for the imagination to freely consider radically different solutions unburdened by the specific history and politics in which the trials took place. In this chapter I would like to use a work of art, the film *Death and the Maiden* (directed by Roman Polanski),[2] to illuminate these dilemmas in a context untrammeled by historical contingencies. I shall consider what this film can teach us about law and its relation to violence and vengeance in transformative trials. What can we learn about the role of the victim? And, finally, how can the insistence on conducting a trial as opposed to the more flexible alternative of a TRC help achieve the political goals of transformative justice?

The film *Death and the Maiden* presents a dramatic case against the solution of a truth commission and confronts viewers with the legal dilemmas it creates in a vivid and concentrated way. The film emphasizes that by giving up the encounter between victim and aggressor in a court of law the truth commission forgoes an important advantage of transformative justice—a collective confrontation, on a public stage, with the moral dilemmas raised by the previous regime. It is this confrontation that can help achieve one of the most important objectives of the trial, namely, the reconciliation between the victims and civil society. After discussing the three dilemmas as they are presented in the film, I return to our real trials to consider how the film can illuminate the common threads connecting them and yield a strong argument in favor of transformative justice.

1. Death and the Maiden

Death and the Maiden creates an unusual encounter between the victim, Paulina Escobar, formerly a political prisoner of the military regime in her country (a South American country, probably Chile), and Roberto Miranda, the doctor who tortured and raped her while in captivity to the music of Schubert's "Death and the Maiden." The encounter takes place in Paulina's beach house years after the military regime has been replaced. The plot begins at the moment when the new regime has just appointed Paulina's husband, Gerardo, to be head of a commission investigating the former regime's violations of human rights. At the time of the military regime Gerardo had been a student leader and editor of an underground newspaper who was being sought by the authorities. Despite the torture she underwent, Paulina had not disclosed his identity, thus saving his life. On the stormy night at the beginning of the film, Gerardo's car breaks down and he is given a lift back home by a passerby (a good Samaritan) who turns out to be the same Dr. Miranda. Once Paulina recognizes the doctor's voice (she had been blindfolded in captivity and never saw him), she flees from the house in his car. In the car, she finds a tape of "Death and the Maiden," which further convinces her that this is indeed the doctor who tortured and raped her. In her rage she pushes his car over a cliff. This is a turning point, however, and instead of continuing to run away from her torturer Paulina returns home to confront her past. Now the judicial drama begins. She returns, ties Dr. Miranda to a chair at gunpoint, blindfolds him, stuffs her panties into his mouth and puts on the music "Death and the Maiden." Gerardo, awakened by the noise, convinces Paulina to let him obtain a confession from Dr. Miranda in exchange for his life. The film follows the quasi-judicial process that ensues during that night.

The opening point of the film is a modern attempt by the new regime to turn the clock back—to take the law out of the courtroom and place it in the hands of a pragmatic truth commission. The pragmatism and utilitarianism that look to the future are represented in the play by Gerardo the lawyer, who takes it upon himself to head the commission, knowing that it will serve as a fig leaf for the criminals of the former regime and will allow their reintegration into the new society.[3] Paulina, presented as a modern-day Fury, reproaches Gerardo for his decision, seeing it as a betrayal of their common path, seemingly preferring the way of violence and revenge. As in Aeschylus's play The Oresteia, the woman represents uncompromising vengeance.[4] In contrast, the men, Gerardo and Dr. Miranda, representing the new and the old regimes respectively, both profess political pragmatism. The men want a truth commission, the woman wants justice. By depicting Paulina as a modern-day Fury, Polanski reminds the viewers that law itself retains an element of vengeance and violence and cannot do without it. Moreover, the reference to *Oresteia* suggests that it is only through this kind of justice that a real halt can come to the cycle of blood feuds. Gerardo, like Athena in the Greek myth, has to persuade Paulina to abandon violence for the sake of establishing a judicial process.[5] During the course of persuasion, however, Gerardo himself changes his position and becomes an active participant in Paulina's trial (despite its violation of human rights). Gerardo persuades Paulina to be satisfied with a confession as a substitute for killing Dr. Miranda—and actually becomes Roberto Miranda's defense lawyer, trying to elicit a confession from him in order to save him. Paulina is the victim who, with the gun in her hand, becomes both prosecutor and judge.

The judicial process in the film is presented as a compromise that requires each of the participants to concede something important. Paulina has to relinquish violence, the will to exact "an eye for an eye." She tells Gerardo she would have liked to repay Dr. Miranda in his own coin, to rape him, but she is unable to do so and does not believe Gerardo will do it for her.[6] Instead, she settles for his promise to extract a recorded and written confession of Dr. Miranda's deeds. Speech itself becomes the symbolic punishment of Dr. Miranda.[7] Gerardo also needs to give something up. He is aware that by initiating a pseudojudicial process that involves extracting a confession at gunpoint he is violating the principles of rule by law to which he is committed. He might jeopardize his political future (the possibility of being appointed minister of justice). Moreover, it is against his principles: the new regime is forbidden to repeat the crimes of the old one—to take part in a process in which prosecutor, judge, and executioner are one and the same. Still, his willingness to take part in this judicial process allows him to hear from Paulina the details of the torture and rape she has suffered. It also gives him the opportunity to prevent the murder of a man who might be innocent. Dr. Miranda is required to relinquish his lie. In order to save his life he must reveal the man behind the mask. The dignified doctor is required to confess his criminal deeds so that they become part of the collective memory.

Although TRCs also require compromises, the trial in the film differs from that format by giving voice to the victim and the perpetrator through a conflictual encounter between them. As the film shows, the truth commission headed by Gerardo is structured so that it silences the human voice. On the one hand, its jurisdiction is limited to investigating only the most severe cases of human rights violations, those resulting in death. In practice, this means that the victims of those crimes are no longer alive to bear witness. Paulina, who survived her ordeal, kept her story concealed for years for fear of being exposed and hurt. Now that she wants to speak out, there is no one on the truth commission who will listen, for the crimes she suffered are outside its jurisdiction.[8] Nonetheless, the voices of the criminals of the former regime are not really heard either. Since the commission's authority is limited to writing a general report about the crimes, without identifying the individual transgressors, there is no need to take individual confessions from the people investigated or have them give evidence publicly. The uniqueness of the compromise proposed by Paulina's trial is in allowing the individual voices of victim and aggressor to be heard through the painful encounter mediated by the lawyer. In this context, the role of the gun (the tool of violence and terror) as an enabler of dialogue is interesting.

Immediately after Gerardo is awakened by the noise in the living room, to find his wife pointing a gun at their guest, the following dialogue takes place between them.

> *Gerardo:* Paulina, I'm asking you to please give me that gun.
> *Paulina:* No.
> *Gerardo:* While you point it at me, there is no possible dialogue.
> *Paulina:* On the contrary, as soon as I stop pointing it at you, all dialogue will automatically terminate. If I put it down you'll use your strength to win the argument.[9]

The existence of a gun, which is physically present at Paulina's trial, is usually out of sight in a regular trial. It is this failure to remember the connection between violence and law that enables different writers to address the similarity between law and literature, and legal and literary interpretation, without drawing the important distinction between them.[10]

The gun reminds us of the element of violence and the asymmetry that characterizes political trials. Every political trial begins with what can be described as a situation of "radical difference" in which two groups holding opposite or irreconcilable ideas about law and society meet in court. The conflict is radical in the sense that the two sides cannot agree about the law that governs the dispute. The controversy cannot be solved solely by legal means since it raises the prior (meta-) questions of what legal system has the right to adjudicate the conflict and what tribunal has jurisdiction over it. In effect, each side calls for the recognition of a different historical narrative according to which the court should adjudicate the case. In such cases the triad structure of a trial collapses into a binary structure of two opposite sides facing each other in a power struggle without an accepted overriding law that can function as arbiter. In an ordinary trial, the two disputing parties can bring their case before a third party whose position as an "outsider" to the dispute can guarantee its impartiality and endow its ruling with legitimacy. In cases of radical difference, there is no third party because the court itself is deemed by one of the parties to be its adversary and the legitimacy of the court itself is called into question. Such a crisis is manifest after a war or revolution when one regime judges its predecessor's crimes. But it can also occur in regular trials within functioning democracies, especially where there is an ongoing conflict among ethnic, religious, and national groups.[11] The doctrine of the "separation of powers" is of little help in situations of radical difference because the controversy concerns the legal foundations of the state and the court is required to judge those who pose a fundamental threat to the state in whose name the court is adjudicating the case.

Paulina's gun forces us not only to be aware of the law's dependence on violence but also to face the unique dilemmas involved in seeking a balance between violence and law in a confrontation between people holding two irreconcilable worldviews. Paulina's trial does not expel violence but puts limits on its legitimate use. In this respect we realize that, despite the fact that extracting a confession from Dr. Miranda at gunpoint is a serious breach of the rules of fair trial, Paulina's gun is not used to kill him. The film introduces the gun to mark the possibility of delineating the narrow but critical line that distinguishes a political trial held by a democratic regime from the show trials of authoritarian regimes. It is the existence of the gun throughout the film in the hands of Paulina, and sometimes in the hands of Gerardo, but never handed back to Dr. Miranda, that forces viewers to reflect on the neutrality of the court in a transitional trial. It also sharpens the dilemmas discussed in this book arising from the marriage of two very different goals of the trial—determining the guilt of the defendant while responding to the needs of the victims of a collective trauma. I will discuss several important dilemmas that highlight the ongoing tension between adherence to reason (rule of law) and the need to open the legal process to other no less important aims such as restoring the integrity of the victims, giving a responsible account of history, and promoting civic reconciliation and democratization in a divided society.

2. Dilemmas

Personal and Public Truth

> PAULINA: It may be a teensy-weensy thing, but it's enough for me. During all these years not an hour has passed that I haven't heard it, that same voice, next to me, next to my ear, that voice mixed with saliva, you think I'd forget a voice like his?[12]

It is customary to think of the judicial process as one aimed at establishing the "objective truth" by means of legal procedures. Objective truth is generally understood as the opposite of a lie. The film undermines this assumption when comparing what is considered by law to be an objective truth with the victim's subjective truth.

Dr. Miranda denies being the doctor who raped Paulina. Paulina cannot provide the "queen of evidence"—the testimony of an eyewitness—as she was blindfolded when she was tortured. Her testimony is at best *hearsay*, not in the legal but in the literal sense of the word, for she initially identified Dr. Miranda when she heard his voice. This voice identification is positive enough to awaken all her past fears and make her flee in panic from her home and refuge. Legally, however, this is not sufficient identification.[13] Paulina's private truth, her positive identification, is based on two other signs that would not hold up in court. She recognizes Dr. Miranda's scent (smell is the most private sense we have, and it cannot be recaptured objectively in court).[14] She identifies him also by the tape of "Death and the Maiden," which she finds in his car, and by his chauvinistic quotes from Nietzsche. These pieces of evidence are also inadmissible in the eyes of the law. Being so widespread—music by Schubert and writings by Nietzsche—they cannot be construed as exclusive to Dr. Miranda. The film enables us to understand that things that cannot be regarded as objective truth by the court are not necessarily lies. We learn that juridical truth is "objective" only in the sense that it can be proven in public. Subjective or personal truth may be a certainty to the victim, but it is an insufficient basis for conviction. The film highlights in this way the high price the victim must pay when entering a judicial process. To achieve public recognition of her status as victim, Paulina must relinquish her private, deepest truth, which is based on her intimate knowledge of the man who raped her—the combination of scent, voice, and music. She must subordinate herself to the judicial demands of objective evidence, that is, she must obtain a written and recorded confession from Dr. Miranda, which can later become a part of history.

Blaming the Victim

> DR. MIRANDA: I don't know you, madam. I have never seen you before in my life. But I can tell you this: you are extremely ill, almost prototypically schizoid.[15]

In exchange for a confession, Gerardo persuades Paulina to give up violence. She is willing to do so if she receives Dr. Miranda's acknowledgment that she has spoken the truth and a detailed confession of his crimes. His confession can be the "objective evidence" needed for conviction. Here, however, Paulina must confront another dilemma. In the competition between the victim's and the defendant's words, the law in many cases prefers those of the latter. The defendant, who is a dignified, civilized doctor, sounds credible, while Paulina, suffering from trauma, seems "crazy" to those around her. This is a dilemma that arises in many trials and hinders the use of victims' testimony, but it is particularly disturbing in a transitional trial in which large segments of society have been victimized by the previous regime. The paradox is that the worse the horrors inflicted on the victims and the greater the mental scars they have left the less credible the victims will seem in the eyes of the law. Paulina tries to make an important distinction between her illness and her ability to be a credible witness when she says to Gerardo: "I can be sick and recognize a voice."[16] Gerardo finally believes Paulina, but it is doubtful that a regular court would have done so.[17]

It is interesting to note that in many instances the need to tell the story is not forced on the victims by the court but is rather an inner need of their own, as in Paulina's case. However, since her story is so painful and threatens to destroy the delicate fabric of normal existence that she has created with her husband, there has to be a good reason for her to tell her story. A truth commission that promises amnesty to the perpetrators cannot induce her to talk since it offers too little. The trial of Dr. Miranda, on the other hand, acts as a trigger that impels her to relate the story of her rape. In order to extract Dr. Miranda's testimony from him, Gerardo has to function as a lawyer, that is, he must learn from Paulina all the details he had previously been reluctant to hear and had refrained from asking her about. Paulina's story is heard differently this time. It is heard as part of the public record and therefore has to be detailed and accurate. Her testimony changes her from that of an archetypal victim to that of a specific victim with a name and a story. Ironically, not only Dr. Miranda's identity is revealed in the course of the trial but Paulina's identity as well, for in order to obtain Miranda's acknowledgment that she is his victim she not only relates the details of her story but also describes herself as a young woman (her long hair, her love of Schubert, her hope to become a doctor) and states her maiden name—Paulina Lorca. The judicial process is therefore essential also for constituting (or, more precisely, for rehabilitating) the victim's individual identity.

Admissibility of Confession: "The Miranda Rules"

> To speak of confessions of crime made after the arrest as being "voluntary" or "uncoerced," this assertion is somewhat inaccurate, although traditional.[18]

Paulina's self-exposure and disclosure, despite the danger they pose to her, are intended to make Dr. Miranda confess his true identity and tell of his part in the previous regime's crimes. He is required to recount what he did to Paulina. Only his recorded and written confession will be considered credible evidence in the eyes of the law and will enable Paulina's story to become part of her country's collective memory. The film raises difficult questions concerning the credibility of the confession extracted from Dr. Miranda. It is given under duress. Dr. Miranda sits frozen, his head bandaged, in front of a video camera and reads aloud a text that has been dictated to him. How can such a confession be given any consideration? There is a slight irony in the play, as Dr. Miranda's name alludes to the well-known Miranda Rules instituted in the United States, which demand that the defendant be made aware of his or her right to representation by a lawyer and of the right to remain silent to avoid self-incrimination.[19] The film, however, reveals a more general truth about confessions in trials, a truth that we usually prefer to forget. Behind the facade of civilized speech that we witness in court always stand the power and violence of the law. Were it not for fear of them, confessions would not be given.[20] Paulina's words about the power of the gun become a metaphor for the entire judicial process.

Civil Society at the Crossroads of the Political Trial

A trial poses questions and demands answers from both victims and perpetrators. In trials of "transitional justice," however, the whole of society is actually put on trial for its past. The most difficult questions are those posed to civil society, to those people who were neither victims nor perpetrators but bystanders. At a certain stage of Paulina's trial she turns the questions back on Gerardo. Gerardo, who functions as the lawyer, suddenly becomes the accused. At the very time Paulina was withstanding torture in order to protect him, he began a relationship with another woman. This is the "original sin" that casts a shadow on their relationship. He owes her his life and is guilty of having betrayed her. Gerardo married Paulina and takes care of her, but he will never be able to repay his debt. Or so it seems until the trial. In the course of that night Paulina asks him for the first time what he did during her abduction, how many times he met the other woman, and how many times they made love.[21] These questions bring to the surface her harsh accusations of him. Her trial, however, affords Gerardo the opportunity to somehow make amends. He had promised her that he would bring the perpetrators to justice and publicize their crimes. Paulina gives him the chance to do the one thing that might induce her to forgive him. The film therefore demonstrates that the true reconciliation facilitated by a trial is that between victims and the general public, not between victims and perpetrators.

3. *In Favor of Political Trials*

Paulina's trial succeeds in achieving its declared objective: the extraction from Dr. Miranda of a confession of his guilt. This success, however, comes at the expense of many deviations from the rules of fair trial and of conventional criminal proceedings. In effect, the trial succeeds only on account of its deviations from the rules of due process.

For example, if proper legal procedure had been strictly observed, either Paulina herself would have been disqualified as a witness or her testimony would have been dismissed as not credible. Had that happened, the trial would not have been able to serve as a medium for the victim's reacceptance into civil society. On the other hand, the film forces us to confront the difficult question of where to draw the line between legitimate political trials and show trials, how to limit the excessive use of force by the state even for the sake of what is seen as a just cause. In the process, we discover that the central goal of the political trial is not to punish the guilty, at least not in the conventional sense of the term. What at the film's outset seems to be the prime objective of the process, namely, to obtain Dr. Miranda's confession of his crimes, later turns out to be less important. The film teaches us that the contribution of the political trial lies in the process itself. The main goal of the political trial is to establish a strong foundation for a democratization process and from it to derive three secondary objectives.

The first objective is to clarify the truth—not truth as established by outside experts but truth as it emerges from the mouths of the victims and perpetrators themselves. "Subjective truth," therefore, is just as important as "objective truth." The importance of the trial lies in its initiating a long and complex process in which, from the testimony of victims and victimizers, a collective memory is founded. Retaining a place for the subjective voice promises a multiplicity of perspectives, which is essential for a genuine political deliberation. Political trials, by offering an opportunity for an individual to bring forth his or her unique story, can become an essential ingredient of the political culture of liberal societies that seek both to enhance the respect for the individual as a unique being and to celebrate public deliberation based on the common knowledge that arises from the victims' experiences. In contrast to history books, the primary power of legal "truth" resides in its being based on a commonly known story that relies on the testimony of victims as an integral component of society's collective memory.

The second objective of the political trial is a public confrontation with the moral dilemma of delineating a border between seeing justice being done and a commitment to the rule of law. This goal can be achieved only if it is understood that general rules and legal precedents cannot dictate the boundary between law and politics. Rather, every society has to redefine that line on the basis of its own particular past and renewed social consensus. This negotiation takes place among civil society, juridical institutions, and the victims. A definition of this boundary universally and in advance, provided by the sages of law, undermines this process. Political trials are dynamic, not the product of some formula either valid for a specific society across time or valid cross-culturally. Rather, since these trials are intertwined with the political, they always have to confront the unique feature of the political: the unexpected and the new, the natality inherent in this sphere of human affairs.

The third objective of the political trial is the process of reconciliation. The crimes that separate the torturer from his or her victim are unforgivable and beyond reconciliation. All that can be done is to know the truth about the crimes and to seek to prevent their recurrence. Thus, the emphasis placed by the literature on reconciliation between victim and victimizer diverts our attention from the processes of reconciliation that are actually accessible through legal channels, that is, those between the victims and civil society. The very fact that the trial takes place signifies society's decision to accept responsibility for the victims of the previous regime. The success of the trial can be measured only by examining to what extent it has encouraged members of society to confront difficult questions regarding their own responsibility for the existence of that oppressive regime. Conducting the trial is tantamount to taking responsibility for the victims, and declaring society's readiness to refrain from blaming them, and instead to begin coping with society's own guilt as well.[22] The great challenge that every such political trial poses is how to achieve these goals without running the risk of adopting the same techniques employed by the previous, oppressive regime.

4. *Transitional Justice and Transformative Trials*

The fictional trial presented in *Death and the Maiden* occurs during the transition from an authoritarian-military regime to a democratic system. The real cases discussed in this book occurred after the establishment of a democratic regime committed to the rule of law. And yet we have seen that these trials could not fit the goals and dilemmas of ordinary criminal trials since here, too, the need to confront the past and address a collective trauma raised the difficult issue of democratization in the shadow of the law. For this reason, I proposed the more inclusive term *transformative trials* to alert our attention to the political transformation sought by the participants and to the constructive process of negotiations over the fundamental values of society that is present in each.

It is important, however, to note the difference between the two situations. Transitional justice proceedings are constitutive of, and prior to, the establishment of a legal system, and as such they enjoy broader legitimacy for deviating from ordinary rules of evidence and procedure. They are seen as exceptional cases that represent the need of society to symbolically draw the line between the past and the present, thus requiring flexibility in the use of the legal tools that are ordinarily used to deal with individual breaches of the law, not with a regime's crimes. Moreover, at this fragile moment there is considerable concern about the ability of the new regime to resist the pressures of the previous power holders so that some political compromise is acceptable.

This is no longer the case after the establishment of a democratic regime with a functioning legal system. On the one hand, every deviation from ordinary procedures threatens to become a precedent, and therefore to undermine the functioning of criminal law, and on the other hand, the opposition represented by the defendant on trial is seen as less dangerous. Hence, there is much less willingness on the part of the court and the legislators to change the rules of procedure or even to admit the legitimacy of seeking to achieve political goals through the trial beyond the establishment of innocence and guilt. However, despite the difference between the two cases, there is continuity between transitional and transformative justice. Democracy is a political system that constantly reinvents itself, and one of its unique features is its ability to create proper institutions that allow such a reinvention to take place without violence and with a necessary degree of continuity. The parliament is an obvious place where such deliberations and changes take place, but due to systematic failures of representation of certain groups and voices marginal groups tend to use some trials as places to voice their criticism of the system that excludes them publicly, even if only in confined and distorted ways.[23]

In each of the four cases discussed in this book, I have pointed out the futility of denying their political element and the need to find ways to go beyond legalistic concerns to accommodate the "external" goals of transformative justice within the framework of the rule of law. In the following pages, I will discuss briefly how the dilemmas of transition illuminated in *Death and the Maiden* were present in each of our trials and how the theory of transformative justice helped resolve them in a more satisfying way than traditional liberal legalism could.

Personal Testimonies in Transformative Trials

Establishing the truth through the testimony of survivors played a role in each of the first three trials we discussed. However, these testimonies were not always intended to disclose a personal truth like the one offered by Paulina but were sometimes used by the lawyers to achieve political goals. Thus, in the Kastner trial the survivors' testimonies were not meant to reveal their personal truths about the failure of the rescue plans during the Holocaust but to enhance an ideological narrative about the failure of the Zionist leadership. For this reason the witnesses were not asked about their experiences but were asked to answer one simple (and misleading) question: if they had known about the destination of the trains, would they have boarded them? We also saw that the adversarial framework of the trial, in which the prosecution summoned public figures to testify while the defense summoned ordinary people, helped reenact the selection between prominent Jews who were saved and ordinary Jews who were sent to their deaths. Since the survivors' testimonies did not enable the public to view reality through eyes of the Other (enlarged mentality) and did not help dismantle ideological blinders, the verdict failed to bring about catharsis or reconciliation and only sharpened the binary view of the Holocaust that was prevalent at the time.

Against this background I discussed the innovative approach taken by the prosecution in the Eichmann trial, which sought to open the legal stage to Holocaust survivors in order to listen to their personal experiences and entertain their points of view as much as possible. However, here, too, the prosecution tended to instrumentalize the testimonies by trying to fit them into the Zionist narrative that represented the establishment of the State of Israel as an act of redemption after the catastrophe. This ideological framework collapsed during the trial under the weight of the testimonies and the refusal of survivors to simplify their experiences (as we have seen in the testimony of Hansi Brand and Moshe Beiski.) Undermining the ideological framework proved to be more difficult with regard to Eichmann's testimony, as the prosecution tried to fit him into the traditional saga of eternal anti-Semitic persecution. However, the courageous decision of the judges to investigate Eichmann in the German language allowed some of the most illuminating moments in the trial and supplied the basis for Arendt's report.

The decisions to set aside the controversial issue of the Judenrate and the Kastner affair in the Eichmann trial and to place the survivors alongside the prosecution were crucial to enabling the survivors to talk about their experiences without feeling that they were being blamed for their own victimization. It is from this vantage point that the Kufr Qassem trial can be seen as falling between these two poles of personal and instrumental truth. The decision to conduct the trial and keep most of its sessions open to the public created the conditions for an Israeli court to listen empathetically to the testimonies of Palestinian victims of the deadly brutality of Israeli soldiers. However, the structural constraints of the case—the fact that this was a military court where all the defendants wore uniforms, spoke in Hebrew, and were represented by their lawyers of choice—had the effect of marking out the Arab witnesses, who were not a formal party to the trial and were represented by the military prosecution, as Others. All of these factors placed constraints on their testimony and caused them to reexperience their trauma during the trial.

These cases teach us that it is not enough to summon the victims to give testimony in a court of law. There must be a genuine commitment of the community to use the trial as part of the reintegration of the victims into society, a commitment that can be translated into changes in the law of procedure, appointing special lawyers, and creating an empathetic atmosphere in the court of law. In other words, maintaining the difference between personal truth and instrumental testimony depends on two elements of reflective judgment—listening to the narrative of the Other and facilitating a process of enlarged mentality in which this narrative is allowed to enter the audience's world and challenge some of its preconceptions. When this happens, political trials can offer a unique opportunity for enlarging the heterogeneity of the public sphere and bringing new perspectives to bear on the democratic deliberation. But when these elements are missing these trials can also perpetuate certain ideologies and prejudices. The result depends on a variety of factors: the judges, the lawyers, those who testify, and the political climate outside the courtroom.

As *Death and the Maiden* shows, since the personal truth of the victim is often too painful to discuss, the law has to create real incentives for the victim to come forward and testify. Although TRCs, which reject the adversarial structure and eliminate cross-examination of the victims, create a more empathetic atmosphere, at the same time they can weaken the incentive to talk altogether since the perpetrator is usually promised amnesty and the court does not function as a meeting place (even if a constrained and adversarial one) between victim and perpetrator. As has been noted by others, the very act of entering into an argument with an antagonist, as is usually the case in the courtroom, establishes relations and is the beginning of a dialogue even when this does not lead to agreement.[24] The question of which format to favor—a political trial or TRC—also depends on variables such as whether the two groups of victims and victimizers are to separate into two political entities or whether they are to share the same political system, whether there are representatives of the two sides in the legal process (as attorneys, judges, or juries) or whether it is dominated by one side, whether there is a strong identification between the court and one of the sides, and so forth. The differences in this regard between the Eichmann and Kufr Qassem trials may have had long-term influences. While the first trial led Israeli society to listen to individual stories of the Holocaust and changed the entire nature of the historiography of this event, the failure of the latter to include the stories of the individual victims as individual human beings in the Israeli collective memory enhanced an abstract moral discourse about Israeli-Palestinian relations.

Drawing the Lines (illiberal foundations)

This dilemma is strongly felt in the transition to democracy when the new regime undertakes to prosecute the crimes of the old regime with the individualizing tools of traditional criminal law, but it is also present when a democracy is forced to confront radically new crimes.[25] The Eichmann case presented this problem to the Israeli court most directly by raising such questions as retroactivity, extraterritorial jurisdiction, collective responsibility, and the law of conspiracy. The other cases also involved deviations from traditional liberal notions of criminal law since they all had to tackle the problem of targeting an individual for the crimes carried out on behalf of a group. Since a criminal trial, unlike a truth commission, cannot resort to different rules of procedure when dealing with the victims and the defendant, the need to draw the line between victims' and defendants' rights, between the demands of justice and the demands of politics, cannot be avoided. Contrary to the prevailing view, I argued that it is precisely this difficulty that constitutes the strength of a criminal trial over a TRC because it forces society to confront publicly the dilemma of how far it is willing to go to achieve important political goals at the cost of its liberal commitments. This problem is connected to the element of natality, present in every reflective judgment, which attempts to transcend traditional concepts in order to address the novelty of the political situation under consideration. In the Kastner trial, Judge Halevi of the district court decided to rely on the Law of Punishment of the Nazis and Their Collaborators in relaxing the rules of evidence (e.g., by allowing testimonies on the paratrooper affair that were not directly connected to the libel charges) and the rules of procedure with regard to the scope and order of the testimonies in the trial. These deviations allowed the judge to seek the historical truth with fewer constraints, but at the same time they jeopardized the rights of the de facto defendant Rudolf Kastner. The appellate court took the opposite direction and drew the line very narrowly, criticizing Judge Halevi for his deviations and limiting the role of the court to establishing the legal truth needed for the trial, thus leaving many of the historical controversies unresolved.

Deciding where to draw the line between creativity and continuity, between the needs of the political situation and the rule of law, was not the prerogative of one actor in any of the trials but was seen as a negotiated process (or an ongoing conversation) between the judges, the attorneys, the government, and the social critics. This negotiation is beautifully captured in *Death and the Maiden* in the negotiation over who should hold the gun. The dialogue among institutions (committed to very different rules of discourse and decision making), which makes this question a matter of vital interest to society as a whole, thus becomes part and parcel of the larger negotiation over the meaning of the democratic system.[26] These negotiations are not always tension free, as we have seen in the Kufr Qassem trial. The court's attempt to draw the line in such a way that the rule of law would override national security arguments and would be applied to the army was resisted both by the army—which asked for closed sessions and the defense of obedience to superior orders—and by the government—which attempted to avoid the trial by conducting a partial reconciliation (forced *sulha*) with the village's leaders prior to the trial—as well as by granting the amnesty to the convicted soldiers after the trial.[27] In terms of transformative justice theory, the court attempted to note the novelty of the situation by resorting to reflective judgment, providing an exemplary narrative about the "black flag," and introducing a new legal concept of the duty to disobey "manifestly illegal" orders. One can only surmise what spurred the court at this specific historic moment to be willing to listen to testimony about the brutality of the IDF soldiers and to intervene in the name of the rule of law.[28] Nonetheless, the political authorities threatened to render this judgment meaningless by mitigating the punishments, promoting the convicted soldiers in the ranks of the civil service, and later appointing a "friendly" court when the highest commander of the massacre was brought to trial, which sentenced him to a fine of one cent. These political interventions signaled to the Israeli public that the court's decision was only symbolic and that crimes committed in the name of "security" were still immune from the rule of law. It also signified that the Arab victims were to be kept outside the domain of the Israeli collective memory. We can trace the long-term effects of this attitude in the de facto exclusion of the Arab citizens of Israel from the political process of decision making and also in the difficulties faced by Prime Minister Yitzhak Rabin when he attempted to change this situation abruptly during the Oslo peace process. Ironically, this exclusion was also manifest in the decision against Yigal Amir, which warned against assassination by invoking the ancient traditions of the Jewish collective memory while entirely ignoring the modern history of political violence in Israel, which is intimately connected to the conflict between Palestinians and Israelis.

The tension between the court and the government explains the dynamic of constraint and legitimation that is present in every political trial. The inability of the political branch to control the court, and the inability of the court to completely constrain the political branch are evident in this struggle. However, much of the struggle occurs away from the public eye, and it is for this reason that the social critic plays such an important role both in reporting the political interventions and in articulating the legal question in terms of where to draw the line of the rule of law and what impact this will have on society's commitment to democracy. The interesting question concerns the relative roles of the court, the government, and civil society in drawing this line and maintaining it over time. I described Arendt's critique of the Eichmann trial in these terms, exposing the "cost" that excluding the story of the Judenrate, resorting to ethnic categorization, and, most importantly, using the trial to create solidarity through an opposition to an Other had for the democratic culture of the state. The Israeli authorities perceived this criticism as too threatening at the time and succeeded in preventing the translation of Arendt's book into Hebrew. In the absence of the most eloquent dissenting voice, these issues did not become part of the Israeli public debate and the implications of the trial for the democratic nature of Israel were not explored.

Reconciliation and Trials

Criminal prosecutions, compared to the alternative of the TRC, are seen as preventing reconciliation among social antagonists because of the trial's backward orientation, its adversary structure, and its retributive goals. The transformative trials discussed in this book cast doubt on this assumption, revealing the ways in which they can promote reconciliation between victims and civil society.[29] We have seen two kinds of reconciliation. The first was present in the Kastner and Eichmann trials, in which the perpetrators were the Nazis and the responsibility of Israeli civil society was viewed in terms of its failure to pursue further lines of rescue during the Holocaust and its tendency to blame the victims for their disaster afterward. The reconciliation that the Kastner trial failed to bring about was later achieved in the Eichmann trial by the very commitment to conduct it in Israel, notwithstanding worldwide criticism, and by the structuring of the trial to facilitate empathetic listening to the testimonies of survivors. The problem of reconciliation was very different in the Kufr Qassem trial since the perpetrators themselves belonged to Israeli society and claimed to have acted on its behalf. Interestingly, in both the Kastner and Kufr Qassem trials Judge Halevi attempted to bring about reconciliation by focusing the blame on specific individuals (Kastner and the soldiers belonging to the Border Police unit) but can be seen as having failed. While in the Kastner trial this focus only underlined political and ideological divisions that finally culminated in the assassination of Kastner, in Kufr Qassem it helped Israeli society swallow the bitter pill of recognizing its own acts of victimization and violence toward its Arab citizens but without having to make an effort to change the basic perceptions and social structures that perpetuated discrimination against them.

Under what conditions, then, can we say that a trial enhances reconciliation between the victims and civil society more successfully than an investigative commission? The various trials show that in a conflict-ridden and multicultural society like the Israeli one trials provide an opportunity for reconciliation that is often impossible in the Knesset or the media. This might be connected to the phenomenon of radical difference. The excluded groups that seek entrance into public debate are often seen as the Other, standing in opposition to the dominant narrative of identity shared by the majority of society. This was the case with Holocaust survivors and the Arab citizens of Israel. Paradoxically, it might be that the constrained nature of the discussions in a court of law—the commitment to create at least a formal symmetry through rules of procedure, the need to allow the other side to be heard before a judgment is reached, and the need to justify this judgment in universal terms—all create opportunities for the underprivileged and marginalized to voice their concerns. The court cannot promise equality between the parties, but it gives a clever lawyer, a subversive defendant, or a group of victims the opportunity to challenge the dominant story and convince the judge. Paradoxically, it seems that the institutional constraints placed on the debate in a court of law can be facilitators of voice, as *Death and the Maiden* illustrates so well.

The finality of a court's judgment is often seen as the main obstacle to an ongoing public debate about fundamental values in a divided society. However, as we have seen, the trials that we discussed were not closed universes, and the judgment of the court, though determining the results of the specific case, did not become the final word on the historical truth. On the contrary, we saw how Alterman's critical intervention, for example, which caused such a public controversy at the time of the Kastner trial, later became the dominant view of the Holocaust in Israel, so that when Arendt attempted to raise the ghosts of the Kastner trial she was strongly condemned by Gershom Scholem. We also saw how political pressures to repress unpleasant facts, such as Halevi's judgment in the Kastner trial, Arendt's book on the Eichmann trial, or the memoirs Eichmann wrote after his trial, failed to create true reconciliation and solidarity in Israeli society, since these could only be based on knowing the facts and maintaining "antagonistic solidarity."[30] This was most clearly demonstrated in Amir's trial, when the defendant relied on the very image of Rabin as a Judenrat member to justify killing him as an act of collective self-defense. The court's judgment, which resorted to a rhetoric of reconciliation based on myths, repressing memories of previous political assassinations, and failing to confront the political meaning of Rabin's murder, could not encourage Israeli society to squarely confront the dilemmas of maintaining both a democratic and a Jewish state.

The four cases we have discussed here can therefore shed new light on the importance of political trials in contemporary politics, where group identity, memory, and victims' rights are receiving more attention. In each case the court had to struggle with one of the most difficult questions faced today, namely, what it means for a politics of identity to respect the individual voice, not only as an abstraction but as an individual who is seen as belonging to a group outside the inclusive "nation." It also helps explore the possibilities of deliberative democracy based on the idea of an "ideal speech situation" in a world whose politics are less than ideal and where the conditions necessary for genuine deliberation about the basic values of a democratic society are threatened by powerful forces from within and without the political sphere.

This book has been devoted to examining the ways in which a transformative trial can enhance a democratic system. We have seen that each trial had its share of failures and successes in that respect. However, it is only by viewing them as an ongoing conversation about the meaning of democracy in a plural and divided society (among ethnicities, nationalities, religions, etc.) that we can begin to formulate a liberal theory of law that can seriously address the transformative trial as a legitimate phenomenon in a democratic society committed to the rule of law.

Notes

Introduction

1. Ehud Sprinzak, *Brother against Brother* (New York: Free Press, 1999), 253–58. Din Rodef is the only case in which the Halakhah allows the killing of a Jew without trial. For elaboration on the Halakhic sources for Din Rodef, see Nachum Racover, *A Bibliography of Jewish Law* (in Hebrew) (Jerusalem: Jewish Legal Heritage Society, 1990), 2:268.

2. Declaration of the Establishment of the State of Israel 14 May 1948, 1 L.S.I. 3 (1948). Notice that in the Hebrew version equal protection of the law is guaranteed to all its "citizens" and not to all its "inhabitants." For further elaboration, see chapter 7.

3. Shulamit Aloni (a jurist and former member of the Knesset) maintains that the omission of the term *democratic* from the declaration was intended to emphasize that by its very nature a Jewish state was also committed to democracy. See Shulamit Aloni, "Basic Law: Human Dignity and Liberty" (in Hebrew), *Teoria u-Bikoret* 12–13 (1999): 367–75. The process of drafting the declaration reveals, however, that there were some strategic reasons for this omission, in particular, the attempt to avoid the legal implications of using the broad term *democracy*, specifying instead the obligations that the State of Israel undertook. For elaboration on the composition of the declaration and its various drafts, see Yoram Shachar, "The Early Drafts of the Declaration of Independence of the State of Israel," *Tel Aviv University Law Review* 26 (2) (2002): 523–600. It should be borne in mind that the Declaration of Independence emphasized the state's Israeli-secular, rather than Jewish-religious, character. The term *Jewish state* referred to the 1947 United Nations' partition resolution to establish two states: one Jewish and one Arab. See Orit Kamir, "The Declaration Has Two Faces: The Interesting Story of the 'Zionist Declaration of Independence' and the 'Democratic Declaration of Independence'" (in Hebrew), *Tel Aviv University Law Review* 23 (2000): 473–538.

4. Berenson's proposal is available at the State Archive, file c/20/5664. See also Shachar, "Early Drafts." In addition to the omission of the word *democratic,* the definition of the state's final borders was also omitted due to the unstable situation at the time. The final version of the declaration also promised that civil and political rights would be guaranteed by a constitution to be drafted by elected members of a Constituent Assembly. Nonetheless, the Constituent

Assembly elected immediately afterward failed to produce a constitution. It transformed itself into a parliamentary legislative body (the Knesset), which retained the power to legislate basic laws and to transfer this power to following Knessets until eventually a constitution would be completed.

The declaration states that "with effect from the moment of the termination of the Mandate . . . (15 May, 1948), until the establishment of the elected, regular authorities of the State *in accordance with the Constitution which shall be adoped by the Elected Constituent Assembly not later than the 1st October 1948,* the People's Council shall act as a Provisional Council of State" (emphasis added). Indeed, two members of the Constitutional Assembly belonging to the Herut party (Ari Jabotinsky and Hillel Kook) claimed that the decision of the constitutive assembly to transform itself into an ordinary parliament retaining the power to enact a constitution in stages through basic laws (known as the Harrari Resolution) was equivalent to a political putsch. See Aloni, "Basic Law," 369. For a short historical overview, see Ruth Gavison, "The Controversy Over Israel's Bill of Rights," *Israel Yearbook of Human Rights* 15 (1985): 113, 115–17.

5. The two basic laws refer to the State of Israel as "Jewish and Democratic" (section 1a. at Basic Law: Human Dignity and Liberty, 1992, S.H. 150; section 2 at Basic Law: Freedom of Occupation, 1994, S.H. 90). For an overview of the enactment of the basic laws, see Judith Karp, "Basic Law: Human Dignity and Liberty—A Biography of Power Struggles" (in Hebrew), *Mishpat U-Mimshal* 1 (2) (1993): 323–84.

6. The most elaborate effort to reconcile the two values was undertaken by the jurist Ruth Gavison in several articles and her book *Can Israel Be Both Jewish and Democratic? Tensions and Prospects* (in Hebrew) (Tel Aviv: Hakibbutz Ha-Meuchad, 1999). But the issue has preoccupied a wide range of writers, including Supreme Court justices such as Aharon Barak, Menachem Elon, and Haim Cohn. See Menachem Mautner, Avi Sagi, and Ronen Shamir, eds., *Multi-culturalism in a Democratic and Jewish State* (in Hebrew) (Tel Aviv: Ramot, 1998). See also *Tel Aviv University Law Review* 19 (3) (1995), a special issue devoted to this problem. Most jurists found it possible to reconcile the two values, but see the contrary opinion of law professor Avigdor Levontin in "Jewish and Democratic: Personal Reflections" (in Hebrew), *Tel Aviv University Law Review* 19 (3) (1995): 521–47; and Hassan Gabareen, "The Future of Arab Citizenship In Israel," *Mishpat u-Mimshal* 6 (1) (2001): 53–86 (all in Hebrew). Other writers, mainly outside of the legal community, claim that Israeli society must choose between being an ethnocracy or "a state of all its citizens." See, for example, Yoav Peled, "Will Israel Be a State of All Its Citizens on Its 100 Anniversary?" *Bar Ilan Law Studies* 17 (2001): 73–89; Oren Yiftachel, "Nation-Building and the Division of Space in the Israeli 'Ethnocracy': Settlement, Land, and Ethnic Disparities" (in Hebrew), *Tel Aviv University Law Review* (1998): 637–63.

7. For recent attempts to distinguish between show trials such as the Moscow trials, which use the court as an means of eliminating political opponents, and legitimate political trials (with theatrical and didactic elements), which maintain the risk element and thus need to be acknowledged by liberal legal theory, see Mark Osiel, *Mass Atrocity, Collective Memory, and the Law* (New

Brunswick, NJ, and London: Transaction Publishers, 1997); and Lawrence Douglas, *The Memory of Judgment: Making Law and History in the Trials of the Holocaust* (New Haven: Yale University Press, 2001).

8. Judges are often reluctant to acknowledge the educational role of their decisions. Osiel, *Mass Atrocity,* 244–45.

9. Ron Christenson, *Political Trials: Gordian Knots in the Law,* 2d ed. (New Brunswick, NJ: Transaction Publishers, 1999), 5.

10. Bruce Ackerman, *The Future of Liberal Revolution* (New Haven: Yale University Press, 1992), 5–24.

11. For elaboration, see chapter 7.

12. Yael Zerubavel, *Recovered Roots: Collective Memory and the Making of Israeli National Tradition* (Chicago: University of Chicago Press, 1995).

13. See, for example, the Martyrs' and Heroes' Commemoration (Yad Vashem) Law, 1953, 7 L.S.I 119 (1952–53); Remembrance Day (War of Independence and Israel Defense Army) Law, 1963, 17 L.S.I. 85 (1962–63); Memorial Day of Yitzhak Rabin Law, 1997, S.H. 186; Presidents and Prime Ministers of Israel (Perpetuation of Memory) Law 1986, 40 L.S.I. 260 (1985–86). For an overview of the large body of literature on collective memory, see, for example, *Representation* 26 (1989), a special issue entitled "Memory and Counter Memory"; and Benedict Anderson, *Imagined Communities: Reflections on the Origin and Spread of Nationalism* (London: Verso, 1991). For the special role of law in creating and maintaining a collective memory, see Osiel, *Mass Atrocity;* and Austin Sarat and Thomas R. Kearns, eds., *History, Memory, and the Law* (Ann Arbor: University of Michigan Press, 1999).

14. For a theoretical elaboration on the marriage of nationalism and liberalism, see Yael Tamir, *Liberal Nationalism* (Princeton: Princeton University Press, 1993). In this book I adopt the Zionist conception that treats Jews as a nation (in the original sense of the word), an ethnos, and not merely a religious group. I adopt the broad definition of *nation* as connoting a group of people who believe they are ancestrally related. See Walker Connor, *Ethnonationalism* (Princeton: Princeton University Press, 1994), xi. According to Alan Dowty the commonly accepted meaning of Jewishness is of a common national or ethnic identity as a historically developed community of people with distinctive cultural, linguistic, and other attributes. This, he argues, includes a distinctive Judaic religion, which makes Jews unusual, though not unique, among ethnic groups. See Alan Dowty, *The Jewish State: A Century Later* (Berkeley: University of California Press, 1998), 3.

15. A distinction, unique to Israel, must be kept in mind regarding the two very different settings in which the Supreme Court functions. In the first, it functions as a court of appeal over decisions made by the various district courts. In the second (as High Court of Justice), it functions as a first and last instance of judicial review over disputes concerning the political administration and the Knesset. This latter function of the Supreme Court is a heritage from the times of the British Mandate that was continued in Israel, and it is on this function of the court that jurists in Israel focus their attention. See, for example, Menachem Mautner, *The Decline of Formalism and the Rise of Values in*

Israeli Law (in Hebrew) (Tel Aviv: Ma'agalay Da'at, 1993); and Gad Barzilai, Ephraim Yaar Yuchtman, and Zeev Segal, *The Israeli Supreme Court and the Israeli Public* (in Hebrew) (Tel Aviv: Papirus, 1994).

16. H.C. 72/62, *Rufeisen v. Minister of Interior*, 16(4) P.D. 2428 (The Story of Brother Daniel); H.C. 58/68, *Shalit v. Minister of Interior and the Population Registrar*, 23(2) P.D. 476. For elaboration, see Amnon Rubinstein, *The Constitutional Law of Israel* (in Hebrew), 5th ed. (Tel Aviv: Shocken, 1996), 1:109–39; and Pnina Lahav, *Judgement in Jerusalem: Chief Justice Simon Agranat and the Zionist Century* (Berkeley, University of California Press, 1997), 196–220. Recently, following the recognition of reform conversion to Judaism by the Israeli High Court of Justice (H.C. 5075/95, *Naamat v. Minister of Interior*, not published), there were suggestions made by Knesset members of the religious parties to drop the nationality rubric from Israeli identity cards altogether. The Orthodox factions supported these suggestions, even though the General Security Service (GSS) claimed it might create some security difficulties. This shows how the two dimensions of the "Jewish" aspect of the state (religious oriented and security oriented) can collide.

17. E.A. 1/65, *Yeredor v. Chairman of the Central Elections Commission*, 19(3) P.D. 365; E.A. 2/84, *Nayman v. Chairman of the Central Election Commission*, 39(2) P.D. 225. For elaboration, see Rubinstein, *The Constitutional Law of Israel*, 537–59, 579–84; and Lahav, *Judgment in Jerusalem*, 185–95.

18. H.C. 910/86, *Resler v. Minister of Defense*, 42(2) P.D. 441 (the drafting of yeshiva boys into the army). See also Rubinstein, *The Constitutional Law of Israel*, 302–5, 195–211 (on civil marriage); 221–24 (on opening stores on the Sabbath); 218–20 (on the importation of pork).

19. H.C. 114/78, *Burkan v. Minister of Treasury*, 32(2) P.D. 800; H.C. 6698/95, *Kaadan v. Israel's Land Administration*, 54(1) P.D. 258.

20. The exception is Lahav, *Judgement in Jerusalem*. This book not only provides a biography of a Supreme Court justice but also a critical examination of the reflection of a century of Zionism in the rulings of the Israeli Supreme Court.

21. However, the same question might come to the attention of the High Court of Justice several times in different petitions, and in this way it could create mobilization over time. For a good example, see the series of petitions by attorney Yehuda Resler regarding the constitutionality of the exemption of yeshiva boys from army service, H.C. 910/86, *Resler v. Minister of Defense*.

22. Pierre Nora, "Between Memory and History: Les Lieux de Mémoire," *Representations* 26 (1989): 7–25; Pierre Nora, "The Era of Commemoration," in *Realms of Memory: The Construction of the French Past*, vol. 3: *Symbols*, under the direction of Pierre Nora, ed. Lawrence D. Kritzman, trans. Arthur Goldhammer (New York: Columbia University Press, 1998), 609–37; Austin Sarat, "Rhetoric and Remembrance: Trials, Transcription, and the Politics of Critical Reading," *Legal Studies Forum* 23 (1999): 355–78.

23. See, for example, Leon Sheleff, "From Schindler's List to Kasztner's Train: On Historical Reality, Media Myths, and Judicial Truth," in *Law and History*, ed. Daniel Gutwein and Menachem Mautner (in Hebrew) (Jerusalem: Zal-

man Shazar Center for Jewish History, 1999), 339–53; Asher Maoz, "Historical Adjudication: Courts of Law, Commissions of Inquiry, and 'Historical Truth,'" *Law and History Review* 18 (3) (fall 2000): 559–606; Michal Shaked, "History in Court and Court in History: The Kastner Trial and the Narratives of Memory" (in Hebrew), *Alpayim* 20 (2000): 36–81; Leora Bilsky, "Kastner Trial" (in Hebrew) *Teoria u-Bikoret* 12–13 (1999): 125–36; and Leora Bilsky, "Judging Evil in the Trial of Kastner," *Law and History Review* 19 (1) (2001a): 117–60.

24. Jacob Robinson, *And the Crooked Shall Be Made Straight: The Eichmann Trial, the Jewish Catastrophe, and Hannah Arendt's Narrative* (Philadelphia: Jewish Publication Society of America, 1965); Gideon Hausner, *Justice in Jerusalem* (New York: Harper and Row, 1966). The first Israeli jurist to acknowledge the wider concerns of the Eichmann trial was Pnina Lahav in "The Eichmann Trial, the Jewish Question, and the American Jewish Intelligentsia," *Boston University Law Review* 72 (1992): 555–78. See also the articles in *Theoretical Inquiries in Law* 1 (2) (2000), a special issue entitled "Judgment in the Shadow of the Holocaust."

25. See, for example, Ilan Shif, "In Favor of the 'Black Flag' Test," in *Kafr Kassem: Myth and History*, ed. Ruvik Rosenthal (in Hebrew) (Tel Aviv: Hakibbutz Hameuchad, 2000), 117–30; Adi Parush, "Critique of the 'Black Flag' Test," in ibid., 131–177; and Adi Parush, *Obedience, Responsibility and Criminal Law: Legal Issues from a Philosophic Perspective* (in Hebrew) (Tel Aviv: Papirus, 1996), 65–116.

26. The division of labor was such that the legal scholars focused on extracting the legal precedent out of the long and detailed verdicts, while the narrative was left for historians and sociologists to examine, as in Yechiam Weitz, *The Man Who Was Murdered Twice* (in Hebrew) (Jerusalem: Keter, 1995); Yehuda Bauer, *Jews For Sale? Nazi-Jewish Negotiations* (New Haven: Yale University Press, 1994); Tom Segev, *The Seventh Million: The Israelis and the Holocaust*, trans. Haim Watsman (New York: Hill and Wang, 1993); and most recently Hannah Yablonka, *The State of Israel v. Adolf Eichmann* (in Hebrew) (Tel Aviv: Yediot Aharonot, 2001). For more journalistic accounts of the trials, see Moshe Kordov, *Kufr Qassem Trial* (in Hebrew) (Tel Aviv: Narkis, 1959); Shalom Rosenfeld, *Tik Plili 124: Mishpat Gruenwald-Kastner* (Criminal Trial 124, the Gruenwald-Kastner Trial) (in Hebrew) (Tel Aviv: Karni, 1955); Imanuel Prat, *The Big Trial: Kastner Affair* (in Hebrew) (Tel Aviv: Or, 1955); Ben Hecht, *Perfidy* (New London: Milah Press, 1997); and Haim Gouri, *The Glass Cage: The Jerusalem Trial* (in Hebrew) (Tel Aviv: Hakibbutz Hameuchad, 1962).

27. The term is taken from Bruce Ackerman, *We the People: Foundations* (Cambridge, MA: Belknap Press, 1991). For a brief application of the theory to the case of the Zionist revolution in Israel, see Ackerman, *The Future of Liberal Revolution*, 63–65. I disagree, however, with Ackerman's contention that the only successful liberal revolution must be consolidated in a constitution and that transitional criminal trials have only a negative impact on the future democratic functioning of the state.

28. Compare the very different attitude toward this risk in Germany with that in the United States. In the aftermath of Nazism, the new West German

Constitution explicitly declared that some fundamental human rights cannot be revised constitutionally (such as the federal structure of governance, protection of human dignity, and the democratic and social character of the state, section 79(3) of the German Basic Law). In contrast, the American system is built so that the Constitution can be amended, though the process is more difficult than enacting ordinary legislation (Art. 5 of the Constitution of the United States). See Ackerman, *We The People*, 15; Aharon Barak, *Interpretation In Law*, vol. 3: *Constitutional Interpretation* (in Hebrew) (Jerusalem: Nevo Press, 1994), 52–6; and Sabine Michalowski and Lorna Woods, *German Constitutional Law* (Ashgate: Dartmouth Publishing, 1999), 29–30, 34.

29. Ruti G. Teitel, *Transitional Justice* (Oxford: Oxford University Press, 2000); Ruti G. Teitel, "Bringing the Messiah through the Law," in *Human Rights in Political Transitions: Gettysburg to Bosnia*, ed. Carla Alisson Hesse and Robert Post (New York: Zone Books, 1999), 177–93; Martha Minow, *Between Vengeance and Forgiveness: Facing History after Genocide and Mass Violence* (Boston: Beacon Press, 1998); Carlos Santiago Nino, *Radical Evil on Trial* (New Haven: Yale University Press, 1996); Carla Alisson Hesse and Robert Post, eds., *Human Rights in Political Transition* (New York: Zone Books, 1999); Neil J. Kritz, ed., *Transitional Justice: How Emerging Democracies Reckon with Former Regimes* (Washington, DC: U.S. Institute of Peace Press, 1995); James McAdams, ed., *Transitional Justice and the Rule of Law in New Democracies* (Notre Dame: University of Notre Dame Press, 1997); Bruce Ackerman, *The Future of Liberal Revolutions* (New Haven: Yale University Press, 1992).

30. Judith N. Shklar, *Legalism* (Cambridge: Harvard University Press, 1964).

31. Otto Kirschheimer, *Political Justice* (Princeton: Princeton University Press, 1961); William E. Scheuerman, ed., *The Rule of Law under Siege* (Berkeley: University of California Press, 1996), 1–25.

32. Robert W. Gordon, "Some Critical Theories of Law and Their Critics," in *The Politics of Law*, ed. David Kairys, 3d ed. (New York: Basic Books, 1998), 641–61.

33. Peter Gabel and Paul Harris, "Building Power and Breaking Images: Critical Legal Theory and the Practice of Law," *Review of Law and Social Change* 11 (1982–83): 369–411.

34. Douglas, *The Memory of Judgment*; Osiel, *Mass* Atrocity; Lahav, *Judgment in Jerusalem*.

35. Douglas, *The Memory of Judgment*, 2.

36. For a reading of Arendt's thesis as adopting a legalist approach to the trial, see Shoshana Felman, "Theatres of Justice: Arendt in Jerusalem, the Eichmann Trial, and the Redefinition of Legal Meaning in the Wake of the Holocaust," *Theoretical Inquiries in Law* 1 (2) (2000): 465–507; Douglas, *The Memory of Judgment*, 111–13.

37. For elaboration, see Seyla Benhabib, *The Reluctant Modernism of Hannah Arendt* (Thousand Oaks, CA: Sage, 1996), 185–203.

38. For elaboration, see chapters 4–6.

39. For elaboration, see chapters 1–3.

40. See, for example, Will Kymlicka, *Liberalism, Community, and Culture* (Oxford: Oxford University Press, 1989); and Will Kymlicka, ed., *The Rights of Minority Cultures* (Oxford: Oxford University Press, 1995).

Chapter 1

1. Nazis and Nazi Collaborators (Punishment) LAW, 5710–1950, 4 L.S.I. 154; Hannah Yablonka, "The Law of Punishment for Nazis and Their Collaborators: History, Implementation, and Point of View" (in Hebrew), *Kathedra* 82 (1996): 135–52; Yehiam Weitz," The Law for Punishment of the Nazis and Their Collaborators as Image and Reflection of Public Opinion," *Kathedra* 82 (1996): 153–64; Tom Segev, *The Seventh Million: The Israelis and the Holocaust*, trans. Haim Watzman (New York: Hill and Wang, 1993), 260–62.

2. The trial began on 1 January 1954, and the verdict was given on 22 June 1955.

3. For detailed descriptions of the Kastner affair, see Segev, *The Seventh Million*, 255–320; Yehiam Weitz, *The Man Who Was Murdered Twice* (Jerusalem: Keter, 1995); and Yehuda Bauer, *Jews for Sale? Jewish Negotiations, 1933–1945* (New Haven: Yale University Press, 1994), 145–71. For a discussion of the decisions in the trial and appellate courts, see Pnina Lahav, *Judgment in Jerusalem: Chief Justice Simon Agranat and the Zionist Century* (Berkeley: University of California Press, 1997), 123–25, 132–33, 142–44.

4. Rudolf Kastner (born in 1906) was a journalist from Cluz in northern Transylvania, a member of the center-left Zionist group Ihud, the diaspora extension of the Palestine Jewish labor party known as Mapai. Before Hungary's annexation of Transylvania in 1940, Kastner had been a parliamentary correspondent in Budapest, and after he became a Hungarian citizen he moved to Budapest. As historian Yehuda Bauer explains, people like Kastner and Brand were unknown in the Jewish community before the invasion of the Nazis, being both foreigners and Zionists (a small minority of no more than 5 percent of the Hungarian Jews). See Bauer, *Jews for Sale?* 152.

5. The exact number of passengers remains unclear according to the different sources. Bauer (pp. 198, 199) mentions 1,684, Segev (265) mentions 1,685, and Weitz (33) mentions 1,685. In the appeal, the figure was given as 1,684 (Cr.A. 232/55, *Attorney General v. Gruenwald*, 12 P.D. 2017, 2046, 2048). Maybe the source of the confusion is Kastner's own report (Israel Kastner, *Report of the Rescue Committee in Budapest, 1942–1945*, submitted to the Zionist Congress, in Hebrew), which states at one point that the number was 1,685 (47) and in other places that it was 1,684 (105, 115).

6. For a detailed examination of the negotiations, see Bauer, *Jews for Sale?* 145–71.

7. Kastner, *Report of the Rescue Committee in Budapest*.

8. Weitz, *The Man Who Was Murdered Twice*, 60–61.

9. Translated by Lahav in *Judgment in Jerusalem*, 123. The Hebrew quotation is from Shalom Rosenfeld, *Tik Plili 124: Mishpat Gruenwald-Kastner* (Crimi-

nal Trial 124, the Gruenwald-Kastner Trial) (Tel Aviv: Karni, 1955), 16–17. The full version is quoted and translated into English in Segev, *The Seventh Million,* 257–58.

10. Kurt Becher, who had joined the SS (Schultzstafell) in 1934 and the Nazi party in 1937, arrived in Hungary a short while after its occupation in the official role of supplying horses and equipment to the SS units there. He played a major role in the Nazi confiscation of the Menfred-Weiss corporation, one of the biggest industrial factories in Hungary. After this "success" Himmler appointed him chief negotiater with Kastner and his committee. In 1945 he was raised to the rank of SS-Standarten-Fuehrer (colonel) and was put in charge of the concentration camps (Weitz, *The Man Who Was Murdered Twice,* 32, 69).

11. Cohn insisted on conducting the trial against the better judgment of the political figures involved in the affair such as the minister of trade and industry, Dov Yosef (see Dov Yosef, *A Dove and a Sword* [in Hebrew] [Ramat Gan: Massadah, 1975], 321–22); and the minister of justice, Pinchas Rosen (see Ruth Bondi, *Felix: Pinchas Rosen and His Time* [in Hebrew] [Tel Aviv: Zmora Bitan, 1990], 490).

12. Shmuel Tamir (Katznelson) was born in Jerusalem and was thirty-two at the time of the trial. In the 1940s, when Kastner was negotiating with Eichmann, Tamir was organizing acts of sabotage against the British in Palestine as a member of the the the underground right-wing movement Etzel. For these activities he was arrested twice by the British and deported to a detention camp in Kenya for a year and a half (a fact he mentioned in his closing arguments).

13. This was not the first time the two protagonists had found themselves on the opposite sides of the bench in a political trial. Tamir had defended Yaakov Heruti, the leader of a the right-wing group known as the Tzrifin Underground that was accused of planting a bomb near the Soviet legation in Tel Aviv and of a series of violent acts aimed at preventing the signing of the reparations agreement with Germany. Cohn had been the prosecutor at the military trial, and Judge Halevi was especially appointed by Prime Minister David Ben-Gurion to preside over the trial. See Segev, *The Seventh Million,* 265.

14. Otto Kirschheimer pointed to the inherent risk to the authorities of conducting political trials, a risk that is often exploited by a clever defense attorney, and saw it as a redeeming feature of the trial. In particular he thought that the authorities ran a great risk in conducting libel trials against a political opponent. See Otto Kirschheimer, "Politics and Justice," reprinted in *Politics, Law, and Social Change: Selected Essays of Otto Kirschheimer,* ed. Frederic S. Burin and Kurt L. Shell (New York: Columbia University Press, 1969), 408, 410–11; and *Political Justice* (Princeton: Princeton University Press, 1961), 246–56.

15. Tom Segev suggests that the debate came as an opportunity for Herut to regain public support. "The fight against negotiations with Germany rescued Menachem Begin from a period of depression and lifted his party from a low point. Begin acted euphoric; his party took on new life" (*The Seventh Million,* 223). Begin attacked Ben-Gurion in public speeches and demonstrations, which culminated in a mass rally in Jerusalem on the day of the vote itself, a rally that turned into a massive attack on the Knesset building. For this involvement in

violence he was later suspended from the Knesset for more than three months (214–22).

16. Oz Almog, *The Sabra: The Creation of the New Jew*, trans. Haim Watzman, (Berkeley: University of California Press, 2000).

17. *Ha-Olam Ha-Ze*, edited by Uri Avneri, was known for its aggressive criticism of the political establishment both in content and in style. It sought to expose corruption on the part of politicians and public figures and became known as a dynamic journal devoted to shattering national myths. The opinions expressed in the journal made it a target of criticism and harassment by the political establishment. It generated many heated controversies during the 1950s and 1960s, including reports on the Kastner affair that supported Tamir's line and gave him a public forum for expressing his views outside the courtroom. See Yoav Yitzhak, *First Class*, vol. 1: *Persons* (in Hebrew) (Tel Aviv: Egel Ha-Zahav Journalism, 1998), 215–16.

18. Segev, *The Seventh Million*, 264, 276, 285.

19. Lahav, *Judgment in Jerusalem*, 141. Judge Halevi even had difficulty remembering Gruenwald's name. See Segev, *The Seventh Million*, 255.

20. Lahav describes him as "the sabra, fair, blue-eyed, and exuding self-confidence, [who] represented the 'new' Jew" (*Judgment in Jerusalem*, 124).

21. Weitz, *The Man Who Was Murdered Twice*, 126.

22. Rosenfeld, *Tik Plili 124*, 342–43.

23. Ibid., 312 (my translation).

24. Quoted in ibid., 36. It should be noted that in the Eichmann trial, during the testimony of Freudiger, who was a member of the Budapest Judenrat, someone from the audience shouted and accused him of collaboration. For a discussion, see chapters 4–6.

25. For elaboration, see chapter 8.

26. Rosenfeld, *Tik Plili 124*, 350.

27. See ibid., 335.

28. See ibid., 315.

29. Ibid., 332: "The tragedy begins with a situation over which no person or leader had control; it begins with the identification of the Jewry of each land with the rulers of that land. This was the tradition of two thousand years [of diaspora] which affected everything and everyone. But the tragedy increases when we reach Eretz Israel. . . . We argue that here, in Israel, the official institutions surrendered to the British. They were not willing to take risks out of obtuseness and reluctance to relinquish their ruling power, and this resulted in what I call the abandonment of the Jews of Europe in their most difficult time."

30. This temporal inversion has been identified by scholars in transitional justice trials in general. See Ruti G. Teitel, *Transitional Justice* (Oxford: Oxford University Press, 2000), 27–67.

31. Dominique LaCapra, *History and Memory after Auschwitz* (Ithaca and London: Cornell University Press, 1998).

32. Psychoanalyst Dori Laub explains that "bearing witness to a trauma is, in fact, a process that includes the listener." See Shoshana Felman and Dori Laub, *Testimony: Crises of Witnesses in Literature, Psychoanalysis, and History*

(New York: Routledge, 1992), 70. However, people are often reluctant to listen to stories of traumatic experiences because the story "forces us to acknowledge that we [the listeners] are not in control of our own lives." See Susan J. Brison, "Outliving Oneself: Trauma, Memory, and Personal Identity," in *Feminists Rethink the Self,* ed. Diana Tietjens Meyers (Boulder: Westview Press, 1997), 26. Israeli society as a whole found it difficult to face a collective experience of such helplessness and horror and preferred to hear about the heroism of the ghetto fighters and Jewish partisans. The solution of using the trial as a controlled environment in which survivors' testimony could gain empathetic listening was not attempted in the Kastner trial but had to wait for *Eichmann* in the 1960s.

33. Weitz, *The Man Who Was Murdered Twice,* 128–29.

34. Ibid., 129. Later, during the trial, Tamir managed to present the actual affidavit that Kastner had written (dated 4 August 1947) on behalf of Becher in which Kastner had claimed that "In my opinion Becher is entitled to the greatest consideration when his case comes before the Allies or the German authorities. Becher should receive the greatest consideration. I give this statement not only on my behalf but also on behalf of the Jewish Agency and the World Jewish Congress. Signed Dr. Rudolf Kastner." For the full text, see Rosenfeld, *Tik Plili 124,* 248–49.

35. Weitz, *The Man Who Was Murdered Twice,* 353. Menachem Bader was a member of the left-wing Mapam party and the Knesset; Ehud Avriel was the Israeli delegate in Budapest and the director general of the Prime Minister's Office and the Finance Ministry.

36. Other witnesses, such as Prof. Benjamin Aktzin, dean of the law school at Hebrew University, and Shmuel Benzur of the Foreign Ministry, were not connected to the affair directly and were summoned by the prosecution as part of its policy of calling important people who would make a better impression on the court because of their public credentials (ibid., 132).

37. Among the survivors were Yechiel Shmueli, Irena Hirsch, Yosef Kats, David Rozner, Paul Gross, Friedrich Mund, Eliezer Rozental. Weitz (ibid.) notes that the idea of bringing these witnesses, all survivors from Kastner's hometown, Cluj, and all simple, hardworking people who had lost many relatives in the Holocaust, was a wise decision. "Their words sounded reliable and authentic, and the story they told was engaging" See also Imanuel Prat, *The Big Trial: Kastner Affair* (in Hebrew) (Tel Aviv: Or, 1955), 195.

38. *McCormick on Evidence,* ed. John W. Strong, 4th ed. (St. Paul: West, 1992), 37–40.

39. Lawrence Douglas, "Wartime Lies: Securing the Holocaust in Law and Literature," *Yale Journal of Law and Humanities* 7 (1995b): 367–96, quotation at 389.

40. Primo Levi, *The Drowned and the Saved,* trans. Raymond Rosenthal (New York: Summit Books, 1988), 82.

41. "This is what a wrong would be: a damage accompanied by the loss of the means to prove the damage. This is the case if the victim is deprived of life, or of all her liberties, or of the freedom to make his or her ideas or opinions public, or simply of the right to testify to the damage, or even more simply if the

testifying phrase itself is deprived of authority. In all these cases, to the privation constituted by the damage there is the added impossibility of bringing it to the knowledge of others, and in particular the knowledge of a tribunal" (Jean-François Lyotard, *The Differend*, trans. G. Van dAbbeele [Minneapolis: University of Minnesota Press, 1988], 5).

42. Rosenfeld, *Tik Plili 124*, 319–20.

43. Ibid., 325.

44. Cited in the court's decision, Cr.C. (Jm.) 124/53 *Attorney General v. Gruenwald*, 44 P.M. (1965) 3, 85–88.

45. Lawrence Langer, *Holocaust Testimonies: The Ruins of Memory* (New Haven: Yale University Press, 1991).

46. For this purpose he relied on the permission given in Article 15 of the Law of Punishment of the Nazis and Their Collaborators (1953), under which Eichmann was tried, which stipulates that the court may deviate from the rules of evidence provided it places on record the reasons which prompted such deviations.

47. Rosenfeld, *Tik Plili 124*, 319–29.

48. Weitz, *The Man Who Was Murdered Twice*, 134.

49. Yoel Palgi, *And Behold, a Great Wind Came* (in Hebrew) (Tel Aviv: Am Oved, [1946] 1977); Yoel Palgi, *Into the Inferno: The Memoir of a Jewish Paratrooper behind Nazi Lines* (New Brunswick, NJ: Rutgers University Press, 2003).

50. Rosenfeld, *Tik Plili 124*, 130–31.

51. The effect of Tamir's cross-examination on the public was profound. See Prat, *The Big Trial*, 72; and Weitz, *The Man Who Was Murdered Twice*, 138. A glimpse of the shock that Palgi's words, "I wrote a novel and not a history book," caused can be seen in a letter to Palgi written on 25 July 1955 by the editor of his publishing house, Menachem Dorman, explaining why he had decided not to reprint his book: "Having read your testimony I have come to the conclusion that for years I have been living in error regarding the nature of your book *And Behold a Great Wind Came*. I do not claim that you gave us a 'legal document' for publication, but between that and a 'novel' there is a large distance. An entire public, myself included, regarded your book as an *almost sacred document* as something entirely true as the whole truth. Someone who remains as the only *witness to testify on matters of life and death has to be accurate to the highest degree. In sum: I do not intend to elaborate on this point. I only wanted to say that the stenogram of your testimony in the Kastner trial, surprisingly has thrown a most negative light on your book*" (quoted in Weitz, *The Man Who Was Murdered Twice*, 19).

52. Interestingly, in this trial, the reconstructed myth of heroism revolved around two women—Katherine Senesh, the mother, a symbol of sacrifice; and Hannah Senesh, the daughter, an Israeli Jeanne d'Arc. The newspapers called Katherine Senesh "a Hebrew mother" (erasing her "diaspora" origins). By contrasting Kastner and Senesh, Tamir succeeded in creating an implied gender opposition between "the heart" (Senesh) and "the brain" (Kastner.)

53. Bandi Grosz, who was sent by Eichmann together with Brand to Palestine, testified that the mission had another aim: to help Himmler create a connection with the West that could lead to a separate peace treaty. However, as a

man who had been a double agent and had a criminal record, his testimony at trial was not regarded as credible. The historian Bauer argues, however, that Grosz's testimony was accurate. The most unreliable witness in the trial turned out to be the one who told the historical truth (*Jews for Sale?* 130–32, 169).

54. Rosenfeld, *Tik Plili 124*, 343.

55. Weitz, *The Man Who Was Murdered Twice*, 168. Only during the Eichmann trial was the prosecution successful in introducing Sharett's report. For elaboration, see chapter 4.

56. See, for example, the trial of Ernst Zundel, a German-born Canadian citizen who had arranged for the publication of *Did Six Million Really Die?* a pamphlet that alleged that the Holocaust was a Zionist hoax (*Regina v. Zundel*, 58 O.R. [2d] 129). Many of the court documents associated with the suit are reproduced in Barbara Kulazka, ed., *Did Six Million Really Die? Report of the Evidence in the Canadian "False News" Trial of Ernst Zundel, 1988* (Toronto: Samisdat Publishers, 1992). For legal articles on the topic of "Holocaust denial trials," see Douglas, "Wartime Lies"; and Eric Stein, "History against Speech: The New German Law against 'Auschwitz' and Other Lies," *Michigan Law Review* 85 (1986): 277–324. For historical assessments of the phenomenon of Holocaust denial, see Pierre Vidal-Naquet, *Assassins of Memory: Essays on the Denial of the Holocaust*, trans. Jeffrey Mehlman (New York: Columbia University Press, 1992); and Gill Seidel, *The Holocaust Denial: Antisemitism, Racism, and the New Right* (Leeds: Beyond the Pale Collective, 1986). See also Lawrence Douglas, *The Memory of Judgment: Making Law and History in the Trials of the Holocaust* (New Haven: Yale University Press, 2001), 226–56. See also the trial of the Holocaust denier David Irving, discussed in Richard J. Evans, *Lying about Hitler: History, Holocaust, and the David Irving Trial* (New York: Basic Books, 2002); and Robert J. Van Pelt, *The Case for Auschwitz: Evidence from the Irving Trial* (Bloomington: Indiana University Press, 2002).

57. At the outset, however, Tamir had requested the establishment of an investigative commission. The government denied this request, as Ben-Gurion was worried that "the political-party interests that exploited the Holocaust for their own purposes" would distort its work (quoted in Segev, *The Seventh Million*, 294). The justices on the appellate court, in retrospect thought that it would have been the better course for investigating the Kastner affair. See, for example, the opinions of Justice Olshan (Cr.A. 232/55, *Attorney General v. Gruenwald*, 2269–70); Cheshin (2282); Goitan (2317); and Agranat (2057).

58. Rosenfeld, *Tik Plili 124*, 283.

59. Alan Dershowitz, "Life Is Not a Dramatic Narrative," in *Law's Stories*, ed. Peter Brooks and Paul Gewirtz (New Haven and London: Yale University Press, 1996), 99–105.

60. Tamir's request to put Kastner on trial for perjury was rejected, and his attempt to file a private criminal suit against Kastner was unsuccessful. See Weitz, *The Man Who Was Murdered Twice*, 307, 316–17.

61. Kastner was shot near his home in Tel Aviv on the night of 3 March 1957. The assassin belonged to an underground right-wing organization that was involved in the planning of terrorist attacks. The assassin (Zeev Ack-

shtein), the driver (Dan Shemer) and the head of the organization (Yosef Menks) were tried and convicted of murder. Weitz, 332–36.

62. Only at a much later stage, in a 1990s television adaptation of a play by Motti Lerner, was there an attempt to deal critically with the Kastner affair by revisiting the myth of Hannah Senesh and to speculate that she might have broken down during her interrogation and divulged the names of her friends. This slanderous insinuation prompted Senesh's brother to bring a petition to the High Court of Justice against the Israel Broadcasting Authority. Although the court rejected his petition, it is interesting to note that the minority opinion of Justice Chesin pointed to the importance of preserving national myths for the sake of collective identity. See H.C 6126/94, *Giorah Senesh v. Chairman of Broadcasting Authority,* 53(3) P.D 817 (in Hebrew).

Chapter 2

1. The exemplary case is the Nuremberg trials. See also the growing literature on "transitional justice," for example, Mark Osiel, *Mass Atrocities, Collective Memories, and the Law* (New Brunswick, NJ, and London: Transaction Publishers, 1997); and Ruti G. Teitel, *Transitional Justice* (Oxford: Oxford University Press, 2000).

2. This was the situation preceding the Chicago Seven trial, when different social movements opposing the Vietnam War and challenging social practices in American life were intensifying their criticism at the Democratic Convention in Chicago. See Janice Schuetz and Kathryn Holmes Snedaker, eds., *Communication and Litigation* (Carbondale: Southern Illinois University Press, 1988), 217–46.

3. Robert Hariman, "Performing the Laws: Popular Trials and Social Knowledge," in *Popular Trials: Rhetoric, Mass Media, and the Law,"* ed. Robert Hariman (Tuscaloosa: University of Alabama Press, 1990b), 17, 20.

4. Hannah Arendt, *Men in Dark Times,* (San Diego: Harcourt, Brace, [1955] 1968), ix. For an elaboration of the epistemic meaning of "dark times" in Arendt's work, see David Luban, "Explaining Dark Times: Hannah Arendt's Theory of Theory," in *Hannah Arendt: Critical Essays,* ed. Lewis P. Hinchman and Sandra K. Hinchman (Albany: State University of New York Press, 1994), 79–109.

5. Hannah Arendt, *Between Past and Future,* (New York: Penguin, [1954] 1993), 3–15.

6. The element of surprise was enhanced, as Judge Halevi was considered by Ben-Gurion to be a trustworthy trial judge who had previously agreed to preside over the unusual setting of a military trial to try the members of a Jewish underground movement and had convicted and sentenced them severely (Segev, *The Seventh Million,* 265).

7. In Israel there is no jury system. Judges of a trial court sit either as sole judges in minor cases or in groups of three judges in the more important or complicated cases (Art. 37 of the Courts Law, consolidated version, 1984). Since Kastner's libel trial fell under the category of minor criminal offenses and did

not seem to involve complicated issues of law at the outset, a sole judge was assigned to it. Even after Tamir had managed to transform the case into one that addressed the extremely complex issue of the behavior of Jewish leaders during the Holocaust, Judge Halevi did not ask for a panel of three judges to be appointed (in contrast to the state prosecution, which replaced attorney Amnon Tel with the attorney general, Haim Cohn.) With the benefit of historical hindsight we see that a panel of the judge's peers could have supplied a deliberative framework for dealing with these sensitive problems by allowing the judges to consult each other. Indeed, at Kastner's appeal five judges were appointed to sit on the case instead of the three who normally preside at the appellate court.

8. Cr.C. (Jm.) 124/53 *Attorney General v. Gruenwald,* 44 P.M. (1965) 3, 8. [hereafter Cr.C. *Gruenwald*]. Unless otherwise noted, all translations from this source are mine.

9. The defense attorney proved allegation 4 by providing the affidavit Kastner had written in support of Kurt Becher. The court decided that allegation 3 had not been proved in the trial.

10. Cr.C. *Gruenwald,* 51.

11. In an interview to the newspaper *Maariv* on 3 October 1969 Judge Halevi stated: "This sentence was misinterpreted. In the judgment's context where it appears it refers to the 600 emigration permits that Kromey gave Kastner in order to bind him to him, to make him dependent on Eichmann and the Gestapo. I explain there the extent of the temptation that was involved in Eichmann's 'gift.' . . . This literary allusion was not understood correctly, and if I had known in advance that it would be understood in this way I would have given up the literary term. It was not necessary" (cited in Weitz, *The Man Who Was Murdered Twice,* 245).

12. Lawrence Douglas, "Wartime Lies: Securing the Holocaust in Law and Literature," *Yale Journal of Law and the Humanities* 7 (1995): 367–95.

13. See, for example, Martha C. Nussbaum, "Poets as Judges: Judicial Rhetoric and the Literary Imagination," *University of Chicago Law Review* 62 (1995): 1477–1519.

14. As early as 1930 the legal realist Jerome Frank identified this function of law: "Man . . . driven by fear of the vaguenesses, the chanciness of life, has need of rest. Finding life distracting, unsettling, fatiguing, he tries to run away from unknown hazards . . . [and] to postulate a legal system . . . free of the indefinite, the arbitrary and the capricious" (Jerome Frank, *Law and the Modern Mind* [New York: Anchor Books, (1930) 1963], 196–97). For an interesting discussion of the relations between law and literature in this respect, see Gretchen A. Craft, "The Persistence of Dread in Law and Literature," *Yale Law Journal* 102 (1992): 521–46.

15. The very structure of the judgment is such that after the "introductory" chapter (7–26), in which the judge presents the unsolved question (How is it that the common people were led to Auschwitz without knowledge of their destination, while the leaders who encouraged them to board the trains found

a safe haven in Switzerland?), he begins the judicial answer (the legal narrative) with a chapter entitled "The Contract between Kastner and the S.S." See Cr.C. *Gruenwald*, 26.

16. Contrast Halevi's binary approach with that of the historian Yehuda Bauer, who discusses the options that were open to the committee within the historical context of the time (*Jews for Sale? Jewish Negotiations, 1933–1945* [New Haven: Yale University Press, 1994], 145–71).

17. Ibid., 154.

18. Cr.C. *Gruenwald*, 29–30.

19. Ibid., 34.

20. Ibid., 111.

21. The judge divided his story into three subchapters: "Preparation for the Temptation," "The Temptation," and "The Dependence of K. on Eichmann." See ibid., 49–51. The description of the temptation is a dramatic moment in the judgment: "The temptation was great. K. was offered the opportunity to save six hundred souls from the impending Holocaust and a chance to somewhat increase their numbers through payment or further negotiations. And not just any six hundred souls, but those very people who were most important and deserving of rescue in his eyes, for whatever reason—if he wished, his relatives; if he wished, members of his movement; and if he wished, the important Jews of Hungary" (51).

22. Ibid., 90–93.

23. A letter dated 14 May 1944, written by Kastner and Brand to Saly Mayer, conveying a report on the development of the matter since their last letter of 25 April 1944, is quoted in Cr.C. *Gruenwald*, 68.

24. Ibid., 93.

25. In her testimony at Eichmann's trial, Hansi Brand, Kastner's partner, testified to Eichmann's moral deficiency, describing the "clean" commercial language that he used to block himself from the reality of his crimes. See *Transcript of Testimonies from Eichmann Trial* (in Hebrew) (Jerusalem: State of Israel, 1974) pt. B, 914: "My impression was that he was asking for a pure commercial environment, a simple transaction, we are two parties to this transaction."

26. Saul Friedlander, *Reflections of Nazism: An Essay on Kitsch and Death* (Bloomington: Indiana University Press, 1993), 95.

27. Cited in ibid., 102–3.

28. Ibid., 103–4.

29. The straightforward application of contract law to the negotiations between Kastner and the Nazis also overlooks the fact that Kastner's contract was with the "law" itself (since the law was Hitler's wishes as interpreted by his officials). For this reason Kastner could not rely on the law to enforce his "contract." Kastner was in the position of an illegal gambler (for whom the law does not offer enforcement). As we shall see, Kastner preferred the metaphor of a "game of roulette" to describe the nature of his relationship with Eichmann much more accurately.

30. Cr.A. (Jm.) 232/55 *Attorney General v. Gruenwald*, 12 P.D. 2017, 2043, (hereafter Cr.A. *Gruenwald*), cited in Pnina Lahav, *Judgment in Jerusalem: Chief Justice Simon Agranat and the Zionist Century* (Berkeley: University of California Press, 1997), 135.

31. Cr.C. *Gruenwald*, 51, 93.

32. Ibid., 111.

33. See, for example, ibid., 92.

34. Ibid., 105.

35. Hannah Arendt, *The Human Condition* (New York: Anchor Books, 1959), 212–19. See also Martha Minow, *Between Vengeance and Forgiveness: Facing History after Genocide and Mass Violence* (Boston: Beacon Press, 1998), 25–51. For a more recent discussion of the law's relation to forgiveness, and in particular in relation to crimes against humanity as a category of crimes to which laws of limitations do not apply, see Jacques Derrida, *On Cosmopolitanism and Forgiveness*, trans. Mark Dooley and Michael Hughes (New York: Routledge, 2001).

36. Cr.C. *Gruenwald*, 54.

37. We can perceive here a connection between time and narrative. Contract law expels time and encourages us to view Kastner as an archetype. When we are introduced to the archetypal story of how he "sold his soul to the Devil" we grasp at once the beginning and end of Kastner's story. There is no need for us to listen to the details as they unfold over time, and there is thus no need to listen to Kastner's narrative. For an elaboration of the connection between time and narrative, see David Carr, *Time, Narrative, and History* (Bloomington: Indiana University Press, 1986).

38. Cr.C. *Gruenwald*, 56 (citing Kastner's report).

39. Cr.C. *Gruenwald*, 90.

40. Ibid., 43.

41. Ironically, Judge Halevi's image of a Jewish Faust is reminiscent of the early anti-Semitic versions of the legend in which Faust is depicted as a Jew or in which a Jew introduces a Christian man to the devil. See Joshua Trachtenberg, *The Devil and the Jews: The Medieval Conception of the Jew and Its Relation to Modern Anti-Semitism* (Philadelphia: Jewish Publication Society of America, 1943), 23–26.

42. Christopher Marlowe, *Doctor Faustus,* with an introduction by Sylvan Barnet (New York: New American Library, 1969); Thomas Mann, *Doctor Faustus,* trans. John E. Woods (New York: Knopf, [1947] 1997).

43. The exact phrase used by Eichmann,"To extract necessary labor from Hungarian Jewry and sell the balance of valueless human material against valuable goods," appears in War Refugee Board [United States], McClelland's report to Washington, 8/11/44, cited in Bauer, *Jews for Sale?* 196.

44. See Elizabeth M. Butler, *The Fortunes of Faust* (State College: Pennsylvania State University Press, 1998); and J. W. Smeed, *Faust in Literature* (Westport, CT: Greenwood Press, 1987).

45. Cr.C. *Gruenwald*, 27.

46. Ibid., 28–30. According to Freudiger's report (cited in agreement by the

judge), Kastner deliberately provided incomplete reports so that no one could have a general perspective like his and compete with him for the leadership role (46). The judge affirmatively quoted Moshe Krausz, the head of the "Palestine office" in Budapest, who was in charge of dispensing Palestine immigration certification and had opposed Kastner's decision to negotiate with the Germans. Krausz found refuge with the Swiss legation, which represented British interests in Hungary, and he persuaded them to issue protection documents to Jews (Bauer, *Jews for Sale?* 158). Krausz explained that Kastner had failed to warn the people about the impeding catastrophe: "When it concerns his own interests . . . he also lacks conscience. He has no conscience and no regard for others" (Cr.C. *Gruenwald*, 93).

47. Ibid., 51.

48. Ibid., 72, 73, 92; Segev, *The Seventh Million*, 265.

49. This is again reminiscent of the Faustian tradition, which depicts the contract with the devil as a kind of infection. See Joseph P. Stern, *History and Allegory in Thomas Mann's Doktor Faustus* (London: H. K. Lewis, 1975), 11.

50. Cr.C. *Gruenwald*, 223. Kastner's travels in his attempts to save the lives of Jewish inmates in concentration camps (especially toward the end of the war) and his moving from one hotel to the next are reminiscent of the life of Faust, who did not have a permanent home and stayed in successive inns. Faust is depicted in the different versions of the story as a loner. He is not married, and his dealings with Satan to further his ambition and interests gradually drive him farther and farther from the company of ordinary people.

51. Such statements include "We could not look behind Eichmann's cards," "[We chose] the German card," and "The loser in this game [of roulette] will also be called a traitor" (Cr.C. *Gruenwald*, 49, 56).

52. Ibid., 228–40.

53. Ibid., 195–206. The judged relied on an analogy to the Nazi and Nazi Collaborators (punishment) Law, 5710–1950, Art. 15, which permits diversions from ordinary rules of evidence in order to get at the historical truth of the period. For this procedural decision Judge Halevi was severely criticized by several justices of the appellate court (Cr. A. *Gruenwald*, 2281 [Justice Cheshin], 2270 [Justice Olshan]).

54. Compare this to Kastner's description of himself as Eichmann's puppet: "We knew that in front of us stands the general director of the destruction of the Jews. But also the possibilities of rescue were in his hands. He—and he alone—decided on life and death" (Kastner's report, p. 38, cited in Cr.C. *Gruenwald*, 52).

55. Ibid., 206–38.

56. "We did not have any illusions about the Nazi proposals, but we did not sit as judges, our role was to save the lives of Jews, and we had a duty to pass the proposal to the Jewish highest authorities for them to decide. We evaluated the chances as balanced, but not impossible. But we hoped that the Jewish agencies together with the Allies would find a way to continue the negotiation that we began, and to buy a lot of time by doing so" (ibid., 66.)

57. Ibid., 68–69.

58. Alfred Hoelzel, *The Paradoxical Quest: A Study of Faustian Vicissitudes* (New York: Peter Lang, 1988), 160.

59. Halevi could have learned from the complex depiction of Faust in the hands of Goethe and Thomas Mann. Thus, for example, Goethe writes in a letter that he means his poem to present "an unresolved problem that constantly entices people to think about it" (letter dated 13 February 1831, quoted in ibid., 106). Likewise Mann finds in the Faust figure the key to understanding the duality in the German people—a deep-seated need for order and strict obedience combined with an equally strong proclivity for fantastic flights of the imagination (169).

60. The saying: "But, *timeo Danaos* et *dona ferentis*," meaning "Don't trust all acts of apparent kindness," comes from a line in book II of Virgil's *Aeneid*, in which the hero Aeneas escapes the fall of Troy. Having besieged Troy for more than nine years because their admired Helen was a captive there, the Greeks pretended to abandon their quest and left the Trojans a gift of a wooden horse; once the horse was taken within the walls of Troy, Greek soldiers poured out of its hollow interior and destroyed the city. See Virgil, *The Aeneid*, book II: *The Fall of Troy*, trans. Rolfe Humphries (New York: Macmillan, 1987), line 58. For a retelling of the story, see Rex Warner, *Greeks and Trojans* (London: Macgibbon and Kee, 1951), 177–84.

61. Cr.C. *Gruenwald*, 36.

62. Carol M. Rose, "Giving, Trading, Thieving, and Trusting: How and Why Gifts Become Exchanges and (More Importantly) Vice Versa," *Florida Law Review* 44 (1992): 295–326. This mistrust of gifts is also apparent in the anthropological literature, which demonstrates how what appears to be a gift can be explained as a contractual exchange (obligatory and self-interested). See, for example, Marcel Mauss, *The Gift: The Form and Reason for Exchange in Archaic Societies*, trans. W. D. Halls (New York: Norton, 1990). The "dark side" of gifts can be traced back to the etymology of the word *dosis* in Latin and Greek, which means both "gift" and "poison." "The Latin and especially Greek use of dosis to mean poison shows that with the Ancients as well there was an association of ideas and moral rules of the kind we are describing" (Jacques Derrida, *Given Time*. I. *Counterfeit Money*, trans. Peggy Kamuf [Chicago: University of Chicago Press, 1992a], 36).

63. Rose, "Giving, Trading, Thieving, and Trusting," 298.

64. Ibid., 300. Rose suggests taking the opposite direction and discovering the "gift' element in ordinary contractual transactions. For a reflective essay about the need to retain the singularity of the gift as a category distinct from that of contracts, see Derrida, *Given Time*.

65. The moral blame of the Trojans is traced back to the warning given to them by the prophet Laocoon: "Are you crazy, wretched people? Do you think they have gone, the foe? Do you think that any Gifts of the Greeks lack treachery? . . . Do not trust it, Trojans, Do not believe this horse. Whatever it may be, I fear the Greeks, even when bringing presents" (lines 50–60). It was a warning they ignored. Likewise, Judge Halevi blamed Kastner for ignoring a warning

given by Moshe Krauz, the head of the "Palestine office" in Budapest, that the negotiations were a "dangerous Nazi plot" (Cr.C. *Gruenwald*, 32).

66. Ibid., 39 (emphasis added).

67. The judge writes: "All the above circumstances come to show that it was very clear to K. from the beginning of his negotiation with the Nazis until the destruction of the ghetto of Cluj, what was the *price* that was expected and taken by the S.S. for saving his relatives and friends in Cluj; this price included, with the full knowledge of Kastner, the cooperation of the leaders in Cluj" (ibid., 105 [emphasis added]).

68. Derrida, *Given Time*, 41.

69. Cr.C. *Gruenwald*, 90–91.

70. The irony in the finding of a conspiracy between Kastner and the Nazi officers is that it returns us to the anti-Semitic image of the Jew as conspirator. See Hannah Arendt, *The Origins of Totalitarianism*, 2d ed. (New York: Harcourt Brace Javanovich, 1951), 76, where she writes: "It is well known that the belief in a Jewish conspiracy that was kept together by a secret society had the greatest propaganda value for anti-Semitic publicity, and by far outran all traditional European superstitions about virtual murder and well poisoning." It may very well be that this perception of the Jew inspired Himmler to come up with the fantastical idea of sending Brand on his mission to Istanbul with an offer to exchange Jews for trucks (Bauer, *Jews for Sale?* 168). Eichmann in fact relied on this perception when explaining his proposal to transfer a group of "prominent Jews" from the town of Cluj to Budapest to the Hungarian authorities. Wisliceny is quoted as saying to Kastner: "We won't have difficulties with the Hungarians. I told the Hungarian officer that we uncovered a dangerous *Zionist conspiracy*. . . . I told him that we cannot put the conspirators together with the rest of the group, otherwise they will create disquiet and interfere with their labor" (Cr.C. *Gruenwald*, 57).

71. Cr.C. *Gruenwald*, 96: "The leaders of Cluj were not heroes, they did not withstand the strong temptation created by the rescue plan designed by K. and the Nazis. This plan acted on the camp of the privileged Jews like a collective bribe, that brought them, whether they noticed it or not, to collaboration with the Nazis." On pages 101–15 of the judgment the judge explains Kastner's full responsibility for securing the collaboration of the Jewish leaders.

72. Like any good conspiracy story, the language of secrecy is dominant in Halevi's narrative. He refers to the "Reich's secret" and "the secret of the rescue was transformed into a secret about the extermination" (Cr.C. *Gruenwald*, 57, 62–63).

73. Ibid., 2076.

74. Lahav, *Judgment in Jerusalem*, 135.

75. Cr.A. *Gruenwald*, 2099. Interestingly, similar questions about the possibility of equality and free will arose in the literary controversy about Faust's moral blame given the trickery and lies of Mephistopheles and the enormous inequality between the parties. There are scholars who argue that Faust was simply blind to the invalidity of the contract. Halevi's blindness is similar in this respect. I thank Carol Rose for suggesting this analogy. Indeed, Goethe,

who was aware of this problem, tried to equalize the position of the parties by transforming the "contract" into a "wager."

76. Cr.A. *Gruenwald*, 2080–82. Judge Halevi acknowledged at one point in the judgment (110) that the relevant legal question was about a breach of trust by a public official (moving him in the direction of public law). However, he did not elaborate this point because the signing of the "contract" constitutes, in his eyes, a breach of this trust (111).

77. The difference between Halevi and Agranat can be attributed to their understanding of Jewish life in Europe. While Agranat was willing to see it in terms of self-governance (hence public law), Halevi remained within the framework of private law. I thank Pnina Lahav for suggesting this point.

78. It should be noted, however, that Justice Agranat himself was critical of the formalistic division into private and public categories. He demonstrated the blurring of the categories in the case of a libel trial, where criminal and civil law come together. The relevant question according to Agranat was about what standard of proof (civil or criminal) to apply to a libel trial defense that claims "I told the truth." Agranat believed that this decision required balancing conflicting interests (free speech and protection of the good name of individuals) and could not be decided by simply choosing the standard of proof according to the legal classification of public and private law. For elaboration, see Lahav, *Judgment in Jerusalem*, 129–30.

79. Cr.A. *Gruenwald*, 2063, citing Glanvile Williams, *Criminal Law—the General Part* (London: Stevens and Sons, 1953), 36.

80. This rupture between the two normative worlds is captured by Hansi Brand in her testimony in the Eichmann trial. See *The Eichmann Trial: Testimonies* (in Hebrew) (Jerusalem: State of Israel, 1974), 911.

81. There is, however, an ambiguity in Agranat's approach in how much legal positivism (i.e., separating law from morality) is required in a judgment that raises such complicated moral dilemmas. On the one hand he insists on their separation (reasonably, for the law is not necessarily morally approvable). See Cr.A. *Gruenwald*, 2120: "[T]here will be those who will argue that from a strictly *moral* point of view, and no matter what the practical considerations are, it was the duty of the head of the Committee to allow the leaders of Cluj to decide for themselves about the significance of the information about Auschwitz and to determine alone the fate of their community members. My answer to this will be that this matter belongs to the question of the *reasonableness* of the means that were chosen by Kastner to save the Jews of Hungary from destruction. It is a question of whether the line of financial negotiations with the Nazis raised the chance of achieving this mission." But at other times Agranat seems to argue that, also from a strictly moral perspective, Kastner should not be condemned. See, for example, 2082: "My opinion is that even if Kastner did not achieve his aim, one cannot condemn him morally, under one condition—that he was allowed to think, given the circumstances at the time, that the way of commercial negotiations with the Germans offered the best chance—even the only chance—of saving the majority of the Ghetto Jews."

82. Ibid., 2064–65. The choice of the word *reconciling* is even more striking

given the fact that Agranat is quoting from an English source that uses the more neutral term balance).

83. Ibid., 2058, translated in Lahav, *Judgment in Jerusalem*, 132.

84. Michael A. Bernstein, *Foregone Conclusions: Against Apocalyptic History* (Berkeley: University of California Press, 1994), 12.

85. Instead of Halevi's dramatic subtitles, such as "Preparation for the Temptation," "The Temptation," "K's Dependency on Eichmann," and "The Origins of Secrecy," Agranat divided the decision chronologically: "From 19.3.44 to 7.7.44" (the Holocaust in the provincial towns), "From 8.7.44 to 14.10.44" (time of recess), and "From 15.10.44 to the end of December 1944" (the partial expulsion of the Jews of Budapest)" (Cr.A. *Gruenwald*, 2022).

86. Ibid.

87. For the difference between narrative and chronology in terms of moral closure, see Hayden White, "The Value of Narrativity in the Representation of Reality," in *On Narrative*, ed. W. J. T. Mitchell (Chicago: University of Chicago Press, 1981), 1–23. For a position that rejects the need to produce historical narratives with closure in order to allow "the point of view of any single moment in the trajectory of an ongoing story [to have] significance that is never annulled or transcended by the shape and meaning of the narrative as a (supposed) whole," see Bernstein, *Foregone Conclusions*, 28.

88. Bauer, *Jews for Sale?* 156: "The official Judenrat leaders were of the upper-middle-class Jewish elite; they were loyal and law-abiding Hungarian citizens whose life styles and views made them utterly unprepared for the calamity." See also Hansi Brand's testimony in Eichmann's trial about the illegal activities of the rescue committee (*The Eichmann Trial: Testimonies*, 911). See also the documentary film *Free Fall* (dir. Peter Forgacs, Hungary 1996) based on home movie footage that was produced between 1939 and 1944 by a Hungarian Jew (Gyorgy Peto) from a wealthy assimilated environment. The film demonstrates these observations by juxtaposing images of private life among Szeged's assimilated Jewish family and written texts (citing the "Jewish laws" passed by the Hungarian Parliament) and voice-overs that situate these happy scenes in their grim historical context.

89. Freudiger, a member of the Budapest Judenrat and an orthodox religious Jew, emphasized this point in his testimony on the trucks for blood plan.

I told him [Kastner] that it would not be any good. First of all, one cannot provide the enemy with trucks . . . money can be exchanged . . . but trucks?! how do you intend to get them? from whom? He [Kastner] said: In Istanbul there is a rescue committee, there are representatives of the Jewish Agency, and we can fix it. I told him that I didn't think this would work. *He said: You are not a Zionist, this is why you think it will not work. I said: Yes, I am not a Zionist, but aside from this I do not think this is possible.* (Cr.C. *Gruenwald*, 66, emphasis added)

90. The Nazis on their part used the grand aims of the Zionists against them. For example, when Kastner and his friends approached Eichmann and sug-

gested allowing a limited number of Jews to emigrate Eichmann reacted by saying that this plan was not big enough to provide a total (in Nazi terms "final") solution to the Jewish problem (Cr.C. *Gruenwald*, 49–50, quoted from Brand's report, 20–22).

91. Ibid., 43.

92. Ibid., 178–89.

93. Ibid., 2176 (conditions such as no statehood, no international support, terror and deception).

94. For elaboration on the distinction between memory and history, see Pierre Nora, "Between Memory and History: *Les Lieux de Memoire*," *Representations* 26 (1989): 7–9.

95. In particular since it appeared in a long and legalistic judgment.

96. This might raise questions regarding Osiel's theory of the proper "liberal narrative" for political trials. According to him, the narrative that is most adequate to the goals of a liberal democracy is the one that encourages critical distance and reflection on events (in the genre of the "theater of ideas") rather than a clear-cut moralizing narrative. See Osiel, *Mass Atrocity*, 244–51, 283–92. In the Israeli context, although Justice Agranat approximated this model, his antinarrative approach could not serve as an antidote to the emotions that were inflamed by the trial court narrative.

97. For a theoretical discussion of the possibilities and limitations of this type of judgment, see Iris Marion Young, *Intersecting Voices* (Princeton: Princeton University Press, 1997), 38–59.

98. Bertolt Brecht, "Little Organon for the Theatre," in *Brecht on Theatre*, ed. John Willet (New York: Hill and Wang, 1964); and "Alienation Effects in Chinese Acting," in *The Modern Theater*, ed. Daniel Seltzer (Boston: Little, Brown, 1967), 276, 277. For an application in the legal context, see Osiel, *Mass Atrocity*, 291.

Chapter 3

1. "When Dreyfus, the innocent, fell victim to a gross miscarriage of justice, the possibility of charges for contempt of the court prevented an immediate public outcry. Clearing his good name and honor was achieved only several years later, and was dependent upon the efforts of Emile Zola. I need no Zola to clear my own name. History and all those who know what really happened in those dark years can testify on my behalf. Now, after the terrible years that I have experienced in which I tried with no success to serve my people and to save at least a small part of my brethren who were condemned to death by the Nazis, I will do all that I can so that my name and honor will be redeemed" (Kastner, "Also Dreyfus Was Finally Acquitted," 23 June, 1955, a press announcement published in all the papers, cited in Yehiam Weitz, *The Man Who Was Murdered Twice* (in Hebrew) (Jerusalem: Keter, 1995), 274.

2. "In January 1898, Émile Zola published an open letter to the president of the Republic that contained grave accusations against the military and the legal system; the following day, a manifesto appeared in the same newspaper, like-

wise protesting against infringements of rights in the trial of Captain Dreyfus, who had been convicted of espionage. It bore over a hundred signatures, including those of prominent writers and scholars. Soon thereafter it was publicly referred as the 'manifesto of the intellectuals.' Anatole France spoke at the time of the 'intellectual' as an educated person acting 'without a political mandate' when, in the interest of public matters, he makes use of the means of his profession outside the sphere of his profession—that is, in the political public sphere." Quoted in Jurgen Habermas, "Heinrich Heine and the Role of the Intellectual in Germany," in *The New Conservatism,* ed. and trans. Shierry Weber Nicholsen (Cambridge: MIT Press, 1996), 72–73.

3. Nancy Fraser, *Unruly Practices: Power, Discourse, and Gender in Contemporary Social Theory* (Cambridge, MA: Polity Press, 1989), 166.

4. Ziva Shamir, *On Time and Place: Poetics and Politics in Alterman's Writing* (in Hebrew) (Tel-Aviv: Ha-Kibbutz Ha-Meuchad, 1999), 27.

5. Ibid., 7–52.

6. *Davar* was the newspaper of the Histadrut, the General Federation of Jewish Labor. It was established in 1925 by Berl Katznelson (1887–1944), one of the founders of the Zionist labor movement, who also served as its first editor.

7. Shamir, *On Time and Place,* 27.

8. For a discussion of Alterman as the poet of the consensus, see Aharon Komem, "The Poet and the Leader," in *Alterman's Writing,* ed. Menachem Dorman and Aharon Komem (in Hebrew) (Tel Aviv: Ha-Kibbutz Ha-Meuchad, 1989), 54; and Dan Laor, "Alterman as a Political Poet" in *The Trumpet and the Sword* (in Hebrew) (Tel-Aviv: Ha-Kibbutz Ha-Meuchad, 1994), 16–18.

9. The general view that Alterman was a court poet of Ben-Gurion, and that in one instance he was manipulated by him to produce a poem that Ben-Gurion used in a Knesset debate to support his military plans, is advanced in Dan Miron, "From Creators and Constructors to Homeless People" (in Hebrew), *Igra* (1985–86): 71, 113–14. See also Michael Keren, *Ben-Gurion and the Intellectuals: Power, Knowledge, and Charisma* (De Kalb: Northern Illinois University Press, 1983), 142–46.

10. Komem, "The Poet and the Leader," 64.

11. This view supported by archival documents and references to Alterman's diaries, which were discovered in the 1980s. See Nathan Alterman, "Tehum Ha-Meshulash" [The Triangle Zone], in *Ha-Tur Ha-Shevii* [The Seventh Column] (Tel Aviv: Hakibbutz Hameuhad, [1956] 1981), 2:355; Dan Laor, ed., *Al Shtei Ha-Drachim* [Between Two Roads] (Tel-Aviv: Ha-Kibbutz Ha-Meuchad, 1989), 148; Komen, "The Poet and the Leader," 59–61; and Shamir, *On Time and Place,* 38–39, 46–47. For later historical research rehabilitating the image of the Judenrate, see Yehuda Bauer, "The Judenrats: A Few Conclusions," in *The Image of the Jewish Leadership under the Nazi Occupation* (in Hebrew) (Jerusalem: Yad Vashem, 1980); and Isaiah Trunk, *Judenrat: The Jewish Counsels in Eastern Europe under Nazi Occupation* (New York: University of Nebraska Press, 1972).

12. Yitzhak Zuckerman and Moshe Basuk, *The Book of the Ghettos' Wars* (in Hebrew) (Tel Aviv: Ha-Kibbutz Ha-Meuchad, 1964). This book culminated a

series of testimonial books by central members of the resistance movement.

13. Avner Holzman, "Nathan Alterman and the 'Two Paths' Controversy" (in Hebrew), *Bizaron* 8, n.s., (1986): 6–15, quoted at 7.

14. Laor, *Al Shtei Ha-Drachim*, 125.

15. Ibid., 158 n. 28.

16. These views are linked to the general poetic approach that Alterman developed at the time, in which he warned against the tendency of art to embellish reality and thus miss the gray colors of lived experience. See Shamir, *On Time and Place*, 20.

17. Laor, *Al Shtei Ha-Drachim*, 119, 122. Laor claims that Alterman had held these views as early as 1947 but that it was only during the trial, and in particular after the publication of Halevi's verdict, that Alterman decided to publicize his private thoughts.

18. "Yom Ha-Zikaron Ve-Ha-Mordim" [Day of Memorial and the Rebels], 30 April 1954, reprinted in Alterman, *Ha-Tur Ha-Shevii*, 2:407–8.

19. Alterman, *Ha-Tur Ha-Shevii*, 2:409–20.

20. Tom Segev, *The Seventh Million: The Israelis and the Holocaust*, trans. Haim Watzman (New York: Hill and Wang, 1993), 285–89.

21. Holzman, "Nathan Alterman," 9.

22. The first poem (1 July 1955), "Around the Trial" [Misaviv la-Mishpat], consists of three parts that are devoted to the different aspects of the trial ("Two Paths" [Al Shtei Ha-Drakhim], "The Nature of The Accusation" [Tiv Ha-Ashma], and "The Tone of Discussion" [Nimat Ha-Diyun]). The second poem is entitled "More about the 'Two Paths'" [Od Al Shtei Ha-Derakhim], 22 July 1955. The third is "Judgment by Principle" [Dino Shel Ikaron], 29 July 1955, and the fourth is "The Moral to the Generation" [Ha-Lekach la-Dor], 12 August, 1955. The poems appear, edited and revised, in Alterman, *Ha-Tur Ha-Shevii*, 2:421–40. For explanations, see Laor, *Al Shtei Ha-Drachim*, 122–23.

23. "More about the 'Two Paths,'" in ibid., 3:426. See also "Judgment by Principle," (3:427).

24. *Davar*, 26 April 1954. The title ("Sheloshim le-Retzah Kastenr") refers to the Jewish tradition of the thirty days of mourning after the funeral (Shloshim). On the thirtieth day the headstone is erected on the grave, and Alterman's poem can be seen as a metaphorical headstone for Kastner.

25. Gershon Shaked, "Light and Shadow, Unity and Plurality: The Hebrew Literature in a Dialectical Confrontation with a Changing Reality" (in Hebrew), *Alpayim* 4 (1991):113–39.

26. Laor, *Al Shtei Ha-Drachim*, 127–28.

27. Ibid., 123.

28. See chapter 1.

29. The only published testimonies available at the time were those of partisans and ghetto fighters. See Haika Grosman, *The Members of the Jewish Underground* (in Hebrew) (Sifriat Po'alim, Merhavia, 1950); and Zuckerman and Basuk, *The Book of the Ghettos' Wars*.

30. Alterman, "Around the Trial."

31. Alterman, "About the Two Paths."

32. Alterman, "More about the Two Paths."

33. The speech was given on 15 July 1955 and reported in *Lamerhav* on 17 July. For a reprint, see Yitzhak Zuckermann, "Between the Judenrat and the Fighters" (in Hebrew), *Edut* 5 (1990): 13–19.

34. Keren, *Ben-Gurion and the Intellectuals.*

35. *On Ha-Olam Ha-Ze,* see chapter 1, n. 17.

36. Alterman's support of Ben-Gurion earned him the titles "The Jew of the *Paritz* (Polish landowner)," "Ben-Gurion's marionette," "court-poet," and so on (Shamir, *On Time and Place,* 37). Alterman's belated response to this accusation can be found in his play *Pundak Ha-Ruhot* (The Inn of the Spirits, 1962), in which he describes the life of an artist (Hananel, literally "gifted by God," just as Faust is literally "the fortunate man"), who enters into a Faustian bargain (selling the soul of his wife in order to become a famous violinist). The play can be read as a fable about the dilemma that occupied Alterman, whether to write symbolic and detached poetry or produce engaged and political poetry, in which he suggests that it is the detached art, which remains blind to the suffering of everyday life, that should be condemned as egoistic and can be compared to a Faustian bargain. For a discussion of the Faustian origins of this play, see Gideon Ofrat, *The Israeli Drama* (in Hebrew) (Jeruslem: Tcharikover Publications, 1975), 117–30. Shamir suggests that Alterman's play was influenced by Halevi's judgment (275).

37. Meir Ben Gur, "The Poet Nathan A. and the 'Two Paths,'" *Lamerhav,* 8 July 1955. Meir Ben Gur and Moshe Carmel, who vehemently criticized Alterman in their newspaper *Lamerhav,* were also senior spokesmen for *Ahdut Ha-Avodah* (Laor, *Al Shtei Ha-Drachim,* 123).

38. David Kenaani, "Like a Shining Light" (Ke-Or Yahel), *Al Ha-Mishmar,* 14 May 1954 (emphasis added).

39. Many of Alterman's insights about the errors of Halevi's verdict (as expressed in his diary and poems) were also shared by Justice Cheshin of the Supreme Court. Among others, there was the understanding that there is a huge difference between knowing about the destination of the trains and acting on this knowledge, the limitations of a court of law to produce an accurate historical narrative, and the fact that the same facts can be interpreted to exculpate and incriminate Kastner. Cheshin, like Alterman, believed that the source of many of these errors resulted from focusing on the Cluj affair. However, while Cheshin's judgment contributed to a more nuanced understanding of the affair, only Alterman's poems were able to offer counterimages about the heroism of the Judenrat leaders to a broad public and to produce a public debate. For an article discussing the merits in Cheshin's approach to the Kastner affair, see Michal Shaked, "History in the Courtroom and the Courtroom in History" (in Hebrew), *Alpayim* 20 (2000): 36–80.

40. "About the 'Moral to the Generation,'" 12 August 1955.

41. "Thirty Days since Kastner's Murder" (Shloshim le-Retzach Kastner), 26 April 1957.

42. Alterman expressed this poetic principle in the poem "In the Dawn of Day" (Be-terem Yom): "To sing what one sees as long as it is free and lives in its

own right / Before it becomes a slave to meaning and symbols." See Nathan Alterman, *Shirim Shemikvar* (in Hebrew) (Tel Aviv: Ha-Kibutz Ha-Meuhad, 1972), 281–19.

43. By saying this I do not mean to suggest that the dilemmas of writing political poetry are identical to the dilemmas of conducting political trials but that we can distill an underlying commonality. In respect to the law, I doubt the popular view (known as liberal legalism) that assumes that a trial can be just only if it is separated completely from political interests. For elaboration, and criticism, of this view, see Judith Shklar, *Legalism* (Cambridge: Harvard University Press, 1964).

44. 22 June 1955, cited in Weitz, *The Man Who Was Murdered Twice*, 256.

45. Unlike ordinary trial reports, it was prefaced by a "warning" to readers that the decision had been overturned by the Supreme Court.

Chapter 4

1. Cr.C. (Jm.) 40/61 *Attorney General v. Adolf Eichmann*, 45 P.M. 3 (1965). The official translation to English was published as "District Court Judgment" in *International Law Reports* 36 (1968): 18–276.

2. A unanimous verdict is a very uncommon practice in Israel. When there is disagreement, judges usually sign their separate opinions.

3. Prosecution's opening statement, in *Attorney General versus Eichmann* (Jerusalem: Ministry of Information, 1961), 7. See also Gideon Hausner, *Justice in Jerusalem* (New York: Harper and Row, 1966), 322–24.

4. Lotte Kohler and Hans Saner, eds., *Hanna Arendt and Karl Jaspers Correspondence* (New York: Harcourt, Brace, 1992) 409–410.

5. The first report was published after the conclusion of the trial on 16 February 1963. See also Idith Zertal, "Hannah Arendt in Jerusalem" (in Hebrew), *Teoria Ve-Bikoret* 12–13 (1999): 159, 165.

6. Hannah Arendt, *Eichmann in Jerusalem: A Report on the Banality of Evil*, rev. ed. (New York: Penguin, 1994), 19–20, 223–25, 268–70, 277–79.

7. Hausner, *Justice in Jerusalem*, 465. In the 1980 Hebrew version he did, however, devote a few pages to refuting Arendt's approach.

8. Otto Kirschheimer, "Politics and Justice," *Social Research* 22 (1955): 408, 410.

9. Hausner, *Justice in Jerusalem*, 340.

10. Tom Segev, *The Seventh Million: The Israelis and the Holocaust*, trans. Haim Watzman (New York: Hill and Wang, 1993), 328.

11. Article 16(b) of Courts Law, 1957 (11 L.S.I. 157 [1957]), authorizes the president of the district court to designate the judges who shall sit in any particular matter.

12. See Segev, *The Seventh Million*, 342–43; Itzhak Olshan *Din Ve-Dvarim: Memoirs* (in Hebrew) (Jerusalem: Schocken, 1978), 315–17; Elyakim Rubinstein, *Shoftey Eretz* (Judges of the Country) (Jerusalem: Schocken, 1980), 162–64; and Hannah Yablonka, *The State of Israel v. Adolf Eichmann* (in Hebrew) (Tel Aviv: Yediot Achronot, 2001), 149–50.

13. Segev, *The Seventh Million*, 343, quoting from an interview with Halevi by Refael Bashan in *Maariv*, 3 October 1969.

14. Article 2 of Courts (Offenses Punishable by Death) Law, 1961 (15 L.S.I. 20 [1960–61]). Initially the intention was that the panel would consist of three Supreme Court justices, but due to the adverse reactions in the Knesset the final proposal was that only the presiding judge would be from the Supreme Court. The debate is reported in D.K. (1961) 754–63 (session of 18 January 1961). For the similarities to the earlier debate around the Kastner trial, see Olshan, *Memoirs*, 316.

15. The amendment was to the general law of offenses punishable by death and not to the specific Law of Punishment of the Nazis and Their Collaborators, according to which Eichmann was judged. See Olshan, *Memoirs*, 316; and Rubinstein, *Shoftey Eretz*, 163.

16. D.K. (1961) 754 (session of 18.1.1961). See especially the speech of Knesset member Eliyahu Meridor of the Herut party (755–56).

17. Justice Olshan wrote in his memoirs that the defense counsel, Dr. Servatius, had intended to ask Halevi to disqualify himself but had later preferred to make a general claim to disqualify all the judges because they were Jewish (Olshan, *Memoirs*, 317). It was this general claim that made it possible for Halevi not to disqualify himself (interview with Hannah Yablonka 16 February 1995, in Yablonka, *The State of Israel v. Eichmann*, 151–52).

18. See, for example, the testimonies of Zivia Lubetkin and Yitzhak (Antek) Zuckerman, leaders of the Jewish resistance in the Warsaw ghetto, both in *The Eichmann Trial: Testimonies* (in Hebrew) (Jerusalem: State of Israel, 1974), 242–61, 262–81, respectively; and the testimony of Abba Kovner, a resistance leader in the Vilna ghetto (335–52). Judge Landau intervened to prevent Kovner from relating the entire story of the underground in the Vilna ghetto (345).

19. Hausner, *Justice in Jerusalem*, 294–95.

20. Pnina Lahav, *Judgment in Jerusalem: Chief Justice Simon Agranat and the Zionist Century* (Berkeley: University of California Press, 1997), 121–65; Hannah Yablonka, "The Law Punishing Nazis and Their Collaborators: Legislation, Implementation, and Attitudes" (in Hebrew) *Cathedra* 82 (1997): 135–52.

21. Hausner, *Justice in Jerusalem*, 341.

22. Ibid. See also Yablonka, *The State of Israel v. Adolf Eichmann*, 136–39.

23. For example, in the book Joel Brand wrote with Hansi Brand, *The Devil and the Soul*, he harshly criticized the leaders of the Yishuv for their behavior during the war and for their numerous attempts to silence him. See Haviv Kena'an, "A Document on the Devil and the Soul" (in Hebrew), *Ha'aretz*, 10 February 1961.

24. For elaboration on this tension, see Lawrence Douglas, *The Memory of Judgment: Making Law and History in the Trials of the Holocaust* (New Haven: Yale University Press, 2001), 150–82.

25. Gideon Hausner was appointed attorney general only a few weeks before the trial opened, and his main legal experience was in civil law, while Tamir had rich experience in criminal law. It is interesting to note that when

Knesset member Elyakim Ha-Etzny approached Ben-Gurion on Tamir's behalf, he was willing to promise that Tamir would not use the trial to bring up the Yishuv leadership's failure to rescue Jews but would deal only with Eichmann (see Yablonka, *The State of Israel v. Adolf Eichmann*, 93). However, when his request was denied, Tamir tried to join the prosecution team by offering archival materials he had collected for the Kastner trial. This attempt failed as well (93–94). See also "Ben-Gurion Prevented Attorney Tamir from Participating in the Preparation of the Eichmann Trial" (in Hebrew), *Haboker*, 19 July 1960.

26. By interrogating Eichmann, Tamir hoped to gain new facts that would support his attempts to gain a retrial for Gruenwald. He applied to the Israeli police and the attorney general several times, asking to meet Eichmann personally, but all his petitions were denied. See Tamir's letter to the Israeli police, 26 December 1960; and Tamir's letter to Hausner, 13 January 1961. Hausner replied (on 18 January 1961) that he did not intend to disrupt the interrogations and that he would not permit any conversations with Eichmann other than the official interrogation. He would allow Tamir to make his request again when the official interrogations were over. Tamir indeed applied again, on 23 January 1961. This time Hausner replied (on 1 February 1961) that it was inappropriate to question Eichmann before the end of the trial since the subject was part of the accusation (the full correspondence is available at the Jabotinsky Archive in Tel Aviv). The request for a retrial for Gruenwald was ultimately filed by Tamir following the completion of the Eichmann trial on the basis that the trial shed new light on the Kastner affair, but it was denied (Tamir's request and the correspondence regarding it are also available at the Jabotinsky Archive).

27. C. C. (Hi.) 75/61, *Yosef Mendel v. Adolf Eichmann* (not published). The court's archive regarding this period is lost, and there are only secondary sources referring to the case. See D.K. (1961), 1714 (session of 16 May 1961); A. Markowitz in *Maariv* (8 February 1961); and Y. Azrieli in *Ha-Zofe* (31 March 1961). The case is also mentioned in Tamir's request for a retrial in the Jabotinsky Archive. This attempt was also frustrated, this time by a legislative amendment that prevented civil parties from joining trials involving capital punishment.

28. Hansi Brand's testimony is reproduced in *The Eichmann Trial: Testimonies*, 933. Halevi presented similar questions to another witness, Moshe Rosenberg, who was a member of the rescue committee and boarded Kastner's train (945, 948). The questions included "Have you ever heard about discussions to kill Eichmann?" and "How do you explain the . . . results of your initiative [to convince the Jews of the periphery to escape to Budapest]?"

29. Hausner, *Justice in Jerusalem*, 341. See Freudiger's testimony in *The Eichmann Trial: Testimonies*, 734–74.

30. Joel Brand's testimony is reproduced in *Protocols of District Court Sessions*, session 57 (30 May 1961), 21. Yablonka argues that the use of the Sharet-Weizmann documents was one of the most dramatic political interventions in the trial (*The State of Israel v. Eichmann*, 137–38).

31. See chapter 2.

32. The documents demonstrated how the British had refused to adopt any of the courses of action suggested by the Yishuv leaders such as bombing Auschwitz or sending large numbers of parachutists to the occupied territories to organize resistance and rescue.

33. Cross-examination of Joel Brand, in *Protocols of District Court Sessions,* session 57 (30 May 1961), 61.

34. Cross-examination of Hansi Brand, in *Protocols of District Court Sessions,* session 58 (30 May 1961), 45.

35. Ibid., session 85 (4 July 1961).

36. Ibid., session 85 (4 July 1961). Nevertheless, the court refused to disqualify the entire testimony on that basis, only agreeing to take the point into account when evaluating the testimony (24).

37. Ibid. It seems that Hausner's fears were quite reasonable. Tamir requested that the German authorities put Becher on trial.

38. Otto Kirschheimer, *Political Justice* (Princeton: Princeton University Press, 1961), 50.

39. Arendt, *Eichmann in Jerusalem* , 112–34.

40. Jennifer Ring, *The Political Consequences of Thinking: Gender and Judaism in the Work of Hannah Arendt* (Albany: State Univerity of New York Press, 1998), 80–84. In my view there are, however, important differences between Tamir's and Arendt's positions. For elaboration, see chapter 6.

41. The criticism of Arendt's book concentrated on two issues: the inclusion of the chapter on the Judenrate and her thesis about the banality of evil. Both issues, the critics argued, obscured the distinction between victims and perpetrators. See, for instance, Lionel Abel, "The Aesthetics of Evil: Hannah Arendt on Eichmann and the Jews," *Partisan Review* (summer 1963): 211–30; Marie Syrkin, "Hannah Arendt: The Clothes of the Empress," *Dissent* (autumn 1963a): 341–53; and Marie Syrkin, "Miss Arendt Surveys the Holocaust," *Jewish Frontier* (May 1963b): 7–14. In some reviews Arendt was even accused of taking on herself the legal defense of Eichmann. See, for example, Norman Podhoretz, "Hannah Arendt on Eichmann: A Study in the Perversity of Brilliance," *Commentary* 6 (September 1963): 201–8. See, for criticism in Israel, Jacob Robinson, *And the Crooked Shall Be Made Straight* (New York: Macmillan, 1965). See also Arie Leon Kobobi, "A Criminal Country versus a Moral Society"; M. Mushkat, "Eichmann in New York"; and Nathan Eck, "Hannah Arendt's Hateful Articles" (in Hebrew), all in *Yediot Yad Vashem* 31 (December 1963); and A. E. Simon, "A Portrait of Hannah Arendt" (in Hebrew), *Molad* 21 (1963): 239–56.

42. Letter from Arendt to McCarthy, 3 October 1963, in *Between Friends: The Correspondence of Hannah Arendt and Mary McCarthy, 1949–1975,* ed. Carol Brightman (New York: Harcourt, Brace, 1995), 151.

43. Arendt, *Eichmann in Jerusalem,* 5.

44. Ibid.

45. Ibid., 119–21, 124, 225.

46. Ibid., 125–26.

47. Hannah Arendt, "Truth and Politics," in *Between Past and Future: Eight Exercises in Political Thought* (New York: Penguin, 1968), 227. Arendt mentions

in a footnote that the controversy "may also serve as an example of what happens to a highly topical subject when it is drawn into that gap between past and future which is perhaps the proper habitat of all reflections."

48. Shklar, *Legalism*, 145.

49. Ibid.

50. Shklar, *Legalism*, 155.

51. Mark Osiel, *Mass Atrocity, Collective Memory, and the Law* (New Brunswick, NJ, and London: Transaction Publishers, 1997), 62.

52. She characterizes her attitude thus: "It is, at its simplest, a defense of social diversity, inspired by that barebones liberalism which, having abandoned the theory of progress and every specific scheme of economics, is committed only to the belief that tolerance is a primary virtue and that a diversity of opinions and habits is not only to be endured but to be cherished and encouraged" (Shklar, *Legalism*, 5).

53. Hausner's preference for the category "crimes against the Jewish people" might be described as a type of affirmative action in a criminal trial on behalf of the victims, using the trial as a type of truth commission. This was needed because the Nazis specifically marked Jews as their enemies and persecuted them as such. A historical narrative that reframes the facts under universalist legal categories will tend to obscure this fact (this point will be elaborated in the following section). Using affirmative action in criminal law raises very difficult questions that will not be discussed here. For an initial discussion of this subject (in relation to Afro-American criminal defendants), see Paul Butler, "Affirmative Action and the Criminal Law," *University of Colorado Law Review* 68 (1997): 841–89, and two replies to his article published in the same issue, Margaret E. Montoya, "Of 'Subtle Prejudices,' White Supremacy, and Affirmative Action: A Reply to Paul Butler," 891–931; and Richard B. Collins, "Race and Criminal Justice," 933–38.

54. Several writers have recently discussed the tension between Hausner's and Arendt's approaches to the trial. While acknowledging the validity of Arendt's critique of the historical narrative, they suggest reconciling it with Hausner's attempts to empower the victims and use the stage of the trial as a truth commission writ large. See, for example, Shoshana Felman, "Theaters of Justice: Arendt in Jerusalem, the Eichmann Trial, and the Redefinition of Legal Meaning in the Wake of the Holocaust," *Theoretical Inquiries in Law* 1 (2) (2000): 465–507; and Douglas, *The Memory of Judgment*, 95–182. Although my discussion aims to highlight the strengths and limitations of both approaches, I think that it was impossible to reconcile them within the framework of the Eichmann trial, as discussed in the next section of this chapter.

55. Hayden White, "The Value of Narrativity in the Representation of Reality," in *On Narrative*, ed. W. J. T. Mitchell (Chicago: University of Chicago Press, 1981), 1, 13.

56. A letter from Arendt to Karl Jaspers, 23 December 1960, in *Hannah Arendt and Karl Jaspers Correspondence, 1926–1969*, ed. Lotte Kohler and Hans Saner, trans. Robert Kimber and Rita Kimber (New York: Harcourt, Brace, 1992), 417.

57. Pharaoh is from the story of the Exodus; Haman is the enemy of the Jews in the story of Esther. Hausner's framework was compatible with the Zionist narrative of "negation of the diaspora," which depicts the life of the Jew in the diaspora as a monolithic story of persecution and assigns to the Jew the role of the eternal passive victim. For discussions of the cyclical structure of traditional Jewish historiography, see Yosef Hayim Yerushalmi, *Zakhor: Jewish History and Jewish Memory* (Seattle: University of Washington Press, 1982); and Amos Funkenstein, *Perceptions of Jewish History* (Berkeley: University of California Press, 1993), 54–55.

58. Hausner tried to prove that the purpose of Eichmann's tour of Palestine in 1937 had been to contact Haj Amin Al-Husseini. See Hausner's cross-examination in *Protocol of District Court Sessions*, session 90 (10.7.61). Arendt was strongly opposed to this line of investigation (*Eichmann in Jerusalem*, 13).

59. For a discussion of the reasons for this omission in the Nuremberg trials, see Lawrence Douglas, "Film as Witness: 'Nazi Concentration Camps' before the Nuremberg Tribunal," *Yale Law Journal* 105 (1995a): 449, 459–463; and Michael R. Marrus, "The Holocaust at Nuremberg," *Yad Vashem Studies* 26 (1998): 5–42.

60. According to the Law of Punishment of the Nazis and their Collaborators, 1950, 4 L.S.I. 154 (1949–50).

61. Arendt, *Eichmann in Jerusalem*, 19. Interestingly, a similar criticism was offered by Ben-Gurion to Hausner after reading a draft of his opening speech. See Yablonka, *The State of Israel v. Eichmann*, 101–2.

62. Arendt, *Eichmann in Jerusalem*, 269.

63. Ibid.

64. Ibid., 273: "It is in the very nature of things human that every act that has once made its appearance and has been recorded in the history of mankind stays with mankind as a potentiality long after its actuality has become a thing of the past."

65. Ibid., 12.

66. A narrative account is authorized at the court by being reproduced as an "eyewitness testimony," by being subjected to cross-examination, and by receiving the stamp of approval from the judgment of the court.

67. She expressed the same attitude in a letter to McCarthy in which she wrote: "As I see it, there are no 'ideas' in this Report, there are only facts with a few conclusions, and these conclusions usually appear at the end of each chapter." Letter from Arendt to Mary McCarthy, 20 September 1963, in Brightman, *Between Friends*, 148. Arendt insists on the "report" nature of her book on several occasions in her correspondence with McCarthy (146, 147, 148, 152).

68. Arendt, "Truth and Politics," 264.

69. Ibid., 238–39.

70. Hausner, *Justice in Jerusalem*, 291 (emphasis added).

71. Arendt, "Truth and Politics," 262 (emphasis added).

72. Arendt explained that recounting the facts is not enough for history telling because "Reality is different from, and more than, the totality of facts and events. . . . Who says what is . . . always tells a story, and in this story the

particular facts lose their contingency and acquire some humanly comprehensible meaning" (ibid., 261–62).

73. Ibid., 262 (emphasis added).

74. Among these deviations were the retroactivity of the law and exclusion of the "act of state" defense. In both cases the prosecution relied on the Nuremberg precedent (Hausner, *Justice in Jerusalem*, 173, 316).

75. Gideon Hausner, *Justice in Jerusalem* Hebrew (Tel Aviv: Ha-Kibbutz Ha-Meuchad, 1980), 462.

76. 1 IMT at 11 (interpretation of Article 6 of the Charter of the International Military Tribunal at Nuremberg). The conspiracy charge was limited to waging an aggressive war and did not include a charge of conspiracy to commit war crimes or other atrocities. Under this interpretation, whatever crimes against humanity the Nazis committed against German citizens before the German army crossed the Polish border did not fall under the jurisdiction of the Nuremberg court (Douglas, "Film as Witness," 461).

77. Lawrence Douglas, "The Memory of Judgment: The Law, the Holocaust, and Denial," *History and Memory* 7 (2) (1996): 100–120, quoted at 105.

78. It is interesting that the first draft of the law made no mention of crimes against the Jewish people. This category was added only after an objection by Knesset member Zerah Verhaftig, who argued that ignoring the specific history of the war against the Jews by the Nazis constituted the greatest omission of the proposed law. D.K. (1950) 1152–53 (session of 27 March 1950).

79. One example Hausner cites to prove the lack of the Jewish narrative at Nuremberg is the plea by Chaim Weizmann, at that time president of the Zionist Confederation, to be allowed to appear as a Jewish witness. The American chief counsel at Nuremberg, Robert Jackson, refused this request, explaining that he was convinced that it would be better to prove the case by means of documents rather than testimonies.

80. Hausner, *Justice in Jerusalem*, 453 (emphasis added).

81. Arendt, *Eichmann in Jerusalem*, 119.

82. Arendt, "Truth and Politics," 236.

83. Ibid., 238 (emphasis added). The connections among speech, community, and reality are captured in Arendt's interpretation of the notion of "common sense" (*sensus communis*); see Arendt, *The Human Condition*, 208.

84. Arendt, "Truth and Politics," 258.

85. Ibid. (emphasis added).

86. Hausner, *Justice in Jerusalem*, Hebrew ed., 452–54. As noted earlier, Hausner's reference to Arendt's criticism only appears in the Hebrew edition of his book. In the English edition he mentions her only in a short footnote.

87. Robert Jackson explains the decision to rely solely on documents at Nuremberg in these terms: "The decision supported by most of the staff, was to use and rest on documentary evidence to prove every point possible. The argument against was that documents are dull, the press would not report them, the trial would become wearisome and would not get across to the people. There was much truth in this position, I must admit. But it seemed to me that witnesses, many of them persecuted and hostile to the Nazis, would always be

chargeable with bias, faulty recollection, and even perjury. The documents . . .
would make the sounder foundation not only for the immediate guidance of
the Tribunal, but for the ultimate verdict of history. The result was that the Tribunal declared, in its judgment, 'The case, therefore, against the defendants
rests in a large measure on documents of their own making, the authenticity of
which has not been challenged except in one or two cases.'" Robert Jackson,
introduction to Whitney R. Harris, *Tyranny on Trial: The Evidence at Nuremberg*,
rev. ed. (Dallas: Southern Methodist University Press, 1999), xxxv–xxxvi.

88. Hausner, *Justice in Jerusalem*, 291.

89. A letter from Arendt to Karl Jaspers, 23 December 1960, in Robert Kimber and Rita Kimber, eds., Arendt and Jaspers, *Correspondence*, 417.

90. Arendt, *Eichmann in Jerusalem*, 211. Arendt explained the need to
exclude victims' testimonies in terms of legalistic considerations. However, the
historical writing of this period reveals the more general approach of not relying on survivors. Raul Hilberg, on whose work Arendt relied in her book,
announced that his was "not a book about the Jews. It is a book about the people who destroyed the Jews. Not much will be read here about the victims. The
focus is placed on the perpetrators" (*The Destruction of the European Jews*
[Chicago: Quadrangle Books, 1961], v).

91. Hannah Yablonka, "Preparing the Eichmann Trial: Who Really Did the
Job?" *Theoretical Inquiries in Law* 1 (2) (2000): 368–92, quotation at 382; Hausner,
Justice in Jerusalem, 291.

92. Hausner, *Justice in Jerusalem*, 291–92.

93. Yablonka, "Preparing the Eichmann Trial," 383–84.

94. Primo Levi, *The Truce*, trans. Stuart Woolf, in *If This Is a Man and The
Truce* (London: Penguin, 1979), 226.

95. For the lawyer's activity as a cultural translator, see James Boyd White,
Justice as Translation (Chicago: University of Chicago Press, 1990), particularly
229–69.

96. Hausner, *Justice in Jerusalem*, 291.

97. Lawrence L. Langer, *Holocaust Testimonies: The Ruins of Memory* (New
Haven: Yale University Press, 1991).

98. Hausner, *Justice in Jerusalem*, 294. Hausner also described the effects of
deep memory on the testimony of Kastner's partner, Joel Brand, who had been
sent from Hungary to promote the trucks for blood plan: "I realized that the
man was no more than a receptacle for memories. He had no present; his life
had stopped long ago . . . for every day ten thousand Hungarian Jews were
being sent to their deaths. . . . All he could do was to keep telling the story of the
mission that had fallen through" (344).

99. *The Eichmann Trial: Testimonies*, 1122–23. See Arendt's sarcastic account
of this event in *Eichmann in Jerusalem*, 223–24. For a new interpretation of the
trial and of this episode in particular, see Shoshana Felman, *The Juridical Unconscious: Trials and Traumas in the Twentieth Century* (Harvard University Press,
2002).

100. This was done in accordance with section 15 of the Law of Punishment
of the Nazis and Their Collaborators. He was also helped by the strategy of the

defense lawyer not to cross-examine the victims since they were irrelevant to proving Eichmann's guilt.

101. Arendt, *Eichmann in Jerusalem*, 121. Arendt was unaware apparently that this procedural decision could have been influenced by the Kastner trial, where the survivors' voices had been distorted by the ordinary framework of lawyer's investigation. See, for example, the testimony of Hillel Danzig, Cr.C. 123/54 (Jm.), *Attorney General v. Gruenwald*, 44 P.M. (1965) 3, 85–88; and Cr.A. 232/55, *Attorney General v. Gruenwald*, 12 P.D. 2017, 2115. For elaboration, see chapter 1.

102. Hausner, *Justice in Jerusalem*, 374.

103. Modern criminal law views the crime as an offense against the public at large, as a violation of the public order, while the victim of the crime is seen as a random victim, as one of many other people who could have been hurt by the criminal. The victim therefore has little control over the direction of the trial. For a historical overview of the status of victims in criminal trials, see Douglas E. Beloof, *Victims in Criminal Procedures* (Durham: Carolina Academic Press, 1998), 19–40.

104. Segev, *The Seventh Million*, 329. Segev cites Ben-Gurion's letter to Nahum Goldmann, president of the World Zionist Organization: "It is the particular duty of the State of Israel, the Jewish people's only sovereign entity, to recount this episode in its full magnitude and horror."

105. Speech of Knesset member Baruch Ozniah of the Mapai party, in D.K. (1961) 758–59 (session of 18.1.1961). Communist members who opposed the amendment viewed it as political, citing the unsuccessful attempt made by Dr. Kaul, a lawyer from East Germany, to meet the justice minister in order to join the trial as a civil prosecutor. See Hausner, *Justice in Jerusalem*, Hebrew ed., 302. In the English version Hausner only mentions Kaul's wish to join the trial and that it was legally impossible (*Justice in Jerusalem*, 466).

106. Draft amendment to Criminal Procedure Law, 1963 H.H., 161, 202. Justice Minister Rosen never explained the specific reasons that roused the government's fears that this rarely used avenue of joining a criminal trial as a civil party would be practiced in Eichmann's trial. Section 6 of the draft amendment of Courts (Offences Punishable by Death) Law, 1961 states that: "no civil party will be heard and no civil law suit will be filed during a trial under this law" (1961 H.H., 72). The official explanation given for the amendment was that "section 6 is to guarantee that the criminal procedures regarding these severe crimes will be exclusively criminal, and that the only litigators will be the State's prosecutor, the defendant and the defense attorney." A different rationale was hinted at during the Knesset debate over the amendment. Moshe Sneh of the Communist party, who opposed the amendment, argued that "those who will come to prosecute are not interested in the monetary value of the suit, the main aim of bringing civil suits against Eichmann is symbolic. Its goal is to allow survivors from Jewish communities from all over Europe to approach the court, and for their historical claim to be heard. The form of civil prosecution is only a legal dress to that larger claim" (D.K. [1961] 857 [session of 31.1.1961]). See also Uriel Gorny, *Criminal Law, Practical Theory* (in Hebrew) (Tel Aviv:

Dinim, 1953), 53–56. The procedural law that enabled this was the Ottoman Procedural Law of 1897. Israeli criminal procedure was based on a British colonial law of 1936, which retained parts of prior Ottoman legislation from 1858 (which was in turn based on a French law of 1810).

107. The amendment blocked Tamir from suing on behalf of a Hungarian survivor, Yosef Mendel; see note 27. It also blocked two additional civil suits filed on behalf of Hungarian survivors, Hava Kakash and Mordechay Litner. See Eithan Benzur, "Servatius Was Rebuked for His Remarks," *Maariv,* 11 April 1961. The route of demanding individual compensation from Eichmann was also denied. See "First Confrontation with Servatius in Court," *Ha'aretz,* 11 April 1961; and *Protocols of the District Court,* session 119 (12 December 1961).

108. For the distinction between a healthy reenactment and a pathological one, see chapter 1. For an elaboration on the performative aspects of trials, see Milner Ball, "The Play's the Thing: An Unscientific Reflection on Courts under the Rubric of Theater," *Stanford Law Review* 28 (1975): 81–115.

109. Shoshana Felman and Dori Laub, *Testimony: Crises of Witnessing in Literature, Psychoanalysis, and History* (New York: Routledge, 1992), 80–82.

110. Arendt discusses this point in her article on concentration camps: Hannah Arendt, "Social Science Techniques and the Study of Concentration Camps," *Jewish Social Studies* 12 (1950): 49–64, quotation at 59–60: "Most difficult to imagine and most gruesome to realize is perhaps the complete isolation which separated the camps from the surrounding world as if they and their inmates were no longer part of the world of the living, . . . From the moment of his arrest, nobody in the outside world was supposed to hear of the prisoner again; it is as if he had disappeared from the surface of the earth."

111. Arendt, *Eichmann in Jerusalem,* 232.

112. Arendt, "Social Science Techniques," 60: "Total domination is achieved when the human person, who somehow is always a specific mixture of spontaneity and being conditioned, has been transformed into a completely conditioned being whose reactions can be calculated even when he is led to certain death." As one witness states in Claude Lanzmann's film *Shoah:* "The Germans even forbade us to use the words 'corpse' or 'victim.' The dead were blocks of wood, shit. The Germans made us refer to the bodies as *figuren,* that is, as puppets, as dolls, or as Schmattes, which means 'rags.'" Claude Lanzsmann, *Shoah* (New York: Da Capo Press, 1995), 9.

113. On the transformations in the legal use of the documentary film *Nazi Concentration Camps,* see Douglas, *The Memory of Judgment,* 23–27, 62–63, 226–27. In the Eichmann trial it had become a "silent movie" since the prosecution erased the interpreter's voice from it. Haim Gouri, *The Glass Cage: The Jerusalem Trial* (in Hebrew) (Tel Aviv: Hakibbutz Hameuchad, 1962), 129.

114. Gouri, *The Glass Cage,* 119.

115. Ibid., 243–44.

116. For an indication of the low status of the testimony of Holocaust victims for writing the history of the period, see Tony Kushner, *The Holocaust and the Liberal Imagination* (Oxford: Blackwell, 1994), 2–11. Kushner writes: "Even though a great number of these texts were produced immediately after the

author's release from camp and thus can be expected to give an authentic record of the writer's experience, historians generally do not trust them when looking for evidence of the historical truth of the camps" (3). See also Leon Poliakov, *Harvest of Hate* (London: Eleck Books, 1956), xiii.

117. The influence can be seen in Claude Lanzmann's film *Shoah*, in which he chose to focus on three survivors who had appeared as witnesses in the Eichmann trial. Likewise, the various Holocaust documentation projects providing video-recorded testimonies (e.g., Yad Vashem, the Yale Project, and the Spielberg Project) can also be seen as heirs to the Eichmann trial's innovative presentation of survivors as authoritative writers of history. Saul Friedländer points to the sharp division that has developed between the two approaches to Holocaust historiography (those based on perpetrators' documents and those based on victims' testimonies) in *Nazi Germany and the Jews*, vol. 1: *The Years of Persecution, 1933–1939* (New York: HarperCollins, 1997), 1–2. Friedländer's book provides the first attempt to integrate the various materials and points of view about the Holocaust.

118. This situation can be demonstrated by comparing two recent documentary films about the trial. *The Trial of Adolf Eichmann* (1997), produced by the American Public Broadcasting Service (PBS), presents the trial from the perspective of the Israeli prosecution, while *The Specialist* (1999), by Israeli director Eyal Sivan, is inspired by Arendt's book. The focus of the PBS film is the prosecution's case, which was built on testimonies of one hundred Holocaust survivors telling the story of the Holocaust as the culmination of anti-Semitic persecutions of Jews for generations. In contrast, *The Specialist* focuses on Eichmann's testimony and develops a counternarrative about the Holocaust as the product of bureaucratic mass murder. As viewers of the films, we are expected to take sides without any serious attempt being made to provide the framework that would make such a comparison possible.

119. For a detailed description, see Hannah Yablonka, *Brothers—Strangers: Holocaust Survivors in Israel, 1948–1952* (in Hebrew) (Jerusalem: Yad Ben Zvi, 1994).

120. Douglas, *The Memory of Judgment*, 161–62.

121. The prosecution fought hard to establish the relevance of his testimony. See Hausner, *Justice in Jerusalem*, 332–33. Hausner explains that "the truth on the revolts was important for its own sake, and also as an educational by-product of the trial for our own youth, who were constantly asking why there were no more revolts than they had heard of. Here was a chance to bring out the countless acts of heroism with which people were generally less acquainted" (333).

122. *The Eichmann Trial: Testimonies*, 344. His testimony helped to rehabilitate the image of the victims but not the Judenrat phenomenon that was debated in the Kastner trial.

123. For obvious reasons juridical testimony cannot replace therapy. However, when the barriers of silence are not only individual but also collective, trials can have a therapeutic function by reconciling the personal traumatic story with the larger framework of collective memory. This function of a trial as a

facilitator of testimony can be seen in the Eichmann trial and also more recently in the Truth and Reconciliation Commission in South Africa. For the Eichmann trial and psychotherapy, see Judith Stern, "The Eichmann Trial and Its Influence on Psychiatry and Psychology," *Theoretical Inquiries in Law* 1 (2) (2000): 393, 409–25. For testimonies of survivors in South Africa, see Martha Minow, *Between Vengeance and Forgiveness* (Boston: Beacon Press, 1998), 61–74.

124. Gouri, *The Glass Cage,* 139

125. In recent years there has been a dispute, also in the common law countries, over the role of the victims in criminal trials. Several countries have reinforced the victims' status by giving them an opportunity to tell their stories (victim impact statements) and by requiring consultation and notification of the victims about the legal procedure. These reforms, however have not dealt with the issue of the victim's self-representation in the criminal process. See Beloof, *Victims in Criminal Procedure;* and George E. Fletcher, *With Justice for Some* (New York: Addison Welsley, 1995). For an early discussion of the opportunities to reinforce victims' status in the common law, see Abraham S. Goldstein, "Defining the Role of the Victim in Criminal Prosecution," *Mississippi Law Journal* 52 (2) (1982): 515–62. For a discussion of the dangers of the victims' rights discourse, see Martha Minow, "Surviving Victim Talk," *UCLA Law Review* 40 (2) (1993): 1411–46; and Lynne N. Henderson, "The Wrongs of Victim's Rights," *Stanford Law Reviews* 37 (2) (1985): 937–1022.

126. See "Conclusion," this volume.

127. Letter from Arendt to Mary McCarthy, 20 September 1963, in Brightman, *Between Friends,* 147; Arendt, *Eichmann in Jerusalem,* 232–33.

128. Arendt, *Eichmann in Jerusalem,* 229.

129. Ibid., 232–33.

130. Recent writings on the Eichmann trial can be understood as opting for one of the two approaches. Douglas and Osiel evaluate the trial in order to "take sides" (Douglas chooses Hausner while Osiel chooses Arendt). Felman, on the other hand, attempts to show that both were right to a degree and therefore can be reconciled. See Osiel, *Mass Atrocity;* Douglas, *The Memory of Judgment;* and Felman, *The Juridical Unconscious.*

Chapter 5

1. See *Estes v. Texas,* 381 U.S. 543, 588 (1965); *In re Oliver,* 333 U.S. 257 (1948). For elaboration on the principle of publicity, see Max Radin, "The Right to a Public Trial," *Temple Law Quarterly* 6 (1932): 381–98; and Gerhard Mueller, "Problems Posed by Publicity to Crime and Criminal Proceedings" *University of Pennsylvania Law Review* 110 (1961): 1–26 (arguing that the reason for publicity goes beyond entertainment and has to do with the fact that a criminal prosecution is carried in the name of the community at large and therefore it concerns everybody). See also Jeremy Bentham, "Rationale of Judicial Evidence," in *The Works of Jeremy Bentham,* ed. John Bowring (New York: Russell and Russell, 1962), 1:511; and John Henry Wigmore, *Evidence,* rev. ed. (Boston: Little, Brown, 1976), especially 438. In the United States the right to a public trial is

constitutionally protected; see Natalia Nicholaidis, "The Sixth Amendment Right to a Speedy and Public Trial," *American Criminal Law Review* 26 (4) (1989): 1489–506.

For a historical study of the relationship between trial and theater in general, see Johan Huizinga, *Homo Ludens: A Study of the Play-Element in Culture* (Boston: Beacon Press, 1955). For a more recent exploration of the topic, see Milner S. Ball, "The Play's the Thing: An Unscientific Reflection on Courts under the Rubric of Theater," *Stanford Law Review* 28 (1975): 81–115. For an examination of trial as theater in the high-profile trial of the Chicago Seven, see Pnina Lahav, "Theater in the Courtroom: The Chicago Conspiracy Trial" *Law and Literature* (forthcoming, 2004). See also Robert Hariman, ed., *Popular Trials: Rhetoric, Mass Media, and the Law* (Tuscaloosa: University of Alabama Press, 1990).

2. Hannah Arendt, *Eichmann in Jerusalem: A Report on the Banality of Evil,* rev. ed. (New York: Penguin, 1994), 5.

3. Ben-Gurion was involved in formulating the concept of the trial. Thus, the opening address of the prosecutor Gideon Hausner was submitted to him before it was delivered in court. See Gideon Hausner to Ben-Gurion, 24 March 1961, and Ben Gurion to Hausner, 28 March 1961, cited in Michael Keren, "Ben-Gurion's Theory of Sovereignty: The Trial of Adolf Eichmann," in *David Ben Gurion: Politics and Leadership in Israel,* ed. Ronald W. Zweig (London: F. Cass, 1991), 46–47, n. 34. In contrast to Arendt, Keren argues that "From Ben-Gurion's standpoint, Chief Justice Landau and his associates served the interests of the state of Israel no less than Hausner" (47). See also Hannah Yablonka, *The State of Israel v. Adolf Eichmann* (in Hebrew) (Tel Aviv: Yediot Ahronot, 2001), 60–67.

4. Arendt, *Eichmann in Jerusalem,* 9.

5. In the epilogue Arendt proposed imagining an inverse Eichmann trial—what would have occurred if one of the Jewish victims had killed Eichmann, given himself up to the police, and insisted on being tried before a public court: "The trial, it is true, is again a 'show' trial, and even a show, but its 'hero,' the one in the center of the play, on whom all eyes are fastened, is now the true hero" (*Eichmann in Jerusalem,* 266). Arendt mentions two historical precedents: the case of Shalom Schwartzbard, who in Paris on May 25, 1926, shot and killed Simon Petlyura, who was responsible for the pogroms during the Russian civil war of 1917–20; and the case of Salomon Tehlirian, who in Berlin in 1921 shot to death Talaat Bey, the infamous Turkish killer in the Armenian pogroms of 1915. Both used their trials to awaken the world to the massacre of their peoples, and both were acquitted (265).

6. Martha Minow, *Between Vengeance and Forgiveness* (Boston: Beacon Press, 1998).

7. Arendt, *Eichmann in Jerusalem,* 9.

8. Judith Shklar, *Legalism* (Cambridge: Harvard University Press, 1964), 153–54.

9. Ronald Beiner, "Hannah Arendt on Judging," in Hannah Arendt, *Lectures on Kant's Political Philosophy,* ed. Ronald Beiner (Chicago: University of Chicago Press, 1982b), 97–101; Elisabeth Young-Bruehl, *Hannah Arendt: For Love*

of the World (New Haven: Yale University Press, 1982), 377. See also Arendt's own testimony on the matter in her *The Life of the Mind* (New York: Harcourt, Brace, [1971] 1978a), 5–6.

10. Lon L. Fuller, *The Morality of Law* (New Haven: Yale University Press, 1964), 59.

11. Immanuel Kant, *Critique of Judgment*, trans. J. H. Bernard (New York: Hafner, 1951), 10. Kant's formulation was "thinking the particular as being contained in the universal." According to Arendt, when Kant was thinking about determinative judgment the lawyer and doctor served as his models (*Lectures*, 36).

12. Ronald Dworkin, *A Matter of Principle* (Cambridge: Harvard University Press, 1985), 9–11, 158–61; Ronald Dworkin, *Law's Empire* (Cambridge, MA: Belknap Press, 1986), 87–88, 244–45, 255–58; Ronald Dworkin, *Taking Rights Seriously* (London: Duckworth, 1977), 81–130; Roscoe Pound, *Jurisprudence* (St. Paul: West Pub., 1959), iv, 3–20. In legal theory, especially when it comes to criminal law, there is a strong need to play down this element of discretion in judgment. See Rosemary Pattenden, *The Judge, Discretion, and the Criminal Trial* (Oxford: Clarendon Press, 1982).

13. Kant, *Critique of Judgment*, 15. Arendt, *Lectures*, 76.

14. I borrow this term from Stanley Fish, *Doing What Comes Naturally:* Stanley Fish, *Doing What Comes Naturally: Change, Rhetoric, and the Practice of Theory in Literary and Legal Studies* (Durham: Duke University Press, 1989), 503–5.

15. Kant, *Critique of Judgment*, 136–37, cited in Arendt, *Lectures*, 43.

16. For an examination of the relations between taste judgments and sociability in Kant's *Critique of Judgment*, see Paul Guyer, "Pleasure and Society in Kant's Theory of Taste," in *Essays in Kant's Aesthetics*, ed. Ted Cohen and Paul Guyer (Chicago: University of Chicago Press, 1982), 21–54.

17. See Arendt, *Eichmann in Jerusalem*, 19. See also the correspondence of Arendt and Jaspers regarding his concern about the demonization of Eichmann, in *Hannah Arendt and Karl Jaspers Correspondence, 1926–1969*, ed. Lotte Kohler and Hans Saner, trans. Robert Kimber and Rita Kimber (New York: Harcourt Brace, 1992), 54, 62, 69.

18. Arendt, *Eichmann in Jerusalem*, 50. The ease with which Eichmann switched language codes was demonstrated time and again at the trial. See Hannah Arendt, "Thinking and Moral Considerations: A Lecture," *Social Research* 38 (3) (fall 1971a): 417, 419.

19. Michael Denneny, "The Privilege of Ourselves: Hannah Arendt on Judgment," in *Hannah Arendt: The Recovery of the Public World*, ed. Melvyn A. Hill (New York: St. Martin's, 1979), 245–74, quotation from 254–55 (emphasis added).

20. As Bernstein points out, the subtitle, *A Report on the Banality of Evil*, did not appear in the original publication in the *New Yorker* articles, and the expression itself appears only once, in the last sentence of the report (just before the epilogue). See Richard J. Bernstein, *Hannah Arendt and the Jewish Question* (Cambridge: MIT Press, 1996), 166.

21. Arendt, *Eichmann in Jerusalem*, 287.

22. See "'Eichmann in Jerusalem': An Exchange of Letters between Gershom Scholem and Hannah Arendt," *Encounter* 21 (January 1964) 51, 56.

23. *Eichmann in Jerusalem*, 290. For an attempt to develop a jurisprudence adequate to deal with bureaucratic crimes, see David Luban, Alan Strudler, and David T. Wasserman, "Moral Responsibility in the Age of Bureaucracy," *Michigan Law Review* 90 (8) (1992): 2348–92.

24. Arendt, *Eichmann in Jerusalem*, 48. Arendt adds that "when he did succeed in constructing a sentence of his own, he repeated it until it became a cliche" (49).

25. Ibid., 49.

26. A similar observation is made in Dagmar Barnouw, *Visible Spaces: Hannah Arendt and the German-Jewish Experience* (Baltimore: Johns Hopkins University Press, 1990), 238.

27. Ibid., 51.

28. Arendt quoted his words: "Whatever I prepared and planned, everything went wrong, my personal affairs as well as my years-long efforts to obtain land and soil for the Jews. I don't know, everything was as if under an evil spell; whatever I desired and wanted and planned to do, fate prevented it somehow. I was frustrated in everything, no matter what" (ibid., 50).

29. Ibid.

30. Ibid., 53.

31. Ibid., 86. For a book discussing changes in the German language under the Third Reich, see Victor Klemperer, *The Language of the Third Reich*, trans. Martin Brady (London: Athlone, 2000).

32. This interpretation of the connection between the failure of language and the failure of judgment can help reconcile Arendt's two different approaches to the problem of judgment: "internal dialogue" and "enlarged mentality." The internal dialogue interpretation is largely based on an article that Arendt wrote in 1971 in which she tried to clarify the philosophical foundations of her phrase "the banality of evil" ("Thinking and Moral Considerations."). The enlarged mentality or "representative thinking" interpretation is largely based on Arendt's essay "The Crisis in Culture," in *Between Past and Future* (New York: Penguin, [1954] 1968), 197–226, especially 220–221, and on her Kant Lectures. See also Seyla Benhabib, *The Reluctant Modernism of Hannah Arendt* (Thousand Oaks, CA: Sage, 1996), 191–93; and Bernstein, *Hannah Arendt and the Jewish Question*, 166–78.

33. Haim Gouri, *The Glass Cage: The Jerusalem Trial* (in Hebrew) (Tel Aviv: Hakibbutz Hameuchad, 1962), 168; see also Hausner, *Justice in Jerusalem*, 344.

34. Gouri, *The Glass Cage*, 169.

35. Ibid.

36. Arendt, *Eichmann in Jerusalem*, 290–94. Cf. Shklar's similar argument regarding the Nuremberg trials in *Legalism*, 157.

37. Arendt, *Eichmann in Jerusalem*, 215. Bruno Bettelheim explains the dilemma as one of incongruity "between all the horrors recounted, and this man in the dock, when essentially all he did was to talk to people, write memoranda, receive and give orders from behind a desk" ("Eichmann, the System,

the Victims," *New Republic,* 15 June 1963, 23).

38. In contemporary Israeli law, the liability for incitement to the crime is the same as that of the main perpetrator's. The liability for accessory, however, is half that of the main perpetrator's (Articles 32, 34d. to Penal Law, 1977 [amend. 1994], S.H. 348). Note that at the time of the trial it wasn't the Penal Law but the Criminal Code Ordinance of 1936 that was in effect, according to which both a person who aids or who counsels a crime is deemed to commit it and may be liable to the same punishment as the actor (Art. 23).

39. Gideon Hausner, *Justice in Jerusalem* (New York: Harper and Row, 1966), 342–43 (the murder of a Jewish boy who was suspected of stealing cherries by Eichmann, testimony of Abraham Gordon). The court was unable to determine the issue beyond a reasonable doubt, as it lacked corroborating evidence.

40. Ibid., 247; Cr.C. (Jm.) 40/61, *Attorney General v. Eichmann,* 45 P.M. 3 (1965), 231. For the official English translation, see "District Court Judgment," in *International Law Reports* 36 (1968): 18, 237.

41. Shklar, *Legalism,* 171.

42. In the United States the conspiracy charge was employed by the government as an instrument for suppression of labor unions in the nineteenth and early twentieth centuries. See Daniel Novak, "The Pullman Strike Cases: Debs, Darrow, and the Labor Injunction," in *American Political Trials,* ed. Michal R. Belknap (Westport, CT: Greenwood Press, 1981), 119–28. On the law of conspiracy, see Peter Gillies, *The Law of Criminal Conspiracy* (Sydney: Law Books, 1981).

43. Michael R. Marrus, "History and the Holocaust in the Courtroom" (manuscript, 1997).

44. "District Court Judgment," 230.

45. Ibid., 231: "We hesitate to adopt the view propounded by the Attorney General as a general rule applicable in all cases. We do not consider that a person who consents to perpetrating a criminal act or acts (for this is the essence of conspiracy) renders himself *ipso facto* liable, without any additional ground of responsibility, as an actual perpetrator of all these acts. . . . Were we to accept the Attorney-General's argument, we would destroy the statutory framework . . . of the Criminal Code Ordinance which defines the responsibility of the various parties to a crime."

46. Ibid., 232–33.

47. See the section "Crimes against Humanity," this chapter.

48. Arendt, *Eichmann in Jerusalem,* 294–95.

49. "District Court Judgment," 262–67, 272.

50. Arendt, *Eichmann in Jerusalem,* 149.

51. Ibid., 146.

52. District Court Judgment, 257, 249. The court referred to the Israeli legal precedent without elaborating on the circumstances in which this case was decided. Arendt provides these missing details in her report and in doing so introduces briefly the Arab-Israeli conflict into the Eichmann trial (*Eichmann in Jerusalem,* 292). For further discussion of the intricate connections between the Eichmann trial and the Kufr Qassem case, see chapter 7.

53. Arendt, *Eichmann in Jerusalem*, 293; Mark Osiel, *Obeying Orders: Atrocity, Military Discipline, and the Law of War* (New Brunswick, NJ: Transaction Publishers, 1997).

54. Arendt, *Eichmann in Jerusalem*, 150.

55. Ibid., 126. Arendt illustrates the failure of respectable society to convey a clear condemnation with the example of a clergyman, Propst Gruber (130–31).

56. Arendt claims that, although the judges in Nuremberg presented themselves as relying on solid legal precedents (crimes against the peace), the fact that they sentenced to death only those who committed the novel and unprecedented "crimes against humanity" demonstrates a willingness to break with precedents (ibid., 294).

57. Ibid., 273.

58. For legal purposes the motivation, as opposed to the immediate intention, of the perpetrator is irrelevant for the establishment of legal responsibility and can therefore remain "unique." See George Fletcher, *Rethinking Criminal Law* (Boston: Little, Brown, 1978), 452. Hence, the court could insist on the uniqueness of Eichmann's motivation (inhuman, beastly), without undermining the legal grounds for punishing him (legal precedents about war crimes and mass murder).

59. Arendt, *Eichmann in Jerusalem*, 268–69.

60. Ibid., 269.

61. Arendt, *The Human Condition*, 194–95. In her lectures, Arendt quotes from Kant, who wrote that "a good constitution is not to be expected from morality, but conversely, a good moral condition of a people is to be expected under a constitution" (*Lectures*, 17). Arendt identifies in the constitutive character of law an important link between law and morality. See also Hannah Arendt, *On Revolution* (New York: Penguin, 1963).

62. In Nazi Germany the rule against retroactivity was one of the first to be abolished in section 2 of the revised Criminal Code, which stated that an act could be punished if "the spirit of a rule of criminal law and healthy folk feelings" justified punishment (1 Reichsgesetzblatt at 839, cited in Ingo Muller, *Hitler's Justice: The Courts of the Third Reich*, trans. Deborah Lucas Schneider [Cambridge: Harvard University Press, 1994], 74).

63. Leaving the legislation of new rules against the new crimes to the legislator is not satisfactory because this still allows the first perpetrators of the crimes to go unpunished. Even outside the scope of criminal law this solution is not wholly satisfactory because legislation is not quick enough to adjust to new economic and social conditions. For an early formulation of the problem, see John Dewey, "Logical Method and Law," *Cornell Law Quarterly* 10 (1924): 17, 26.

64. Arendt, *Eichmann in Jerusalem*, 254.

65. This line of argument is still missing from Arendt's report, but it is developed later in her lectures on Kant. For her solution to this problem, which involves a thorough examination of the role of common sense (sensus communis) in judgment, see Leora Bilsky, "The Narrative Turn in Legal Scholarship," J.S.D. diss., Yale Law School, 1995, 319–50.

66. S. Z. Feller, *Elements of Criminal Law* (in Hebrew) (Jerusalem: Hebrew

University of Jerusalem, 1984), 1:248; S. Z. Feller "Jurisdiction over Offenses with a Foreign Element," in *A Treatise on International Criminal Law*, ed. M. C. Bassiouni and V. P. Nanda (Springfield: Charles and Thomas Books, 1973), 2:5–64; Malcolm N. Shaw, *International Law*, 4th ed. (Cambridge: Cambridge University Press, 1997), 467–68.

67. Cr.A. 336/61, *Eichmann v. Attorney General*, 16(3) P.D. 2033, 2053, 2060–61. For the official English translation, see "Supreme Court Judgment" in *International Law Reports* 36 (1968): 277, 291–92, 298–99.

68. Ibid., 300, 303.

69. Arendt, *Eichmann in Jerusalem*, 261.

70. Ibid., 262.

71. Arendt would have preferred Eichmann to be judged by an international criminal court, but such a court did not exist at the time. The Rome status that created this court was enacted only in 1998, and as of April 2002 sixty states had signed the treaty and made the tribunal a reality.

72. Arendt, *Eichmann in Jerusalem*, 262–63.

73. Ibid., 263.

74. I therefore reject Benhabib's criticism that Arendt adopted an ethnic categorization in justifying Israel's jurisdiction over Eichmann. See Benhabib, *The Reluctant Modernism*, 183.

75. Arendt's decision to seek an answer to the crisis of moral judgment in Kant's Third Critique (the critique of aesthetic judgment) may have been induced by Eichmann's testimony, in which he gave his distorted interpretation of Kant's categorical imperative. See Eichmann's testimony in *Protocols of District Court Sessions*, session 105 (20.7.61), 17. Arendt explained that in Nazi Germany Eichmann's "household use" of Kant's moral philosophy had allowed people to salve their conscience (*Eichmann in Jerusalem*, 136–37). The trial therefore impelled her to search not so much for a new formula of the categorical imperative as for a moral philosophy that would base moral judgment on a different basis—on the ability of human beings to "visit" in their imagination the viewpoints of others. She found the seeds of this new theory in Kant's Third Critique.

76. Arendt, *The Life of the Mind*, 109.

77. Arendt, *The Human Condition*, 177.

78. As explained in her essay, Hannah Arendt, "Social Science Techniques and the Study of Concentration Camps," *Jewish Social Studies* 12 (1950): 49, 60–63, it was the novel purpose of Nazi totalitarianism to experiment with the human condition itself, that is, to eradicate the conditions of natality and plurality for the occupants of the camps by erasing their individuality and spontaneity.

79. "Even though we have lost yardsticks by which to measure, and rules under which to subsume the particular, a being whose essence is beginning may have enough of origin within himself to understand without preconceived categories and to judge without the set of customary rules which is morality" (Hannah Arendt, "Understanding and Politics," *Partisan Review* 20 [1953]: 377, 391).

80. Muller, *Hitler's Justice*, 70–81. This charge was raised by one of the critics of Arendt's report, Jacob Robinson, in *And the Crooked Shall Be Made Straight: The Eichmann Trial, the Jewish Catastrophe, and Hannah Arendt's Narrative* (New York: Macmillan, 1965), 66–67, 134.

81. Arendt, *Lectures*, 42–43.

82. Arendt, "Truth and Politics," 241.

83. Arendt, *Lectures*, 42–44, 58–65. These changes are also apparent in the following passage from Arendt's essay "The Crisis in Culture": Judgment is endowed with a certain specific validity but it is never universally valid. Its claim can never extend further than the others in whose place the judging person has put himself for his considerations. Judgment, Kant says, is valid 'for every single judging person,' but the emphasis in this sentence is on 'judging'; it is not valid for those who do not judge or for those who are not members of the public realm where the objects of judgment appear" (221). See also Arendt, *Lectures*, 72 ("when one judges one judges as a member of a human community"); and Ronald Beiner, "Rereading Hannah Arendt's Kant Lectures," in *Judgment, Imagination, and Politics*, ed. Ronal Beiner and Jennifer Nedelsky (Lanham, MD: Rowman and Littlefield, 2001), 91–102.

84. See Jennifer Nedelsky, "Communities of Judgment and Human Rights," *Theoretical Inquiries in Law* 1 (2) (2000): 245–82.

85. If, for example, Kurt Becher had been allowed to testify in the court, the differences between his and Eichmann's approach could have been evaluated by the Israeli audience.

86. Arendt, *Eichmann in Jerusalem*, 3.

87. Note that Arendt limited her observations of Eichmann to the manuscript of the police investigation and to the court's proceedings, unlike others, who in trying to understand the mental constitution of Nazi criminals went beyond the court's materials and conducted personal interviews with the defendant, his relatives, and his friends. For this approach, see, for example, Gitta Sereny, *Into That Darkness: From Mercy Killing to Mass Murder* (London: Deutsch, 1974), a book about Franz Stangl, the *kommandant* of Sobibor and Treblinka. Arendt's insistence on limiting her investigation to the court materials obeys the dictate that "the conclusions reached in a case will be induced only by evidence and argument in open court, and not by any outside influence" (Justice Holmes, in *Patterson v. Colarado*, 205 U.S. 454, 462 [1907]). It may also show her belief that the court could have formed a similar judgment of Eichmann solely on the basis of the evidence presented at the trial. Her judgment, therefore, competes with that of the court in a very deep sense.

88. This confusion led many of Arendt's critics to accuse her of sympathizing with Eichmann. See Marie Syrkin, "Hannah Arendt: The Clothes of the Empress," *Dissent* (autumn 1963): 342, 346–47, 348; Marie Syrkin, "Miss Arendt Surveys the Holocaust," *Jewish Frontier* (May 1963): 7, 9–10; Jacob Robinson, "A Report on the Evil of Banality: The Arendt Book," *Facts* 15 (1) (July–August 1963): 263; and Richard I. Cohen, "Breaking the Code: Hannah Arendt's *Eichmann in Jerusalem* and the Public Polemic: Myth, Memory, and Historical Imagination," in *Michael: On the History of the Jews in the Diaspora*, ed. Dina Porat and Shlomo Simonsohn (Tel Aviv: Diaspora Research Institute, 1993), 13:29, 61.

89. Arendt, *Eichmann in Jerusalem*, 251–52. She returns to this issue in her postscript (295–98).

90. In her *Lectures on Kant* Arendt explains the connection between communication, common sense, and sanity in a way that might suggest that Eichmann according was not sane: "Kant . . . remarks in his *Anthropology* that insanity consists in having lost this common sense that enables us to judge as spectators. . . . *Our* logical faculty, the faculty that enables us to draw conclusions from premises, could indeed function without communication—except that then, namely, if insanity has caused the loss of common sense, it would lead to insane results precisely because it has separated itself from the experiences that can be valid and validated only in the presence of others" (64).

91. See Young-Bruehl, *Hannah Arendt*, 343; Daniel Bell, "The Alphabet of Justice: Reflections on 'Eichmann in Jerusalem,'" *Partisan Review* 30 (fall 1963): 417–429; and Benhabib, *The Reluctant Modernism*, 185.

92. Ball, "The Play's the Thing," 88–89.

93. Arendt, *Eichmann in Jerusalem*, 206. Arendt was still critical of the court for not rejecting the whole "Eastern" chapter of the story as irrelevant to proving Eichmann's guilt and basing the conviction solely on his activities in Central and Western Europe (208). Note that Arendt's narrative follows the structure of the court's judgment (beginning with Eichmann's activities in Germany and Austria and ending with "The Killing Centers in the East").

94. Ron Christenson, *Political Trials: Gordian Knots in the Law*, 2d ed. (New Brunswick, NJ: Transaction Publishers, 1999), 5.

95. Hariman, "Performing the Laws," 1–8.

96. On the narratological methodology that Arendt employs in *The Origins of Totalitarianism*, see Lisa Jane Disch, *Hannah Arendt and the Limits of Philosophy* (Ithaca: Cornell University Press, 1996), 121–40.

97. Benhabib, *Reluctant Modernism*, 107–13; Luban, *Legal Modernism*, 179–208; Disch, *Hannah Arendt and the Limits of Philosophy*, 106–40.

98. Arendt, *Eichmann in Jerusalem*, 229–30.

99. Arendt discusses the power of the exemplar in the process of arriving at a valid reflective judgment (*Lectures*, 76–77, 79–85). See also Arendt, "Thinking and Moral Considerations."

100. Walter Benjamin, *Illuminations*, ed. Hannah Arendt, trans. Harry Zohn (New York: Schocken Books, 1969), 89.

101. Arendt, *Men in Dark Times*, 21 (emphasis added).

102. For an elaboration of the humanizing effect of public judgment, see Arendt's essay on Doris Lessing in "On Humanity in Dark Times: Thoughts about Lessing," in ibid., 3–31.

103. Martha L. Minow and Elizabeth V. Spelman, "Passion for Justice," *Cardozo Law Review* 10 (1988): 37–76.

Chapter 6

1. Before the war, Arendt had been engaged in Zionist activities, for which she was arrested by the Gestapo. After fleeing from Germany to France, she worked for Youth Aliyah (dealing with youth immigration to Israel). See

Elisabeth Young-Bruehl, *Hannah Arendt: For Love of the World* (New Haven: Yale University Press, 1982), 105–15. Later, however, Arendt became critical of certain Zionist policies. In an 11 June 1963 letter to the anti-Zionist American Council for Judaism refusing the council's invitation to lecture on her views about the Eichmann controversy, she explained:

> I am not against Israel on principle, I am against certain important Israeli policies. I know, or believe I know, that should catastrophe overtake this Jewish state, for whatever reasons (even reasons of their own foolishness) this would be the perhaps final catastrophe for the whole Jewish people, no matter what opinions every one of us might hold at the moment. (361)

2. Gouri is a poet, writer, and publicist. Born in Tel Aviv and educated at the famous agricultural school Kaduri (among its graduates was Yitzhak Rabin), he joined the Palmach (an elite fighting unit of Israeli youth and precursor to the Israeli army) and later joined the left-wing Mapam party. For a comparison between Gouri's and Arendt's reports of the trial, see Anita Shapira, *Hannah Arendt and Haim Gouri: Two Perceptions of the Eichmann Trial* (in Hebrew) (Jerusalem: Yad Va-Shem, 2002). Guri's reports were published in *Lamerchav* (a daily newspaper) from 12 April 1961 to 30 March 1962 under the title "In Front of the Glass Booth." They were widely read and were later published in a book bearing the same title.

3. The correspondence was published in European newspapers and the American journal *Encounter;* see Young Bruehl, *For Love of the World,* 332. The letters are reprinted in Hannah Arendt, *The Jew as Pariah: Jewish Identity and Politics in the Modern Age,* ed. Ron H. Feldman (New York: Grove Press, 1978b), 241. All my references to the correspondence are from Arendt's book.

4. Letter from Scholem, 23 June 1963, in Arendt, *The Jew as Pariah,* 241–43.

5. As we saw, Eichmann was also charged with crimes against humanity, but this crime was presented by the prosecution as a subcategory of crimes against the Jewish people. The appellate court opinion reversed this order of importance. Justice Agranat wrote that "the category of 'crimes against the Jewish people' is nothing but . . . the gravest type of 'crime against humanity.' Although certain differences exist between them . . . these are not differences material to this case" (Cr.A. 336/61, *Adolf Eichmann v. Attorney General,* 16[3] P.D. 2033, 2048). For the English translation, see "Supreme Court Judgment" in *International Law Reports* 36 (1968): 288. For further discussion, see Pnina Lahav, *Judgment in Jerusalem: Chief Justice Simon Agranat and the Zionist Century* (Berkeley: University of California Press, 1997), 152–55.

6. Hannah Arendt, *Eichmann in Jerusalem,* rev. ed. (New York: Penguin, 1994), 7. As we have seen, Arendt did not see a problem in giving jurisdiction to Jewish judges over a Nazi criminal; rather, she criticizes the choice of the legal category "crimes against the Jewish people."

7. Ibid., 6–7.

8. On this issue, like on many others, Arendt was able to see ahead of her time. As of the year 2004 Israel still does have a written constitution. Instead,

the Knesset had legislated over the years a series of Basic Laws, which deal with constitutional issues and are supposed to be eventually gathered together into a constitution. See Ruth Gavison, "The Controversy over Israel's Bill of Rights," *Israel Yearbook on Human Rights* 15 (1985): 113–54.

9. Arendt makes a similar observation in her discussion of the Dreyfus affair. She explains that for the future of the French Republic the important fact was not whether one supported Dreyfus but on what grounds this support was based: did it stem from a particular group interest or was it based on a broader understanding that infringing the rights of one is to infringe the rights of all? See Hannah Arendt, *The Origins of Totalitarianism*, 2nd ed. (New York: Harcourt Brace Jovanovich, 1951), 106.

10. See chapter 4.

11. Arendt, *Eichmann in Jerusalem*, 11 (emphasis added).

12. Ibid., 13. See also a letter from Arendt to Jaspers, 23 December 1960, in Hannah Arendt and Karl Jaspers, *Correspondence, 1926–1969*, ed. Lotte Kohler and Hans Saner, trans. Robert Kimber and Rita Kimber (New York: Harcourt Brace, 1992), 416. The discussion of the relations between the Eichmann trial and the Israeli-Arab conflict has only recently begun. See Hannah Yablonka, *The State of Israel v. Adolf Eichmann* (in Hebrew) (Tel Aviv: Yediot Achronot, 2001). About the Holocaust and the Arabs, see Azmi Beshara, "The Arabs and the Holocaust," *Zemanim* 53 (1995): 54–72; and the various responses to it in *Zemanim* 54 (1996): 117–19; *Zemanim* 55 (1996): 102–7; and *Zemanim* 56 (1996): 113–18. See also Salem Jubran, "The Arabs and the Holocaust: Historical and Current Perspective," *Bishvil Ha-Zikaron* 17 (1996): 15–18.

13. See chapter 7.

14. Arendt, *Eichmann in Jerusalem*, 10.

15. *The Eichmann Trial: Testimonies* (in Hebrew) (Jerusalem: State of Israel, 1974), 185.

16. Haim Gouri, *The Glass Cage: The Jerusalem Trial* (in Hebrew) (Tel Aviv: Hakibbutz Hameuchad, 1962), 107.

17. For elaboration, see Shoshana Felman, *The Juridical Unconscious* (Cambridge: Harvard University Press, 2002).

18. Arendt, *Eichmann in Jerusalem*, 224.

19. Ibid., 227–30.

20. On the night of 9 November 1938, in retaliation for the assassination carried out by Herschel Grynszpan two days earlier, organized terror attacks were made on Jewish synagogues and stores in Germany and Austria. The assault had been long in the works, but the assassination provided the opportunity to begin the attack. During that night, 101 synagogues were destroyed by fire, 76 were demolished, and 7,500 Jewish-owned stores were systematically destroyed by gangs of Nazis.

21. Arendt, *Eichmann in Jerusalem*, 227–28.

22. Ibid., 8 (emphasis added). This exposure of the personal could not have been easy for Arendt, who warned against such "transgression" in her other works. See Hannah Arendt, *The Human Condition* (Chicago: University of Chicago Press, 1958), 68–78.

23. The possibility of textual resistance, as opposed to the military resistance that was extolled by Israeli society at the time, is a crucial move toward building a society that tolerates criticism. I will return to this subject later in my discussion on the meaning Arendt gives to "patriotism."

24. Arendt, *Eichmann in Jerusalem*, 122 . Nonetheless, she does not think this would have been a strong point for the defense and provides an answer to it.

25. Ibid., 124.

26. Ibid.

27. Ibid., 20.

28. For an elaboration of the gray zone of cooperation under Nazi regime and the challenges it presents to those who try to judge the people who acted under it, see David Luban, "A Man Lost in the Gray Zone," *Law and History Review* 19 (1) (2001): 161–76. Luban's expression is taken from Primo Levi, *The Drowned and the Saved*, trans. Raymond Rosenthal (New York: Summit Books, 1988), 36–69.

29. Gouri, *The Glass Cage*, 108.

30. Ibid., 108–9.

31. Arendt did not think to criticize herself or those of her friends who were able to escape to the safe shores of America and did not do enough to save the Jews left behind in Europe. See Shapira, *Hannah Arendt and Haim Gouri*, 17.

32. Young-Bruehl, *For Love of the World*, 347–55.

33. Norman Podhoretz, "Hannah Arendt on Eichmann: A Study in the Perversity of Brilliance," *Commentary* 36 (1963): 201: "In the place of the monstrous Nazi, she gives us the Jew as accomplice in evil; and in the place of the confrontation of guilt and innocence, she gives us the 'collaboration' of criminal and victim." See also Lionel Abel, "The Aesthetics of Evil: Hannah Arendt on Eichmann and the Jews," *Partisan Review* 30 (summer 1963): 211; Marie Syrkin, "Hannah Arendt: The Clothes of the Empress," *Dissent* 10 (autumn 1963): 341; and Marie Syrkin, "Miss Arendt Surveys the Holocaust,"*Jewish Frontier* 30 (May 1963): 7. For a reflective essay on the two controversial issues raised by Arendt's book, see Richard Bernstein, "The Banality of Evil Reconsidered," in *Hannah Arendt and the Meaning of Politics*, ed. Craig Calhoun and John McGowan (Minneapolis: University of Minnesota Press, 1997), 297–322.

34. See, for example, Podhoretz, "Hannah Arendt on Eichmann."

35. Letter from Scholem, 23 June 1963, in Arendt, *The Jew as Pariah*, 241–43.

36. Ibid., 248.

37. The structural similarity of the controversies is remarkable given the very different historical contexts in which they took place. See Segev, *The Seventh Million*, 255–310, 323–84.

38. Kenaani, "Ke-Or Yahel" (Like a Shining Light), *Al Ha-Mishmar*, 14 May 1954, 5.

39. For elaboration, see chapters 1–3.

40. See Arendt, *Eichmann in Jerusalem*, 112–34.

41. Nathan Alterman, "Pney Ha-Mered u-Pney Zmano" (The Resistance Memorial Day and Its Time), in, *Writings in Four Volumes* (Tel Aviv: Ha-Kibbutz Hameuhad, 1962), 3:415–16 (originally published in *Davar*, 28 May 1954).

42. Abba Kovner, *Hitvadut* (Acquaintance), in *On a Narrow Bridge: Oral Essays* (in Hebrew) (Tel Aviv: Poalim, 1981), 111, cited in Dan Laor, "Od Al Shtei Ha-Derachim" (More on the Two Roads), in Nathan Alterman *Al Shtei Ha-Derachim* (Between Two Roads), ed. Dan Laor (Tel Aviv: Hakibbutz Ha-Meuhad, 1989), 116. Laor writes that this incident was also confirmed in a letter that Kovner sent to him on 21 May 1987 (151 n. 18).

43. Daniel Boyarin, *Unheroic Conduct: The Rise of Heterosexuality and the Invention of the Jewish Man* (Minneapolis: University of Minnesota Press, 1997); David Biale, *Eros and the Jews* (Berkeley: University of California Press, 1992); Paul Breines, *Tough Jews: Political Fantasies and the Moral Dilemma of American Jewry* (New York: Basic Books, 1990).

44. Jennifer Ring, *The Political Consequences of Thinking: Gender and Judaism in the Work of Hannah Arendt* (Albany: State University of New York Press, 1997), 111. See also p. 153, on which Ring writes:

> The surprising singularity of the agreement of the New York and Israeli Jews over Arendt's report is not so paradoxical once gender is factored in. . . . Both . . . were responding to the gentile racism that associated Judaism with femininity, accepting the challenge to be "real" men, and in that sense, desiring to assimilate to the non-Jewish standards of masculine deportment. Hannah Arendt touched *that* nerve.

45. Raul Hilberg, *The Destruction of the European Jews* (New York: Holmes and Meier, 1985). Ring (*The Political Consequences of Thinking*, 39–40) compares the two. Hilberg's work was historical, and Arendt was writing on political theory. Hilberg wrote for a professional audience, Arendt for a general audience, Jews and non-Jews. Hilberg was not responding to a particular public event, while Arendt was reporting on a highly publicized trial with the intention of producing a counternarrative. Ring herself recognizes some of these factors, but she does not see them as undermining her thesis. See Ring, *The Political Consequences of Thinking*, 39–40.

46. Arendt, *The Jew as Pariah*, 246, 241.

47. Ibid., 246. Bonnie Honig argues that Arendt relies on an essentialist understanding of gender (one cannot escape one's gender) and applies the same essentialist understanding to Jewish identity in order to resist Scholem's attack. Honig is critical of this move and suggests that the opposite approach would have been preferable (i.e., analogizing womanhood to Jewishness and noticing the element of performativeness and construction in both). See Bonnie Honig, "Toward an Agonistic Feminism: Hannah Arendt and the Politics of Identity," in *Feminists Theorize the Political*, ed. Judith Butler and Joan W. Scott (New York: Routledge, 1992), 215, 230.

48. Arendt's essay on Rosa Luxembourg shows an acute awareness of the unsettling effects of a woman's "masculine" intervention in public debate. See Hannah Arendt, *Men in Dark Times* (New York: Harcourt, Brace, 1968), 37.

49. Arendt, *The Jew as Pariah*, 250.

50. Ibid., 247.

51. Ibid.

52. Arendt, *Eichmann in Jerusalem*, 117.

53. Arendt, *The Jew as Pariah*, 247.

54. Here I disagree with Bonnie Honig, who sees the controversy between Arendt and Scholem in terms of the private-public divide. Honig argues that Scholem believed that certain *public* responsibilities stemmed from one's Jewish identity, while Arendt rejected this attitude, considering her Jewishness to be a *private* matter. I think that both Arendt and Scholem agreed that one's Jewish identity could sometimes become a political (public) matter (indeed, Arendt explicitly says so in her letter, reproduced in Arendt, *The Jew as Pariah*, 246), but they disagreed about the nature of the obligations that stemmed from recognizing one's Jewishness (love vs. judgment). See Honig, "Toward an Agonistic Feminism," 215–30.

55. Nathan Alterman, "Ha-Lekach La-Dor" (About the Moral to the Generation), in Alterman, *Writings in Four Volumes*, 434. See also chapter 3.

56. It is interesting that while she controls her emotions and measures her words throughout the report, at this point Arendt suddenly gives vent to fierce feelings of vengeance, allowing them to dictate her sentence of Eichmann (*Eichmann in Jerusalem*, 277).

57. Ibid., 279.

58. See, for example, Abel, "The Aesthetics of Evil," 227–28: "Every point Miss Arendt maintained in her book on totalitarianism she would today have to retract and deny in order to seriously criticize the decisions made by the leaders of the Jewish councils between 1941 and 1944." During the Arendt controversy, Mary McCarthy questioned the technique of uncovering contradictions: "Supposing Abel is right and there is a contradiction between the earlier book and the present one, what would it prove? That she was right then and wrong now or vice versa?" See Mary McCarthy, "The Hue and Cry," *Partisan Review* 31 (1) (1964): 82–94. McCarthy misses the quasi-legal nature of the debate, which allows each contradiction to be resolved in favor of an earlier statement. In a recent book, Richard Bernstein suggests that there is no real contradiction between the thesis of "radical evil" in the *Origins of Totalitarianism* and the thesis of the banality of evil in the Eichmann report; see Richard J. Bernstein, *Hannah Arendt and the Jewish Question* (Cambridge: MIT Press, 1996), 137–53.

59. Gouri's reports can be understood as a work of cultural translation. Thus, Gouri made the connection between the biblical story of Joseph and the striped cloth of the Auschwitz inmates; between one of the testimonies and a popular story, "Hanna'le's Sabbath Dress" (Gouri, *The Glass Cage*, 49–52); between Eichmann's defense of obeying orders and the "black flag" image of the Kufr Qassem trial (218–22); and so forth.

60. For further writing in favor of agonistic politics in a liberal democratic context, exploring Arendt's political theory of action as a viable alternative, see Dana R. Vila, *Politics, Philosophy, Terror* (Princeton: Princeton University Press, 1999), 107–127; Bonnie Honig, *Political Theory and the Displacement of Politics* (Ithaca: Cornell University Press, 1993), 76–125; Bonnie Honig, "Difference,

Dilemmas, and the Politics of Home," in *Democracy and Difference*, ed. Seyla Benhabib (Princeton: Princeton University Press, 1996); Chantal Mouffe, "Democracy, Power, and the 'Political,'" in *Democracy and Difference*, ed. Seyla Benhabib (Princeton: Princeton University Press, 1996), 245–56; and William E. Connolly, *Identity/Difference: Democratic Negotiations of Political Paradox* (Ithaca: Cornell University Press, 1991).

61. Bernstein, *Hannah Arendt and the Jewish Question*, 157. He explains that Arendt never thought of herself as an anti-Zionist but rather as a member of the "loyal opposition." To support this view he quotes from one of her earlier articles: "Every believer in a democratic government knows the importance of a loyal opposition. The tragedy of Jewish politics at this moment is that it is wholly determined by the Jewish Agency that and no opposition to it of any significance exists either in Palestine or America" (209, n, 2), quoting from Arendt, *The Jew as Pariah*, 184.

62. Cr.C. 124/53, *Attorney General v. Gruenwald*, 44 P.D. 3 (1965), 7.

63. Hannah Arendt, *Eichmann in Jerusalem* (in Hebrew), trans. Arie Uriel (Tel Aviv: Babel, 2000). Segev argues that Arendt attributed the nonpublication of her book in Hebrew to the efforts of Ben-Gurion to repress the issue (*The Seventh Million*, 465). Arendt also points out the fact that Eichmann's autobiography, which he wrote while in prison in Israel, was confiscated by the Israeli authorities and deposited with the Israeli National Archives (*Eichmann in Jerusalem*, 222). Segev writes that this action was taken after Hausner explained to Ben-Gurion that Eichmann's book was intended to compete with the court's verdict and, if published, could raise doubts as to the correctness of the court's judgment (*The Seventh Million*, 360). The decision to seal the memoirs from public view was revoked only recently by the attorney general in response to a petition from Eichmann's children to receive the memoirs. The manuscript was released in March 2000 in response to a request from the lawyers of Prof. Deborah Lipstadt, a defendant in a libel suit brought against her by David Irving. See Tom Segev, "Adolf Eichmann's Idols," *Ha'aretz*, 3 March 2000, B4.

64. Jacob Robinson, *And the Crooked Shall Be Made Straight: The Eichmann Trial, the Jewish Catastrophe, and Hannah Arendt's Narrative* (New York: Macmillan, 1965). The Hebrew translation of this book appeared under the title *He-Akov le-mishor* in 1966.

65. We can consider the way in which Justice Agranat chose to relate the Kastner affair as a similar attempt to broaden the range of possible narratives so as to free the Israeli public from the grip of the ideological worldview. Likewise, in the Eichmann trial Hausner's decision to base the prosecution's case on the live testimonies of survivors broadened the stock of stories available for the Israeli public to make sense of the Holocaust and the reactions of the Jewish population to it. As we have seen, both had to transgress the traditional boundaries of legal discourse in attempting to change the prevailing narrative of the Holocaust.

66. For the new historian debate, see "Israeli History Revisited," *History and Memory* 7 (1) (1995), a special issue edited by Gulie Ne'eman Arad; Anita Shapira and Derek J. Penslar, eds., *Israeli Historical Revisionism: From Left to*

Right (London: Frank Cass, 2002); and Laurence J. Silberstein, *The Postzionism Debates* (New York: Routledge, 1999).

Chapter 7

1. Cr.C. (Jm.) 40/61, *Attorney General v. Adolf Eichmann*, 45 P.M. (1965) 3, 248–49. For the English translation, see *International Law Reports* 36 (1968): 18, 256–57.

2. Military Court 3/57, *Military Prosecutor v. Major Melinki*, 17 P.M. (1958–59) 90 (hereafter *Melinki*).

3. For this trial the civil judges (Halevi and Cohen) were given army ranks.

4. The judgment of the court lists forty-three victims, while according to the Kufr Qassem villagers forty-nine people were murdered. The court excluded four villagers whose circumstances of death remained unclear. The people of Kufr Qassem included an elderly man who died of a stroke the day after the massacre and the death of the unborn baby of one of the victims, Fatma Daud Sarsur. See Ruvik Rosenthal, "Who Killed Fatma Sarsur," in *Kafr Kassem: Myth and History* (in Hebrew), ed. Ruvik Rosenthal (Tel Aviv: Hakibbutz Hameuchad, 2000a), 11, 14.

5. He was tried later in a separate trial, as a direct result of the harsh condemnation of Judge Halevi in the Kufr Qassem decision.

6. M.C. 3/57 *Melinki*, 213–14. The translation is in Tom Segev, *The Seventh Million: The Israelis and the Holocaust*, trans. Haim Watzman (New York: Hill and Wang, 1993), 301.

7. In 1953 Halevi had agreed to serve as judge in the military court in the trial of what came to known as the "Tsrifin Underground" (an underground of Jewish nationalist-religious extremists whose members were accused of planting bombs near the Russian consulate in Tel Aviv). Other Supreme Court judges, citing the Israeli public's mistrust of the military court, refused to participate in that trial. Ben-Gurion turned to Judge Halevi, who returned to active duty especially for the trial and was given the temporary rank of colonel for a period of two months. See Segev, *The Seventh Million*, 267; and Ehud Sprinzak, *Brother against Brother* (New York: Free Press, 1999), 66–70. During the Kufr Qassem trial Halevi was criticized for agreeing to put on army uniform and participate again in a military court. For elaboration, see Ron Linenberg, "The Kfar Kassem Affair in the Israeli Press," *Medina U-Memshal* 2 (1972): 48, 55.

8. See chapters 4–6.

9. Otto Kirschheimer, *Political Justice* (Princeton: Princeton University Press, 1961), 49.

10. Peter Gabel and Paul Harris, "Building Power and Breaking Images: Critical Legal Theory and the Practice of Law," *Review of Law and Social Change* 11 (1982–83): 369–411; David Kairys, ed., *The Politics of Law*, 3rd ed. (New York Basic Books, 1998).

11. Robert W. Gordon, "Some Critical Theories of Law and Their Critics," in

The Politics of Law, 641, 647. See also Duncan Kennedy, *A Critique of Adjudication* (Cambridge, Harvard University Press, 1997), 236–63.

12. Ronen Shamir, "'Landmark Cases' and the Reproduction of Legitimacy: The Case of Israel's High Court of Justice," *Law and Society Review* 24 (3) (1990): 781–82.

13. Cf. Bruce Ackerman's distinction between ordinary and constitutive politics in *We the People* (Cambridge, MA: Belknap Press, 1991); and Bruce Ackerman, "Constitutional Politics/Constitutional Law," *Yale Law Journal* 99 (3) (1989): 453–547. Within the "dualist democracy" framework that Ackerman describes, ordinary political and constitutional change proceed on separate tracks. Ordinary decision making is accomplished by the government while "higher" lawmaking is accomplished by "the people." Moreover, Ackerman focuses on lawmaking by the people, not by the courts. My discussion extends Ackerman's framework to the politics of criminal trials that offer "transformative" decisions.

14. For a discussion of this phenomenon in the Israeli context (five landmark cases that produced legitimization without any material change), see Shamir, "'Landmark Cases' and the Reproduction of Legitimacy." For a similar exploration in South Africa during the apartheid regime, see David Dyzenhaus, *Judging the Judges, Judging Ourselves: Truth, Reconciliation, and the Apartheid Legal Order* (Oxford: Hart Publishing, 1998), 136–83; and David Dyzenhaus, "With the Benefit of Hindsight: Dilemmas of Legality," in *Lethe's Law*, ed. Emilios Christodoulidis and Scott Veithch (Oxford: Hart Publishing, 2001), 65–89. Dyzenhaus addresses the same problem from the opposite direction, stating that "the more successful they [opposition groups] were at using the law to challenge the law, the more they legitimated the legal order by helping to vindicate the government's claim to be part of the family of states committed to such fundamental Western values as the rule of law" (78).

15. H.C. 125/51, *Muhammad Ali Hassin v. Minister of Interior*, 5 P.D. 1386 (hereafter H.C. 125/51, *Hassin*).

16. About half the Arab population (estimates varies between 630,000 and 760,000) left the country during the war. After the war and the redivision of Palestine, about 156,000 Arabs were left under Israeli government (compared to 714,000 Jews). See Benny Morris, *The Birth of the Palestinian Refugee Problem, 1947–1949* (Cambridge: Cambridge University Press, 1987), 297. Mark Tessler observes that, in spite of the disputes over the exact number of refugees, "both sides concur that only about 150,000 Palestinians remained inside Israel by the end of 1949" (*A History of the Israeli-Palestinian Conflict* [Bloomington: Indiana University Press, 1994], 279).

17. Benny Morris, *Israel's Border Wars, 1949–1956: Arab Infiltration, Israeli Retaliation, and the Countdown to the Suez War* (Oxford: Clarendon, 1993) 97–115. The proportion of terrorist-motivated infiltrations slightly increased during 1954–56, in part due to Fedayeen activity, but the majority remained socially or economically motivated. See also David Tal, *Israel's Day-to-Day Security Conception: Its Origin and Development, 1949–1956* (in Hebrew) (Beer Sheba: The Ben-

Gurion Research Center and Ben-Gurion University of the Negev Press, 1998), 23–26. Moshe Dayan, who was the chief of staff at the time, agrees that the infiltration phenomenon was at first socially and economically motivated, but he strongly disagrees with the claim that it remained the primary cause of infiltration: "It has been asserted quite wrongly that this infiltration is conducted primarily by refugees. The nightly incursions into Israel territory, which in most cases show careful planning, are not the work of destitute refugees but of highly trained gunmen acting on paramilitary lines" ("Israel's Border and Security Problems," *Foreign Affairs* 33 (1955): 251, 260. For a similar view, see Yigal Allon, *Shields of David: The Story of Israel's Armed Force* (London: Weidenfeld and Nicolson, 1970), 230.

18. The Fedayeen was composed of units of terrorists recruited and trained by Egyptian military intelligence and sent into Israel to exact revenge and terrorize the Israeli borders settlers. During 1954–56 Fedayeen squads murdered Israeli citizens, attacked IDF patrols, and caused great damage to property and targets. See Morris, *Israel's Border Wars*, 35.

19. Ibid., 116–73.

20. Oren Bracha, "Unfortunate or Perilous: The Infiltrators, the Law, and the Supreme Court, 1948–1954" (in Hebrew), *Tel Aviv University Law Review* 21 (2) (1998): 333–85, quoted at 369.

21. Ibid., 379–89.

22. The formalist approach of the court during these years is further discussed in Menachem Mautner, *The Decline of Formalism and the Rise of Values in Israeli Law* (in Hebrew) (Tel Aviv: Ma'agalay Da'at, 1993). For elaboration on the way in which the Israeli Supreme Court established its authority in the early days of the state, see Pnina Lahav, "The Formative Years of Israel's Supreme Court, 1948–1955" (in Hebrew), *Tel Aviv University Law Review* 14 (3) (1989): 479–502. See also Pnina Lahav, *Judgement in Jerusalem: Chief Justice Simon Agranat and the Zionist Century* (Berkeley: University of California Press, 1997), 79–120.

23. H.C. 125/51, *Hassin*. For elaboration, see Morris, *The Birth of the Palestinian Refugee Problem*, 228. The village was conquered on 30 October, and the act of retaliation by the Israeli army took place six days later, on 5 November 1949.

24. Ibid., 1391.

25. Morris bases this conclusion on an investigative report of the United Nations. This report appears only in the extended Hebrew version of his book (Tel Aviv: Am Oved, [1991] 2000, 304), while in the earlier English version he did not yet have this source and therefore refrained from a positive conclusion, merely citing the account of one of the villagers (*The Birth of the Palestinian Refugees Problem*, 228). For a recent elaboration of the historiographical issues involved in ascertaining the commitment of a massacre, see Benny Morris, *Jews and Arabs in Palestine/Israel, 1936–1956* (in Hebrew) (Tel Aviv: Am Oved, 2000), 146–47. The historian Yoav Gelber mentions Majd-El-Kurum as one of several Arab villages in which "alleged massacres" took place. He refrains from drawing a positive conclusion about the events but notes that the Israeli soldiers tried to frustrate the inquiry and destroy the evidence, if there was any. See

Yoav Gelber, *Palestine 1948: War, Escape, and the Emergence of the Palestinian Refugees Problem* (Brighton: Sussex Academic Press, 2001), 226–27.

In a telephone interview I conducted (on 12 September 2001) with one of the soldiers who participated in this military act (who preferred to remain anonymous), I was told that the unit was sent to the village after it had surrendered to find weapons and suspects of collaboration with the enemy on the basis of intelligence information. The unit was ordered to execute these suspects. The person whom I interviewed refused to take part in the execution. He explained to me that he did not think of the issue in legal terms but as a moral question. The commander granted his request. The issue of refusal to obey an illegal order in this case never reached the court.

26. Note that the court tried to mitigate the effect of its acceptance of the version of the petitioners against that of the army by saying that in fact there was no contradiction between the two versions (H.C. 125/51, *Hassin*, 1391).

27. For elaboration, see Bracha, "Unfortunate or Perilous," 356–58. Compare this to other "landmark" cases in which the court ruled against the authorities but at the same time created a legal framework that facilitated the "legalization" of the policy in future cases. The most famous is the 1979 Elon Moreh case (H.C. 619/78, *Dawikat v. Government of Israel* 34[1] P.D. 505), in which the court ordered the evacuation of a Jewish settlement in the occupied territories on the basis that the order of seizure of land was not justified by military needs and was therefore null and void. At the same time this decision paved the way for future alternative forms of land seizures and Jewish settlements in the occupied territories. For elaboration, see Shamir, "'Landmark Cases' and the Reproduction of Legitimacy," 786–89.

28. H.C. 125/51, *Hassin*, 1392. Lahav maintains that Justice Shneur Z. Cheshin considered to carry a voice of Jewish particularism and nationalism in the court. See Lahav, "The Formative Years," 492.

29. From the perspective of the legitimization effect it is important to compare the *Hassin* case to the landmark constitutional case *El-Karabutly* of 1948, in which the Supreme Court accepted a petition to release a Palestinian prisoner who had been arrested for security reasons without trial or due process. While *El-Karabutly* is celebrated as a landmark case and is taught in the law schools as part of the basic constitutional law class, *Hassin* is mostly forgotten. In this way, the liberal line in Supreme Court decisions is given special emphasis and becomes part of the collective memory of the Israeli legal elite.

In *El-Karabutly* the court based its intervention on legalistic grounds but nevertheless established in firm words the superiority of the rule of law over security interests. See H.C. 7/48 *El-Karabutli v. Minister of Defense*, 2(1) P.D., 5 (on the bench sat justices Moshe Zemora, Yitzhak Olshan, and Shneur Z. Cheshin). How can we account for these very different attitudes toward the Arabs by the Israeli Supreme Court? One explanation is given by Lahav, who points to two very different conceptions in Zionism: "utopia Zionism," which stresses the liberal and egalitarian foundations of the Zionist movement, and "catastrophe Zionism," which emphasizes the goal of the State of Israel in providing shelter for Jews. See Pnina Lahav, "A 'Jewish State . . . to Be Known as the State of Israel': Notes on Israeli Legal Historiography," *Law and History Review* 19 (2) (2001): 387–433. Historian Elie Rekhes refers to these two tendencies as "egalitarian" and "security oriented." He claims that both views were upheld by important political figures and were often in conflict. The narrative told by Judge Cheshin in *Hassin* gives preference to the security-oriented view of Zionism, although other, more liberal conceptions existed at the time. See Elie Rekhes, "The Underlying Principles of the Policy towards the Arabs in Israel," in *Transition from "Yishuv" to State, 1947–1949: Continuity and Change* (in Hebrew), ed. Varda Pilowsky (Haifa: University of Haifa Press, 1990), 291–97.

30. Similar views were expressed in the Israeli parliament during the debates regarding the Nationality Law (1950–52). The different proposals of the law sought to distinguish between Arab inhabitants who had not left the country during the war and those who had. While the former were eligible for automatic citizenship, the latter had to go through a long process to prove their loyalty to the state before citizenship would be granted (see n. 34). During all the debates, the accusations against the Arab population for abandoning the country in its time of trouble and for cooperating with the enemy were raised time and again. For example, see the declaration of Minister of Interior Shapira, delivered in July 1950, that "those who deserted the country or left it in order to fight it . . . should undergo this minimal effort. . . . It is not such an unreasonable demand from those who forsook their country while it was in flames to make the effort and acquire citizenship in the normal way without expecting the privilege of automatic citizenship" (D.K [1950] 2134–35, session of 10 July 1950). See also remarks by Minister of Justice Haim Cohen, two years later, in a debate over a proposed amendment to this law, which proposed granting any Israeli Arab automatic citizenship. Interestingly, Cohen cites with approval the short narrative of Justice Cheshin in the *Hassin* case (D.K. [1952] 2701–2 [session of 23.7.1952]).

31. For examples of legal scholarship, see Shif, "In Favor of the 'Black Flag' Test," 117–30; Parush, "Critique of the 'Black Flag' Test," 131–77; and Adi Parush, *Obedience, Responsibility, and Criminal Law: Legal Issues from a Philosophic Perspective* (in Hebrew) (Tel Aviv: Papirus, 1996), 65–116.

32. For example, Halevi rejected the lawyers' attempt to classify the affair under the law of war and to employ the many distinctions following from it, such as that between warrior and hostage, between the one who surrenders and the one who runs away, and so on. See, for example, M.C. 3/57, *Melinki*, 186, 192.

33. For further discussion, see Ilan Pappé, "An Uneasy Coexistence: Arabs and Jews in the First Decade of Statehood," in *Israel: The First Decade of Independence*, ed. S. Ilan Troen and Noah Lucas (Albany: State University of New York Press, 1995), 617, 633–34. For a detailed discussion of the contrasting narratives about Jews and Arabs in the Declaration of Independence, see Lahav, "A Jewish State." See also Orit Kamir, "The Declaration Has Two Faces: The Interesting Story of the 'Zionist Declaration of Independence' and the 'Democratic Declaration of Independence'" (in Hebrew), *Tel Aviv University Law Review* 23 (2000): 473–538. Kamir notes that, while the declaration treats Jewish citizens

both as a national collective with collective rights and as individuals, other citizens are recognized only as individuals with rights (498). For a fascinating recounting of the history of writing the Israeli Declaration of Independence, see Yoram Shachar, "The Early Drafts of the Declaration of Independence" (in Hebrew), *Tel Aviv University Law Review* 26 (2) (2000): 523–600.

34. During the Knesset debate on the Nationality Law, Communist members estimated that the law would bar half the country's Arabs from citizenship, although the minister of interior stated that no more than six thousand would be barred. See Don Peretz, *Israel and the Palestine Arabs* (Washington, DC: Middle East Institute, 1958), 124–26. The Nationality Law deals with Israeli citizenship granted to people who are not entitled to it through the right of return, that is (at that time), those who are not Jews. The statute outlines a process of acquiring citizenship by residents of Israel, and a much more complicated process for those who are not entitled to citizenship by way of residency or right of return, which applied to many of the Arab applicants. By contrast, Jewish people, whether born in Israel or having immigrated on the basis of the Law of Return (4 L.S.I. 114 [1949–50]), are automatically granted Israeli citizenship. When it was amended in 1980, the law granted more discretion to the minister of interior in matters of citizenship. See Amnon Rubinstein, *The Constitutional Law of Israel,* 5th ed. (in Hebrew) (Tel Aviv: Schocken Publishing House, 1996), 892; and Haim Ganz, "Law of Return and Affirmative Action" (in Hebrew), *Tel Aviv University Law Review* 19 (1995): 683–97.

35. Ron Harris, "Jewish Democracy and Arab Politics: The El-Ard Movement in the Israeli Supreme Court" (in Hebrew), *Plilim* 10 (2002): 107–56; Lahav, *Justice in Jerusalem,* 185–92; Sabri Jiryis, *The Arabs in Israel* (New York: Monthly Review Press, 1976), 9–55; Ian Lustik, *Arabs in the Jewish State* (Austin: University of Texas Press, 1980), 122–45; for a general discussion of the initial years, see Elie Rekhes, "Initial Israeli Policy Guidelines towards the Arab Minority," in *New Perspectives on Israeli History,* ed. Lawrence J. Silberstein (New York: New York University Press, 1991), 103–19.

36. On 29 October 1956, the IDF invaded the Sinai Peninsula in response to an escalation of Fedayeen attacks activated by Egypt and an Egyptian blockade of the Suez Canal. The campaign was coordinated with France and Britain, which saw their interests harmed by the nationalization of the Suez Canal by President Nasser. They joined Israel and attacked Egyptian targets in and around Port Said. The Sinai war ended the Fedayeen attacks, as well as the entire infiltration phenomenon. See Morris, *Israel's Border Wars,* 403–9. On the Sinai war, see also Tessler, *A History of the Israeli-Palestinian Conflict,* 336–39; and Charles D. Smith, *Palestine and the Arab-Israeli Conflict,* 3rd ed. (New York: St. Martin's Press, 1996), 171–75.

37. Rosenthal, "Who Killed Fatma Sarsur?" 18. Rosenthal explains that the fifth-column explanation was delivered in one of the closed sessions of the trial. In his public testimony, on the other hand, Colonel Shadmi explained that he had ordered an early curfew in order to enable the soldiers to distinguish infiltrators from Arab citizens (who would remain at home). See also Moshe Kordov, *Kufr Qassem Trial* (in Hebrew) (Tel Aviv: Narkis, 1959), 169.

38. Morris, *Israel's Border Wars*, 131–34.

39. On 9 April 1948, units of the right-wing underground Etzel and Lehi attacked Deir Yassin, calling on its citizens to surrender. During the fighting that followed, approximately two hundred Arabs were killed, among them women and children. This had an enormous effect on the morale of the Arabs in Israel and "convinced" many of them to flee the country.

On the night of 15 October 1953, in response to the murder of a Jewish woman and her children by infiltrators, IDF troops attacked Qibya, killing a few dozen villagers (estimations vary between sixty and two hundred), most of them women and children. For elaboration, see Morris, *Israel's Border Wars*, 225–62.

In general, trials of Israeli soldiers for war crimes were very rare until the late 1980s. When these crimes were finally brought to trial the court did not recognize them as war crimes under international law. The only case from 1948 that I managed to find concerns the murder of three elderly Arab villagers by an Israeli lieutenant (see Appeal no. 43/49 + 45/49, *Farchi v. Chief Military Prosecutor*, Military Appellate Court Verdicts, 1948–1950, 24). Benny Morris mentions this case and adds that the soldier was later amnestied (*Jews and Arabs in Palestine/Israel*, 146). Later, following the Lebanon war of 1982, an Israeli officer, Dani Pinto, was put on trial for murdering five South Lebanon inhabitants and disposing of their bodies in a well. During the first Intifada (1988) many soldiers were put on trial in military courts for manslaughter and negligent killing. The Intifada was also the first time in which the Supreme Court intervened in the decision of the military attorney general not to try a soldier who had allegedly broken the law and ordered the army to try him. The possibility of a judicial review of the military prosecution's decisions may be one of the factors responsible for the considerable rise in the number of cases brought to court.

40. Compare the two contrasting narratives advanced by the U.S. Supreme Court regarding the Japanese American citizens in the *Korematsu* trial (upholding the constitutionality of the evacuation of all persons of Japanese ancestry from the Pacific Coast on a plea of military necessity to "relocation centers"). While the opinion of the court (delivered by Justice Black) depicted them as a "suspect fifth column," the dissenting judge (Justice Murphy) insisted on treating them as equal citizens and declared that such a perception "falls into the ugly abyss of racism" See *Korematsu v. United States* 323 U.S. 214 (1944).

41. On 23 November 1956, Tubi distributed a personal letter to the public, citing at length testimonies of survivors and eyewitnesses and demanding that blame be laid not only on the Border Police but also on the IDF and the government itself. Later a private bulletin with more facts and commentaries on the massacre was published by a group of left-wing politicians and publicists. See Rosenthal, "Who Killed Fatma Sarsur?" 35.

42. Knesset Deliberation, 12 December 1956. Moshe Sharett wrote his response in his diaries: "This attitude always enrages me, as if the command 'do not murder' was pronounced only in our ears, as if only we are obliged and know how to respect human life, and as if when a terrible and horrifying act of

murder is committed by non-Jews, it is less astonishing" (*Personal Diary* [Tel Aviv: Ma'ariv, 1978], 7:1915). We will see how the same kind of rhetoric reappeared years later in the judgment of the court during the murder trial of the assassin of Israeli prime minister Yitzhak Rabin (chapter 8).

43. Indicative of the army's trust in Judge Halevi was his meeting with the chief of staff, Moshe Dayan, where Dayan agreed to leave the discretion to Halevi. When this meeting was discovered, one of the defense attorneys asked Halevi to disqualify himself, a request that was refused after the testimony of Dayan was given (*Protocols of Military Court Sessions*, session 3, [26 March 1957], 17, available in IDF archive file no. 18–165/1992, 43). Note also that legally the commander of a jurisdictional region had the power to overturn the decision of the court. See articles 308, 441, and 442 to Military Justice Law, 1955, 9 L.S.I 184, (1954–55). See also note 99.

44. M.C. 3/57 *Melinki*, 108.

45. The ethos "purity of arms" expresses the strong commitment of Israeli soldiers to moral standards and their obligation to refrain from excessive and unnecessary use of weaponry or force. The purity of arms ethos has recently been included among the eleven basic values of the IDF. See Asa Kasher, *Military Ethics* (in Hebrew) (Tel Aviv: Ministry of Defense, 1996), 52–59, 232.

46. *Protocols of Military Court Sessions*, session 2 (25 March 1957), IDF archive file no. 18–165/1992, 28–29.

47. See, for example, the testimony of Ismail Aqeb Badir in ibid., session 28 (17 May 1957), 7, IDF archive file no. 5–165/1992, 78. A typical question was: "I agree you were shot, but I tell you you were shot while you were running away." See testimony of Tawfiq Ibrahim Badir, session 29 (22 May 1957), 103–4, IDF archive file no. 5–165/1992, 69–70). See Halevi's rejection of these accusations in M.C. 3/57 *Melinki*, 126.

48. Testimony of Ismail Aqeb Badir, *Protocols of Military Courts Sessions*, session 29 (22 May 1957), 70, IDF archive file no. 5–165/1992, 47); testimony of Sallah Halil Issa, session 31 (23 May 1957), 23–26, IDF archive file no. 6–165/1992, 113). The testimonies reveal that the people who returned from the fields trusted the soldiers and were completely surprised by the sudden shooting. See, for example, the testimony of Tawfiq Ibrahim Badir, session 29 (22 May 1957), 103, IDF archive file no. 5–165/1992, 69, who claimed that he would not have believed that Israeli soldiers could murder for no apparent reason, and even if he had been told of the massacre taking place in the village before he himself returned he would have still not believed it. Beshara argues that in this period the main concern of the Arab population was its personal security. The Arabs, most of whom were under military rule, tried to maintain good relations with the army authorities. See Azmi Beshara, "On the Question of the Palestinian Minority," in *Israeli Society: Critical Perspectives* (in Hebrew), ed. Uri Ram (Tel Aviv: Brerot, 1993), 203, 207.

49. Testimony of Abdallah Samir Badir, *Protocols of Military Court Sessions*, session 26 (16 May1957), 24, IDF archive file no. 4–165/1992, 27.

50. See, for example, the testimony of Wadia Ahmad Mahmud Sarsur, the village leader (mukhtar) who asserted several times that he would like to tell

the whole story, while Judge Halevi instructed him to answer only the questions he was asked (*Protocols of Military Court Sessions*, session 25 [15 May 1957], for example, 62, 68, 76, IDF archive no. 4–165/1992, 140, 143, 147, respectively). The uninterrupted narration of witnesses in the Eichmann trial was partly due to the specific law applied—Law of Punishment of Nazis and Their Collaborators, 1950, 4 L.S.I 154 (1949–50). It was also due to the legal strategy of the defense attorney, Servatius, who decided not to question the witnesses in order to demonstrate their irrelevance to proving Eichmann's guilt. See Douglas, *The Memory of Judgment,* 129.

51. For example, when one of the witnesses was overheard in the corridor saying that the defense attorney had "defeated me," Judge Cohen explained that the Arabic word used by the witness could also be translated as "tired me." See *Protocols of Military Court Sessions*, session 32 (28 May 1957), IDF archive file no. 6–165/1992, 50–55. By contrast, defense attorney Oren attempted to conduct the inquiry as much as possible in Hebrew and often emphasized that since the trial was being conducted in Hebrew, it was preferable for the witnesses also to testify in that language.

52. None of the Arab witnesses blamed the shooters personally. They mourned the horrible murder but tended to emphasize their confidence and trust in the Israeli army. By contrast over forty years later, during the sessions of the investigative committee that was established after the killing of thirteen Arab citizens by Israeli policemen during the turbulent demonstrations of October 2000 (Vaadat Or), the families of the victims attempted to attack one of the policemen who testified. After two such attempts a glass wall was built to separate the witnesses from the audience. Such assertiveness, of course, did not exist in the first decades of the state, especially under military rule.

53. For current literature that extends the category of political trials to include those that are politicized by victims and their communities, which are not formal parties to trials, see George P. Fletcher, *With Justice for Some* (New York: Addison-Wesley, 1995).

54. See, for example, the cross-examination of Tufik Ibrahim Badir by defense attorney Oren about Tawfiq Tubi's visit to the village in *Protocols of Military Court Sessions,* session 29 (22 May 1957), 96–103, IDF archive file no. 5–165/1992, 63–69.

55. Ibid., session 29 (22 May 1957), 82, IDF archive file no. 5-165/1992, 53. See, for example, session 31 (27 May 1957), 13, IDF archive file no. 6–165/1992, 105.

56. Ibid., session 32 (28 May 1957), 41, IDF archive file no. 6–165/1992, 30.

57. Article 5(a)(5) of the Nationality Law, 1952.

58. It should be noted that since most of the defendants (all but Melinki) preferred not to testify before the court and only submitted written declarations they were not cross-examined. Other examples of this kind of "Hebrew test" included the use of the word *kelev* (dog) by the soldiers when addressing one of the Arab victims ("dog, move to the center of the line"). See the testimonies of Saleh Halil Issa, *Protocols of Military Court Sessions*, session 30 (23 May

1957), 47, IDF archive file no. 6–165/1992, 198; and As'ad Salim Issa, session 31 (27 May 1957), 57, IDF archive file no. 6–165/1992 140–41. The word *haval* (a pity) was also used in reference to a truck that had passed without being stopped and in reference to "wasting" too many bullets on the victims. See the testimony of Mahmud Muhammad Farij, session 35 (3 June 1957), 81, IDF archive file 7–165/1992, 60.

59. "Poem of Blood" (Shirat Ha-Dam), my free translation. The Hebrew translation of the poem appears in Rosenthal, "Who Killed Fatma Sarsur?" 243–44.

60. For elaboration, see Kordov, *Kefar Kassim's Trial,* 95–97, 168–71.

61. This was particularly evident in the testimony of Colonel Shadmi, who was a highly respected officer in the IDF and the very incarnation of the New Jew, the Sabra. He had graduated from the Kadury agriculture school and commanded the Harel Brigade during the 1948 war. Melinki testified about Shadmi's colorful language, which was spiced with many Arabic expressions. For example, in order to explain to his soldiers that they should not hurt anyone who stayed at home, he used the Arabic expression "kali yishrabu qahwa, kali basir mabsut" (they can drink coffee if they want, and be happy). See ibid., 95.

62. M.C. 3/57, *Melinki,* 166. Compare this to Halevi's critique of the "neutralizing effect" of the use of contract law terminology by Kastner and his partners in chapter 2. Also compare it to Arendt's critique of Eichmann's bureaucratic language in chapter 5.

63. Ibid., 158. Melinki explained that this was his interpretation of Shadmi's words (159).

64. Lt. Gabriel Dahan was the commander in charge of the unit that committed the massacre.

65. M.C. 3/57, *Melinki,* 162.

66. Pappé, "An Uneasy Coexistence," 636.

67. For example, see Mariam Mar'i, "The New Status" (in Hebrew), *Politica* 21 (1988): 33–35.

68. Indeed, Morris attributes the roots of the Kufr Qassem massacre to the Border Police's attitude toward the infiltrators, which was backed by the tough policy of "free shooting" (*Israel's Border Wars,* 445).

69. M.C. 3/57, *Melinki,* 152.

70. Ibid., 154.

71. Ibid., 223. Dalia Karpel also explains that the direct commander, Dahan, was famous for killing many infiltrators. His photograph even appeared on the cover of the magazine—*Ha-Olam Ha-Ze*—with his foot on the body of a dead infiltrator. See Dalia Karpel, "Yes, We Are from the Same Village," in Rosenthal, *Kafr Kassem,* 178, 181.

72. The force of this rhetorical change is illuminated when contrasted to the opinion of the dissent, in which the word *Arab citizen* does not appear even once.

73. M.C. 3/57, *Melinki,* 105.

74. Compare this to William Felstiner, Richard Abel, and Austin Sarat, "The Emergence and Transformation of Disputes: Naming, Blaming, Claiming," *Law and Society Review* 15 (1980–81): 631–54.

75. This practice was referred to in the trial as *vidu harigah* (confirmation of killing), and whenever the issue arose in the testimony of the Arab victims the judges intervened and questioned them, clearly astounded by the horror. See, for example, the testimony of Abed El-Rahim Salim Taha, in *Military Court Sessions,* session 33 (29 May 1957), 80, IDF archive file no. 7–165/1992, 190. In his judgment Halevi accepted the contention that the soldiers "assured the death" of the victims by shooting those who had merely been injured in the first round, preferring the testimony of the Arab victims to that of the soldiers (see M.C. 3/57, *Melinki,* 118–19.)

76. M.C. 3/57, *Melinki,* 109.

77. Ibid., 115 (Ofer's statement).

78. Ibid., 116.

79. This issue had first reached the court in 1949 during the trial of Iser Beeri (C.C. 47/49 [T.A.], *Attorney General v. Iser Beeri* [not published, given on 22 November 1949]) for ordering the execution of a fellow Jew, Meir Tubianski, who was suspected of spying for the British. The court's decision has never been published, but one historian reports that the issue of obeying an illegal order was pushed aside during the trial. See Shabtai Teveth, *Shearing Time/Firing Squad at Beth-Jiz* (in Hebrew) (Tel Aviv: Ish Dor Publications, 1992), 87.

80. See Kim Lane Scheppele, "The Quarantined Past: The Collective Construction of Regimes of Horror and the Creation of New Constitutions," paper presented at the annual conference Law and Society, Budapest, July 2001 (on file with the author).

81. M.C. 3/57, *Melinki,* 181.

82. This emphasis on the law of the heart resonates with the literary archetype for refusing to obey a king's order: the story of Antigone. See Sophocles, *Antigone,* in *The Theban Plays,* trans. E. F. Walting (New York: Penguin, 1974).

83. M.C. 3/57, *Melinki,* 178. For a critique of the moral criterion and its applicability in military conditions, see Parush, "Critique of the 'Black Flag' Test."

84. M.C. 3/57, *Melinki,* 172–73 (emphasis added).

85. The legal literature examines several examples of an illegal order that does not amount to a manifestly illegal order such as obeying an order to drive an officer's car above the legal speed limit. See Shif, "In Favor of the 'Black Flag' Test," 118; and Adi Parush, "Kfar Kasem Case, the Black Flag Test, and Its Concept of the Manifestly Illegal Order" (in Hebrew), *Tel Aviv University Law Review* 15 (2) (1990): 245, 265–67.

86. M.C. 3/57, *Melinki,* 237–46. Referring to the soldiers who disobeyed the order, the judge in the dissent writes: "We treat with great caution all that we have heard from these witnesses. My impression is that everybody became wise in hindsight, *after learning about the dimensions of the Kufr Qassem incident.* Each one undeservedly crowned himself with wisdom and responsibility only after the fact" (238, emphasis added).

87. A similar pattern of giving wide publicity to Supreme Court decisions intervening in the decisions of the political and military authorities (often in favor of Arab petitioners) can be seen in recent years. Thus, for example, we can find on the Supreme Court Internet site two landmark cases (translated to English) in which the court intervened to guarantee the equal rights of Israeli Arabs. The first case guaranteed the ability of an Arab Israeli to purchase a house in a Jewish village (see H.C. 6698/95, *Adel Qaadan v. Minhal Mekarkey Israel* 54[1] P.D. 258). The second case rejected the constitutionality of the methods of interrogation of the Israeli General Security Service (see H.C. 5100/94, *The Israeli Committee against Torture v. The Israeli Government* 53 [4] P.D. 817). Compare this to Mari Dudziak's thesis about the instrumentalization of the American Supreme Court decision in *Brown v. Board of Education* (347 U.S. 483 [1954]) in furthering the foreign policy of the United States during the cold war and creating positive public international opinion about the U.S. policy of civil and minority rights. See Mari Dudziak, *Cold War Civil Rights* (Princeton: Princeton University Press, 2000), 79–114 (chapter 3, "Fighting the Cold War with Civil Rights Reform"). The Brown decision, however, did not bring about real social change for a long time. See Gerald N. Rosenberg, *The Hollow Hope: Can Courts Bring about Social Change?* (Chicago: University of Chicago Press, 1991).

88. As mentioned earlier, only a third of the sessions were closed. Ruvik Rosenthal argues that what was discussed behind the closed doors was a secret military plan with the code name Hafarperet (Mole) in which the possibility of transferring the Arab inhabitants of the little triangle in case of a war with Jordan was discussed. The plan was canceled a day before the beginning of the Sinai war. See Rosenthal, "Who Killed Fatma Sarsur?" 14–21, 37–39.

89. This is evident from the coverage of the trial in the Hebrew press. For example, the editorial in *Davar* (associated with the ruling party, Mapai) on 17 October 1958, the day of the verdict, stressed that the "germs of murder" had infiltrated Israel from beyond its borders, where they were officially bred by the dominant ideology. The article also stressed that the frequent murder of Israelis by Fedayeen had caused a numbing of human sensitivity among the soldiers. This rhetoric is based on the logic of "blaming the victim," attributing the murders committed by Israeli soldiers to the Arabs. See Linenberg, "The Kfar Kassem Affair in the Israeli Press," 51; Merav Muymon Shnizer, "Between Shock and Oblivion: On the Historiography of the Kufr Qassem Massacre in Israeli Newspapers," in Rosenthal, *Kafr Kassem*, 52–86.

90. Yigal Elam, *The Orders' Obeyers* (in Hebrew) (Jerusalem: Keter, [1959] 1990), 58.

91. Rosenthal, "Who Killed Fatma Sarsur?" 44–45. In his speech at the Knesset after the massacre, Ben-Gurion emphasized the responsibility of the Border Police and at the same time mentioned that the interrogation committee had praised the actions taken by the IDF immediately after the event. See D.K. (1956), 462 (session 12 December 1956). Moshe Sharett, the minister of foreign affairs, resisted this distinction and criticized Ben-Gurion for his willingness to place the blame solely on the Border Police, without assigning any responsibility to the IDF. See Elam, *The Orders' Obeyers*, 57. The historians are quite united

in their conclusion that the political authorities sought to clear the IDF from any responsibility for the massacre (58; see also Kordov, *Kefar Kassim's Trial*, 44).

92. The Shadmi case was not published.

93. Rosenthal suggests that Ben-Gurion was afraid that the accusation of Shadmi would frustrate the efforts to leave the case solely within the realm of the Border Police and was therefore reluctant to bring him to trial. He mentions that Ben-Gurion was directly involved in choosing and appointing the presiding judge in Shadmi's military trial. For the Arab reaction, see, for example, Jiryis, *The Arabs in Israel*, 153–55; and Muztafa Kabha, "The Conspiracy and the Victim: Kufr Kassem Massacre in the Palestinian Arab Historiography," in Rosenthal, *Kafr Kassem*, 87–116. Kabha cites various Arab writers who emphasize the shameful punishment of Shadmi, among them the *Palestinian Encyclopedia*, published in Damascus. However, one must bear in mind the historical context of the court's lenient attitude toward the military authorities, which was also demonstrated when the victims were Jews. The most famous case is perhaps the trial of Iser Beeri, (see note 79). Beeri was found responsible for Tubiansky's execution in a "field court" but was sentenced to a single day of imprisonment, due to the high regard in which he was held in the Haganah, and eventually was granted amnesty by the president. For elaboration, see Teveth, *A Firing Squad in Beth Jiz*, 30–33.

94. See interviews with the defendants and their families conducted thirty years after the massacre in Karpel, "Yes, We Are from the Same Village."

95. For further details, see Rosental, "Who Killed Fatma Sarsur?" 46. Palestinian historian Sabri Jiryis emphasizes the fact that in September 1960 the Ramla municipality announced that it was placing Gabriel Dahan in charge of "Arab affairs" in the city (which was a mixed city of Arabs and Jews). See Jiryis, *The Arabs in Israel*, 150. This pattern repeated itself in other "security" scandals that granted amnesty to all those involved, who were later promoted to high public positions. The most important struggle against this pattern was against the appointment of Yossi Ginosar (who was responsible for misleading an inquiry into the Security Forces' methods of investigation and for forcing a confession from Eizat Nafso in his trial for treason) as the director general of the Ministry of Housing. The affair is described in the decisions of the Israeli Supreme Court to intervene and forbid this appointment. See H.C. 6163/92, *Eizenberg v. Minister of Construction* 47(2) P.D. 229. The court continued this line in a recent decision preventing Ehud Yatom—who had allegedly killed a captured terrorist in an action seventeen years previously—from being appointed by Prime Minister Ariel Sharon as head of the Department of the Fight against Terrorism. See H.C. 4668/01, *Sarrid v. Prime Minister Ariel Sharon* 56(2) P.D. 265.

96. For the changing attitudes of Israeli Arabs toward the Kufr Qassem affair, see Kabha, "The Conspiracy and the Victim."

97. H.C.J 6698/95, *Qaadan*. For a discussion and criticism of its limitations in effecting a real change in the status of Arab citizens in Israel, see Ruth Gavison, "Zionism in Israel? A Note on Qaadan" (in Hebrew), *Mishpat U-Memshal: Law and Government in Israel* 6 (1) (2001): 25–52; and Hassan Gabareen, "The Future

of Arab Citizenship in Israel" (in Hebrew), *Mishpat U-Memshal: Law and Government in Israel* 6 (1) (2001): 53–86.

98. This differential attitude might be traced back to Israel's Declaration of Independence, which recognizes the national group rights of Jews while promising to protect the rights of Arab citizens as individuals. See Yoav Peled, "Strangers in Utopia: The Civic State of Israel's Palestinian Citizens" (in Hebrew), *Theoria U-Bikoret* 3 (1993): 21–35; and Avigdor Feldman, "The Democratic State v. The Jewish State: Space without Place, Time without Duration" (in Hebrew), *Tel Aviv University Law Review* 19 (3) (1995): 717–27. Only recently have court decisions begun to recognize the collective rights of the Arabs in Israel. Examples include the Supreme Court decision to order the Ministry of Transportation to add Arabic to every road sign (see H.C. 4438/97, *Adalah v. The Ministry of Transportation* [not yet published, given on 25 February 1999]; and the Supreme Court order to the Ministry of Religious Affairs to equally allocate budgets to Jewish and Arab cemeteries (H.C. 1113/99, *Adalah v. the Minister of Religious Affairs*, 54[2] P.D. 164). However, in most cases the court is still reluctant to recognize the collective discrimination of the Arab minority. See, for example, Samera Esmair, "On the Legal Space and the Political Ghosts" (in Hebrew), *Adalah's Review* 2 (2000): 52–57. See also Ruth Gavison and Issam Ibu-Ria, *The Jewish-Arab Conflict in Israel: Characteristics and Challenges* (Jerusalem: Research Institution of Israel Democracy, 1999), 39–46.

99. The Military Justice Law, 1955 (9 L.S.I. 184 [1954–55]), allows the political and military authorities to intervene in the military legal process. For example; the military commander of the region can order sessions to be conducted in camera for security reasons (Article 324), the military commander retains the discretion to confirm the verdict and has the power to mitigate the penalty of the court (Articles 441–42), and the military commander also has the power to quash the file altogether, with the consent of the military prosecutor or the chief military prosecutor (Article 308).

100. See Linenberg, "The Kfar Kassem Affair in the Israeli Press"; and Muymon-Shnitzer, "Between Shock and Oblivion."

101. Shif, "In Favor of the 'Black Flag' Test," 129–30; Merav Muymon Shnizer, "Between Shock and Oblivion: On the Historiography of the Kufr Qassem Massacre in Israeli Newspapers," in Rosenthal, *Kafr Kassem*, 72–79.

102. For the dispute over Sarid's decision, see Muymon-Shnitzer, "Between Shock and Oblivion," 81. The most recent book on the massacre, *Kafr Kassem: Myth and History*, published in 2000, which was edited by publicist Ruvik Rosenthal, made a first contribution to transforming Israeli collective consciousness regarding the massacre.

103. Compare this to the recent heated public debate about an alleged massacre in the Arab village of Tantura during the 1948 war by the Alexandroni Brigade, which resulted in a libel trial against a student, Theodor Katz, who made this allegation in his master's thesis. During the trial Katz agreed to withdraw the accusation from the thesis and to publish a public apology to the members of the Alexandroni Brigade. However, he subsequently reneged on

this agreement, claiming that he had signed it under coercion. The district court, as well as the Supreme Court, denied his appeal. See C.A. 456/01, *Theodor Katz v. Alexandroni Association* (not yet published, given on 8 November 2001).

104. Rosenthal, "Who Killed Fatma Sarsur?" 12–13. It is interesting to note a counternarrative about the Kufr Qassem massacre that was advanced at the time by the right-wing youth movement Beitar linking the massacre not to the alleged massacre of Deir Yassin but to the bombing by Israeli soldiers of the *Altalena*, a ship bringing Jewish refugees from Europe to Palestine with a cargo of arms being smuggled by Etzel to assist in the 1948 war. In a pamphlet to Beitar youth instructors it was written: "The Deir Yassin action which is so condemned by our opponents was an action taken in the midst of a cruel war and came after a warning and a request to the inhabitants to surrender that was ignored. While the pupils of the left-wing youth movements were willing to shoot not only the 'Deir Yassiniates.' They raised their fists and weapons against their own brethren. They bombed a Hebrew ship, waving a white flag, and tens of warrior brothers paid with their lives for this insane action. Indeed, there is a connecting thread between the *Altalena* and Kufr Qassem incidents ("The Kufr Qassem Affair and Its Lessons" (in Hebrew), reproduced in *Homa* 70–71 (1983): 129–32.

105. The subcommittee worked on this Basic Law for a few years (1971–73) and eventually published the proposal on August 1973 (1973 H.H., 448). The proposal was brought to the Knesset in September 1973 (D.K. [1973] 4439) and several times during 1974 (D.K. [1974] 1192, 1565, 1752, 2484, 2731). Since the resignation of Halevi on 17 January 1977, the proposal hasn't been discussed by the Knesset and in fact was never enacted. It is worth mentioning that the proposal explicitly declares (in Article 2) the principle of equality, which was never included in Basic Law: Human Dignity and Freedom (1992).

Chapter 8

The quotation from Judge Edmond Levy at the beginning of this chapter is from Cr.C. (T.A.) 498/95, *State of Israel v. Yigal Amir*, 1996 (2) P.M. 49, 52 (hereafter Cr.C. *Amir*).

The quotation from Yigal Amir is from Cr.C. (T.A.) 498/95, reproduced in *Protocols of District Court Sessions*, session of 27 March 1996, 285–86 (hereafter *Protocols of District Court Sessions*).

1. An amateur photographer, Roni Kempler, videotaped the scene of the murder and caught Amir on his camera, pacing up and down for a long time in front of the steps leading from the speakers' stage to the car park behind the municipality. He eventually captured Amir on film shooting Rabin in the back. See *Protocols of District Court Sessions*, 107 (1 February 1996).

2. He relied on a "defense" from the Halakhah known as Din Rodef, a rule that permits the killing of a Jew who is about to commit or facilitate the murder of another Jew in order to save Jewish life. See Ehud Sprinzak, *Brother against Brother* (New York: Free Press, 1999), 253–58; and Nachum Racover, *A Bibliog-*

raphy of Jewish Law: Modern Books, Monographs, and Articles in Hebrew (in Hebrew) (Jerusalem: Jewish Legal Heritage Society, 1990), 2:268.

3. *Protocols of District Court Sessions*, 45 (28 January 1996); also cited by the judgment (Cr.C. *Amir*, 18).

4. As early as 1905 Lenin pointed out the inevitable conflict between the political defendant and his or her lawyer. Lenin suggested that the lawyer be limited to cross-examination of the prosecution witnesses and that the defendant be allowed to question the defense witnesses and present the full version of the defense in his or her own words. See Otto Kirschheimer, *Political Justice* (Princeton: Princeton University Press, 1961), 245.

5. He repeatedly asked to tell the court in his own words what had led him to kill the prime minister, requested that he be allowed to submit his own reaction to the bill of indictment, testified about the political background that had led to the assassination, and refused to show any remorse.

6. *Protocols of District Court Sessions*, 52 (28 January 1996).

7. Ibid., 53–54 (28 January 1996).

8. Cr.C. *Amir*, 9.

9. During the trial Amir was nonetheless given several opportunities to present his worldview: first, in his reaction to the indictment; second, in his testimony; and, finally, in his concluding remarks. The judgment, however, did not provide the public with Amir's complete narrative, but use sporadic quotations from his testimony in support of the court's findings.

10. Cited by Ariella Azulay, "The Ghost of Yigal Amir" (in Hebrew), *Teoria u-Bikoret* 17 (2000): 9, 14. This exchange is not mentioned in the protocols, but it should be noted that there was no recording in the trial and the protocol is not always accurate.

11. Article 90A, 300(a)(2) the Penal Law, 1977 (6 L.S.I. 18 [1977]); George Fletcher, *Rethinking Criminal Law* (Boston: Little Brown, 1978), 452.

12. Cr.C. *Amir*, 9 ("the deed attributed to the defendant is so exceptionally severe, that we thought it was appropriate to examine his mental state in order to dismiss any doubt concerning his capacity to stand trial"). It should be noted that the court initiated this examination despite the protest of the prosecution. Furthermore, it relied on this evaluation to later reject the defense's request for extra time in order to conduct its own psychological evaluation.

13. Ibid., 22.

14. Ibid., 27.

15. Ibid., 10.

16. Ibid., 21.

17. Yaacov Yadager, "'The Rabin Myth': Zionist Nationalism in the '90s" (in Hebrew), *Democratic Culture* 1 (1999): 23–36.

18. In early June 1948 the newly formed government of Israel faced a critical internal challenge to its authority. Although the militant right-wing underground organization Etzel had undertaken to stop all independent arms purchases, it was learned that a ship called the *Altalena* was on its way from France carrying not only nine hundred Holocaust survivors but also weapons. The government demanded that the ship, with its cargo, be placed unconditionally

at its disposal, but the Etzel leaders refused. The ship was set on fire just off the Tel Aviv beach by IDF troops, who then waded into the water to rescue Etzel personnel. There were casualties on both sides. The incident left deep bitterness but made it clear that no sectional armed force competing with the IDF would be tolerated.

19. *Protocols of District Court Sessions*, 184 (7 March 1996).

20. Inquiry of the psychiatrist Dr. Gabriel Weil, *Protocols of District Court Sessions*, 240 (12 March 1996).

> Q: How did you interpret his smile, which was apparent in the talks with him?
>
> A: He is pleased with what he has done. He is even proud of it. . . . I did not see any sign of remorse. I think it is connected to his feelings of superiority and contempt for the masses and this sense of mission in conducting his deed. . . . I think the basis is an extreme national identification with the people of Israel. . . . It has nothing to do with whether he understood what he was doing or not.

Note that the last sentence reveals that the whole inquiry was completely irrelevant to establishing Amir's legal sanity. The issue of the smile also came up during the cross-examination of Amir (*Protocols of District Court Sessions*, 192 (27 March 1996).

> Q: Throughout the interrogation we see you laughing and relaxed; what is so funny?
>
> A: The absurdity is funny. Here is a person who was willing to sacrifice his people for his seat, as opposed to someone who sacrificed himself for the people. . . . I am laughing at the absurdity. There are thousands of terrorists sent to Israel and I am a risk to the security of the state. Can you see it? I am a risk to the security of the government. That is true. But not to the security of the state.

21. Ben Yehuda uses the phrase "an alternative system of justice" and explains that "perpetrators of assassinations have claimed that 'political assassination' should be recognized as a special type of killing that is justified as a legal proceeding. This is done, for example, when assassins feel that their hopes of getting political or social justice are blocked, or that they are prevented access to legitimate avenues" (Nachman Ben-Yehuda, *Political Assassinations by Jews: A Rhetorical Device for Justice* [Albany: State University of New York Press, 1993], 78–79).

22. Ibid., 65.

23. There were several petitions to the High Court of Justice that contested the legitimacy of different aspects of the Oslo process. All petitions were rejected by the court by invoking doctrines of "nonjusticiability," "the political question," and so on. See, for example, H.C. 6592/94, *Hebron Municipality v.*

Minister of Defence, 50(2) P.D. 617 (on the legality of a town plan regarding Hebron that violates the Oslo agreement); H.C. 4877/93, *The Organization of Terror Casualties v. State of Israel*, not published, available in electronic form in 31 *Dinim Elyon* 317, in Hebrew (an attempt to prevent the Israeli government from signing the Oslo accord); H.C. 4354/92, *Ne'emaney Har HaBayit v. Prime Minister Yitzhak Rabin*, 47(1) P.D. 37 (a petition contesting the government's authority to negotiate with Syria); H.C. 2456/94, *Dor On v. Prime Minister*, not published, available in electronic form in 94(3) *Takdin Elyon* 794, in Hebrew (a petition seeking a declaration that the Oslo accord is not obligatory as long as the PLO Convention is not reformed and the Israeli law declaring the PLO to be a terrorist organization is not amended); H.C. 4064/95, *M.K. Porat v. The Knesset Spokesman*, 49(4) P.D.177 (a petition to allow several members of the Knesset to put forward a proposal for a referendum on the second Oslo accord a reasonable time before signing it); and H.C. 5934/95, *Dov Shilansky v. Prime Minister*, not published, available in electronic form in 41 *Dinim Elyon* 801, in Hebrew (a petition to prohibit the respondents from signing, on behalf of the Israeli government, the second Oslo accord unless it is ratified in advance by the Knesset). For elaboration on the constitutional issues raised by these petitions, see section 3 of this chapter.

24. *Protocols of District Court Sessions*, 204 (7 March 1996).

25. Cr.C. *Amir*, 11. The philosopher Giorgio Agamben explains the distinction between the physical and symbolic aspects of a prime minister as stemming from a long tradition of the "king's two bodies." See Giorgio Agamben, *Homo Sacer: Sovereign Power and Bare Life*, trans. Daniel Heller-Roazen (Stanford: Stanford University Press, 1998), 91–103.

26. This also puts Amir in competition with the court. Compare the words of Judge Edmond Levy, who states that "retribution as revenge is not a virtue of punishment . . . and we should not on any account be vengeful. . . . When deciding the punishment the court should be moderate, to consider carefully, and dismiss all anger from its heart" (Cr.C. *Amir*, 53).

27. Article 1 to Rabbinical Courts Jurisdiction (Marriage and Divorce) Law, 1953, 7 L.S.I. 139 (1953), states that: "Marriages and divorces of Jews shall be performed in Israel in accordance with Jewish religious law." See also Menachem Alon, *Jewish Law: History, Sources, Principles* (in Hebrew) (Jerusalem: Jewish Publication Society, 1994), 4:1624.

28. Cr.C. *Amir*, 20. Hellenists were Jews who, in the period when Palestine was part of the Hellenistic Kingdom, adapted Greek language and culture and turned away from their own religious traditions. The antagonism between the traditional Jewish masses and the Hellenizing Jews who came to power in Jerusalem led to the Maccabean revolt of 167 B.C.E.

29. Cr.C. *Amir*, 28.

30. *Protocols of District Court Sessions*, 178 (4 March 1996).

31. Cr.C. *Amir*, 26. Amir's contention might have been motivated by a desire to clear the rabbis. For a discussion of the positions held by different rabbis regarding the interpretation of Din Rodef in the period preceding the Rabin

assassination, see Sprinzak, *Brother against Brother*, 253–58. In the judgment, however, the question of whether Amir had received explicit permission from any competent Halakhic authority remained open (Cr.C. *Amir*, 24).

32. *Protocols of District Court Sessions*, 177 (4 March 1996): "Regarding the issue of Din Rodef you do not ask rabbis but rather you ask an army general . . . even if all the rabbis in the world would have answered in the negative, I would have done it anyway. You do not need a rabbi in order to know the answer."

33. Agamben, *Homo Sacer*, 83: "The sovereign sphere is the sphere in which it is permitted to kill without committing homicide and without celebrating a sacrifice, and sacred life—that is, life that may be killed but not sacrificed—is the life that has been captured in this sphere."

34. It is interesting to note that one of the three original crimes in Roman law that removed an individual from the protection of law, thus enabling him to be killed by any person in the community, was *terminum exarare*, the cancellation or negation of borders (ibid., 85).

35. Robert Cover, "Nomos and Narrative," in *Narrative, Violence, and the Law: The Essays of Robert Cover*, ed. Martha Minow, Michael Ryan, and Austin Sarat (Ann Arbor: University of Michigan Press, 1992a), 147–48.

36. The Great Sanhedrin was the supreme political, religious, and judicial body in Palestine during the Roman period, both before and after the destruction of the Temple. See *Encyclopaedia Judaica*, vol. 14 (Jerusalem: Keter Publishing, 1971), 836–40.

37. Cr.C. *Amir*, 45. Jewish Law scholar Eliav Schuchtman agrees with the court's ruling that Din Rodef does not apply to Rabin, but he objects to the court's reasoning in this regard. He maintains that Din Rodef should be viewed as similar to the laws of "self-defense" and "necessity" in Israeli criminal law, whose conditions were not met in this case. See Eliav Shochtman, "A Jewish Regime Cannot Be 'Rodef.'" (in Hebrew), *Tehumin* 19 (1999): 40–47.

38. Cr.C. *Amir*, 46.

39. My translation. For another, see Chaim Nachman Bialik, *Selected Poems*, trans. Ruth Nevo, bilingual ed. (Jerusalem: Dvir, 1981), 42.

40. Cr.C. *Amir*, 54.

41. On the dangerous supplement, see Jacques Derrida, "Signature Event Context," in *Margins of Philosophy*, trans. Alan Bass (Chicago: University of Chicago Press, 1982), 307–30; and *Of Grammatology*, trans. Gayatri Chakravorty Spivak (Baltimore: Johns Hopkins University Press, 1998), 141–65.

42. Cr.C. *Amir*, 49.

43. Ibid., 50 (emphasis added).

44. James Boyd White, *Heracles' Bow: Essays on the Rhetoric and Poetics of Law* (Madison: University of Wisconsin Press, 1985), 28.

45. On the liminal, see Victor W. Turner, *The Ritual Process* (Chicago: Aldine, 1969). On the relationship between Turner's theory of the liminal and identity politics enhancing the concept of borders, see Donald Weber, "From Limen to Border: A Meditation on the Legacy of Victor Turner for American Cultural Studies," *American Quarterly* 47 (1995): 525–36.

46. Cover, "Nomos and Narrative," 105–6.

47. Yoram Peri, "Rabin: Between Commemoration and Denial," in *The Assassination of Yitzhak Rabin*, ed. Yoram Peri (Standford: Stanford University Press, 2000b), 180–81.

48. Judge Edmond Levy explicitly relates to this fear by saying that "it is a small consolation that the murder not only failed to achieve its aim, but united the hearts for a moment" (Cr.C. *Amir*, 54).

49. Ibid., 51.

50. Ibid., 50.

51. The power to decide the composition of the panel is given to the president or vice president of the district court (Article 38[a] Courts Law [Consolidated Version], Laws of the State of Israel, vol. 38, 5744–1984/4, 281–282). The presiding judges in both Amir's trial and that of Aryeh Deri, a leader of the Shas party, were religious Mizrahi Jews like the defendants. For the Deri trial, see Leora Bilsky, "I Accuse: Deri, Political Trials, and Collective Memory," in *Shas: The Challenge of Israeliness*, ed. Yoav Peled (Tel Aviv: Miskal-Yedioth Ahronoth Books, 2001b), 279–320.

52. Ibid., 52.

53. For a warning against a politics of "love" instead of one based on friendship and respecting boundaries, see Hannah Arendt, *The Jew as Pariah: Jewish Identity and Politics in the Modern Age* (New York: Grove Press, 1978), 247. For a discussion of the public discourse on Amir in terms of "family honor," see Tamar Elor, "Like Murder for Family Honor" (in Hebrew), *Meimad* 13 (1998): 24–26.

54. Cr.C. *Amir*, 52.

55. Ibid., 51.

56. The declaration contains only one other reference to the Bible, again from a universalist perspective, when it identifies the core values of the State of Israel as "freedom, justice and peace as envisioned by the prophets of Israel." See Amnon Rubinstein, *From Herzl to Rabin* (in Hebrew) (Tel-Aviv: Schocken Publishing House, 1997), 144–45; and *From Herzl to Gush Emunim and Back: The Zionist Dream Revisited* (New York: Schocken Publishing House, 1984), 41–46.

57. However, as Rubinstein explains, rabbis from Amir's political camp had been promoting the radical interpretation that the precept "Do not kill" did not apply to the murder of non-Jews (*From Herzl to Rabin*, 160–68). If the court intended to address this audience it should have undertaken to refute this dangerous Halakhic interpretation. Interestingly, this question was addressed by the court for the first time after Rabin's murder when criminal charges of incitement were brought against a rabbi who advanced such an interpretation. See Cr.A. 2831/95, *Alba v. State of Israel*, 50(5) P.D. 221.

58. For a theoretical elaboration on the symbolic functions of sacrifice for the unity of the community, see Rene Girard, *Violence and the Sacred* (Baltimore: Johns Hopkins University Press, 1977).

59. Cr.C. *Amir*, 50.

60. Ibid., 52.

61. Ibid.

62. The origin of the word *sacred* lies in the religious ritual of sacrifice. According to Agamben (in *Homo Sacer*), the real meaning of determining that a person was sacred was not only legal but also religious (unworthy of being sacrificed). In this regard, the attempt of the court to depict Rabin's death as a sacrifice for the sake of peace is a rebuttal of Amir's attempt to exclude Rabin from the protection of law and religion alike. The motif of Rabin as a sacrifice was common in the public discourse as expressed, for example, in the popular slogan "In his death he commanded peace" (a paraphrase of the expression used with regard to fallen soldiers in Israel: "In their death they commanded us life"). See Yoram Peri, "Rabin: Between Commemoration and Denial," in *The Assassination of Yitzhak Rabin*, ed. Yoram Peri (Stanford: Stanford University Press, 2000), 348, 353–54.

63. For a premonition about the danger inherent in using Hebrew as a secular language, see a letter from Gershom Scholem, the famous Kabbalah scholar, to his friend, the Jewish philosopher Franz Rosenzweig, on 26 December 1926. (first published in English in 1990): "But if we transmit the language to our children as it was transmitted to us, if we, a generation of transition, revive the language of the ancient books for them, that it may reveal itself anew through them, shall not the religious power of that language explode one day? And when that explosion occurs, what kind of a generation will experience it? As for us, we live within that language above an abyss, most of us with the steadiness of blind men. But when we regain our sight . . . shall we not fall into that abyss? And we cannot know if the sacrifice of those who will perish in that fall will be enough to close it again." See Gershom Scholem, "On Our Language: A Confession," trans. Ora Wiskind, *History and Memory* 2 (2) (1990): 97–99. For an explanatory essay, see Stéphane Mosès, "Scholem and Rosenzweig: The Dialectics of History," *History and Memory* 2 (2) (1990): 100–116. Scholem's premonition is especially striking given Amir's corrupt use of the term *Din Rodef*.

64. Kierkegaard's answer to this dilemma is that we should nonetheless continue to study the story of the binding of Isaac, but we should also learn to distinguish the false believer from the authentic one.

65. Søren Kierkegaard, *Fear and Trembling*, ed. and trans. Howard V. Hong and Edna V. Hong (Princeton: Princeton University Press, 1983), 30.

66. The desire to "tear the mask" from Amir's face can be understood as a counterresponse to Amir's own use of this theme:

Q: When you considered whether to kill Rabin or [Foreign Minister Shimon] Peres, did you decide to focus on the prime minister because he symbolizes security and the people trust him?

A: He [Rabin] is the mask. When you watch Peres on T.V. you see "Mr. Unreliability." With Rabin there is some kind of an illusion. He was security oriented in the beginning, he was the Chief of Staff. Only because of him they [Labor party] won the election (*Protocols of District Court Sessions*, 194 [7 March 1996])

67. Cr.C. *Amir*, 52.

68. Ibid., 55.

69. Ibid., 56.

70. Amir told the court that he was a student who always strove for excellence, that his army service had combined studies in a yeshiva with serving in a combat unit, that he had been sent to Russia to help establish a Zionist youth movement, and that he had studied criminology and law at the university while continuing to study in the yeshiva. Moreover, he believed in and promoted the ideals of pioneering (labor and settlement) throughout the Land of Israel. See Protocols of District Court Sessions, 170 (4 March 1996).

71. For elaboration, see Anita Shapira, New Jews, Old Jews (in Hebrew) (Tel Aviv: Am Oved, 1997), 155–74.

72. Oz Almog, The Sabra: The Creation of a New Jew, trans. Haim Watzman (Berkeley: University of California Press, 2000), 18.

73. Pnina Lahav, "A 'Jewish State . . . to be Known as the State of Israel': Notes on Israeli Legal Historiography," Law and History 19 (2) (2001): 387–434.

74. Daniel Boyarin, Unheroic Conduct: The Rise of Heterosexuality and the Invention of the Jewish Man (Berkeley: University of California Press, 1997), 369.

75. See Ehud Sprinzak, The Ascendance of Israel's Radical Right (New York: Oxford University Press, 1991), 48.

76. For elaboration on the origins of the Zionist-religious messianic ideology of Gush Emunim, following the spiritual leadership of Rabbi Kook, see Aviezer Ravitzky, Messianism, Zionism, and Jewish Religious Radicalism (in Hebrew) (Tel Aviv: Am Oved, 1997), 111–200; and Sprinzak, The Ascendance of Israel's Radical Right, 43–51. For a discussion of the connection between these ideologies and the murder of Rabin, see Shlomo Avineri, "Rabin's Murder and the Problem of the Authority of the Government," in Political Assassination: The Rabin Assassination and other Political Assassinations in the Middle East (in Hebrew), ed. Charles S. Liebman (Tel Aviv: Am Oved, 1998), 49, 55–66.

77. Sprinzak warns against confusing the New Jew ideal embraced by Gush Emunim with that of secular Zionism, since it lacks one of the fundamental elements of the original ideology, the commitment to the secular character of the state. See Sprinzak, The Ascendance of Israel's Radical Right, 114–17.

78. Rabin's conduct was also compared to that of the French marshal Pétain and the Vichy government, which collaborated with the Nazis. See Rubinstein, From Herzl to Rabin, 172. For further examples from Israeli media at the time, see Idith Zertal, Death and the Nation: History, Memory, Politics (in Hebrew) (Or Yehuda: Dvir Publishing House, 2002), 272–79.

79. During the trial Amir relied heavily on a book by Uri Milstein, Rabin File: How the Myth Swelled (in Hebrew) (Tel Aviv: Yaron Golan Publications, 1995), in which the author attempts to "prove" that Rabin was not an authentic Sabra hero. A similar argument can be found in the rhetoric of Shmuel Tamir, the defense lawyer in the Kastner trial, who accused the Israeli leadership and the Mapai party of betraying the Zionist values of the New Jew and claimed that only the right-wing undergrounds (of which he had been a member) preserved this ideal. See chapter 2.

80. A difficult question is whether it is possible to create an identity narrative that is not based on a contrast to a certain Other. In South Africa there was an attempt to build such an identity through the commitment to a pluralistic

society and the distinction between past (apartheid) and present (multicultural democracy). For elaboration, see Richard Wilson, "The Sizwe Will Not Go Away: The Truth and Reconciliation Commission, Human Rights, and Nation Building in South Africa," *African Studies* 55 (2) (1996): 1–20.

81. See, for example, historian Anita Shapira's dedication of her book, *New Jews Old Jews*, to Yitzhak Rabin, "who embodied the image of the new Jew, a son of the land who knows every wadi and every rock, forthright and honest, speaking his mind, shy and modest, a lover of deeds not words."

82. Yaron Ezrahi, *Rubber Bullets: Power and Conscience in Modern Israel* (Berkeley: University of California press, 1997), 9–10.

83. Ackerman, *We the People*, 36:

But must all myths be mystifications? The Greek *mythos* points in a different direction: the narrative we tell ourselves about our Constitution's roots is a deeply significant act of collective self definition; its continual retelling plays a critical role in the ongoing construction of national identity.

84. Ibid., 50

85. These words echo also the ancient national trauma of the expulsion from the Land of Israel following the rebellion against the Roman Empire, when the defeated were bound in chains.

86. Yael Zerubavel, *Recovered Roots: Collective Memory and the Making of Israeli National Tradition* (Chicago: University of Chicago Press, 1995). Bar Kochba was a leader of the revolt in Judea against Rome (132–35 C.E.). Judah Maccabee led the revolt against the Greek ruler Antiochus Epiphanes. Joseph Trumpeldor (1880–1920) perished in the battle of Tel Hai in the Upper Galilee in 1920. His death, with his reputed last words, "Ein davar, tov lamut be'ad artzenu" (Never mind, it is good to die for our country"), became a symbol for heroism and patriotism in Israeli collective memory.

87. It is interesting that the declaration, which seeks to establish the "right" of the Jews to the Land of Israel, states that the Jewish people were constituted in the Land of Israel, while according to the Jewish tradition the transformation into a people occurred outside the land, in the Sinai desert through the commitment of the people of Israel to the commandments of the Torah.

88. Judge Levy crafts the story of Rabin's life to match the archetypal narrative of Moses: Bialik's poem, quoted at the beginning of this chapter, evokes the tragic end of Moses, who, having led the people of Israel out of Egypt and given them the Torah, did not have the privilege of entering the Holy Land himself: "His life's song was stopped in the middle." Readers are invited to fill in the rest: Rabin's promised land was the land of peace, which he, the veteran leader, did not live to enter. The analogy between the figures is augmented through the emphasis on a key trait they shared: neither was a man of words. It was said of Moses that he was "heavy of mouth and heavy of tongue" (usually interpreted as meaning that he stammered), and similarly the judge quotes from two poems that suggest Rabin's typical Sabra image of a man of deeds not of words (Yevgeny Yevtushenko and Leah Goldberg). By writing that he would

like to be Rabin's mouthpiece, the judge invokes the image of Aaron, Moses's brother, who spoke in his name before Pharaoh.

89. Cr.C. *Amir*, 56.

90. Hannah Arendt, *Eichmann in Jerusalem* (New York: Penguin, 1964), 11.

91. Cr.C. *Amir* 55. See also Albert Camus, *The Rebel: An Essay on Man in Revolt* (New York: Vintage International, [1951] 1991), 247.

92. An early argument for restricting the theory to times of transition can be found in Judith Shklar, *Legalism* (Cambridge: Harvard University Press, 1964), 209–21. I follow and expand on Kirschheimer's criticism of the tendency of liberal theory to distinguish between political trials in authoritarian and democratic societies and between trials in times of transition and trials in established democracies. Kirschheimer noted that democratic societies also tend to use courts as a way of enhancing the legitimacy of political acts and that in pluralist societies fundamental disputes about the constitutive values of the state are often brought to the courts for adjudication. See Kirschheimer, "Politics and Justice," 424.

93. Intranormative defense arguments include contentions of mistaken identity ("I am not the murderer"), contentions regarding the absence of one of the elements defining the crime of murder (absence of premeditation, absence of preparation, provocation), or reliance on sundry defenses (e.g., obedience to an order, self-defense, or legal incompetence).

94. Walter Benjamin, "Critique of Violence," in *Reflections*, ed. Peter Demetz (New York: Schocken, 1978), 277.

95. Carl Schmitt, *The Concept of the Political*, trans. George Schwab (New Brunswick, NJ: Rutgers University Press, 1976), 26. Schmitt criticized the weakness of the parliamentary liberalism of Weimar and later became a theorist of the Third Reich. His writings on the crisis of democracy can be useful here, although this reference to Schmitt does not mean endorsing the solutions he offered. For elaboration, see his biography: Joseph W. Bendersky, *Carl Schmitt: Theorist for the Reich* (Princeton: Princeton University Press, 1983). For a comparison between the crisis of Israeli democracy and that of the Weimar Republic (especially the development of political discourse that relates the term *opponent* to the terms of *friend* and *foe*), see Michael Walzer, "Democracy and the Politics of Assassination" (in Hebrew), in Liebman, *Political Assassination*, 13–21.

96. For elaboration, see Amnon Kapeliouk, *Rabin: Political Murder in the Name of God* (in Hebrew) (Tel Aviv: Poalim, 1996), 50–56.

97. But Eyal Benvenisti warns against assuming a causal link between the demonstrations and the murder, which may lead to a sharp change in the judicial policy regarding the freedom of speech. See Eyal Benvenisti, "Regulating Speech in a Divided Society" (in Hebrew), *Mishpatim* 30 (1999): 29–67.

98. Cr.C. *Amir*, 20 (quoting Amir's response to the request to extend his arrest).

99. Nachman Ben Yehuda, who studied political assassinations in Israeli culture in 1882–1988 (including an analysis of eighty-seven murder cases), discovered a considerable increase in the number of political assassinations in

1939–48 (especially in 1939, 1944, 1947). These years represent a period of intense national struggle over the definition of the boundaries of the collective. See Nachman Ben-Yehuda, "One More Political Murder by Jews," in Peri, *The Assassination of Yitzhak Rabin*, 63–95, 88.

100. Israeli law was amended in August 1986, and a criminal sanction was applied to any person who had contact with a member of a "terrorist organization." The PLO was specifically included among these organizations (Prevention of Terrorism Ordinance Law [amendment no. 2], 1986, S.H. 1179). This prohibition was the basis for a criminal prosecution of several Israeli citizens who met with representatives of the PLO in Romania (among others with Muhammad Abass, known as Abu Mazen) in order to promote a peace dialogue. The Israeli defendants' contention that the meeting was intended to promote peace and hence was not included under the broad prohibition of the law on the prevention of terrorism was rejected. See Cr.C. (Ramla) 76/87, *State of Israel v. Dori*, 1989(1) P.M. 289. After the prohibition was canceled on 19 January 1993, the defendants' appeal was accepted and the prison sentence was changed to a fine of one thousand shekels each. See Cr.A. 621/88, *Feiler v. State of Israel*, 47(3) P.D.112.

101. See the articles in Lev Greenberg, ed., *Contested Memory: Myth, Nation, and Democracy* (in Hebrew) (Beer-Sheva: Humphrey Institute for Social Research, 2000a): Amnon Raz-Krakotzkin, "The Legacy of Rabin," 89–107; Yossi Yona, "Israel after Rabin's Assassination: State of the Jewish People or State of Its Citizens?" 107–21; and Lev Greenberg, "Why Didn't We 'Follow His Route'? On Peace, Democracy, Political Assassination, and the Post-conflict Agenda," 123–51. See also Jamal Zahlaka's comments on pp. 159–64.

102. Sprinzak, *Brother against Brother*, 249–50.

103. Dani Korn and Boaz Shapira, *Coalition Politics in Israel* (in Hebrew) (Tel Aviv: Zmora-Bitan, 1997), 389–90.

104. For elaboration on the Law of Return, see chapter 7. The combination of the two values that was already described in the Declaration of Independence received a formal formulation in the twin terms *Jewish* and *democratic*, which began to appear in the new Basic Laws that were enacted during the 1990s. See Article 1A of Basic Law: Human Dignity and Freedom, 1992, S.H. 150; Article 2 of Basic Law: Freedom of Occupation, 1994, S.H. 90; Article 7a of Basic Law: The Knesset, 1958 (amend. 1985), 39 L.S.I. 216 (1984–85); and Article 5 of the [Political] Parties Law, 1992, S.H. 190. See also E.A. 2/84, *Neiman v. Chairman of Central Elections Committee for the Tenth Knesset*, 39(2) P.D. 225; E.A. 1/88, *Neiman v. Chairman of Central Elections Committee for the Twelfth Knesset*, 42(4) P.D.177; and Law of Return, 1950, S.H. 114.

105. For the opinion that there is no necessary contradiction between the democratic and Jewish values of the state, see Ruth Gavison, *Can Israel Be Both Jewish and Democratic? Tensions and Prospects* (in Hebrew) (Tel Aviv: Hakibbutz Ha-Meuchad, 1999). For the opinion that there is a contradiction between the two, which can be reconciled only if the State of Israel becomes either a state of all its citizens or a binational state, see Nadim N. Rouhana, "Coping with the Contradiction of Ethnic Policies: How Israeli Society Maintains a Democratic

Self-Image" (manuscript, on file with the author). For elaboration, see "Introduction."

106. Interestingly, Arab and Jewish citizens of Israel have different views of the process. Arab Israelis see the solution to the conflict as a necessary condition for achieving civic equality in Israel but think that a subsequent internal struggle over the Jewish character of the state is still required in order to turn it into a state of all its citizens. Many Jewish citizens, on the other hand, think that the territorial partition of the country would preserve the Jewish character of the state, since the Palestinian right to self-determination would be fulfilled outside its borders. See Majid Al-Haj, "An Illusion of Belonging: Reactions of the Arab Population to Rabin's Assassination," in Yoram Peri, *The Assassination of Yitzhak Rabin*, 163–74.

107. Yoram Peri, "The Media and the Rabin Myth: Reconstruction of the Israeli Collective Identity," in Peri, *The Assassination of Yitzhak Rabin*, 175–94. On the relationship between geographical boundaries and collective identity, see Oren Yiftachel, "Nation-Building and the Division of Space in the Israeli 'Ethnocracy': Settlement, Land, and Ethnic Disparities" (in Hebrew), *Tel Aviv University Law Review* 21 (1998): 637–63.

108. Sprinzak, *Brother against Brother*, 248. Among the rabbis were Shlomo Goren, Abraham Shapiro, Shaul Yisraeli, and Moshe Tzvi Nerial. Rabbi Goren, Israel's former chief rabbi and a highly regarded Halakhic authority, wrote that "The criminal initiative to evacuate Hebron ought to be met with *mesirut hanefesh* [total devotion]. The ruling on such a heinous crime, as the ruling on saving life, is *yehareg velo ya'avor* [be killed but do not sin]. According to the Halakhah, the meaning of the destruction of Hebron, God forbid . . . is like the killing of people, which requires *kri'ah* [tearing one's clothes—a sign of death in a family] like on the dead. . . . This is why we have to give our life in the struggle against this vicious plan of the government of Israel, which relies on the Arabs for its majority, and be ready to die rather than allow the destruction of Hebron" (quoted by Sprinzak [248]). In fact, during the evacuation of Hebron no religious soldier refused to obey an order. However, the ruling indicates another significant development: the rabbis, who had always sought to stay detached from the political realm, now undertake to rule on crucial political issues. The decision of the attorney general not to prosecute Rabbi Shlomo Goren for incitement (publicly calling on soldiers to disobey an order of evacuation) was challenged in the High Court of Justice, which, however, decided not to intervene in this decision. See H.C. 588/94, *Shlenger v. Attorney General*, 48(3) P.D. 40.

109. Dina De-Malkhuta Dina—the positive law of the country—is binding and in certain cases is to be preferred to Jewish law. Orthodox Jewish law acknowledges the legitimacy of the elected government, even when the latter exceeds its authority or violates the religious law (Din Torah). See Eliav Shochtman, "The Halachic Acknowledgement of the State Laws of Israel" (in Hebrew), *Hebrew Law Yearbook* 16–17 (1990–91): 417, 466–69. The problem of this rule is similar but not identical to the problem of conflict of laws in other legal systems. For elaboration on the accommodation of the two systems, see

Alan Dowty, *The Jewish State: A Century Later* (Berkeley: University of California Press, 1998), 159–83.

110. Hannah Arendt, *The Life of the Mind*, vol. 2: *Willing* (New York: Harcourt Brace, 1978), 214.

111. Jacques Derrida, "Force of Law: The 'Mystical Foundation of Authority,'" in *Deconstruction and the Possibility of Justice*, ed. Drucilla Cornell, Michel Rosenfeld, and David G. Carlson (New York: Routledge, 1992), 3–67.

112. Article 97(b) of the Penal Code, 1977 (6 L.S.I. 18 [1977]), states: "A person who, with intent that any area be withdrawn from the sovereignty of the State or placed under the sovereignity of foreign state, commits an act calculated to bring this about is liable to the death penalty or to imprisonment for life."

113. The court based its ruling on two doctrines: first, the doctrine of the "political question" (nonjusticiability), according to which the court will refrain from intervening in matters concerning the policy of foreign relations of the government; and, second, the prerogative authority of the government to enter into peace negotiations and the exemption of the Penal Code of the government from its prohibition. See H.C. 4354/92, *Ne'emaney Har Habayit v. The Prime Minister*, 47(1) P.D 37, 42. For other petitions challenging the different aspects of the Oslo accords, see note 23. A few years later, petitioners were successful in formulating their challenge in a legal way that forced the court to address its merits. The petition challenged the authority of Ehud Barak's "transitional government" (a government that has been defeated in a vote of no confidence by the Knesset but continued to function until the new elections) to sign a peace agreement. The court rejected the petitioners' claim of "no authority" and explained that the government has the authority to enter into such an agreement, but that this is a question of discretion that depends on different variables (such as the closeness of the elections and the threat to the security of the state) and the court would intervene only in situations of extreme "irreasonableness." The dissenting judge, however, accepted the petition, arguing that since at this specific period the Knesset had no effective control over the government (since it had already voted no confidence) the government should refrain from bringing about far-reaching changes such as a change of borders. See H.C. 5167/00, *Weiss v. Prime Minister*, 55(2) P.D 455.

114. See Ackerman, *We the People*. For a normative criticism, see Jennifer Nedelsky, "The Puzzle and Demands of Modern Constitutionalism," *Ethics* 104 (1994): 500–515. For Ackerman's response, see Bruce Ackerman, "Rooted Cosmopolitanism," *Ethics* 104 (1994): 516–35. For a historical criticism, see Jack N. Rakove, "The Super-Legality of the Constitution; or, a Federalist Critique of Bruce Ackerman's Neo-Federalism," *Yale Law Journal* 108 (1999): 1931–57.

115. C.A. 6821/93, *Bank Ha-Mizrahi Ltd. v. Migdal*, 49(4) P.D 221. For elaboration on the Harrari decision, which conferred the constitutional authority to successive Knessets, see "Introduction." Note, however, that in *Bank Ha-Mizrahi* Justice Cheshin strongly opposed this interpretation and held that the first Knesset could not have passed its constitutive powers to successive Knessets. For a critique of this decision, see Claude Klein, "After the *Bank Hamizrahi*

Case: The Constituent Power as Seen by the Supreme Court" (in Hebrew), *Mishpatim* 28 (1997): 341–58. It should be noted that in the absence of a definition of Israel's borders the jurisdiction of the laws of Israel is determined by the government's declarations or (if it chooses so) by laws (e.g., the law including the Golan Heights under the jurisdiction of Israel).

116. See Greenberg, "Why Didn't We Follow His Route?"

117. Ackerman distinguishes two kinds of collective choices with different binding authority: ordinary decisions made by the democratic government and constitutional decisions made by "we the people." Only the latter can be an amorphous body, which is created ad hoc during a process of public mobilization to effect constitutional change, legitimately engage in transformative politics. See Ackerman, *We the People*.

118. Greenberg, "Why Didn't We Follow his Route?"; Yona, "Israel after Rabin's Assassination."

119. *Reference re Secession of Quebec*, [1998] 2 S.C.R. 217. The Canadian court in effect divided its decisions into those concerning ordinary politics, in which it would refrain from intervening, and those concerning constitutive matters, in which it has the authority and duty to intervene in order to determine for the political actors the framework in which they could exercise their authority within the powers endowed to them by the constitution. In contrast, the Israeli High Court rejected the various "Oslo" petitions by invoking the doctrine of institutional nonjusticiability, referring to them as concerning issues of "internal governance" of the Knesset and not as raising fundamental constitutional issues.

120. Alexander M. Bickel, *The Least Dangerous Branch* (Indianapolis: Bobbs-Merril, [1962] 1978), 111–98.

121. H. C. 588/94, *Shlenger v. Attorney General*, 48(3) P.D. 40. See also Cr. A. 2831/95, *Alba v. State of Israel*, in which Rabbi Ido Alba was convicted for expressing his opinion that according to the Halakhah the prohibition "Do not kill" does not apply to the killing of Gentiles (decided after Rabin's murder); see also F.H. 8613/96, *Muhammad Yusef Jabareen v. State of Israel*, 54(5) P.D. 193, in which the court acquitted Muhammad Jabareen—who had published several articles in support of throwing stones at IDF soldiers—of supporting a terror organization, according to the Prevention of Terrorism Ordinance; and the current trial against a member of the Knesset, Azmi Beshara, for publicly expressing his support for Palestinians' actions of resistance to the occupation.

122. The issue of civil disobedience, in the sense of a politically motivated breach of law designed either to contribute directly to a change in a law or public policy or to express one's protest against, and dissociation from, a law or a public policy, has been raised in Israel by two distinct groups: by those who oppose the occupation of the territories and refuse to serve in the army there, and by those who oppose withdrawal from the territories. For the first, see H.C. 470/80, *Algazi v. Minister of Defense* (not published). For a theoretical discussion of the case, see Yoram Shachar, "The Algazi Trials: Selective Conscientious Objection in Israel," *Israel Yearbook on Human Rights* 12 (1982): 214–58. For a

general discussion, see Leon Sheleff, *The Voice of Honor: Civil Disobedience and Civic Loyalty* (in Hebrew) (Tel Aviv: Tel Aviv University Press, 1989). For the latter, see H.C. 588/94, *Shlenger v. Attorney General;* and Sprinzak, *Brother against Brother,* 245–53. For the distinction between civil disobedience and conscientious objection, see Joseph Raz, *The Authority of Law: Essays on Law and Morality* (Oxford: Clarendon Press, 1979), 272–73. On civil disobedience in general, see Ronald Dworkin, *Taking Rights Seriously* (Cambridge: Harvard University Press, 1977), 206–22; and John Rawls, "The Justification of Civil Disobedience," in *Collected Papers,* ed. Samuel Freeman (Cambridge: Harvard University Press, 1999), 176–89.

123. For a similar claim regarding the collective memory (and oblivion) of Rabin's assassination among the Israeli public and a suggestion to replace the mythical memory with a political one, see Avishay Margalit, "How Are We to Remember Yitzhak Rabin?" (in Hebrew), in Liebman, *Political Assassination,* 59–68.

124. On Rudolf Kastner, see chapters 1–3. Haim Arlosoroff (1899–1933), a statesman and leader of the Zionist labor movement, was assassinated in June 1933 by unknown assailants while walking with his wife on the seashore at Tel Aviv. The Arlosoroff murder trial (1933–34) did not solve the mystery of the assassination but greatly exacerbated political relations in the yishuv and the Zionist movement. See Asher Maoz, "Historical Adjudication: Courts of Law, Commissions of Inquiry, and 'Historical Truth,'" *Law and History Review* 18 (2) (2000): 559–606. Emil Grunzveig, a political activist of Peace Now movement, was killed on 10 February 1983 during a peace assembly organized by the movement. The murderer, Yona Avrushmi, threw a grenade at the participants of the assembly, killing Grunzveig and injuring nine others. See Cr.A. 154/85, *Avrushmi v. State of Israel,* 41(1) P.D. 387.

125. Ben-Yehuda, *Political Assasinations by Jews;* Shabtai Teveth, *The Arlosoroff Assassination* (in Hebrew) (Jerusalem: Schocken, 1982); Yehiam Weitz, *The Man Who Was Murdered Twice* (in Hebrew) (Jerusalem: Keter, 1995).

126. Kapeliouk, *Rabin,* 35. A close reading of the reports of the commissions of inquiry following both cases reveals major similarities between the courses of action and ideological worlds of Amir and Goldstein. See *Report of the Commission of Inquiry regarding the Machpela Cave Massacre* (Jerusalem: State of Israel, 1994), 76–80; and *Report of the Commission of Inquiry regarding the Assassination of Prime Minister Yitzhak Rabin* (Jerusalem: State of Israel, 1996), 24–32.

127. The court's approach also prevented a comparison with the processes that led to the assassination of Egyptian president Anwar Sadat in 1981, also as a result of the peace treaty with Israel. For a discussion of Rabin's assassination in the broader context of political assassination in the Middle East, see Liebman, *Political Assassination.*

128. Kapeliouk, *Rabin,* 35. For elaboration, see Jose Brunner, "Yigal Amir" (in Hebrew) *Teoria u-Bikoret* 12–13 (1998): 441–49; Ariella Azulay, "A Sign from Heaven: A Murder in a Shiny Scene" (in Hebrew), *Teoria u-Bikoret* 9 (1996): 241–74; and Azulay, "The Ghost of Yigal Amir."

Conclusion

1. There are a wide variety of truth commissions. See Priscilla B. Hayner, *Unspeakable Truths: Confronting State Terror and Atrocity* (New York: Routledge, 2001); and Robert I. Rotberg and Dennis Thompson, eds., *Truth v. Justice: The Morality of Truth Commissions* (Princeton: Princeton University Press, 2000).

2. The film is based on a play by Ariel Dorfman, *Death and the Maiden* (London: Nick Hern Books, 1996) (translated from the Spanish original, *La Muerte y La Doncella*, by Ariel Dorfman). I chose the film over the play because of its different emphasis on the role of the gun in the trial, as I shall elaborate subsequently. The quotations are taken from the play.

3. We can say that this is a kind of "reconciliation" between society and the old regime's criminals in which the victims are abandoned. There can, however, be another reconciliation between civil society and the victims. I will expand on this in the following pages.

4. Aeschylus, *Eumenides* (Chicago: University of Chicago Press, 1953). For elaboration, see Froma I. Zeitlin, "The Dynamics of Misogyny: Myth and Mythmaking in the Oresteia," *Arethusa* 11 (1978): 149–83; David Luban, "Some Greek Trials: Order and Justice in Homer, Hesiod, Aeschylus, and Plato," *Tennessee Law Review* 54 (1987): 279–325; and Paul Gewirtz, "Aeschylus' Law (Law in 'Oresteia')." *Harvard Law Review* 101 (1988): 1043–55.

5. Although Gerardo, the man, takes the place of the goddess Athena, their character presents more similarities than differences. Athena, after all, had androgynous qualities: born from man, a warrior, and one who "identifies with the male in all things." It has been suggested that Athena's androgynous nature allows her to listen emphatically and understand the Furies in a way that the god Apollo could not. See Adi Parush, "Revenge, Justice, and the Function of the Court in Aeschylus' Play *Eumenides*" (in Hebrew), *Bar Ilan Law Studies* 18 (1–2) (2002): 147–212, 202 n. 190. Gerardo's relation to both worlds—the public world of high politics and the private world of intimate connection with Paulina, the victim of the former regime—allows him to listen to her emphatically and establish a judicial process capable of taking account of her rape.

6. Dorfman, *Death and the Maiden*, 27–28. Note that in the film Paulina claims that no revenge can satisfy her, while in the play she tells Gerardo that what she really wants is a confession.

7. This element resembles the unique solution of the South African TRC that made individual amnesty conditional on the full disclosure (confession) of the truth about the crimes committed by the accused. In this regard it differs from the blanket amnesties granted by various South American truth commissions. See the literature discussed in note 1.

8. The subject of rape was also excluded, for a very long time, from the discussion of war crimes and crimes against humanity in international tribunals. This has changed in the international court in The Hague that is judging the war in the former Yugoslavia and in the international tribunal in Rwanda. See Kelly D. Askin, *War Crimes against Women: Prosecution in International War*

Crimes Tribunals (The Hague: Martinus Nijhoff, 1997). For the significance of this change, see Catharine E. MacKinnon, "Crimes of War, Crimes of Peace," in Steven A. Shute, ed., *On Human Rights: The Oxford Amnesty Lectures, 1993* (New York: HarperCollins, 1993), 83–109; Fionnuala Ni Aolain, "Rethinking the Concept of Harm and Legal Categorization of Sexual Violence during War," *Theoretical Inquiries in Law* 1 (1997): 63–96; and Rhonda Copelon, "International Conference: Gender Crimes as War Crimes—Integrating Crimes against Women into International Criminal Law," *McGill Law Journal* 46 (2000): 217–53.

9. Dorfman, *Death and the Maiden*, 16–17.

10. See, for example, Ronald Dworkin, *Law's Empire* (Cambridge: Harvard University Press, 1986); James Boyd White, *Justice as Translation* (Chicago: University of Chicago Press, 1990). For a criticism of this emphasis of law and literature scholarship, see Robert Cover, "Violence and the Word," in Martha Minow, Michael Ryan, and Austin Sarat, eds., *Narrative, Violence, and the Law: The Essays of Robert Cover* (Ann Arbor: University of Michigan Press, 1992b), 203–38, 204, n. 2; and Robin L. West, *Narrative, Authority, and Law* (Ann Arbor: University of Michigan Press, 1993), 419–39. For a law and literature approach that is well aware of the violent component of law and helps to expose it, see Martha Minow, "Words and the Door to the Land of Change: Law, Language, and Family Violence," *Vanderbilt Law Review* 43 (6): (1990): 1665–99; Austin Sarat and Thomas Kearns, eds., *Law's Violence* (Ann Arbor: University of Michigan Press, 1992); and Paul Gewirtz," Aeschylus' Law (Law in 'Oresteia')," *Harvard Law Review* 101 (1988): 1043–55.

11. David Kretzmer, *The Occupation of Justice* (Albany: State University of New York Press, 2002) (discussing the Israeli High Court of Justice rulings on petitions concerning the occupied territories). For a view expressing doubts about the feasibility of the attempt to distinguish clearly between transitional regimes and "presumably 'mature' liberal regimes," see Sanford Levinson, "Trials, Commissions, and Investigating Committees: The Elusive Search for Norms of Due Process," in Rotberg and Thompson, *Truth v. Justice*, 221.

12. Dorfman, *Death and the Maiden*, 16.

13. Generally speaking, a person can be identified and even convicted on the basis of voice alone, but the court is more suspicious toward this than toward visual identification, especially if there was no previous acquaintance between victim and accused, and the evidential requirements tend to be higher See Ron Brent and Sima Segev, "The Spectographic Method of Voice Identification" (in Hebrew), *Plilim* 4 (1994): 121, 124. In a recent case, a British court referred specifically to the unique difficulties that voice identification raised compared to visual identification. See R. V. Roberts, Court of Appeal (Criminal Division) 1999. Israeli law permits voice identification but requires it to be spontaneous, certain, and definite. See Yaakov Kedmi, *On Evidence* (in Hebrew) (Tel Aviv: Dyonun, 1999), 851–52, 915–18. American law enables voice identification as well: "It has been properly held . . . that a witness may testify to a person's *identity* from his *voice* alone" (J. H. Wigmore, *Evidence in Trials at Common Law* [Boston: Little, Brown, 1961], 660).

14. Israeli law acknowledges body scent as an element of identification in

special circumstances of previous and intimate acquaintance (Kedmi, *On Evidence*, 920). Nevertheless, Israeli judges have never relied solely on body scent, not even under such circumstances.

15. Dorfman, *Death and the Maiden*, 21.

16. Ibid., 16.

17. Note the impressive developments in the law of evidence and procedure in prosecuting rape in international law. For example, in *Furundzija*, the defense questioned the credibility of the raped woman on the ground that she was suffering from post-traumatic stress disorder. After hearing experts, the chamber rejected this contention. See *Prosecutor v. Anto Furundzija*, judgment, International Criminal Tribunal for the Former Yugoslavia (ICTY), Trial Chamber II (10 December 1998), Case No. IT–95–17/1 at paras. 108, 109. In *Tadic*, the decision of the tribunal outlined the criteria for keeping the identities of witnesses confidential, and under special circumstances anonymous, even to the defense. See *Prosecutor v. Dusko Tadic*, ICTY Trial Chamber (10 August 1995), Case No. IT–94–1. Rule 96 of the status of jurisdiction for the criminal tribunal for the former Yugoslavia forbids the harassment of and discrimination against victims and witnesses by admitting evidence of prior sexual conduct or permitting unexamined consent defenses in sexual violence cases. The ICTY rules also authorize protective measures at trial and the creation of a victim and witnesses unit. For further elaboration of the changes in the rules of evidence in prosecuting rape, see Fionnuala Ni Aolain, "Radical Rules: The Effects of Evidential and Procedural Rules on the Regulation of Sexual Violence in War," *Albany Law Review* 60 (3) (1997): 883–905.

18. *Ashcraft v. Tennessee*, 322 U.S. 143, 160 (1944) (Justice Jackson dissenting).

19. These rules were instituted in a famous court ruling as a means of differentiating between a forced confession and one given "of free will" (*Miranda v. Arizona*, 384 U.S. 436 [1966]). For the significance of this verdict regarding defendant confessions, see Peter Brooks, *Troubling Confessions* (Chicago: University of Chicago Press, 2000), 8–34.

20. This is the significance of the sword held by the goddess of justice. Several judges who have dealt with this dilemma have admitted that a confession given in a police investigation cannot be truly of free will. In this respect the Miranda Rules never claimed to examine whether a confession was indeed made of free will but only to establish a legitimate way of obtaining it. Justice Harlen explicitly expressed this approach.

> The atmosphere and questioning techniques, proper and fair though they be, can in themselves exert a tug on the suspect to confess, and in this light [here he quotes Justice Robert Jackson dissenting in *Ashcraft v. Tennessee*], "to speak of any confessions of crime made after arrest as being 'voluntary' or 'uncoerced' is somewhat inaccurate, although traditional." . . . Until today, the role of the Constitution has been only to sift out *undue* pressure, not to assure spontaneous confessions.

21. Dorfman, *Death and the Maiden*, 35–36.

22. Erin Daly, "Transformative Justice: Charting a Path to Reconciliation," *International Legal Perspectives* 12 (2001–2): 73–80

23. George P. Fletcher, *With Justice for Some: Protecting Victims' Rights in Criminal Trials* (New York: Addison-Wesley, 1996).

24. Mark Osiel, *Mass Atrocity, Collective Memory, and the Law* (New Brunswick, NJ: Transaction Publishers, 1997), 40.

25. The term *illiberal foundations* in the preceding heading is taken from Mark Osiel, "Why Prosecute? Critics of Punishment for Mass Atrocity," *Human Rights Quarterly* 22 (2000): 118–47.

26. Carlos Nino, *Radical Evil on Trial* (New Haven: Yale University Press, 1996), 133, 147.

27. Ruvik Rosenthal, "Who Killed Fatma Sarsur?" in Ruvik Rosenthal, ed., *Kafr Kassem: Myth and History* (in Hebrew) (Tel Aviv: Hakibbutz Hameuchad, 2000), 44. *Sulha* is a local form of Arabic community mediation between parties in conflict. The mediator is usually a revered elder in the community or village who is acquainted with sulha rules.

28. The recent victory in the Sinai war and the increased security felt by Israelis as a result of their success in stopping infiltrations may have been important factors. See chapter 7. For a discussion of the political and legal conditions that allowed the Israeli Supreme court to advance a transformative judgment on the issue of the legality of the use of force in interrogations conducted by the General Security Services, see David Kretzmer, *The Occupation of Justice* (Albany: State University of New York Press, 2002), 135–43.

29. For the view that trials can help restore solidarity, see Osiel, *Mass Atrocity*, 36–56.

30. For the vision of a limited solidarity that respects differences and conflicts in worldviews in a democratic society, see Osiel, *Mass Atrocity;* and Dana Vila, *Politics, Philosophy, Terror: Essays on the Thought of Hannah Arendt* (Princeton: Princeton University Press, 1999), 107–27.

Bibliography

Abel, Lionel. 1963. "The Aesthetics of Evil: Hannah Arendt on Eichmann and the Jews." *Partisan Review* 30:211–30.

Ackerman, Bruce. 1989. "Constitutional Politics/Constitutional Law." *Yale Law Journal* 99 (3): 453–547.

———. 1991. *We the People: Foundations*. Cambridge: Belknap Press.

———. 1992. *The Future of Liberal Revolution*. New Haven: Yale University Press.

———. 1994. "Rooted Cosmopolitanism." *Ethics* 104:516–35.

Aeschylus. 1953. *Eumenides*. Chicago: University of Chicago Press.

Agamben, Giorgio. 1998. *Homo Sacer: Sovereign Power and Bare Life*, trans. Daniel Heller-Roazen. Stanford: Stanford University Press.

Al-Haj, Majid. 2000. "An Illusion of Belonging: Reactions of the Arab Population to Rabin's Assassination." In *The Assassination of Yitzhak Rabin*. ed. Yoram Peri, 163–74. Stanford: Stanford University Press.

Allon, Yigal. 1970. *Shield of David: The Story of Israel's Armed Forces*. London: Weidenfeld and Nicolson.

Almog, Oz. 2000. *The Sabra: The Creation of the New Jew*, trans. Haim Watzman. Berkeley: University of California Press.

Alon, Menachem. 1994. *Jewish Law: History, Sources, Principles* (in Hebrew). Jerusalem: The Jewish Publication Society.

Aloni, Shulamit. 1999. "Basic Law: Human Dignity and Liberty" (in Hebrew). *Teoria u-Bikoret* 12–13:367–75.

Alterman, Nathan. 1962. *Writings in Four Volumes*. Tel Aviv: Ha-Kibbutz Ha-Meuchad.

———. 1972. *Shirim Shemikvar* (in Hebrew). Tel-Aviv: Ha-Kibbutz Ha-Meuchad.

———. 1973. *The Inn of the Spirits* (in Hebrew). Tel-Aviv: Ha-Kibbutz Ha-Meuchad.

———. 1981. *Ha-Tur Ha-Shevii* (The Seventh Column). Tel Aviv: Ha-Kibbutz Ha-Meuchad.

———. 1989. *Al Shtei Ha-Drachim* (Between Two Roads), ed. Dan Laor. Tel-Aviv: Ha-Kibbutz Ha-Meuchad.

Anderson, Benedict. 1991. *Imagined Communities: Reflections on the Origin and Spread of Nationalism*. London: Verso.

Arendt, Hannah. 1950. "Social Science Techniques and the Study of Concentration Camps." *Jewish Social Studies* 12:49–64.

———. 1951. *The Origins of Totalitarianism.* 2nd ed. New York: Harcourt Brace Jovanovich.

———. [1955] 1968. *Men in Dark Times.* San Diego: Harcourt, Brace.

———. 1958. *The Human Condition.* Chicago: University of Chicago Press.

———. 1963. *On Revolution.* New York: Penguin.

———. [1968] 1993. *Between Past and Future: Eight Exercises in Political Thought.* New York: Penguin.

———. 1971a. "Thinking and Moral Considerations: A Lecture." *Social Research* 38 (3): 417.

———. 1971b. *The Life of the Mind.* New York: Harcourt, Brace.

———. 1978a. *The Life of the Mind.* Vol. 2: *Willing.* New York: Harcourt Brace.

———. 1978b. *The Jew as Pariah: Jewish Identity and Politics in the Modern Age,* ed. Ron H. Feldman. New York: Grove Press.

———. 1982. *Lectures on Kant's Political Philosophy,* ed. Ronald Beiner. Chicago: University of Chicago Press.

———. 1994. *Eichmann in Jerusalem: A Report on the Banality of Evil.* Rev. ed. New York: Penguin.

———. 2000. *Eichmann in Jerusalem* (in Hebrew), trans. Arie Uriel. Tel Aviv: Babel.

Askin, Kelly D. 1997. *War Crimes against Women: Prosecution in International War Crimes Tribunals.* The Hague: Martinus Nijhoff.

Attorney General versus Eichmann. 1961. Jerusalem: Ministry of Information.

Avineri, Shlomo. 1998. "Rabin's Murder and the Problem of the Authority of the Government." In *Political Assasination: The Rabin Assassination and other Political Assassinations in the Middle East* (in Hebrew), ed. Charles S. Liebman, 49–58. Tel Aviv: Am Oved.

Azulay, Ariella. 1996. "A Sign from Heaven: A Murder in a Shiny Scene" (in Hebrew). *Teoria u-Bikoret* 9:241–74.

———. 2000. "The Ghost of Yigal Amir" (in Hebrew). *Teoria u-Bikoret* 17:9–26.

Ball, Milner. 1975. "The Play's the Thing: An Unscientific Reflection on Courts under the Rubric of Theater." *Stanford Law Review* 28:81–115.

Barak, Aharon. 1994. *Interpretation In Law.* Vol. 3: *Constitutional Interpretation* (in Hebrew). Jerusalem: Nevo Press.

Barnouw, Dagmar. 1990. *Visible Spaces: Hannah Arendt and the German-Jewish Experience.* Baltimore: Johns Hopkins University Press.

Barzilai, Gad, Ephraim Yaar-Yuchtman, and Zeev Segal. 1994. *The Israeli Supreme Court and the Israeli Public* (in Hebrew). Tel Aviv: Papirus.

Bassiouni, M. C., and, V. P. Nanda, eds. 1973. *A Treatise on International Criminal Law.* Vol. 2. Springfield: Charles and Thomas Books.

Bauer, Yehuda. 1994. *Jews For Sale? Nazi-Jewish Negotiations.* New Haven: Yale University Press.

Beiner, Ronald, ed. 1982a. *Lectures on Kant's Political Philosophy.* Chicago: University of Chicago Press.

————. 1982b. "Hannah Arendt on Judging." In *Lectures on Kant's Political Philosophy*, ed. Ronald Beiner, 97–101. Chicago: University of Chicago Press.

————. 2001. "Rereading Hannah Arendt's Kant Lectures." In *Judgment, Imagination, and Politics*, ed. Ronald Beiner and Jennifer Nedelsky. Lanham, MD: Rowman and Littlefield.

Beiner, Ronald, and, Jennifer Nedelsky, eds. 2001. *Judgment, Imagination, and Politics*. Lanham, MD: Rowman and Littlefield.

Belknap, Michal R., ed. 1981. *American Political Trials*. Westport, CT: Greenwood Press.

Bell, Daniel. 1963. "The Alphabet of Justice: Reflections on 'Eichmann in Jerusalem.'" *Partisan Review* 30:417–29.

Beloof, Douglas E. 1998. *Victims in Criminal Procedures*. Durham: Carolina Academic Press.

Bendersky, Joseph W. 1983. *Carl Schmitt: Theorist for the Reich*. Princeton: Princeton University Press.

Ben Gur, Meir. 1955. "The Poet Nathan A. and the 'Two Paths,'" *Lamerhav*, 8 July.

Benhabib, Seyla, ed. 1996a. *Democracy and Difference*. Princeton: Princeton University Press.

————. 1996b. *The Reluctant Modernism of Hannah Arendt*. Thousand Oaks, CA: Sage.

Benjamin, Walter. 1969. *Illuminations*, ed. Hannah Arendt, trans. Harry Zohn. New York: Schocken Books.

————. 1978. *Reflections*, ed. Peter Demetz, trans. Edmund Jephcott. New York: Harcourt Brace Jovanovich.

Bentham, Jeremy. 1962. "Rationale of Judicial Evidence." In *The Works of Jeremy Bentham*, vol. 6, ed. John Bowring, 189–585. New York: Russell and Russell.

Benvenisti, Eyal. 1999. "Regulating Speech in a Divided Society" (in Hebrew). *Mishpatim* 30:29–67.

Ben-Yehuda, Nachman. 1993. *Political Assassinations by Jews: A Rhetorical Device for Justice*. Albany: State University of New York Press.

————. 2000. "One More Political Murder by Jews." In *The Assassination of Yitzhak Rabin*, ed. Yoram Peri, 63–95. Stanford: Stanford University Press.

Benzur, Eithan. 1961. "Servatius Was Rebuked for His Remarks." *Ma'ariv*, 11 April.

Bernstein, Michael A. 1994. *Foregone Conclusions: Against Apocalyptic History*. Berkeley: University of California Press.

Bernstein, Richard J. 1996. *Hannah Arendt and the Jewish Question*. Cambridge: MIT Press.

————. 1997. "The Banality of Evil Reconsidered." In *Hannah Arendt and the Meaning of Politics*, ed. Craig Calhoun and John McGowan, 297–322. Minneapolis: University of Minnesota Press.

Beshara, Azmi. 1993. "On the Question of the Palestinian Minority." In *Israeli Society: Critical Perspectives* (in Hebrew), ed. Uri Ram, 203–21. Tel Aviv: Brerot.

————. 1995. "The Arabs and the Holocaust" (in Hebrew). *Zemanim* 53:54–72.

Bettelheim, Bruno. 1963. "Eichmann, the System, the Victims." *New Republic*, 15 June.

Biale, David. 1992. *Eros and the Jews*. Berkeley: University of California Press.

Bialik, Chaim Nachman. 1981. *Selected Poems*. Bilingual ed., trans. Ruth Nevo. Jerusalem: Dvir.

Bickel, Alexander M. [1962] 1978. *The Least Dangerous Branch*. Indianapolis: Bobbs-Merrill.

Bilsky, Leora. 1995. "The Narrative Turn in Legal Scholarship." J.S.D. diss., Yale Law School.

———. 1999. "Kastner Trial" (in Hebrew). *Teoria u-Bikoret* 12–13:125–36.

———. 2001a. "Judging Evil in the Trial of Kastner." *Law and History Review* 19 (1): 117–60.

———. 2001b. "I Accuse: Deri, Political Trial, and Collective Memory." In *Shas: The Challenge of Israeliness* (in Hebrew), ed. Yoav Peled, 279–320. Tel Aviv: Miskal-Yedioth Ahronoth Books.

Bondi, Ruth. 1990. *Felix: Pinchas Rosen and His Time* (in Hebrew). Tel Aviv: Zmora Bitan.

Boyarin, Daniel. 1997. *Unheroic Conduct: The Rise of Heterosexuality and the Invention of the Jewish Man*. Minneapolis: University of Minnesota Press.

Bracha, Oren. 1998. "Unfortunate or Perilous: The Infiltrators, the Law, and the Supreme Court, 1948–1954" (in Hebrew) *Tel Aviv University Law Review* 21 (2): 333–85.

Brecht, Bertolt. 1964. "A short Organum for the Theatre." In *Brecht on Theatre*, ed. John Willet, 179–205. New York: Hill and Wang.

———. 1967. "Alienation Effects in Chinese Acting." In *The Modern Theater*, ed. Daniel Seltzer. Boston: Little Brown.

Breines, Paul. 1990. *Tough Jews: Political Fantasies and the Moral Dilemma of American Jewry*. New York: Basic Books.

Brent, Ron, and, Sima Segev. 1994. "The Spectographic Method of Voice Identification" (in Hebrew). *Plilim* 4:121.

Brightman, Carol, ed. 1995. *Between Friends: The Correspondence of Hannah Arendt and Mary McCarthy, 1949–1975*. New York: Harcourt, Brace.

Brison, Susan J. 1997. "Outliving Oneself: Trauma, Memory, and Personal Identity." In *Feminists Rethink the Self*, ed. Diana Tietjens Meyers, 12–39. Boulder: Westview Press.

Brooks, Peter. 2000. *Troubling Confessions*. Chicago: University of Chicago Press.

Brooks, Peter, and Paul Gewirtz, eds. 1996. *Law's Stories*. New Haven and London: Yale University Press.

Brunner, Jose. 1998. "Yigal Amir" (in Hebrew). *Teoria u-Bikoret* 12–13:441–49.

Burin, Frederic S., and Kurt L. Shell, eds. 1969. *Politics, Law, and Social Change: Selected Essays of Otto Kirschheimer*. New York: Columbia University Press.

Butler, Elizabeth M. 1998. *The Fortunes of Faust*. State College: Pennsylvania State University Press.

Butler Judith, and, Joan W. Scott, eds. 1992. *Feminists Theorize the Political*. New York: Routledge.

Butler, Paul. 1997. "Affirmative Action and the Criminal Law." *University of Colorado Law Review* 68:841–89.

Calhoun, Craig, and, John McGowan, eds. 1997. *Hannah Arendt and the Meaning of Politics*. Minneapolis: University of Minnesota Press.

Camus, Albert. [1951] 1991. *The Rebel: An Essay on Man in Revolt*. New York: Vintage International.

Carr, David. 1986. *Time, Narrative, and History*. Bloomington: Indiana University Press.

Christenson, Ron. 1999. *Political Trials: Gordian Knots in the Law* 2d ed. New Brunswick, NJ: Transaction Publishers.

Christodoulidis, Emilios, and Scott Veithch, eds. 2001. *Lethe's Law*. Oxford: Hart Publishing.

Cohen, Richard I. 1993. "Breaking the Code: Hannah Arendt's *Eichmann in Jerusalem* and the Public Polemic: Myth, Memory, and Historical Imagination." In *Michael: On the History of the Jews in the Diaspora*, vol. 13, ed. Dina Porat and Shlomo Simonsohn, 29–85. Tel Aviv: Diaspora Research Institute.

Cohen, Ted, and, Paul Guyer, eds. 1982. *Essays in Kant's Aesthetics*. Chicago: University of Chicago Press.

Collins, Richard B. 1997. "Race and Criminal Justice," *University of Colorado Law Review* 68: 933–38.

Connolly, William E. 1991. *Identity/Difference: Democratic Negotiations of Political Paradox*. Ithaca: Cornell University Press.

———. 1995. *The Ethos of Pluralization*. University of Minnesota Press.

Connor, Walker. 1994. *Ethnonationalism*. Princeton: Princeton University Press.

Copelon, Rhonda. 2000. "International Conference: Gender Crimes as War Crimes: Integrating Crimes against Women into International Criminal Law." *McGill Law Journal* 46: 217–53.

Cornell, Drucilla, Michel Rosenfeld, and David G. Carlson, eds. 1992. *Deconstruction and the Possibility of Justice*. New York: Routledge.

Cover, Robert M. 1975. *Justice Accused: Antislavery and the Judicial Process*. New Haven: Yale University Press.

———. 1993a. "Nomos and Narrative." In *Narrative, Violence, and the Law: The Essays of Robert Cover*, ed. Martha Minow, Michael Ryan, and Austin Sarat, 95–172. Ann Arbor: University of Michigan Press.

———. 1993b."Violence and the Word." In *Narrative, Violence, and the Law: The Essays of Robert Cover*, ed. Martha Minow, Michael Ryan, and Austin Sarat, 203–38. Ann Arbor: University of Michigan Press.

Craft, Gretchen A. 1992. "The Persistence of Dread in Law and Literature." *Yale Law Journal* 102:521–46.

Daly, Erin. 2001–2. "Transformative Justice: Charting a Path to Reconciliation." *International Legal Perspectives* 12:73–183.

Dayan, Moshe. 1955. "Israel's Border and Security Problems." *Foreign Affairs* 33:250–67

Denneny, Michael. 1979. "The Privilege of Ourselves: Hannah Arendt on

Judgment." In *Hannah Arendt: The Recovery of the Public World*, ed. Melvyn A. Hill, 245–74. New York: St. Martin's.

Derrida, Jacques. 1981. "Plato's Pharmacy." In *Dissemination*, trans. Barbara Johnson, 61–172. Chicago: University of Chicago Press.

———. 1982. "Signature Event Context." In *Margins of Philosophy*, trans. Alan Bass, 307–30. Chicago: University of Chicago Press.

———. 1992a. *Given Time: I. Counterfeit Money*, trans. Peggy Kamuf. Chicago: University of Chicago Press.

———. 1992b. "Force of Law: The 'Mystical Foundation of Authority.'" In *Deconstruction and the Possibility of Justice*, ed. Drucilla Cornell, Michel Rosenfeld, and David G. Carlson, 3–67. New York: Routledge.

———. 1998. *Of Grammatology*, trans. Gayatri Chakravorty Spivak. Baltimore: Johns Hopkins University Press.

———. 2001. *On Cosmopolitanism and Forgiveness*, trans. Mark Dooley and Michael Hughes. New York: Routledge.

Dershowitz, Alan. 1996. "Life Is Not a Dramatic Narrative." In *Law's Stories*, ed. Peter Brooks and Paul Gewirtz, 99–105. New Haven and London: Yale University Press.

Dewey, John. 1924. "Logical Method and Law." *Cornell Law Quarterly* 10:17–27.

Disch, Lisa Jane. 1996. *Hannah Arendt and the Limits of Philosophy*. Ithaca: Cornell University Press.

Dorfman, Ariel. 1996. *Death and the Maiden*. London: Nick Hern Books.

Dorman, Menachem, and Aharon Komem, eds. 1989. *Alterman's Writing* (in Hebrew). Tel Aviv: Ha-Kibbutz Ha-Meuchad.

Douglas, Lawrence. 1995a. "Film as Witness: Screening 'Nazi Concentration Camps' before the Nuremberg Tribunal." *Yale Law Journal* 105:449–81.

———. 1995b. "Wartime Lies: Securing the Holocaust in Law and Literature." *Yale Journal of Law and Humanities* 7:367–96.

———. 1996. "The Memory of Judgment: The Law, the Holocaust, and Denial." *History and Memory* 7 (2): 100–120.

———. 2001. *The Memory of Judgment: Making Law and History in the Trials of the Holocaust*. New Haven: Yale University Press.

Dowty, Alan. 1998. *The Jewish State: A Century Later*. Berkeley: University of California Press.

Dudziak, Mari. 2000. *Cold War Civil Rights*. Princeton: Princeton University Press.

Dworkin, Ronald. 1977. *Taking Rights Seriously*. London: G. Duckworth.

———. 1985. *A Matter of Principle*. Cambridge: Harvard University Press.

———. 1986. *Law's Empire*. Cambridge: Belknap Press.

Dyzenhaus, David. 1998. *Judging the Judges, Judging Ourselves: Truth, Reconciliation, and the Apartheid Legal Order*. Oxford: Hart Publishing.

———. 2001. "With the Benefit of Hindsight: Dilemmas of Legality." In *Lethe's Law*, ed. Emilios Christodoulidis and Scott Veithch, 65–89. Oxford: Hart Publishing.

Eck, Nathan. 1963. "Hannah Arendt's Hateful Articles" (in Hebrew). *Yediot Yad Vashem* 31:15–20.

———. 1964. "'Eichmann in Jerusalem': An Exchange of Letters between Gershom Scholem and Hannah Arendt." *Encounter* 22.

The Eichmann Trial: Testimonies (in Hebrew). 1974. Jerusalem: State of Israel.

Elam, Yigal. [1959] 1990. *The Orders' Obeyers* (in Hebrew). Jerusalem: Keter.

Elor, Tamar. 1998. "Like Murder for Family Honor" (in Hebrew). *Meimad* 13:24–26.

Encyclopaedia Judaica. 1971. Jerusalem: Keter.

Esmair, Samera. 2000. "On the Legal Space and the Political Ghosts" (in Hebrew). *Adalah's Review* 2:52–57.

Evans, Richard J. 2002. *Lying about Hitler: History, Holocaust, and the David Irving Trial.* New York: Basic Books.

Ezrahi, Yaron. 1997. *Rubber Bullets: Power and Conscience in Modern Israel.* Berkeley: University of California Press.

Feldman, Avigdor. 1995. "The Democratic State v. The Jewish State:Space without Place, Time without Duration" (in Hebrew). *Tel Aviv University Law Review* 19 (3): 717–27.

Feller, S. Z. 1973. "Jurisdiction over Offenses with a Foreign Element" In *A Treatise on International Criminal Law,* ed. M. C. Bassiouni and V. P. Nanda, 2:5–64. Springfield: Charles and Thomas Books.

———. 1984. *Elements of Criminal Law* (in Hebrew). Jerusalem: Hebrew University Press.

Felman, Shoshana. 2000. "Theatres of Justice: Arendt in Jerusalem, the Eichmann Trial, and the Redefinition of Legal Meaning in the Wake of the Holocaust." *Theoretical Inquiries in Law* 1 (2): 465–507.

———. 2002. *The Juridical Unconscious: Trials and Traumas in the Twentieth Century.* Cambridge: Harvard University Press.

Felman, Shoshana, and, Dori Laub. 1992. *Testimony: Crises of Witnesses in Literature, Psychoanalysis, and History.* New York: Routledge.

Felstiner, William, Richard Abel, and Austin Sarat. 1980–81. "The Emergence and Transformation of Disputes: Naming, Blaming, Claiming." *Law and Society Review* 15:631–54.

Finkielkraut, Alain. 1989. *Remembering in Vain: The Klaus Barbie Trial and Crimes against Humanity.* New York: Columbia University Press.

Fish, Stanley. 1989. *Doing What Comes Naturally: Change, Rhetoric, and the Practice of Theory in Literary and Legal Studies.* Durham: Duke University Press.

Fletcher, George P. 1978. *Rethinking Criminal Law.* Boston: Little, Brown.

———. 1995. *With Justice for Some.* New York: Addison-Wesley.

Frank, Jerome. [1930] 1963. *Law and the Modern Mind.* New York: Anchor Books.

Fraser, Nancy. 1989. *Unruly Practices: Power, Discourse, and Gender in Contemporary Social Theory.* Cambridge, MA: Polity Press.

Friedlander, Saul. 1993. *Reflections of Nazism: An Essay on Kitsch and Death.* Bloomington: Indiana University Press.

———. 1997. *Nazi Germany and the Jews.* Vol. 1: *The Years of Persecution, 1933–1939.* New York: HarperCollins.

Fuller, Lon L. 1964. *The Morality of Law*. New Haven: Yale University Press.

Funkenstein, Amos. 1993. *Perceptions of Jewish History*. Berkeley: University of California Press.

Gabel, Peter, and, Paul Harris. 1982–83. "Building Power and Breaking Images: Critical Legal Theory and the Practice of Law." *Review of Law and Social Change* 11:369–411.

Ganz, Haim. 1995. "Law of Return and Affirmative Action" (in Hebrew). *Tel Aviv University Law Review* 19:683–97.

Gavison, Ruth. 1985. "The Controversy over Israel's Bill of Rights." *Israel Yearbook of Human Rights* 15:113–54

———. 1999. *Can Israel Be Both Jewish and Democratic? Tensions and Prospects* (in Hebrew). Tel Aviv: Ha-Kibbutz Ha-Meuchad.

———. 2001. "Zionism in Israel? A Note on Qaadan" (in Hebrew). *Mishpat U-Memshal* 6 (1): 25–52.

Gavison, Ruth, and, Issam Abu-Ria. 1999. *The Jewish-Arab Conflict in Israel: Characteristics and Challenges* (in Hebrew). Jerusalem: Israeli Research Institution of Democracy.

Gelber, Yoav. 2001. *Palestine 1948: War, Escape, and the Emergence of the Palestinian Refugees Problem*. Brighton: Sussex Academic Press.

Gewirtz, Paul. 1988. "Aeschylus' Law (Law in 'Oresteia')." *Harvard Law Review* 101:1043–55.

Gillies, Peter. 1981. *The Law of Criminal Conspiracy*. Sydney: Law Books.

Girard, Rene. 1977. *Violence and the Sacred*. Baltimore: Johns Hopkins University Press.

Goldstein, Abraham S. 1982. "Defining the Role of the Victim in Criminal Prosecution." *Mississippi Law Journal* 52 (2): 515–62.

Gordon, Robert W. 1998. "Some Critical Theories of Law and Their Critics." In *The Politics of Law,* ed. David Kairys, 3d ed., 641–61. New York: Basic Books.

Gorny, Uriel. 1953. *Criminal Law—Practical Theory* (in Hebrew). Tel Aviv: Dinim.

Gouri, Haim. 1962. *The Glass Cage: The Jerusalem Trial* (in Hebrew). Tel Aviv: Ha-kibbutz Ha-Meuchad.

———. 2004. *Facing the Glass Booth: Reporting the Eichmann Trial*. Detroit: Wayne State University Press.

Greenberg, Lev, ed. 2000a. *Contested Memory: Myth, Nation, and Democracy* (in Hebrew). Beer-Sheva: Humphrey Institute for Social Research.

———. 2000b."Why Didn't We 'Follow His Route'? On Peace, Democracy, Political Assassination, and the Post-conflict Agenda." In *Contested Memory: Myth, Nation, and Democracy* (in Hebrew), ed. Lev Greenberg, 123–51. Beer-Sheva: Humphrey Institute for Social Research.

Grosman, Haika. 1950. *The Members of the Jewish Underground* (in Hebrew). Merhavia: Sifriat Po'alim.

Guyer, Paul. 1982. "Pleasure and Society in Kant's Theory of Taste." In *Essays in Kant's Aesthetics,* ed. Ted Cohen and Paul Guyer, 21–54. Chicago: University of Chicago Press.

Habermas, Jürgen. 1984. *The Theory of Communicative Action*, trans. Thomas McCarthy. Boston: Beacon Press.

———. 1996. "Heinrich Heine and the Role of the Intellectual in Germany." In *The New Conservatism*, ed. and trans. Shierry Weber Nicholsen, 71–99. Cambridge: MIT Press.

Hariman, Robert, ed. 1990a. *Popular Trials: Rhetoric, Mass Media, and the Law."* Tuscaloosa: University of Alabama Press.

———. 1990b. "Performing the Laws: Popular Trials and Social Knowledge." In *Popular Trials: Rhetoric, Mass Media, and the Law,"* ed. Robert Hariman, 17–30. Tuscaloosa: University of Alabama Press.

Harris, Ron. 2002. "Jewish Democracy and Arab Politics: The El-Ard Movement in the Israeli Supreme Court" (in Hebrew). *Plilim* 10:107–56.

Harris, Whitney R. 1999. *Tyranny on Trial: The Evidence at Nuremberg*. Rev. ed. Dallas: Southern Methodist University Press.

Hausner, Gideon. 1966. *Justice in Jerusalem*. New York: Harper and Row.

Hayner, Priscilla B. 2001. *Unspeakable Truths: Confronting State Terror and Atrocity*. New York: Routledge.

Hecht, Ben. 1997. *Perfidy*. New London, CT: Milah Press.

Henderson, Lynne N. 1985. "The Wrongs of Victim's Rights." *Stanford Law Review* 37 (2): 937–1022.

Hesse, Carla, and, Robert Post, eds. 1999. *Human Rights in Political Transition*. New York: Zone Books.

Hilberg, Raul. 1961. *The Destruction of the European Jews*. Chicago: Quadrangle Books.

Hill, Melvyn A., ed. 1979. *Hannah Arendt: The Recovery of the Public World*. New York: St. Martin's Press.

Hinchman, Lewis P., and Sandra K. Hinchman, eds. 1994. *Hannah Arendt: Critical Essays*. Albany: State University of New York Press.

History and Memory 1995. 7 (1). Special issue on "Israeli History Revisited," ed. Gulie Ne'eman Arad.

Hoelzel, Alfred. 1988. *The Paradoxical Quest: A Study of Faustian Vicissitudes*. New York: Peter Lang.

Holzman, Avner. 1986. "Nathan Alterman and the "Two Paths" Controversy" (in Hebrew). *Bizaron*, 8 (new series) 29–30: 6–15.

Honig, Bonnie. 1992. "Toward an Agonistic Feminism: Hannah Arendt and the Politics of Identity." In *Feminists Theorize the Political*, ed. Judith Butler and Joan W. Scott, 215–41. New York: Routledge.

———. 1993. *Political Theory and the Displacement of Politics* Ithaca: Cornell University Press.

———. 1996. "Difference, Dilemmas, and the Politics of Home." In *Democracy and Difference*, ed. Seyla Benhabib, 257–77. Princeton: Princeton University Press.

Huizinga, Johan. 1955. *Homo Ludens: A Study of the Play-Element in Culture*. Boston: Beacon Press.

Jabareen, Hassan. 2001. "The Future of Arab Citizenship in Israel" (in Hebrew). Mishpat U-Memshal 6 (1): 53–86.

Jackson, Robert. 1999. "Introduction." In Whitney R. Harris, Tyranny on Trial: The Evidence at Nuremberg. Rev. ed. Dallas: Southern Methodist University Press.

Jiryis, Sabri. 1976. The Arabs in Israel. New York: Monthly Review Press.

Jubran, Salem. 1996. "The Arabs and the Holocaust: Historical and Current Perspective" (in Hebrew). Bishvil Ha-Zikaron 17:15–18.

Kabha, Muztafa. 2000. "The Conspiracy and the Victim: The Kufr Kassem Massacre in Palestinian Arab Historiography" (in Hebrew). In Kafr Kassem: Myth and History, ed. Ruvik Rosenthal, 87–116. Tel Aviv: Ha-Kibbutz Ha-Meuchad.

Kairys, David, ed. 1998. The Politics of Law. 3rd ed. New York: Basic Books.

Kamir, Orit. 2000. "The Declaration Has Two Faces: The Interesting Story of the 'Zionist Declaration of Independence' and the 'Democratic Declaration of Independence'" (in Hebrew). Tel Aviv University Law Review 23:473–538.

Kant, Immanuel. 1951. Critique of Judgment, trans. J. H. Bernard. New York: Hafner.

Kapeliouk, Amnon. 1996. Rabin: Political Murder in the Name of God (in Hebrew). Tel Aviv: Poalim.

Karp, Judith. 1993. "Basic Law: Human Dignity and Liberty—a Biography of Power Struggles" (in Hebrew). Mishpat U-Mimshal 1 (2): 323–84.

Karpel, Dalia. 2000. "Yes, We Are from the Same Village." In Kafr Kassem: Myth and History (in Hebrew), ed. Ruvik Rosenthal, 178–95. Tel Aviv: Ha-Kibbutz Ha-Meuchad.

Kasher, Asa. 1996. Military Ethics (in Hebrew). Tel Aviv: Ministry of Defense.

Kastner, Israel. Report of the Rescue Committee in Budapest, 1942–1945 (submitted to the Zionist Congress, translated to Hebrew by Benjamin Gat-Rimon and published by the Association in the memory of Dr. Israel Kastner).

Kedmi, Yaakov. 1999. On Evidence (in Hebrew). Tel Aviv: Dyonun.

Kena'an, Haviv. "A Document on the Devil and the Soul" (in Hebrew). Ha'aretz, 10 February 1961.

Kenaani, David, "Like a Shining Light" [Ke-Or Yahel]. Al Ha-Mishmar, 14 May 1954.

Kennedy, Duncan. 1997. A Critique of Adjudication. Cambridge: Harvard University Press.

Keren, Michael. 1983. Ben-Gurion and the Intellectuals: Power, Knowledge, and Charisma. De Kalb: Northern Illinois University Press.

———. 1991. "Ben-Gurion's Theory of Sovereignty: The Trial of Adolf Eichmann." In David Ben Gurion: Politics and Leadership in Israel, ed. Ronald W. Zweig, 38–51. London: F. Cass.

Kierkegaard, Søren. 1983. Fear and Trembling, ed. and trans. Howard V. Hong and Edna V. Hong. Princeton: Princeton University Press.

Kirschheimer, Otto. 1961. Political Justice. Princeton: Princeton University Press.

———. 1969. "Politics and Justice." In Politics, Law, and Social Change: Selected

Essays of Otto Kirschheimer, ed. Frederic S. Burin and Kurt L. Shell, 408–27. New York: Columbia University Press.

Klein, Claude. 1997. "After the Bank Hamizrahi Case: The Constituent Power as Seen by the Supreme Court" (in Hebrew). *Mishpatim* 28:341–58.

Klemperer, Victor. 2000. *The Language of the Third Reich*, trans. Martin Brady. London: Athlone Press.

Kobobi, Arie Leon. 1963. "A Criminal Country versus a Moral Society" (in Hebrew). *Yediot Yad Vashem* 31: 1–7.

Kohler, Lotte, and, Hans Saner, eds. 1992. *Hannah Arendt/Karl Jaspers Correspondence, 1926–1969*. New York: Harcourt Brace Jovanovich.

Komem, Aharon. 1989. "The Poet and the Leader." In *Alterman's Writing*, ed. Menachem Dorman and Aharon Komem, 47–87 (in Hebrew). Tel Aviv: Ha-Kibbutz Ha-Meuchad.

Kordov, Moshe. 1959. *Kfar Qassem Trial* (in Hebrew). Tel Aviv: Narkis.

Korn, Dani, and, Boaz Shapira. 1997. *Coalition Politics in Israel* (in Hebrew). Tel Aviv: Zmora-Bitan.

Koselleck, Reinhart. 1985. *Futures Past: On the Semantics of Historical Time*, trans. Keith Tribe. Cambridge: MIT Press.

Kovner, Abba. 1981. "Hitvadut" [Acquaintance]. In *On a Narrow Bridge: Oral Essays* (in Hebrew), 109–12. Tel Aviv: Poalim.

Kretzmer, David. 2002. *The Occupation of Justice*. Albany: State University of New York Press.

Kritz, Neil J., ed. 1995. *Transitional Justice: How Emerging Democracies Reckon with Former Regimes*. Washington, DC: U.S. Institute of Peace Press.

Kritzman, Lawrence D., ed. 1998. *Realms of Memory: The Construction of the French Past*. Vol. 3: *Symbols*, under the direction of Pierre Nora, trans. Arthur Goldhammer, ed. New York: Columbia University Press.

The Kfar Qassem Affair and Its Lessons (in Hebrew). 1983. *Homa* 70–71:129–32.

Kulazka, Barbara ed. 1992. *Did Six Million Really Die? Report of the Evidence in the Canadian "False News" Trial of Ernst Zundel—1988*. Toronto: Samisdat Publishers.

Kushner, Tony. 1994. *The Holocaust and the Liberal Imagination*. Oxford: Blackwell.

Kymlicka, Will. 1989. *Liberalism, Community, and Culture*. Oxford: Oxford University Press.

———. 1995. *The Rights of Minority Cultures*. Oxford: Oxford University Press.

LaCapra, Dominique. 1998. *History and Memory after Auschwitz*. Ithaca and London: Cornell University Press.

Lahav, Pnina. 1989. "The Formative Years of Israel's Supreme Court, 1948–1955" (in Hebrew). *Tel Aviv University Law Review* 14 (3): 479–502.

———. 1992. "The Eichmann Trial, the Jewish Question, and the American Jewish Intelligentsia." *Boston University Law Review* 72:555–78.

———. 1997. *Judgment in Jerusalem: Chief Justice Simon Agranat and the Zionist Century*. Berkeley: University of California Press.

———. 2001. "A 'Jewish State . . . to Be Known as the State of Israel': Notes on Israeli Legal Historiography." *Law and History Review* 19 (2): 387–433.

————. Forthcoming. "Theater in the Courtroom: The Chicago Conspiracy Trial." *Law and Literature.*

Langer, Lawrence L. 1991. *Holocaust Testimonies: The Ruins of Memory.* New Haven: Yale University Press.

Lanzsmann, Claude. 1995. *Shoah.* New York: Da Capo Press.

Laor, Dan. 1989. "Od Al Shtei Ha-Derachim" [More on the Two Roads]. In Nathan Alterman, *Al Shtei Ha-Derachim* [Between Two Roads] (in Hebrew), ed. Dan Laor, 113–55. Tel Aviv: Ha-Kibbutz Ha-Meuchad.

————. 1994. "Alterman as a Political Poet." In *The Trumpet and the Sword* (in Hebrew), 9–24. Tel Aviv: Ha-Kibbutz Ha-Meuchad.

Levi, Primo. 1979. *The Truce,* trans. Stuart Woolf. London: Penguin.

————. 1988. *The Drowned and the Saved,* trans. Raymond Rosenthal. New York: Summit Books.

Levinson, Sanford. 2000. "Trials, Commissions, and Investigating Committees: The Elusive Search for Norms of Due Process." In *Truth v. Justice: The Morality of Truth Commissions,* ed. Robert I. Rotberg and Dennis Thompson, 211–34. Princeton: Princeton University Press.

Levontin, Avigdor. 1995. "Jewish and Democratic: Personal Reflections" (in Hebrew). *Tel Aviv University Law Review* 19 (3): 521–47.

Liebman, Charles S., ed. 1998. *Political Assassination: The Rabin Assassination and Other Political Assassinations in the Middle East* (in Hebrew). Tel Aviv: Am Oved.

Linenberg, Ron. 1972. "The Kfar Kassem Affair in the Israeli Press" (in Hebrew). *Medina U-Memshal* 2:48–64.

Luban, David. 1987. "Some Greek Trials: Order and Justice in Homer, Hesiod, Aeschylus, and Plato." *Tennessee Law Review* 54:279–325.

————. 1994. "Explaining Dark Times: Hannah Arendt's Theory of Theory." in *Hannah Arendt: Critical Essays,* ed. Lewis P. Hinchman and Sandra K. Hinchman, 79–109. Albany: State University of New York Press.

————. 2001. "A Man Lost in the Gray Zone." *Law and History Review* 19 (1): 161–76.

Luban, David, Alan Strudler, and David T. Wasserman. 1992. "Moral Responsibility in the Age of Bureaucracy." *Michigan Law Review* 90 (8): 2348–92.

Lustik, Ian. 1980. *Arabs in the Jewish State.* Austin: University of Texas Press.

Lyotard, Jean-François. 1988. *The Differend,* trans. G. Van dAbbeele. Minneapolis: University of Minnesota Press.

MacKinnon, Catharine E. 1993. "Crimes of War, Crimes of Peace." In *On Human Rights: The Oxford Amnesty Lectures, 1993,* ed. Steven A. Shute, 83–109. New York: HarperCollins.

Mann, Thomas. [1947] 1997. *Doctor Faustus,* trans. John E. Woods. New York: Knopf.

Maoz, Asher. 2000. "Historical Adjudication: Courts of Law, Commissions of Inquiry, and "Historical Truth," *Law and History Review* 18 (3): 559–606.

Margalit, Avishay. 1998. "How Are We to Remember Yitzhak Rabin?" (in Hebrew). In *Political Assassination: The Rabin Assassination and Other Political*

Assassinations in the Middle East (in Hebrew), ed. Charles S. Liebman, 59–68. Tel Aviv: Am Oved.

Mar'i, Mariam. 1988. "The New Status" (in Hebrew). *Politica* 21:33–35.

Marlowe, Christopher. 1969. *Doctor Faustus*. New York: New American Library.

Marrus, Michael R. 1997. "History and the Holocaust in the Courtroom." Manuscript.

———. 1998. "The Holocaust at Nuremberg." *Yad Vashem Studies* 26:5–42.

Mauss, Marcel. 1990. *The Gift: The Form and Reason for Exchange in Archaic Societies,* trans. W. D. Halls. New York: Norton.

Mautner, Menachem. 1993. *The Decline of Formalism and the Rise of Values in Israeli Law* (in Hebrew). Tel Aviv: Ma'agalay Da'at.

Mautner, Menachem, Avi Sagi, and Ronen Shamir, eds. 1998. *Multi-culturalism in a Democratic and Jewish State* (in Hebrew). Tel Aviv: Ramot.

McAdams, James, ed. 1997. *Transitional Justice and the Rule of Law in New Democracies.* Notre Dame: University of Notre Dame Press.

McCarthy, Mary. 1964. "The Hue and Cry." *Partisan Review* 31 (1): 82–94.

McCormack on Evidence, ed. John W. Strong. 4th ed. St. Paul: West, 1992.

Michalowski, Sabine, and, Lorna Woods. 1999. *German Constitutional Law.* Ashgate, England: Dartmouth Publishing.

Minow, Martha. 1990. "Words and the Door to the Land of Change: Law, Language, and Family Violence." *Vanderbilt Law Review* 43 (6): 1665–99.

———. 1993. "Surviving Victim Talk." *UCLA Law Review* 40 (2): 1411–46.

———. 1998. *Between Vengeance and Forgiveness: Facing History after Genocide and Mass Violence.* Boston: Beacon Press.

Minow, Martha, Michael Ryan, and Austin Sarat, eds. 1992. *Narrative, Violence, and the Law: The Essays of Robert Cover.* Ann Arbor: University of Michigan Press.

Minow, Martha L., and Elizabeth V. Spelman. 1988. "Passion for Justice." *Cardozo Law Review* 10:37–76.

Miron, Dan. 1985–86. "From Creators and Constructors to Homeless People" (in Hebrew). *Igra* 71:71–135

Mitchell, W. J. T., ed. 1981. *On Narrative.* Chicago: University of Chicago Press.

Montoya, Margaret E. 1997. "Of 'Subtle Prejudices,' White Supremacy, and Affirmative Action: A Reply to Paul Butler." *University of Colorado Law Review* 68:891–931.

Morris, Benny. 1987. *The Birth of the Palestinian Refugee Problem, 1947–1949.* Cambridge: Cambridge University Press.

———. 1991. *The Birth of the Palestinian Refugee Problem, 1947–1949* (in Hebrew). Tel Aviv: Am Oved.

———. 1993. *Israel's Border Wars, 1949–1956: Arab Infiltration, Israeli Retaliation, and the Countdown to the Suez War.* Oxford: Clarendon Press.

———. 2000. *Jews and Arabs in Palestine /Israel, 1936–1956* (in Hebrew). Tel Aviv: Am Oved.

Mosès, Stéphane. 1990. "Scholem and Rosenzweig: The Dialectics of History." *History and Memory* 2 (2): 100–16.

Mouffe, Chantal. 1996. "Democracy, Power, and the 'Political.'" In *Democracy and Difference*, ed. Seyla Benhabib, 245–56. Princeton: Princeton University Press.

———. 2000. *The Democratic Paradox*. London: Verso.

Mueller, Gerhard. 1961. "Problems Posed by Publicity to Crime and Criminal Proceedings." *University of Pennsylvania Law Review* 110:1–26.

Muller, Ingo. 1994. *Hitler's Justice: The Courts of the Third Reich*, trans. Deborah Lucas Schneider. Cambridge: Harvard University Press.

Mushkat, M. 1963. "Eichmann in New York" (in Hebrew). *Yediot Yad Vashem* 31:8–15.

Muymon Shnizer, Merav. 2000. "Between Shock and Oblivion: On the Historiography of the Kufr Qassem Massacre in Israeli Newspapers." In *Kafr Kassem: Myth and History* (in Hebrew), ed. Ruvik Rosenthal, 52–86. Tel Aviv: Ha-Kibbutz Ha-Meuchad.

Nedelsky, Jennifer. 1994. "The Puzzle and Demands of Modern Constitutionalism." *Ethics* 104:500–515.

———. 2000. "Communities of Judgment and Human Rights." *Theoretical Inquiries in Law* 1 (2): 245–82.

Ne'eman Arad, Gulie, ed. 1995. "Israeli History Revisited." Special issue, *History and Memory* 7 (1).

Ni Aolain, Fionnuala. 1997. "Radical Rules: The Effects of Evidential and Procedural Rules on the Regulation of Sexual Violence in War." *Albany Law Review* 60 (3): 883–905.

———. 1997. "Rethinking the Concept of Harm and Legal Categorization of Sexual Violence During War." *Theoretical Inquiries in Law* 1:63–96.

Nicholaidis, Natalia. 1989. "The Sixth Amendment Right to a Speedy and Public Trial." *American Criminal Law Review* 26 (4): 1489–1506.

Nino, Carlos Santiago. 1996. *Radical Evil on Trial*. New Haven: Yale University Press.

Nora, Pierre. 1989. "Between Memory and History: Les Lieux de Mémoire." *Representations* 26:7–25.

———. 1998. "The Era of Commemoration." In *Realms of Memory: The Construction of the French Past*. Vol. 3: *Symbols*, under the direction of Pierre Nora, ed. Lawrence D. Kritzman, trans. Arthur Goldhammer, 609–37. New York: Columbia University Press.

Novak, Daniel. 1981. "The Pullman Strike Cases: Debs, Darrow, and the Labor Injunction." In *American Political Trials*, ed. Michal R. Belknap, 119–28. Westport, CT: Greenwood Press.

Nussbaum, Martha C. 1995. "Poets as Judges: Judicial Rhetoric and the Literary Imagination." *University of Chicago Law Review* 62:1477–1519.

Ofrat, Gideon. 1975. *The Israeli Drama* (in Hebrew). Jerusalem: Tcharikover Publications.

Olshan, Itzhak. 1978. *Din Ve-Dvarim: Memoirs* (in Hebrew). Jerusalem: Schocken.

Osiel, Mark. 1997a. *Mass Atrocity, Collective Memory, and the Law*. New Brunswick, NJ, and London: Transaction Publishers.

———. 1997b. *Obeying Orders: Atrocity, military discipline and the Law of War.* New Brunswick, NJ, and London: Transaction Publishers.

———. 2000. "Why Prosecute? Critics of Punishment for Mass Atrocity." *Human Rights Quarterly* 22:118–47.

Palgi, Yoel. [1946] 1977. *And Behold, a Great Wind Came* (in Hebrew). Tel Aviv: Am Oved.

———. 2003. *Into the Inferno: The Memoir of a Jewish Paratrooper behind Nazi Lines.* New Brunswick, NJ: Rutgers University Press.

Pappé, Ilan. 1995. "An Uneasy Coexistence: Arabs and Jews in the First Decade of Statehood." In *Israel: The First Decade of Independence,* ed. S. Ilan Troen and Noah Lucas, 617–58. Albany: State University of New York Press.

Parush, Adi. 1990. "Kfar Kasem Case, the Black Flag Test and Its Concept of Manifestly Illegal Order" (in Hebrew). *Tel Aviv University Law Review* 15 (2): 245–72.

———. 1996. *Obedience, Responsibility, and Criminal Law: Legal Issues from a Philosophic Perspective* (in Hebrew). Tel Aviv: Papirus.

———. 2000. "Critique of the 'Black Flag' Test" (in Hebrew). In *Kafr Kassem: Myth and History,* ed. Ruvik Rosenthal, 131–77. Tel Aviv: Hakibbutz Hameuchad.

———. 2002. "Revenge, Justice, and the Function of the Court in Aeschylus' Play *Eumenides*" (in Hebrew). *Bar Ilan Law Studies* 18 (1–2): 147–212.

Pattenden, Rosemary. 1982. *The Judge, Discretion, and the Criminal Trial.* Oxford: Clarendon Press.

Peled, Yoav. 1993. "Strangers in Utopia: The Civic State of Israel's Palestinian Citizens" (in Hebrew). *Theoria U-Bikoret* 3:21–35.

Peled, Yoav, ed. 2001a. *Shas: The Challenge of Israeliness* (in Hebrew). Tel Aviv: Miskal-Yedioth Ahronoth Books.

Peled, Yoav. 2001b. "Will Israel Be a State of All Its Citizens on Its 100 Anniversary?" (in Hebrew). *Bar Ilan Law Studies* 17:73–89.

Peretz, Don. 1958. *Israel and the Palestine Arabs.* Washington, DC: Middle East Institute.

Peri, Yoram, ed. 2000a. *The Assassination of Yitzhak Rabin.* Stanford: Stanford University Press.

———. 2000b. "Rabin: Between Commemoration and Denial." In *The Assassination of Yitzhak Rabin,* ed. Yoram Peri, 348–76. Stanford: Stanford University Press.

———. 2000c. "The Media and the Rabin Myth: Reconstruction of the Israeli Collective Identity." In *The Assassination of Yitzhak Rabin,* ed. Yoram Peri, 175–94. Stanford: Stanford University Press.

Pilowsky, Varda, ed. 1990. *Transition from "Yishuv" to State, 1947–1949: Continuity and Change* (in Hebrew). Haifa: University of Haifa Press.

Podhoretz, Norman. 1963. "Hannah Arendt on Eichmann: A Study in the Perversity of Brilliance." *Commentary* 6:201–8.

Poliakov, Leon. 1956. *Harvest of Hate.* London: Eleck Books.

Porat, Dina, and, Shlomo Simonsohn, eds. 1993. *Michael: On the History of the Jews in the Diaspora.* Tel Aviv: Diaspora Research Institute.

Pound, Roscoe. 1959. *Jurisprudence*. St. Paul: West Pub.

Prat, Imanuel. 1955. *The Big Trial: Kastner Affair* (in Hebrew). Tel Aviv: Or.

Racover, Nachum. 1990. *A Bibliography of Jewish Law*. 2 vols. Jerusalem: Jewish Legal Heritage Society.

Radin, Max. 1932. "The Right to a Public Trial." *Temple Law Quarterly* 6:381–98.

Rakove, Jack N. 1999. "The Super-legalty of the Constitution; or, a Federalist Critique of Bruce Ackerman's Neo-Federalism." *Yale Law Journal* 108:1931–57.

Ram, Uri, ed. 1993. *Israeli Society: Critical Perspectives* (in Hebrew). Tel Aviv: Brerot.

Ravitzky, Aviezer. 1997. *Messianism, Zionism, and Jewish Religious Radicalism* (in Hebrew). Tel Aviv: Am Oved.

Rawls, John. 1999. "The Justification of Civil Disobedience." In *Collected Papers*, ed. Samuel Freeman, 176–89. Cambridge: Harvard University Press.

Raz, Joseph. 1979. *The Authority of Law: Essays on Law and Morality*. Oxford: Clarendon Press.

Raz-Krakotzkin, Amnon. 2000. "The Legacy of Rabin: On Secularism, Nationality, and Orientalism." In *Contested Memory: Myth, Nation, and Democracy* (in Hebrew), ed. Lev Greenberg, 89–107. Beer-Sheva: Humphrey Institute for Social Research.

Rekhes, Elie. 1990. "The Underlying Principles of the Policy towards the Arabs in Israel." In *Transition from "Yishuv" to State, 1947–1949: Continuity and Change* (in Hebrew), ed. Varda Pilowsky, 291–97. Haifa: University of Haifa Press.

———. 1991. "Initial Israeli Policy Guidelines towards the Arab Minority." In *New Perspectives on Israeli History*, ed. Lawrence J. Silberstein, 103–19. New York: New York University Press.

Report of the Commission of Inquiry regarding the Assassination of Prime Minister Yitzhak Rabin. 1996. Jerusalem: State of Israel.

Report of the Commission of Inquiry regarding the Machpela Cave Massacre. 1994. Jerusalem: State of Israel.

Representation 1989. 26. Special issue, "Memory and Counter Memory."

Ring, Jennifer. 1998. *The Political Consequences of Thinking: Gender and Judaism in the Work of Hannah Arendt*. Albany: State University of New York Press.

Robinson, Jacob. 1963. "A Report on the Evil of Banality: The Arendt Book." *Facts* 15 (1): 263–70.

———. 1965. *And The Crooked Shall Be Made Straight: The Eichmann Trial, the Jewish Catastrophe, and Hannah Arendt's Narrative*. Philadelphia: Jewish Publication Society of America.

———. 1966. *Ha-Akov Le-Mishor* (in Hebrew). Zvi Bar Meir d Aryeh Mor trans. Jerusalem: Mosad Bialik.

Rose, Carol M. 1992. "Giving, Trading, Thieving, and Trusting: How and Why Gifts Become Exchanges, and (More Importantly) Vice Versa." *Florida Law Review* 44:295–326.

Rosenberg, Gerald N. 1991. *The Hollow Hope: Can Courts Bring about Social Change?* Chicago: University of Chicago Press.

Rosenfeld, Shalom. 1955. *Tik Plili 124: Mishpat Gruenwald-Kastner* (in Hebrew). Tel Aviv: Karni. Criminal Trial 124, the Gruenwald-Kastner trial.

Rosenthal, Ruvik, ed. 2000a. *Kafr Kassem: Myth and History* (in Hebrew). Tel Aviv: Ha-Kibbutz Ha-Meuchad.

———. 2000b. "Who Killed Fatma Sarsur?" In *Kafr Kassem: Myth and History* (in Hebrew), ed. Ruvik Rosenthal, 11–51. Tel Aviv: Ha-Kibbutz Ha-Meuchad.

Rotberg, Robert I., and Dennis Thompson, eds. 2000. *Truth v. Justice: The Morality of Truth Commissions.* Princeton: Princeton University Press.

Rouhana, Nadim N. "Coping with the Contradiction of Ethnic Policies: How Israeli Society Maintains a Democratic Self-Image." Manuscript.

Rubinstein, Amnon. 1984. *From Herzl to Gush Emunim and Back: The Zionist Dream Revisited.* New York: Schocken.

———. 1996. *The Constitutional Law of Israel* (in Hebrew). 5th ed. Tel Aviv: Shocken.

———. 1997. *From Herzl to Rabin* (in Hebrew). Tel-Aviv: Schocken.

Rubinstein, Elyakim. 1980. *Shoftey Eretz* [Judges of the Country] (in Hebrew). Jerusalem: Schocken.

Sarat, Austin. 1999. "Rhetoric and Remembrance: Trials, Transcription, and the Politics of Critical Reading." *Legal Studies Forum* 23:355–78.

Sarat, Austin, and Thomas Kearns, eds. 1992. *Law's Violence.* Ann Arbor: University of Michigan Press.

———. 1999. *History, Memory, and the Law.* Ann Arbor: University of Michigan Press.

Scheppele, Kim Lane. 2001. "The Quarantined Past: The Collective Construction of Regimes of Horror and the Creation of New Constitutions." Paper presented at the annual conference Law and Society, Budapest. Manuscript.

Scheuerman, William E., ed. 1996. *The Rule of Law under Siege.* Berkeley: University of California Press.

Schmitt, Carl. 1976. *The Concept of the Political,* trans. George Schwab. New Brunswick, NJ: Rutgers University Press.

Scholem, Gershom. 1990. "On Our Language: A Confession." *History and Memory* 2 (2): 97–99.

Schuetz, Janice, Kathryn Holmes Snedaker, and Peter E. Kane, eds. 1988. *Communication and Litigation.* Carbondale: Southern Illinois University Press.

Segev, Tom. 1993. *The Seventh Million: The Israelis and the Holocaust,* trans. Haim Watsman. New York: Hill and Wang.

———. 2000. "Adolf Eichmann's Idols." *Ha'aretz,* 3 March.

Seidel, Gill. 1986. *The Holocaust Denial: Antisemitism, Racism, and the New Right.* Leeds: Beyond the Pale Collective.

Sereny, Gitta. 1974. *Into That Darkness: From Mercy Killing to Mass Murder.* London: A. Deutsch.

Shachar, Yoram. 1982. "The Algazi Trials: Selective Conscientious Objection in Israel." *Israel Yearbook on Human Rights* 12:214–58.

———. 2002. "The Early Drafts of the Declaration of Independence of the State of Israel" (in Hebrew). *Tel Aviv University Law Review* 26 (2): 523–600.

Shaked, Gershon. 1991. "Light and Shadow, Unity and Plurality: The Hebrew Literature in a Dialectical Confrontation with a Changing Reality" (in Hebrew). *Alpayim* 4:113–39.

Shaked, Michal. 2000. "History in Court and Court in History: Kastner Trial and the Narratives of Memory" (in Hebrew). *Alpayim* 20:36–81.

Shamir, Ronen. 1990. "'Landmark Cases' and the Reproduction of Legitimacy: The Case of Israel's High Court of Justice." *Law and Society Review* 24 (3): 781–805.

Shamir, Ziva. 1999. *On Time and Place: Poetics and Politics in Alterman's Writing* (in Hebrew). Tel-Aviv: Ha-Kibbutz Ha-Meuchad.

Shapira, Anita. 1997. *New Jews, Old Jews* (in Hebrew). Tel Aviv: Am Oved.

———. 2002. *Hannah Arendt and Haim Gouri: Two Perceptions of the Eichmann Trial* (in Hebrew). Jerusalem: Yad Va-Shem.

Shapira, Anita, and Derek J. Penslar, eds. 2002. *Israeli Historical Revisionism: From Left to Right.* London: Frank Cass.

Sharett, Moshe. 1978. *Personal Diary* (In Hebrew). Tel Aviv: Ma'ariv.

Shaw, Malcolm N. 1997. *International Law,* 4th ed. Cambridge: Cambridge University Press.

Sheleff, Leon. 1989. *The Voice of Honor: Civil Disobedience and Civic Loyalty* (in Hebrew). Tel Aviv: Tel Aviv University Press.

———. 1993. "The Green Line Is the Border of Judicial Activism: Queries about Supreme Court Judgments in the Territories" (in Hebrew). *Tel Aviv University Law Review* 17:757–809.

———. 1999. "From Schindler's List to Kasztner's Train: On Historical Reality, Media Myths, and Judicial Truth" (in Hebrew). In *Law and History,* ed. Daniel Gutwein and Menachem Mautner, 339–53. Jerusalem: Zalman Shazar Center for Jewish History.

Shif, Ilan. 2000. "In Favor of the 'Black Flag' Test" (in Hebrew). In *Kafr Kassem: Myth and History,* ed. Ruvik Rosenthal, 117–30. Tel Aviv: Ha-Kibbutz Ha-Meuchad.

Shklar, Judith N. 1964. *Legalism.* Cambridge: Harvard University Press.

Shochtman, Eliav. 1990–91. "The Halachic Acknowledgment of the State Laws of Israel" (in Hebrew). *Hebrew Law Yearbook* 16–17.

———. 1999. "A Jewish Regime Cannot Be 'Rodef'" [Persecutor] (in Hebrew). *Tehumin* 19:40–48.

Shute, Steven A., ed. 1993. *On Human Rights: The Oxford Amnesty Lectures, 1993.* New York: HarperCollins.

Silberstein, Laurence J., ed. 1991. *New Perspectives on Israeli History.* New York: New York University Press.

———. 1999. *The Postzionism Debates.* New York: Routledge.

Simon, A. E. "A Portrait of Hannah Arendt" (in Hebrew). *Molad* 21:179–80, 239.

Smeed, J. W. 1987. *Faust in Literature* . Westport, CT: Greenwood Press.

Smith, Charles D. 1996. *Palestine and the Arab-Israeli Conflict.* 3d ed. New York: St. Martin's Press.

Sophocles. 1974. *Antigone.* In *The Theban Plays,* trans. E. F. Walting. New York: Penguin.

Sprinzak, Ehud. 1991. *The Ascendance of Israel's Radical Right.* New York: Oxford University Press.

———. 1999. *Brother against Brother.* New York: Free Press.

Stein, Eric. 1986. "History against Speech: The New German Law against 'Auschwitz' and Other Lies." *Michigan Law Review* 85:277–324.

Stern, Joseph P. 1975. *History and Allegory in Thomas Mann's Doktor Faustus.* London: H. K. Lewis.

Stern, Judith. 2000. "The Eichmann Trial and Its Influence on Psychiatry and Psychology." *Theoretical Inquiries in Law* 1 (2): 393–428.

"Symposium: The Trial of the Deported" (in Hebrew). *Plilim* 4:9–66.

Syrkin, Marie. 1963a. "Hannah Arendt: The Clothes of the Empress." *Dissent* 10:341–53.

———. 1963b. "Miss Arendt Surveys the Holocaust." *Jewish Frontier,* 7–14.

Tal, David. 1998. *Israel's Day-to-Day Security Conception: Its Origin and Development, 1949–1956* (in Hebrew). Beer Sheba: Ben-Gurion Research Center and Ben-Gurion University of the Negev Press.

Tamir, Shmuel. 2002. *Son of This Land.* (in Hebrew). Tel Aviv: Zemora Bitan.

Tamir, Yael. 1993. *Liberal Nationalism.* Princeton: Princeton University Press.

Taylor, Charles. 1994. *Multiculturalism.* Princeton: Princeton University Press.

Teitel, Ruti G. 1999. "Bringing the Messiah through the Law." In *Human Rights in Political Transitions: Gettysburg to Bosnia,* ed. Carla Alisson Hesse and Robert Post, 177–93. New York: Zone Books.

———. 2000. *Transitional Justice.* Oxford: Oxford University Press.

Tel Aviv University Law Review 1995. 19 (3). Special issue, "A Jewish and Democratic State."

Tessler, Mark. 1994. *A History of the Israeli-Palestinian Conflict.* Bloomington: Indiana University Press.

Teveth, Shabtai. 1982. *The Arlosoroff Assassination* (in Hebrew). Jerusalem: Schocken.

———. 1992. *Shearing Time/Firing Squad at Beth-Jiz* (in Hebrew). Tel Aviv: Ish Dor Publications.

Theoretical Inquiries in Law. 2000. 1 (2). Special issue, "Judgment in the Shadow of the Holocaust."

Tietjens Meyers, Diana, ed. 1993. *Feminists Rethink the Self.* Boulder: Westview Press.

Trachtenberg, Joshua. 1943. *The Devil and the Jews: The Medieval Conception of the Jew and Its Relation to Modern Anti-Semitism.* Philadelphia: Jewish Publication Society of America.

Troen, Ilan S., and Noah Lucas, eds. 1995. *Israel: The First Decade of Independence.* Albany: State University of New York Press.

Trunk, Isaiah. 1972. *Judenrat: The Jewish Counsels in Eastern Europe under Nazi Occupation.* New York: University of Nebraska Press.

Turner, Victor W. 1969. *The Ritual Process.* Chicago: Aldine.

Van Pelt, Robert J. 2002. *The Case for Auschwitz: Evidence from the Irving Trial.* Bloomington: Indiana University Press.

Vidal-Naquet, Pierre. 1992. *Assassins of Memory: Essays on the Denial of the Holocaust,* trans. Jeffrey Mehlman. New York: Columbia University Press.

Vila, Dana R. 1999. *Politics, Philosophy, Terror: Essays on the Thought of Hannah Arendt.* Princeton: Princeton University Press.

Virgil. 1987. *The Aeneid.* Book II: *The Fall of Troy,* trans. Rolfe Humphries. New York: Macmillan.

Walzer, Michael. 1998. "Democracy and the Politics of Assassination." In *Political Assassination: The Rabin Assassination and Other Political Assassinations in the Middle East* (in Hebrew), ed. Charles S. Liebman, 13–21. Tel Aviv: Am Oved.

Warner, Rex. 1951. *Greeks and Trojans* . London: Macgibbon and Kee.

Weber, Donald. 1995. "From Limen to Border: A Meditation on the Legacy of Victor Turner for American Cultural Studies." *American Quarterly* 47:525–36.

Weber Nicholsen, Shierry, ed. and trans. 1996. *The New Conservatism.* Cambridge: MIT Press.

Weitz, Yechiam. 1995. *The Man Who Was Murdered Twice* (in Hebrew). Jerusalem: Keter.

———. 1996. "The Law for Punishment of the Nazis and Their Collaborators as Image and Reflection of Public Opinion" (in Hebrew). *Kathedra* 82:153–64.

West, Robin L. 1993. *Narrative, Authority, and Law.* Ann Arbor: University of Michigan Press.

White, Hayden. 1981. "The Value of Narrativity in the Representation of Reality." In *On Narrative,* ed. W. J. T. Mitchell, 1–23. Chicago: University of Chicago Press.

White, James Boyd. 1985. *Heracles' Bow: Essays on the Rhetoric and Poetics of Law.* Madison: University of Wisconsin Press.

———. 1990. *Justice as Translation.* Chicago: University of Chicago Press.

Wigmore, John Henry. 1961. *Evidence in Trials at Common Law.* Boston: Little, Brown.

———. 1976. *Evidence.* Rev. ed. Boston: Little, Brown.

Willet, John, ed. 1964. *Brecht on Theatre.* New York: Hill and Wang.

Williams, Glanvile. 1953. *Criminal Law: The General Part.* London: Stevens and Sons.

Wilson, Richard. 1996. "The Sizwe Will Not Go Away: The Truth and Reconciliation Commission, Human Rights, and Nation Building in South Africa." *African Studies* 55 (2): 1–20.

Yablonka, Hannah. 1994. *Brothers—Strangers: Holocaust Survivors in Israel, 1948–1952* (in Hebrew). Jerusalem: Yad Ben Zvi.

———. 1996. "The Law of Punishment for Nazis and Their Collaborators:

History, Implementation, and Point of View" (in Hebrew). *Kathedra* 82:135–52.

———. 2000. "Preparing the Eichmann Trial: Who Really Did the Job?" *Theoretical Inquiries in Law* 1 (2): 368–92.

———. 2001. *The State of Israel v. Adolf Eichmann* (in Hebrew). Tel Aviv: Yediot Aharonot. English language edition, New York: Schocken, 2004.

Yadager, Yaacov. 1999. "'The Rabin Myth': Zionist Nationalism in the '90s" (in Hebrew). *Democratic Culture* 1:23–36.

Yerushalmi, Yosef Hayim. 1982. *Zakhor: Jewish History and Jewish Memory.* Seattle: University of Washington Press.

Yiftachel, Oren. 1998. "Nation-Building and the Division of Space in the Israeli 'Ethnocracy': Settlement, Land, and Ethnic Disparities" (in Hebrew). *Tel Aviv University Law Review* 21 (3): 637–63.

Yitzhak, Yoav. 1998. *First Class.* Vol. 1: *Persons* (in Hebrew). Tel Aviv: Egel Ha-Zahav Journalism.

Yona, Yossi. 2000. "Israel after Rabin's Assassination: State of the Jewish People or State of Its Citizens?" In *Contested Memory: Myth, Nation, and Democracy* (in Hebrew), ed. Lev Greenberg, 107–21. Beer-Sheva: Humphrey Institute for Social Research.

Yosef, Dov. 1975. *A Dove and a Sword* (in Hebrew). Ramat Gan: Massadah.

Young, Iris Marion. 1997. *Intersecting Voices.* Princeton: Princeton University Press.

Young-Bruehl, Elisabeth. 1982. *Hannah Arendt: For Love of the World.* New Haven and London: Yale University Press.

Zeitlin, Froma I. 1978. "The Dynamics of Misogyny: Myth and Mythmaking in the Oresteia." *Arethusa* 11:149–83.

Zertal, Idith. 1999. "Hannah Arendt in Jerusalem" (in Hebrew). *Teoria Ve-Bikoret* 12–13:159–67.

———. 2002. *Death and the Nation: History, Memory, Politics* (in Hebrew). Or Yehuda: Dvir Publishing House.

Zerubavel, Yael. 1995. *Recovered Roots: Collective Memory and the Making of Israeli National Tradition.* Chicago: University of Chicago Press.

Zuckerman, Yitzhak. 1990. "Between the Judenrat and the Fighters" (in Hebrew). *Edut* 5:13–19.

Zuckerman, Yitzhak, and Moshe Basuk. 1964. *The Book of the Ghettos' Wars* (in Hebrew). Tel Aviv: Ha-Kibbutz Ha-Meuchad.

Zweig, Ronald W., ed. 1991. *David Ben Gurion: Politics and Leadership in Israel.* London: F. Cass.

Table of Cases

H.C 6126/94, *Giorah Senesh v. Chairman of Broadcasting Authority*, 53(3) P.D. 817.
H.C. 5100/94, *The Israeli Committee against Torture v. The Israeli Government*, 53(4) P.D. 817.
H.C. 5075/95, *Naamat v. Minister of Interior*, not published.
H.C. 6698/95, *Kaadan v. Israel's Land Administration*, 54(1) P.D. 258.
H.C. 1113/99, *Adalah v. The Minister of Religious Affairs*, 54(2) P.D. 164.
F.H. 8613/96, *Muhammad Yusef Jabareen v. State of Israel*, 54(5) P.D. 193.
H.C. 4438/97, *Adalah v. The Ministry of Transportation* (not yet published, given on 25 February 1999).
H.C. 5167/00, *Weiss v. Prime Minister*, 55(2) P.D 455.
C.A. 456/01, *Theodor Katz v. Alexandroni Association* (not yet published, given on 8 November 01).
H.C. 4668/01, *Sarrid v. Prime Minister Ariel Sharon*, 56(2) P.D. 265.

District Court Cases

C.C. 47/49 (T.A.), *Attorney General v. Iser Beeri* (not published, given on 22 November 1949).
Cr.C. (Jm.) 124/53, *Attorney General v. Gruenwald*, 44 P.M. 1965.
Cr.C. (Jm.) 40/61, *Attorney General v. Adolf Eichmann*, 45 P.M. 3. 1965, *International Law Reports* 36 (1968): 18–276.
C.C. (Hi.) 75/61, *Yosef Mendel v. Adolf Eichmann* (not published).
Cr.C. (Ramla) 76/87, *State of Israel v. Dori*, 1989(1) P.M. 289.
Cr.C. (T.A.) 498/95, *State of Israel v. Yigal Amir*, 1996(2) P.M. 3.

Military Cases

Appeal no. 43/49 + 45/49, *Farchi v. Chief Military Prosecutor*, Military Appellate Court Verdicts (1948–1950), 24.
Military Court 3/57, *Military Prosecutor v. Major Melinki*, 17 P.M. (1958–59) 90.

Foreign Cases

Patterson v. Colorado, 205 U.S. 454, 462 (1907).
Korematsu v. United States, 323 U.S. 214 (1944).
In re Oliver, 333 U.S. 257 (1948).
Brown v. Board of Education, 347 U.S. 483 (1954).
Estes v. Texas, 381 U.S. 543, 588 (1965).
Miranda v. Arizona, 384 U.S. 436 (1966).
Regina v. Zundel, 58 O.R. (2d) 129.
Reference re Secession of Quebec, [1998] 2 S.C.R. 217.
Prosecutor v. Dusko Tadic ICTY Trial Chamber (10 August 1995), Case No. IT–94–1.
Prosecutor v. Anto Furundzija, judgment, ICTY Trial Chamber II (10 December 1998), Case No. IT–95–17/1.

Statutes

Criminal Code Ordinance of 1936.
Declaration of the Establishment of the State of Israel, 14 May 1948, 1 L.S.I. 3 (1948).
Law of Return, 1950 4 L.S.I 114 (1949–50).
Nazis and Nazi Collaborators (Punishment) Law S710–1950, 4 L.S.I. 154.
The Nationality Law, 1952, S.H. 146.
The Martyrs' and Heroes' Commemoration (Yad Va-Shem) Law, 1953, 7 L.S.I. 119 (1952–53).
Rabbinical Courts Jurisdiction (Marriage and Divorce) Law, 1953, 7 L.S.I. 139 (1953).
The Military Justice Law, 1955, 9 L.S.I. 184 (1954–55).
The Courts Law, 1957, 11 L.S.I. 157 (1957).
The Courts (Offences Punishable by Death) Law, 1961, 15 L.S.I. 20 (1960–1961).
The Remembrance Day (War of Independence and Israel Defense Army) Law, 1963, 17 L.S.I. 85 (1962–63).
The Penal Law, 5737–1977 31 (spec. vol.) L.S.I. (1997) at p. 82.
The Penal Law, 1977 (amend. 1994), S.H. 348.
The Courts Law (consolidated version), 5744–1984, 38 L.S.I. 271.
Basic Law: The Knesset, 1958 (amend. 1985), 39 L.S.I. 216 (1984–85).
Prevention of Terrorism Ordinance (Amendment No. 2) Law, 5746–1986, 40 L.S.I. 163.
The Presidents and Prime Ministers of Israel (Perpetuation of Memory) Law 1986, 40 L.S.I. 260 (1985–86).
Basic Law: Human Dignity and Liberty, 1992, S.H. 150.
The [Political] Parties Law, 1992, S.H. 190.
Basic Law: Freedom of Occupation, 1994, S.H. 90.
The Memorial Day of Yitzhak Rabin Law, 1997, S.H. 186.

Foreign Legislation

German Basic Law.
The Constitution of the United States.

Legislative History

Legislative Draft Bills

Draft bill of Courts (Offences Punishable by Death) Law, 1961 H.H., 72.
Draft bill to Criminal Procedure Law, 1963 H.H., 161.

Protocols of Knesset Proceedings

D.K. (1950) 1152–53 (session of 27 March 1950)
D.K. (1950) 2134–35 (session of 10 July 1950).

Index

Ackerman, Bruce, 8, 263n. 27, 311n. 13, 337n. 117

Agamben, Giorgio, 211; Rabin as "homo sacer," 211, 330n. 62

Agranat, Simon: judgment in Kastner trial of, 61, 82, 278nn. 77–78, 81; narrative in Kastner trial of, 64–66

Ahdut Ha-Avodah party, 73, 77–78

Aid and Rescue Committee. See Va'adat Ezrah Vehatzalah

Aloni, Shulamit, 259n. 3

Altalena, 207, 209, 324n. 104, 325n. 18

Alterman, Nathan, 8, 69; Abba Kovner and, 156; Arendt compared to, 153–55, 157, 160–61, 164; being criticized, 77–79, 154, 161; Ben-Gurion and, 281n. 9, 283n. 36; criticism of Kastner trial, 67, 69, 71, 73, 75–76, 79, 81, 160, 282n. 22, 283n. 39; criticism of Kufr Qassem massacre, 195–96; gender analysis regarding, 157; "Ha-Tur ha-Shevii" (The Seventh Column), 69, 75, 78; historical time, reintroduction of, 79–80; as the Judenrat's voice, 73–78; notebooks of, 70; *Pundak Ha-Ruhot*, 283n. 36; "Simhat Aniim," 78; "Thirty Days since Kastner's Murder," 73, 80; "two paths" concept, 69–72, 74–77, 80, 156, 163

Amir, Yigal, 210; narrative of, 203–4, 206–8, 325nn. 5, 9; political defense of, 204–6; quasi-legal defense of, 208–9

Arab Israelis, 177–78, 187, 194, 311n. 16; conception of, in Hassin trial, 192; conception of, in Kufr Qassem trial, 192; Declaration of Independence and, 178; exclusion from crucial political decisions, 232; forced deportation vs. voluntary emigration of, 174–76; granting citizenship to, 187, 192, 194, 197, 229; in Kufr Qassem trial, 15; landmark cases regarding, 321n. 87; liberal approach toward, 194; Nationality Law and, 314n. 30, 315n. 34; perception of Kufr Qassem trial, 194, 197; Rabin and, 225, 229; rights of, 195, 229–30, 232, 323n. 98; testimonies in Kufr Qassem trial, 178, 180–83

Arendt, Hannah, 11–12, 41–42, 52, 86, 303n. 1; on banality of evil, 122–24, 144, 153; being criticized, 94, 104, 153, 158, 161, 164, 287n. 41, 302n. 88, 306n. 33; as critic, 146; criticism of Eichmann trial, 14, 87, 93, 99, 105, 108, 111, 114–15, 118–19, 126–27, 129, 131, 133, 141, 146–51, 155, 160, 164, 296n. 5, 299n. 52, 301n. 71, 302n. 87, 303n. 93; criticism of ethnic distinctions in Israeli law, 147–48; criticism of Hausner, 86, 94; on Eichmann, 122–25,